DREAMING IN THE LOTUS

DREAMING IN THE LOTUS

Buddhist Dream Narrative, Imagery, & Practice

Serinity Young

Foreword by Carol Schreier Rupprecht

Wisdom Publications • Boston

Wisdom Publications
199 Elm Street
Somerville MA 02144 USA

Library of Congress Cataloging-in-Publication Data
Young, Serinity.
Dreaming in the lotus : Buddhist dream narrative, imagery, and practice / by Serinity Young ; foreword by Carol Schreier Rupprecht.
p. cm.
Includes bibliographical references and index.
ISBN 0-86171-158-0 (alk. paper)
1. Dreams—Religious aspects—Buddhism. 2. Gautama Buddha. 3. Mi-la-ras-pa, 1040–1123. 4. Buddhist hagiography. I. Title.
BF1078.Y68 1999
294.3'4446—dc21 99-33959

ISBN 0-86171-158-0

05 04 03 02 01
6 5 4 3 2

Cover by Gopa & The Bear
Interior by Gopa Design
Cover image © Photodisc

Wisdom Publications' books are printed on acid-free paper and meet the guidelines for the permanence and durability of the Committee on Production Guidelines for Book Longevity of the Council on Library Resources.

Printed in the United States of America

For Geshe Lozang Jamspal

⌘ *Table of Contents*

Illustrations

Black and White Figures

Color Plates *(between pages 106 and 107)*

Publisher's Acknowledgment

The Publisher gratefully acknowledges the generous help of the Hershey Family Foundation in sponsoring the publication of this book.

Foreword

Dreaming in the Lotus is a special gift to scholars and dreamworkers of the world from an outstanding specialist of Asian culture. This compelling study explores the genre of sacred biography in Indo-Tibetan Buddhism to arrive at a startling conclusion: without dreams there would be no Buddha and no Buddhism. On the way to this conclusion, author Serinity Young unravels some of the mysteries of dreaming and weaves a pattern of insight into others. With this foreword, I invite readers to pick up any thread of interest or expertise they have and follow where she goes. Whether scholar of religion or of literature, novelist or historian of Asia, psychotherapist or physician, feminist or mystic, all will find here new information, unexpected connections, intriguing suggestions, and remarkable dreams. Much of the material, from Sanskrit and Tibetan-language texts, has been previously unavailable to the general reader in English translation.

With uncommon good sense and refreshingly clear prose, Young presents a comparative analysis of biographies of the historical Buddha Gautama (c. 562–482 B.C.E.) and the poet-yogin Milarepa (1040–1123 C.E.). Commentary is included also on Gampopa, Tsongkhapa, and Buton. The unique distinctiveness of *Dreaming in the Lotus* among the current flood of books about dreaming, Eastern and Western, lies in the author's finely tuned comparative methodology, her depth of knowledge about cross-currents in Western research on dreaming, the cultural and chronological range of her sources, and her expertise in Asian languages.

The methodology is anchored in the initial comparison between dream-centered texts originating in India and those that evolved over centuries in Tibet from the convergence of Buddhism with pre-Buddhist indigenous dream beliefs and practices. Young's frequent reach toward more global comparison enhances the book's contributions to oneiric history and theory. She demonstrates, for example, that in Tibetan Buddhism sleep is not just a metaphor for death, as it seems to be in much Graeco-Roman and

Western European literature, but rather a "training ground" for it, since dreaming, wakefulness, and death are seen as equally illusory states needing to be transcended. Tibetan medical text observations on dreaming are linked to those of Galen and Hippocrates. The way the dream of a private individual in sacred biography becomes transformed into a cultural institution is elucidated by analogies with the founding of the cargo cults of Melanesia and the Native American Ghost Dance Movement. Just as dream ideologies cross religious lines between Judaism, Christianity, and paganism, Young says, so do they from Hinduism to Buddhism.

The heuristic nature of such comparison inspires readers to undertake their own search for affinities. I found fascinating, for example, the way the manipulation or rejection of their wives' dreams by the Buddha, Padmasambhava, and Marpa was partially echoed in Milton's *Paradise Lost* by Adam's unwise and fateful dismissal of Eve's premonitory dream of their temptation. I also found similarities and illuminating dissimilarities between the sacred biography subject's dreams of disheveled women and Dante's pilgrim's dream of the deformed female, whose clothes are torn by a dream-Virgil, in canto XIX of *Purgatorio.*

Since no systematic methodology for the exploration of dreaming or any set of principles governing dream interpretation emerges in Buddhism, Young serves as a necessary guide for our initiation into a "culturally complex process fraught with contradiction." She insistently rejects oversimplification with frequent caveats about the multiple shades of variation in Buddhist dream thought even within the single genre of sacred biographies that foreground dreaming no matter how different the lives of the individuals or the compositional backgrounds of the texts. She observes calmly that apparently contending dream beliefs within Buddhism are sometimes only a matter of emphasis, that the coexistence of attitudes that seem mutually exclusive may only reflect ongoing differences between concurrent elite and popular traditions. Apparent inconsistencies in theory and discrepancies between theory and practice, she notes, sometimes have the desired function in the monastic world of requiring the presence of a guru on whom initiates must rely for interpretation.

Young takes a similarly clear-headed stance on the central paradox of dreaming in Buddhism: it is seen simultaneously as one of the most powerful forms of human cognition and as the principal example of the illusory nature of the world.

> Buddhism valorized dreaming in the popular tradition of biography while the elite monastic tradition used the dream experience to emphasize

> the illusory nature of reality. Their point is not that a dream experience is less real than waking life but that both states, dreaming and waking, are equally illusory.

This paradox shows that radically disparate notions of what constitutes self, cognition, and the "real" are at the core of Eastern and Western oneiric thought. Such difference should prohibit the facile assimilation of Asian practices by Euro-American dreamers, such as equating the mastery over dreaming in Dream Yoga techniques with North American dream control systems like Lucidity. As Young points out, Tibetan Buddhist dream work does not translate wholesale into North American self-help movements, an argument she makes in a thoughtful appendix on the Lucidity Movement headed by Stephen LaBerge.

In working on her extraordinary materials, Young has not succumbed to the seductions of what Carl Jung called "going Eastern." Instead she has combined rigorous academic training with an intuitive grasp of the otherness of her subject and a deep respect for difference. Thus she escapes the essentialist fallacy of thinking that we all mean the same thing when we use words like dream, shaman, and real. She calls attention to the way in most Western languages one "has a dream," while in many Eastern languages one "sees a dream." In the former, the dreamer is the creator of the dream; in the latter, "the passive recipient of an objective vision." In an especially interesting aside, she explains how some Asian dreamers use eye ointment to protect themselves against "seeing" bad dreams. As a comparative literature scholar who has taught and written on the interface between dream theory and translation theory, I am convinced that one major source of certain kinds of recurrent misunderstanding are the inadequate and often misleading translations of foreign texts on which so many North American dreamworkers depend. The translator's world view inevitably skews the original material, and dream texts are especially susceptible to conscious and unconscious distortion. Young's linguistic expertise allows her to work with primary sources and to perform the kind of detailed textual analysis that can limit misrepresentation. This leads to more subtle and sensible communication across cultures about the process of dreaming.

In addition, Young does not atomize the dream experience by isolating single dreams as the crux of analysis. She recognizes the dream experience as a sequence, a dynamic process that moves along a continuum from dream stimulus and setting, to the dream itself (mentation during sleep), telling of the dream, interpretation, and outcome, including ritual attempts to ward off evil effects or efforts to carry out what are perceived to be dream's directives or explicit instructions. She does not excerpt or abstract dream samples from one culture or one historical moment and then generalize, but traces over centuries the evolution of beliefs and practices. As the structure of her book indicates, Young has particular interest in when and how oneiric traditions persist and innovations make their appearance.

Dreaming in the Lotus has its own set of traditional and innovative materials, both of which have value for post-modern dreamers and professional dreamworkers. I plan myself to follow up on Young's brief but provocative remarks about the role that degrees of orality and literacy play in shaping the oneiric mindset of a society. As I have written elsewhere, in many diverse cultures during the transition from an oral to a primarily written tradition the earliest recorded texts always include dreams (like the Old English "Dream of the Rood") or key dream episodes (like Duzumi's dream in the Sumerian "Inanna"). Dreaming seems to be one of the driving forces that sparks the desire in humans for the preservation in concrete form of their experience.

Readers will find many familiar themes in instructively unfamiliar contexts: incubation, dreams as medical diagnosis and prognosis, taxonomies of kinds of dreaming, shared dreams, sought or induced dreams, debate over divine or demonic origin. The chapter on gender especially bears reading for the perspective it adds to the vexing question of male/female difference in the realm of dreaming. I do not know of any other woman's dream, in any society, that had the endlessly adumbrating influence of Queen Maya's dream of the conception of the Buddha: "a magnificent white elephant, striking her right side with its trunk, is able to enter her womb." Young documents the way this dream, along with its various versions, interpretations, and iconographic representations, significantly affected the development of Buddhism. Like Maya's dream in biographies of the Buddha, the majority of females' dreams appearing in the lives of male Buddhist saints are those of conception.

On the other hand, the biographies are full of men's dreams about women, many following what I call the fear/revere pattern, a corollary to the Eve/ Mary pattern of female representation in Christianity. In men's dreams, awesome, often divine women play a crucial role in ensuring the man's salvational goals, while the true dreams of real women, usually wives, about such men are dismissed, as happens also in versions of the Buddha's biography. In these sacred biographies, as in Indian and Tibetan medical texts, men's dreams also include figures of threatening women, such as the demonized Lilith of the Talmud. Young also finds in the Indo-Tibetan world the contradiction, which seems to recur worldwide and across millennia, whereby women are endowed with tremendous power in men's dreams and psychic experiences while the concomitant social reality renders them powerless or at least confines them to considerably weakened positions.

Throughout North America, starting as early as the Winget-Kramer study in 1933, gender in dreaming has been a subject for investigation among researchers in clinical, experimental, and academic settings. Virtually without exception these studies have identified differences between males and females in the attitude, content, interpretation, effect, and use of dreams. In the 1970s feminist scholars like me began challenging the conclusions about gender difference in areas of study like content analysis as being the result of social constructions of femaleness and maleness. As decades pass, however, many feminist investigators are finding that dramatic changes in the social realities of North American women and men along the lines of work, education, and income have not necessarily made their dreaming lives more commensurate.

Dreaming is one of the few truly universal human phenomena yet evidence from many corners of the world like that presented in *Dreaming in the Lotus* can persuade us that dreams of individuals are shaped substantially by specific cultural, social, religious, and political contexts. Can it be true that in dreaming gender overrides all these distinctions among people? Do the dream lives of men in ancient Tibet and post-modern Canada have more in common with each other than they do with the dream lives of ancient Tibetan and post-modern Canadian women despite the great contrast between the waking lives of such people? And if so, what does such commonality demonstrate? Young introduces into this ongoing debate some unusual new material, which in its complexity argues strongly for more cross-cultural studies of gender in dreaming.

The ultimate excellence of *Dreaming in the Lotus* is that it provides a valuable model for dream study that does not domesticate the esoteric but enlarges the oneiric world view of those who consult it. It also incorporates the personal life of the author in subtle but essential ways as she tests her own conclusions about early Buddhist literature during her field work in India, Nepal, and Tibet, speaking with Tibetans from different backgrounds about their own dreams, beliefs, and practices. Her work will remind us as we enter the new millennium that the dream is both a personal and collective experience, both an immanent and a transcendent phenomenon. In this way, Serinity Young earns a place in the most recent wave of dreamworkers who are making this turn of the century as remarkable in the history of oneirology as the last one was in its time.

Carol Schreier Rupprecht
July 1999

Acknowledgments

I FIRST EXPLORED the meaning of Buddhist dreams in my 1990 dissertation and I owe thanks to several members of the Columbia University faculty. I worked most closely with my adviser, Alex Wayman, and Geshe Lozang Jamspal; each in his own way gave generously of his time and advice. Robert Thurman, Peter Awn, and Brian Smith offered insightful comments, while Ainslie Embree, as ever, provided historical perspective and encouragement. That dissertation has been, however, so substantially revised and restructured as to render this a distinct work. I was able to accomplish this, in part, through the generosity of a Research Assistance Grant from the American Academy of Religion, which enabled me to pursue research in the Tibetan communities of India in the spring of 1995. At the Central Institute of Higher Tibetan Studies in Sarnath I am particularly grateful to Samdong Rinpoche for facilitating my research; to Geshe Tsulthim Phuntsok, who went through the *Kangyur* texts on dreams with me and put his vast knowledge of Tibetan history at my disposal; and to Geshe Thapkay, who brought many texts to my attention and shared his knowledge of the world of Tibetan dreaming. I am indebted also to His Holiness Thrangu Rinpoche, who made time for me in his busy schedule in order to clarify the meaning of dreams in the Kagyu tradition, and to the Venerable Rashmi of the Thai Monastery in Sarnath for his enthusiasm, warm hospitality, and introductions to learned Theravāda monks. At the Library of Tibetan Works and Archives in Dharamsala, Research Librarian Lozang Shastri and Reference Librarian Pema Yeshi went far beyond the call of duty in assisting me. I received additional support in the form of a grant from the International Research and Exchanges Board, with funds provided by the U.S. Department of State (Title VIII) and the National Endowment for the Humanities, which enabled me to do research in several Russian archives. It is a pleasure to thank Natalia Zhukovskaia, who generously arranged an invitation for me from the Institute of Ethnology and

Anthropology of the Russian Academy of Sciences in Moscow, and who shared her expertise on Buryatia culture. In Ulan Ude many thanks to Sesegma Zhambalova, director of the Buryat Historical Museum, for allowing me to see their edition of Tibetan medical paintings and to Lama Tenzin Samayev, who gave so generously of his time and resources. In St. Petersburg special thanks to the members of the Kuntsechoinei Datsan for their warm welcome and hospitality, and to Dr. Vladimir Uspensky of the Institute of Oriental Studies of the Russian Academy of Sciences for taking the time to show me their Tibetan manuscript collection and for interesting discussions about the meaning of dreams.

In Kathmandu, while beginning another project with the support of the Asian Arts Council in 1997, I was able to meet with several Tibetan scholars and advanced practitioners to discuss this work. Among these I am indebted to Khenpo Tsultrim Gyamtso Rinpoche for profound teachings on the Six Yogas of Nāropa and his beautiful singing of Milarepa songs. Penelope Walker of the United States Education Foundation in Nepal provided a warm welcome and support, while Sienna Craig was an endless source of practical information and good humor. I especially want to thank Sue Ridley and Bob Chesteen for their hospitality and friendship at a crucial time in my research.

Closer to home, the Southern Asian Institute of Columbia University, where I was a visiting scholar from 1994 to 1996, and later a research associate, provided me with a congenial and stimulating environment; many thanks to the directors of the institute, John Stratton Hawley and Philip Oldenberg. Thanks also go to the staff of the Columbia University libraries, all of whom were unflagging in their efforts on my behalf. I presented various parts of this study at the Southern Asian Institute, the Hagiography Society of New York, the Jacques Marchais Museum of Tibetan Art, Feminist Scholars of Religion, the University of Pennsylvania, and the Buddhist Studies Seminar of Columbia University. I thank the members of these groups and organizations for their warm interest and lively discussions, which contributed significantly to the final shape of this work. I am additionally indebted to the Schoff Publication Grant of the University Seminars at Columbia University for assistance in the preparation of the manuscript for publication. Special thanks to Dean Aaron Warner, whose encouragement came at an important time.

Sections of this work have appeared in *Dreaming: The Journal of the American Association of Dreams* 8, no. 4 (summer 1998).

I also owe a debt of gratitude to the Association for the Study of Dreams, which facilitated my attendance at one of their conferences and introduced me to the larger world of dream studies. I am particularly grateful to Carol Schreier Rupprecht and Kelley Bulkeley, whose continued friendship and exchange of ideas have been so important in sustaining me in this work. Carol went so far as to read the entire manuscript in two different versions, and her insightful comments contributed to the clarity of this work.

I am truly blessed with generous friends and colleagues who read various parts and versions of this book, helped me think through some of the more difficult sections, and in all ways encouraged and supported this work: Grace Burford, Robley Evans, Ellison Banks Findly, Eugene Gallagher, Naomi Goldenberg, Barbara Gombach, Richard Grigg, Lu Hamlin, Rawn Harding, Tim Harwood, Susannah Heschel, Marguerite Holloway, Laurel Kendall (who suggested the title), Steven Kossak, Bruce Lincoln, Ralph Martin, Jo Ann McNamara, Vivian-Lee Nyitray, Daniel Potter, Aracelia Pearson-Brok, Clint Shaw, Stratford Sherman, Francis Tiso, Marya Ursin, James Waller, Homer Williams, and Kenneth Zysk. Natalie Maxwell Hauptman spent hours going over the entire manuscript with me as well as reading revisions of several chapters. It is a better work because of her wisdom and compassion. Let me hasten to say, though, that full responsibility for the views expressed herein is mine.

Things seem to happen in their own time. This book has been a long and winding road for me, but it was finally brought to a safe harbor at Wisdom Publications when E. Gene Smith became an acquisitions editor there. Gene is a legendary figure among Tibetan scholars, and I cannot imagine having been in better hands. He immediately grasped the concept of this work and gently prodded me to finish it. His kindness, expertise, and worldwide connections have been a true blessing.

Abbreviations

AN	*Aṅguttara Nikāya*, ed. E. Hardy (London: Pali Text Society, 1896)
AS	*Abhiniṣkramaṇasūtra*, trans. by Samuel Beal from the Chinese edition as *The Romantic Legend of Śākya Buddha* (1875; Delhi: Motilal Banarsidass, 1985)
BC	Aśvaghoṣa, *Buddhacarita*, ed. and trans. E. H. Johnston (1936; Delhi: Motilal Banarsidass, 1984)
CS	*Caraka Saṃhitā*, ed. and trans. Ram Karan Sharma and Vaidya Bhagwan Das (Varanasi: Chowkhamba Sanskrit Series, 1977)
EOR	*Encyclopedia of Religion*, ed. Mircea Eliade (New York: Macmillan, 1987)
'Jam mgon	*'Jam mgon chos kyi rgyal po tsoṅ ka pa chen po'i rnam thar thub bstan mdzes pa'i rgyan gcig ṅo mtshar nor bu'i 'phreṅ ba* (Sarnath, Varanasi: Mongolian Lama Guru Deva, 1967)
Jātaka	*The Jātaka Together with Its Commentary*, ed. V. Fausbøll (London: Trübner, 1877)
LV	*Lalitavistara*, ed. P. L. Vaidya (Darbhanga: Mithila Institute, 1958)
Mgur 'bum	*Mi la'i mgur 'bum*, comp. Gtsaṅ smyon He ru ka (Delhi: Sherab Gyaltsen, 1983)

Mi la	*Mi la ras pa'i rnam thar*, comp. Gtsaṅ smyon He ru ka, ed. J. W. de Jong ('s-Gravenhage: Mouton, 1959)
MSV	*Mūlasarvāstivāda Vinaya: The Gilgit Manuscript of the Saṅghabhedavastu, Being the 17th and Last Section of the Vinaya of the Mūlasarvāstivādin*, ed. Raniero Gnoli (Rome: Istituto italiano per il medio ed estremo oriente, 1977)
MV	*Le Mahāvastu*, ed. É. Senart (Paris: L'Imprimerie nationale, 1890)
NK	*Nidānakathā*, in *The Jātaka Together with Its Commentary*, ed. V. Fausbøll (London: Trübner, 1877)
Padma	*Padma bka' thang shel brag ma* (Leh, India: 1968)
SS	*Suśrutasaṃhitā of Suśruta*, ed. and trans. Vidya Jādavji Trikamji Āchārya, 4th ed. (Varanasi: Chowkhamba Orientalia, 1980)
Vinaya	*Vinaya Piṭaka*, ed. Hermann Oldenberg, vol. 1. (1879; London: Pali Text Society, 1969)

Introduction

THE SACRED BIOGRAPHIES of Indo-Tibetan Buddhism are filled with dream narratives that foretell the births of important religious figures, describe their spiritual accomplishments, and reveal esoteric teachings. In these texts dreams are first and foremost an accepted form of cognition, one that can provide access to powerful states of consciousness. I approach this material as a historian of religion, though many of my questions are sociological. The goal of this work is not only to illustrate some of the ways in which dreaming functions in these texts but also to show how certain private dreams were translated into social reality for the larger community—that is, to show what changes occur because of them. Primarily, I am looking at the intersection of biography, history, and religious belief in relation to dreams, and correspondingly in relation to Buddhist ideas about consciousness and cognition. I do not attempt to psychoanalyze the dreams but rather provide a cultural context for them through references to additional contemporary biographical materials and through explorations of related literature, such as philosophical texts that theorize about the meanings of dreams. In the course of my research I have uncovered a network of core issues influenced by belief in the significance of dreams, such as the relation between consciousness and reality, the sources of religious authority, and ways to achieve enlightenment. Dream narratives shed light on these issues in very useful ways.

A central thesis of this study is that while dreams had important functions in early Buddhist biographies, there was an efflorescence of dream narrative in Tibetan biographical literature, especially that of Milarepa and his disciples. Ritual texts from the Tibetan canon and esoteric teachings such as Dream Yoga indicate that this increase in literary dream narrative was accompanied by the conscious pursuit of dream experience. In order to highlight these two poles of Buddhist dreaming, textual dreams and dream practices, I have chosen to focus on dream experiences in the biographies of the Buddha (562–462 B.C.E.) and the Tibetan teacher Milarepa (1040–1123 C.E.). These biographies present a rich and culturally varied picture of Buddhist dream experience, which I compare in terms of continuities and innovations in dream narrative. In this way the reader is first familiarized with the ongoing tradition of Buddhist dream experience and is then presented with a particularly telling example of developments in that tradition.

Dreams are a given in Buddhist biographies. Aside from occasional disparaging remarks about the illusory nature of dreams (and indeed of waking life), their validity is neither questioned nor discussed. Part of their cultural context can be found in early texts that present formal analyses of dreams, such as Buddhaghosa's (fifth century C.E.) canonical commentaries and in later Tibetan texts such as Sangye Gyatso's (1653–1705) commentary on the *Rgyud bzhi*, a famous medical text. What these texts have in common is an understanding of the physical bases of dreams—that many are caused by bodily disturbances and illness or are based on previous waking experiences. A related belief is that dreams can be carried on the internal winds of the body and that these winds can be clarified and controlled through ascetic practices such as breath control and meditation. These practices also clarify consciousness: they give rise to a pure consciousness that is able to break free of physical and emotional limitations, enabling one to enjoy true prophetic dreams. These texts assert that some dreams are sent by the gods, and may be prophetic. They also assert a belief in purely prophetic dreams. Buddhaghosa, for one, limits pure prophetic dreams to very special people, like the Buddha, his mother, and the king of Kosala, thereby creating a dreaming elite similar to that found in many other ancient cultures. The idea is that not just anyone's dream is meaningful. Prophetic dreams come to people who have accrued merit, either in a past or in their present life.

I use the ubiquitous Buddhist symbol of the lotus in my title to evoke several things. The lotus is a pan-Indian symbol of fertility and life to such an extent—indeed it even symbolizes a womb—that it also can represent the entire created universe. (One has only to recall Viṣṇu's famous dream of a lotus growing out of his navel from which the universe arises.) It is also a symbol of purity, spiritual perfection and religious authority par excellence. In South Asian art lotuses usually form the seat or stand of a deity or buddha to signify their transcendence of the material world. They also represent one of the highest teachings of Indo-Tibetan Buddhism, that we all innately possess Buddha Nature as our natural, primordial state of being.

This state is beyond dualities, beyond discursive thought. It just is. However, in ordinary people it is obscured because of defilements, a concept frequently expressed through the image of a pure white lotus (Buddha Nature) emerging from a muddy pond (*saṃsāra*, the world of suffering). Defilements also obscure dreams, which is the reason prophetic dreams are thought to arise from pure consciousness or the pure mind of Buddha Nature. Indeed, one of the dream rituals translated below recommends focusing consciousness in the center of a lotus so that the adept's mind becomes completely purified (see p. 142). Many of the dreams recounted in the present work are those of individuals who dream within this consciousness, a consciousness aspired to by many.

Part I introduces Indian biographical dream narratives, most particularly those appearing in the biographies of the Buddha, and various Buddhist theories about dreaming, both Indian and Tibetan. Chapter 1 sets forth the importance of sacred biography to Buddhist salvational goals, both Theravāda and Mahāyāna, and elucidates the function of dream narratives in biographical texts within the context of the meaning they had, and continue to have, in the traditions of Indo-Tibetan Buddhism. Chapter 2 discusses dream narratives in the ancient Indian biographies of the Buddha. These include the most famous dream narrative in Buddhism, the conception dream of the Buddha's mother, Queen Māyā, and the rarely studied dreams attributed to the Buddha. This chapter concludes with an examination of the dreams other people had about the Buddha, including those from his past lives preserved in the Pali *jātakas* (birth stories). These dreams did not occur in an oneiric vacuum, and chapter 3 introduces early, mainly Theravāda, Buddhist dream theory culled from a variety of textual sources and presents dream narratives from other early Buddhist biographical texts such as the biography of Emperor Aśoka. Chapter 4 explores some of the indigenous, pre-Buddhist, dream practices of Tibet, presents Mahāyāna and Vajrayāna views of dreaming, and concludes with an examination of dream theory in Indo-Tibetan medical texts.

Parts II and III are structured by the comparison of dream narratives from the life of the Buddha with those of Milarepa and his disciples in terms of continuities and innovations. Three categories that demonstrate continuity are conception dreams, shared dreams, and dreams that reveal spiritual accomplishments. Conception dreams refer to dreams parents have around the time their children are conceived (chapter 5). Conception dreams are often shared dreams—those that occur when two or more people have a dream about the same person, thing or event—but shared dreams are treated as an independent category (chapter 6). The third category refers to dreams that portend, and in some cases stimulate, the spiritual accomplishments of the dreamer (chapter 7). These categories are present in Buddhist biographies from the time of the Buddha up to the present. Innovations that appear in the Tibetan biographies are teachings about Dream Yoga (chapter 8), ritual dreaming (chapter 9), and the increased presence of females in male dream experience (chapter 10). The conclusion summarizes my findings, and an appendix explores the Western practices of lucid dreaming in relation to traditional Buddhist dream practices.

This study has inevitably led me to investigate the living tradition of dream beliefs and practices among Tibetan Buddhists. Whenever possible I have sounded out my understanding of Buddhist dream experience with the holders of this tradition, and I frequently refer to their comments.

Most of the original-language texts I cite are available in critical editions, so I have limited original-language quotations to particularly relevant passages. For the convenience of nonspecialist readers, whenever possible I also refer to English translations. In order to produce a reader-friendly text, I have dropped silent Tibetan letters when discussing key terms and persons, though full spellings using the Wylie transliteration system appear in parentheses the first time a name or term is used. In the spirit of friendly redundancy, though, and with the full awareness that not everyone reads a book from beginning to end, these are sometimes repeated, as is other relevant information, such as birth and death dates.

In the bibliography I use the Library of Congress form of transliterated Tibetan citations of titles and authors in order to assist readers in finding references in public catalogs.

❋ PART ONE

Indo-Tibetan Dreaming

FIGURE 1

Queen Māyā's dream.

Bharhut. Indian Museum, Calcutta. Photograph by Mary Storm.

1 *Dreams, Religion, & Sacred Biography*

DREAMS IN WORLD RELIGIONS

In all times and places people have dreamed, and most have tried to understand their dreams.[1] The belief that at least some dreams contain prophecies was and remains an acceptable idea to many people. For instance, the Hebrew Bible records Joseph's prophetic dreams about his future (Gen. 37: 5–11), as well as his correct interpretations of the prophecies contained in the baker's dream (Gen. 40) and Pharaoh's dreams (Gen. 41); in the Christian Bible both the Magi and Mary's husband Joseph are warned in dreams to beware of King Herod (Matt. 2: 12–13); and the vision quests of Native Americans often lead to dreams in which young people are given new names indicative of their future role in society.[2] A widespread type of prophetic dream is the conception dream that parents, mainly mothers, have before the birth of extraordinary children. Examples of such dreams are found all over the world, such as that of the Buddha's mother who dreamed a white elephant entered her womb.[3] In the modern West, Carl Jung gave fresh credence, and a scientific patina, to dreams as a form of prophecy.[4]

Underlying the belief in dreams as a source of prophecy is the ancient idea that some dreams are sent by the gods as messages. For example, Jahweh says to Moses, "If there be a prophet among you, I will make myself known unto him in a vision and will speak to him in a dream" (Num. 12: 6–7); the Book of Acts (16: 9 and 18: 9) records several of the apostle Paul's dreams that he interprets as signs of God's will or in which God actually appears; two accepted *ḥadīths* record that Muhammad received the first revelation of the *Qur'ān* in a dream;[5] and Athena sent Penelope a dream to reassure her about Odysseus (*Odyssey* 4.795–807). Such beliefs affirm dreams as a source of divine communication and in some cases confer religious authority on the dreamer, especially one who can correctly interpret dreams.

Theoretically, prophesying the future is open to anyone who dreams. In reality, however, dreams are connected to the social and religious status of the dreamer. For instance, the dreams of kings were generally believed to have meaning for the whole kingdom, while it is usually the great heroines and heroes of antiquity who are blessed with god-sent dreams. In the religious realm it is almost universally believed that the dreams of saints and other religious virtuosi, such as shamans, ascetics, yogis, prophets, and messiahs, are of great importance not only to themselves but to the religious life of the entire community.

Some of the most valuable sources for religious dreams are the sacred biographies and hagiographies of world religions.[6] They often begin with the mother's auspicious dream before the birth of her child and continue to introduce dreams at pivotal points in the story. Though sacred biographies have distinct meanings in different traditions, their universal role is to portray the ideal type, or saint, through the events of her or his life and spiritual progress, including visions and dreams that reveal the inevitability of that life story. Biographers organized dream experience into narratives, often including dream interpretations, and thereby affirmed dream consciousness.[7] Such narratives provided models against which the faithful could measure their own dreams. As we shall see, the Buddhist biographical tradition exemplifies this process.

DREAMS IN BUDDHIST SACRED BIOGRAPHY

Sacred biographies[8] are central to the salvational goals of Buddhism because they tell the story of those who have achieved enlightenment, and they provide models that others can follow. Buddhist sacred biographies are by definition stories about enlightenment and are believed to possess an intrinsic power capable of leading the hearer or reader to enlightenment.[9] They are simply told guides to the spiritual life, and yet, for those who have received advanced training, they are also rich in esoteric meaning. They come alive to all practitioners, whatever their level of religious expertise. Dreams play a prominent role in these texts; they provide dramatic shifts in the action, underscore the inevitability of subsequent events, and precipitate significant changes in the spiritual and temporal life of the dreamer.

In what follows, I investigate the sociological and religious functions of Buddhist biographical dreams within the context of the meanings they had (and continue to have) in ancient and medieval South Asia. To this end, my decision has been to emphasize what these dreams meant and continue to mean—both within the individual texts in which they appear and within the larger Indo-Tibetan Buddhist tradition.

An obvious, yet important, point about these biographical dreams is that the compilers considered them relevant to the spiritual development of their biographical subjects. Sacred biographies reveal the religious instruction and evolution of an individual, and dreams are an important part of that process. The textual survival of the dreams through the vicissitudes of initially oral transmissions and later handwritten or carved editions in geographically diverse areas among contending schools and orders is in itself a significant indicator of the perceived value of dreams. They are present in Buddhist biographies from the first biography, that of the Buddha, and they persist in modern Buddhist biographies. Further, the relationship between biography and dream experience is reciprocal: the biography confirms the prophecy of dreams by dramatizing their fulfillment while prophetic dreams confirm that it is the biography of someone worthy, someone who possesses religious authority or charisma.

Before going further, it is useful to reflect on the consistent use of the verb "seeing" *(darśana, mthong ba)* rather than "having" a dream in all South Asian texts. Such language expresses the fact that dreams are experienced as given to the dreamer rather than created by them and emphasizes the external origin of the dream, thereby lending them a divine or demonic authority.[10] To say one has *seen* rather than *had* a dream is to suggest that the dreamer is the passive recipient of an objective vision.[11] The literalness of this thinking is expressed in hymn 4.9 of the *Atharva Veda,* which recommends an eye ointment, *aṣana,* for protection from troubled dreams, and in a Tibetan text from the *Tangyur* that also recommends using a certain eye ointment when seeking an auspicious dream.[12] Such ideas are connected to the powerful and pervasive South Asian belief in the redemptive value of *darśana*—seeing—particularly in the sense that the deity or holy person *gives* darśana while the worshipper *takes* it; the devotee both sees the deity and is seen by the deity.[13] When this word is used for dreams, instead of the more usual *svapna* (derived from the verb √*svap,* to sleep), one begins to sense the power of the dream in South Asia: the dreamer not only sees the dream but can be seen by it. Seeing is a powerful force that is equated with the experience of touching and even of knowing.[14] Appropriately enough, this belief is expressed visually in the enlarged eyes of Hindu deities and in the huge Buddha eyes on Himalayan stupas. The *ṛṣis*—literally, the seers—saw the Vedic hymns through an inner vision, an idea that is carried out by the further use of the word *darśana*, in the sense of doctrine, to designate philosophy.[15]

Within the Buddhist tradition, what the Buddha saw is foundational to Buddhism: for instance, the four visions that turned him to the ascetic path and his visions on the night of his enlightenment. Throughout South Asia seeing has deeply religious meanings, especially in Indo-Tibetan Buddhism with its emphasis on visualization practices.[16]

In this book I examine dreams in the biographical literature of two important figures from the Indo-Tibetan Buddhist tradition, the historical Buddha Gautama (c. 566–486 B.C.E.)[17] and Milarepa (Mi la ras pa, 1040–1123 C.E.).[18] Despite significant cultural differences in their lives and in the compositional history of their biographies,[19] dreams are pervasive in both sets of texts.

There are many important religious figures in Indo-Tibetan Buddhism, and a great deal of their biographical literature is available. The historical Buddha, being the founder and primary role model for Buddhism, is an obvious choice for inclusion. The most famous dream in Buddhism is the conception dream of his mother, Queen Māyā, and the Buddha himself dreams and interprets the dreams of others. For purposes of a Tibetan comparison I chose the much loved poet and yogi Milarepa, whose songs and biography are well known throughout Tibet. He is a unique and pivotal figure whose lineage eventually became the Kagyu *(bka' brgyud)* Order. His biographies are particularly rich in dream material, including those of his guru Marpa and of his disciples.

One of the first things I noticed about the Buddhist view of dreams is that it distinguishes dream *consciousness*, the cognitive state of dreaming, from dream *content*, the events or subject matter of a dream.[20] Beginning with the dreams of the Buddha, dream content is important in defining which dream symbols or events are religiously significant.[21] The dreams preserved in the biographies provide a map of the Buddhist dream world, acting as signposts for those who would follow the same path. For instance, Tibetan Buddhists often dream of *stūpas*, *dorjes*, and other common Buddhist symbols and deities, images that are pervasive in their iconography and visualization practices. The idea of a dream map is extended in the belief that all buddhas, whether of the past, the present, or the future, have the same story and consequently the same dream.[22] Indeed, according to the *Mahāvastu*,[23] even the mothers of buddhas have the same dream when they conceive. The idea is that all buddhas are exactly the same down to the most minute details.[24] Underlying this notion is the cyclical nature of the Buddhist concept of time: the same events can and do happen in different times and places, including the same dream. Thus, the *Lotus Sūtra* (XIII.60–70) offers a typology of dreams that precede enlightenment, while the *Ārya Svapna Nirdeśa Sūtra*, in its description of 108 auspicious dreams, suggests both the common dream world that is available to striving Buddhists and the value of dreams as signs of spiritual progress and accomplishment.

Overall, Tibetan Buddhists are not interested in the psychological interpretation of dreams; rather they are interested in dreams as prophecies, and they use dreams to achieve a more awakened state of being. I have chosen to follow the emphasis on dream *consciousness*, since it reflects this traditional understanding of dreams and because it allows us to use the biographies not necessarily as records of what actually happened, a highly questionable enterprise especially for the earliest texts, but for what they reveal about the beliefs and practices of their compilers and their audiences.

One of the functions of dream consciousness in the biographies is to provide the dreamer with cognitive experiences that are beyond everyday notions of spatial and temporal reality—such as receiving prophecies about the future, communicating with deities, and gaining access to realms beyond the world of normal waking consciousness.[25] Ancient Indian cosmology was elaborate in its constructions, porous in its boundaries, and not overly concerned with consistency.[26] The same may be said of Tibetan cosmology.[27] This contributed to the value placed on knowledge of these realms,[28] whether gained from dreams or other visionary experiences.[29] Such knowledge, combined with the ability to foresee the future and having access to deities, helped to establish the spiritual and, where these two merge, the political authority of the dreamer in large part because the possession of such knowledge and abilities was a sign of extraordinary power, or charisma.[30]

The successful dreamer is able to call forth a deep response in others by giving voice to their unconscious concerns, or at least by expressing such concerns in a way that the listeners find satisfying enough to act on the dream. Whether the dreamer interprets her or his own dream or someone else is called upon to do this, all the dream material (by which I mean at least the three stages of having the dream, narrating it, and receiving an interpretation)[31] must combine in such a way that the dream elicits belief and motivates people to act according to it. The right set of dream material confers charismatic or religious authority on the dreamer. Although any religiously significant dream confers some charisma on the dreamer, a dream that is supported and acted upon by the larger community—whether it be a village on the Amazon, a small religious community in medieval Tibet, or a royal court in ancient Egypt—confirms the dreamer as having access to highly significant information not readily available to others.[32]

Just as for other signs of charisma, though, the dreams must be "proved," that is, they must be realized and borne out in real life, especially in a way that is of benefit to the community.[33] For instance, shamans[34] often have their first contacts with supernatural beings through dreams, and one way of proving the extraordinary quality of their dreams and looking after the welfare of their community is to become effective at healing. Another well-known historical example occurs in the life of the biblical figure Joseph. His dreams of sheaves of wheat and stars (Gen. 37: 5–11) are clear signs of his charismatic authority, at least over his brothers, who understood all too well the meaning of his dreams and attempted to prevent his ascendancy by selling him into slavery in Egypt. Once there, Joseph's ability to interpret the dreams of others (Gen. 40, 41), especially those of the Pharaoh,[35] led the Pharaoh to confer both religious and political authority on him, a position that eventually enabled Joseph to provide for the welfare of his community. As these examples suggest, granting a dream religious authority, acknowledging its charisma, is not such a radical idea because the charisma has to be proved. The life of the dreamer is the proof of the dream, either because the dream comes true or because the dreamer lives out its spiritual impact. An example of the latter can be found in Islam, where a ḥadīth from Tabari describes Muhammad's call to apostleship through a dream in which the angel Gabriel appears.[36] Muhammad's tremendous success, especially his military victories, were taken as a sign of Allah's favor. In other words his charisma was proved. In varying degrees, the biographical subjects of this study, the Buddha and Milarepa, were such charismatic leaders.

An example of rejected charisma in the life of the Buddha demonstrates this point. After achieving enlightenment, one of the first people to whom he announces his revelation, the Ājīvika Upaka, merely said, "That may be so," and just walked away.[37] The Buddha then encountered the five men who had accompanied him during his years of asceticism; they became his disciples, thereby confirming his charisma and thus beginning his ministry. These two contrasting events show that charisma is essentially a relational term; it is confirmed by the charismatic's followers and denied by others. This recognition is essentially tentative, however, in that the leader is required to prove his or her charisma by displaying magical powers or attending to the welfare of the community of believers. If charisma is not proved, the followers leave.

In Indian and Tibetan biographies there are two categories of dreamers. First, there are the heroes—those who have shaped the tradition—whose dreams are as important as their words and deeds. Second, there are the people closely associated with the hero—his parents, gurus, and disciples—whose dreams serve to reveal various aspects of his spiritual powers, such as his connections to divine realms, his prescience, or his ability to interpret dreams. Both categories of dreamers contribute to the establishment of Buddhist dream maps not only through the content of their dreams but by the interpretations that often accompany them.

My thesis about dreams in these biographical texts is fivefold. First, dreams are an accepted form of cognition.[38] A clear division between the waking world as reality and the world of dreams as illusion, or unreality, is a fairly recent development, and one that is not shared by all cultures.[39] Many ancient people believed dreams to be an acceptable form of cognition about other realities; for instance, dreams about the dead were thought to reveal information about the afterlife.[40] Further, information gathered in dreams could be, and often was, applied to the waking world.[41] As the biographies make clear, dreams help one to *see* other realms and the future, to learn about salvation and a higher reality.

Second, control over dream cognition establishes religious authority. Examples of such control are correctly interpreting dreams (one's own or other people's), causing other people to dream, dreaming solutions to problems or questions, and ultimately controlling the contents and events of one's own dreams. In stressing cognition I am in part capitalizing on the language of dreaming used in most ancient texts: people say they have *seen* a dream, not they have *had* a dream. But further, ancient Indian and medieval Tibetan texts themselves discuss dreaming as a cognitive experience.

Third, *some* dreams provide access to the charisma associated with religious authority.[42] Telling a dream is a narrative, and when someone narrates their dream they reveal something about who they are. Buddhist saints tend to narrate their dreams from a position of authority, as an event that they fully understand. This is partly due to the way the dream narrative fits in with the larger narration of their lives; the dream reveals a significant shift—

it is a moment when, for the dreamer, the world changed. The saints met that change with confidence and authority because they could interpret their dreams; they knew what the dreams portended, and they were ready for it. This confidence and authority contrast with the uncertain dream narrations of other people in the biographies—parents, disciples, and others—who suspect their dreams portend something but must seek the advice of an expert to understand them.

Fourth, in all cases the dreams preserved in the biographies are highly relevant to Buddhist experience; they are understood to be meaningful encounters with spiritual realms or beings—the dreamer crosses a threshold and is often transformed. The dream is perceived as a direct religious experience that the dreamer translates into the waking social world, whether by recounting and interpreting it or by acting upon it. To interpret a dream is to provide a cultural context for the dream experience; the interpretation mediates between the dreaming and waking realms. Significant dreams are never just self-referential: they are a bridge between these two realms, between subjective experience and social existence.[43]

My fifth and final thesis is that dreams are a vital part of the functioning of sacred biography. The biographies of founders, such as Buddha, Muhammad, and Jesus, establish patterns that become guides for the behavior and spiritual aspirations of the faithful, while the biographies of those who come after introduce a tension between innovation and continuity.[44] Continuity is maintained by faithfully following the model established in the life of the founder, yet innovations slip in when an attempt is made to express the uniqueness of those who come after[45]—especially when the tradition moves into different cultural settings. The biographies under study here contain examples of both these points of view. Dreams provide a means for examining such tension because they both dramatize continuities—with, for instance, dreams in the biographies of the Buddha—and yet highlight differences, as when they introduce new religious practices, such as Dream Yoga.

Sacred biography is a particularly accessible way to study a religion, and a revealing one. Reginald Ray has noted that in biographies "one finds a Buddhism that is alive and in evolution, and also relatively unselfconscious"; indeed, they often reveal "deep-seated beliefs and values."[46] Since more than a thousand years of Buddhist history separate the composition dates of the Buddha's and Milarepa's biographies, the texts cannot help but disclose the evolution of Buddhist beliefs and values. Buddhist biographies are the lived reality of Buddhism, and they describe beliefs and practices, such as the pervasive belief in the importance of dreams, that are not readily apparent in other types of Buddhist literature.

My approach to the biographies has been to take them at face value as cultural documents that reveal the spiritual life of Indo-Tibetan Buddhists. This method has also been used to great advantage in the study of Christian hagiography by Donald Weinstein and Rudolph Bell, who explain their approach as follows: "Our method is the traditional one of examining the texts and letting the stories speak for themselves wherever possible. What matters in this endeavor is not so much whether the stories are true as that they were told and retold."[47] In the Buddhist case what matters is that faithful Buddhists believe that the dreams and other events in the biographies actually occurred, and this belief shapes their understanding of what is relevant to the path of enlightenment.

ELITE VERSUS POPULAR VIEWS OF DREAMING

Buddhism advocates following a course of spiritual practices that will precipitate a change of consciousness leading to a direct, personal realization of the illusory nature of attachment, desire, and reality.[48] In other words, aspirants need to change the way they experience the world, the way they cognize or make sense of it. This emphasis on individual experience goes back to the earliest texts, such as the *Mahāparinibbāna Sutta*, in which the dying Buddha tells his disciples to rely on two things: their own experience and the Dharma (the Buddhist teachings),[49] the two bases of religious authority in Buddhism. So, while the teachings of the Buddha (his revelation as it was preserved in the canons)[50] are the best guide to having this personal experience, the focus is on a personal experience of the doctrine, not doctrine for its own sake. This is critical to any understanding of Buddhism: enlightenment can only be achieved by individual experience—no one else can do it for you (although others, such as those who have themselves achieved enlightenment because they are believed capable of pointing the way, can help).[51] Consequently, there is a great reliance on biography, especially that of the Buddha,[52] which reveals an individual's successful struggle toward enlightenment. Of course, the living guru is also critical, but she or he can only offer guidance, not realization itself.

Religious authority is thus traditionally defined as whatever the historical Buddha is believed to have done in his life, all of which is thought to be appropriate and to carry the weight of his example. Thus, the greatest authority for the validity of dreams comes from the Buddha's biographical literature because he himself both dreams and validates the dreams of others when he interprets them. Tibetan biographies follow this pattern when they record their subjects' dreams. These biographies are part of an evolving, legitimate tradition;[53] indeed they became part of the extended Buddhist canon, which is itself a tremendous source of religious authority. As will be shown, though, the biographies maintained their connection to the popular or folk tradition that contributed so much to their composition.

Dreams also have an important position in the nonbiographical and elite texts of Buddhism, such as the commentaries, the *sūtras,* the *tantras,* and so on. Given the range of texts that refer to dreaming, it should come as no surprise that there are contending ideas about its meaning and function. In fact, contradictory views can appear within the same text, even the biographies. For instance, after a dream is recited, discussed, interpreted, and acted upon as a vital, meaningful communication, a warning may be included about the deceptive nature of dreams. Such a warning makes the point that only some, but not all, dreams are significant. It also represents dreams as an example of the illusory and empty nature of reality.[54] Essentially, these seemingly contending beliefs about dreams are really a matter of emphasis between elite and popular views.

Elite views are most often those of literate scholar-monastics who pursue esoteric studies, while popular views are those of the laity and nonliterate monastics who are often dependent on oral presentations of texts.[55] Popular views mix Buddhist and indigenous beliefs[56]—this has certainly been the case for all the countries to which Buddhism spread—and most indigenous traditions accepted some dreams as meaningful events.[57] From its very beginnings, Buddhism has both drawn on indigenous dream traditions, such as the Brahmanical interpretation of Queen Māyā's dream, and created its own, as in the Buddha's interpretation of his wife's dream that flies in the face of Brahmanical dream interpretation. In Tibet the elite/popular distinction is further extended by the diversity of religious virtuosi among Buddhist, Bon, and folk traditions such as wandering monks and yogis, exorcists, hermits, and so on.

The situation I am describing is perhaps best summed up by Clifford Geertz: "What a given religion is—its specific content—is embodied in the images and metaphors [popular tradition] its adherents use to characterize reality.... But such a religion's career—its historical course—rests in turn upon the institutions [elite tradition] which render these images and metaphors available to those who thus employ them."[58] In pursuing the images and metaphors of Buddhist dreamers I have encountered the ideology of elite Buddhist institutions as well as spontaneous bursts of popular piety.

It is helpful to bear in mind that there was and is no central Buddhist authority ruling on new doctrines. Paul Williams has characterized the growth of Mahāyāna as a "'doctrinal widening,' rendering doctrinally respectable certain activities and beliefs that some monks viewed with disdain, and associated primarily with the ultimately useless activities of lay people."[59] Buddhist doctrine was never a uniform monolith. From its earliest days Buddhism adapted to the local conditions to which its missionary activities inevitably led, and Mahāyāna developed more as a highly diverse federation of cults based on different sūtras and their attendant practices than as a univocal movement.[60] Finally, throughout its long history in many diverse cultures there was never an attempt to *impose* uniform views on anyone. There is no central Buddhist authority to do so, and even a cursory look at Buddhism around the world or even in one culture reveals a tremendous diversity. Although I have attempted to trace some of the causes for the contradictory opinions about dreaming in Buddhism, underlying these causes is the simple fact that Buddhism is comfortable with such contradictions. Dreaming, like everything else, can and should be used to help individuals achieve enlightenment in whatever way best suits them: a dedicated practitioner may be led toward the esoteric practice of Dream Yoga, while those with other concerns and obligations may be reminded that since all experience is dreamlike they should apply themselves to being less attached to worldly phenomena.

The main point is that there were continual interactions between monastics and laity in the religious, economic, political, and cultural life of India and Tibet.[61] Consequently, these biographies are not the exclusive materials of one or the other of these divisions, but are read or heard by all practitioners, lay or monastic, rich or poor, literate or not. The conflicting statements that often surround dreams within the same text illustrate these different views of the elite and the popular traditions. Both traditions accepted dreams as a meaningful form of cognition, but the elite tradition maintained an additional position on dreams, that they are a prime example of the empty and illusory nature of this world.[62] I will have more to say about the relation of dreams, illusion, and emptiness in chapter 4.

THE PSYCHOANALYTIC STUDY OF DREAMS

Before turning to the dreams themselves, a few words need to be said about the psychoanalytic study of dreams. Even though my own thinking has been sharpened by that methodology, I have not attempted to use it here. Freud's basic idea in *The Interpretation of Dreams* was that dreams reveal unconscious wishes and motivations,[63] the meaning of which can be revealed in psychoanalysis by the patient's free associations to the various images of the dream. Consequently, the meaning of the dream is personal and highly subjective. In the case of historical dreamers, who are not available to uncover their subjective or unconscious meanings, scholars of historical texts often had to find different paths.[64] Significantly, it was the absence of such associations that led Freud to exclude literary dream material from his own work on dreams.[65] Of course, one can no longer *not* be influenced by Freud's ideas, and, in fact, we cannot help but see some of the "Freudian" implications of these dreams. As W. H. Auden has succinctly put it, Freud "is no more a person now but a whole climate of opinion."[66]

While Jung agreed with Freud regarding the need for the associations of the dreamer,[67] one of his expansions on Freud's theory of dreaming is his distinction between big and little dreams. Little dreams are limited to the affairs of everyday life, while big dreams have such a lasting impact on individuals that they are often remembered for a lifetime.[68] Big dreams are rich in the symbols of myth and religion—archetypes—that arise from the collective unconscious of humanity rather than from the personal unconscious of the individual. The associations of the individual dreamer are therefore not helpful in interpreting such dreams because they are essentially about the process of individuation, or the integration of the conscious and the unconscious.[69] The confidence with which various Jungian studies, for instance, those of Jung himself, interpret literary dreams (those dreams preserved in literary texts of both fiction and purported truth) leads me to suppose they believe these are big dreams that can be interpreted without the associations of the dreamer. The reader is, of course, free to pursue such interpretations of Buddhist dream material,[70] though caution should be exercised before wholeheartedly accepting these accounts as the faithful reproduction of the actual dreams of the Buddha or Milarepa. And, as fascinating as Jung's theory of individuation is, one should pay close attention to the Buddhist notion of the self discussed below. If indeed Buddhists experience individuation, they certainly begin from a very different existential base than Westerners.[71] Lastly, Jung himself was quite clear about the need for extensive training before undertaking dream interpretation, including being psychoanalyzed. Perhaps more important, he recommended meeting the dream with the expectation that one has absolutely no idea what it could mean![72]

The dream process adumbrates a large, meaningful space in Buddhist religious experience that rewards attention. The purpose of this study is to elucidate that space through the sociological and religious functions of Buddhist dreams rather than their psychological and individual meanings[73]—in ways that, I hope, will illuminate their historical and cultural situation more than my own. Of course, it is the nature of dreams to be rich and fluid in meaning, and frequently I will examine the same dream differently in different contexts. For instance, when I discuss Emperor Aśoka's dream in chapter 3 it is largely in terms of the relation of dreams and karma, while in chapter 10 I discuss it in relation to gender ideologies. There simply is no accurate monolithic viewpoint on the meaning of any one dream, just as there is no unitary view in Buddhist dream theory.

2 Dreams in the Biographies of the Buddha

QUEEN MĀYĀ'S DREAM

THE BIOGRAPHIES OF THE BUDDHA present a rich assortment of dream experiences and their interpretations. Some of these are used to assert Buddhist ideas that depart from the Brahmanical tradition. For example, Queen Māyā's conception dream is presented and interpreted in a straightforward Brahmanical style, except for the proviso that the child predicted by the dream will be either a great king or a great renouncer—Brahmanical dream interpretations do not usually offer alternative outcomes. This proviso interrupts the traditional setting of the righteous king celebrating the birth of his son and heir who, when he has sons of his own and performs the correct rituals, will maintain his father and other ancestors in their afterlife. All this is thrown into jeopardy by the alternative and anti-Brahmanical prediction that the Buddha may become a celibate renouncer, a *śramaṇa.* This, the best known dream in Buddhist literature, sets the stage for the religious innovations that will follow.

The core elements of Māyā's dream are that she sees a magnificent white elephant which, by striking her right side with its trunk, is able to enter her womb. This is often referred to as Queen Māyā's conception dream, and many versions of this dream are preserved in early Buddhist iconography and texts. In fact, it is one of the earliest images of Buddhist iconography,[1] and representations of this dream kept up an even pace with the spread of Buddhism. It appears in various important sites throughout Buddhist history, such as Sānchī, Bharhut, Sarnath, Amāravati, Nāgārjunakonda, Ajaṇṭā, Gandhara, and sites in Central, Southeast and East Asia.[2]

The importance of this dream, and of dreams in general, is further suggested by its inclusion in most of the biographical sources on the Buddha.[3]

In addition to the *Lalitavistara,*[4] the dream and its interpretation are preserved in the *Abiniṣkramaṇasūtra,*[5] the *Buddhacarita,*[6] the *Mahāvastu,*[7] and the *Mūlasarvāstivāda Vinaya,*[8] from which it enters the Tibetan canon.[9] It is mentioned in other Tibetan biographies as well; for instance, two editions of Padmasambhava's biography contain references to it.[10]

One of the most elaborate versions of Māyā's dream is contained in the *Nidāna-Kathā,* hereinafter the *NK,* the standard Theravāda biography of the Buddha:

> At that time the Midsummer festival [Asālaha] was proclaimed in the city of Kapilasvatthu....During the seven days before the full moon Mahāmāyā had taken part in the festivities....On the seventh day she rose early, bathed in scented water, and distributed alms....Wearing splendid clothes and eating pure food, she performed the vows of the holy day. Then she entered her bed chamber, fell asleep, and saw the following dream.
>
> The four guardians of the world [gods] lifted her on her couch and carried her to the Himālaya mountains and placed her under a great sāla tree....Then their queens bathed her...dressed her in heavenly garments, anointed her with perfumes and put garlands of heavenly flowers on her....They laid her on a heavenly couch, with its head towards the east. The Bodhisattva, wandering as a superb white elephant...approached her from the north. Holding a white lotus flower in his trunk, he circumambulated her three times. Then he gently struck her right side, and entered her womb. *(Dakkhinapassaṁ tāḷetva kucchim paviṭṭhasadiso.)*[11]

When Māyā wakes up she tells the dream to her husband, who sends for learned Brahmans to interpret it. They predict that Queen Māyā will give birth to a son who will become a universal ruler *(cakkavatti),* unless he abandons his home for the religious life, in which case he will become a buddha.[12] An alternative outcome is as unusual in Buddhist dream interpretation[13] as it is in the Brahmanical system: it suggests that possibilities exist within the Buddha, but that he will need help to get in touch with them. Such help occurs through the gods who, as we just saw, aided in his conception and who later cause his four visions of the sick man, the old man, the dead man, and the monk, visions that turn the Buddha from a worldly life to one of asceticism.[14] What is more, the full potential of Māyā's dream is realized through another set of dreams, those of the Buddha, which I will discuss shortly.

Another text, the *Mahāvastu*, hereinafter the *MV*, challenges the alternative interpretation. This text contains two versions of the dream and its interpretation, that of the soothsayers *(vaipañcikas)*,[15] who offer two different outcomes, and that of the god Brahmā[16] who corrects their interpretation by stating unequivocally that the child will become a buddha.[17] Further, Brahmā's interpretation actually provides a guide to the symbols of the conception dream:

> The woman who saw in a dream the sun from the sky enter her womb will give birth to one who is the woman's jewel, her husband's treasure. He will be a universal king, a protector of men.
>
> The woman who saw in a dream the moon from the sky enter her womb will give birth to one who is a godlike man. He will be a powerful universal king.
>
> The woman who saw in a dream the sun from the sky enter her womb will give birth to one who bears the marks of excellence. He will be the best and most powerful universal king.
>
> The woman who saw in a dream a white elephant enter her womb will give birth to one as select as the elephant is among animals. He will be a Buddha who understands the meaning of Dharma.[18]

It is of interest that the *MV*, along with other Buddhist texts that preserve this dream, changes the elephant's traditional association with royalty[19] to that of buddhahood, a clear case of shifting Brahmanical dream imagery to make room for new Buddhist interpretations.[20]

From the time of the Indus valley civilization until the present, the elephant has been a rich and enduring motif in Indian art and literature, in which it usually symbolizes majesty, raw power, and great dignity.[21] In Indian myth an elephant, Airāvata, is the mount *(vāhana)* of Indra, king of the gods. Indra is also a rain god, which heightens the elephant's traditional connection with rain; a connection furthered by frequent representation of clouds as celestial elephants.[22] That the Buddhists shared this idea is brought out in the *Vessantara Jātaka,* where a white elephant guarantees the prosperity of the kingdom through its magical ability to bring rain.

Interestingly, a close reading of Māyā's dream in the *NK*, *LV*, and *MV* suggests that the dream elephant is the progenitor of the Buddha, not King Śuddhodana.[23] The *NK* specifies that the elephant is the Buddha, so he is incarnating himself. Additionally, many ancient people believed that women could conceive through dreams,[24] and some women slept in temples in order to have dreams as a cure for infertility.[25] Such a dream cure is a provocative concept when applied to Queen Māyā, particularly since H. W. Schumann says she was forty years old when her first child, the Buddha, was born, and according to the *NK* it is while participating in a religious festival that she dreams of being carried to heaven.[26] The *MV* in particular argues for Śuddhodana not being the biological father when it has Māyā pointedly ask his permission to remain celibate for one night, the night she has the dream.[27] This belief in conception through dreams is well documented in later Tibetan biographies, especially Padmasambhava's, probably as much due to earlier beliefs as to the popularity of Māyā's dream.

It is quite remarkable that this dream in all its variants is so widespread both textually and iconographically, and from such an early period. Here, at the very beginnings of Buddhism, dreaming is central. Indeed, without Māyā's dream there would be no Buddha and hence no Buddhism. And, as we are about to see, the dreams of the Buddha are deeply related to Māyā's dream in that they announce its fulfillment as well as continue its motif of birth.

THE DREAMS OF THE BUDDHA

Chapter 14 of the *LV* describes the events leading up to the Buddha's departure from home, among which is a remarkable series of dreams, including those of the Buddha. The chapter begins with the dream of the Buddha's father, King Śuddhodana, that portends the imminent departure of his son. In it he sees his son leaving the palace surrounded by gods, and then he sees him dressed in the red-brown garments of a wandering ascetic *(pravrajitaṃ)*. The text says this dream was *caused (upadarśayati)* by the Buddha,[28] which gives a positive value to this dream and sets a receptive stage for those that follow. It is also the first of many signs of the Buddha's mastery of the dream realm—here as the instigator of his father's dream, later as the interpreter of his wife's dream, and finally as a receiver of significant dreams.

The next person to dream in this chapter is the Buddha's wife Gopā. On the night the Buddha is preparing to leave home, she is awakened by a terrifying dream, which she asks the Buddha to interpret. He interprets the frightening imagery of her dream (she is naked, her hands and feet have been cut off, Mt. Meru is shaken, and so on) positively and then describes to her the dreams that holy men *(narapuṁgavānām)*[29] have when it is time to abandon their home life for the ascetic life. These holy men are defined as those who have accumulated virtuous deeds in the past *(purvaśubha-karmasamuccajānāni)*, a reference to past buddhas,[30] all of whom are believed to have these specific dreams at the same time in their lives.[31] Consequently, the Buddha uses the third person *(so = saḥ)* in his speech, though he is describing his own dreams:

1. He saw [his] hands and feet stir the water of the four great oceans, and the whole earth became a well-adorned bed with Mount Meru as a pillow.
2. He saw a light spread throughout the world, dispelling darkness, and a parasol came out of the earth,[32] spreading light in the three worlds and extinguishing suffering.
3. Four black and white animals licked his feet.
4. Birds of four colors became a single color.
5. He climbed a mountain of repulsive dung, and was not soiled by it.[33]

The *LV* continues with more of his dreams, but since only the first five dreams appear in other early Buddhist texts, I will limit my discussion to these for the present.

The *Aṅguttara-Nikāya (AN)* also records these dreams, referring to them specifically as the actual dreams of the Buddha, calling him by his title of Tathāgata: "When the Tathāgata...was not yet wholly awakened, but a being awakening, there came five great dreams."[34] The *AN*'s presentation of these five dreams provides some insight into one of the functions of dreams in Buddhist biographical narratives: they can be stimulators of enlightenment. The *AN* refers to the Buddha as *anabhisambuddha* (not yet wholly awakened, not yet enlightened) when he has the first of these five dreams, but says he is *abhisambuddha* (wholly awakened) after the dream.[35] So, as a consequence of having one of these dreams something is awakened within him, as is shown in the interpretation of the first dream: "When the Tathāgata...dreamed that the earth was his bed of state...[then] full awakening to the highest was wholly awakened [within him]."[36] Here the text is using waking up from dreams and sleep as a metaphor for waking up to the equally illusory nature of everyday reality. In fact, it suggests that in sleep, in dreams, one comes closer to understanding the nature of reality than in waking consciousness. This play of tension between dreaming, waking reality, illusion, and enlightened awareness continues throughout the Buddhist tradition.

The second dream in the *AN* differs slightly from the *LV* in that it has *tiriya* grass, rather than a parasol, grow out of the Buddha's navel.[37] It interprets this as a reference to the Eightfold Path, which was "wholly awakened" in him by this dream.[38] The *AN* suggests a causal relation for these two dreams: they contain signs that both cause the Buddha to "awaken" and cause the Eightfold Path to awaken within him. This term *sambuddha*, "awakened," suggests that the seed for awakening and the seed of the Eightfold Path were lying dormant in the Buddha—they only needed to be stimulated by dreams. It also subtly harkens back to Queen Māyā's dream, in the sense that the interpretation of her dream emphasized its potential. The dream could mean two things; either the child she conceived would become a great king or he would become a Buddha. The Buddha's dreams reflect her dream in that her dream's promised potential is now made active, or awakened and brought to life, by his dreams.

Belief in the activating function of dreams is also contained in a jātaka tale from the *Divyāvadāna* about a previous life in which Gautama Buddha met a buddha of another time, Dīpaṃkara, who predicted his future buddhahood. This is a necessary step on the long path to buddhahood: one must meet a buddha, be inspired by him, and receive a prediction from him that buddhahood will eventually occur. In this story Gautama Buddha is a young Brahman who has ten dreams: "that he drank the great ocean; that he flew through the air; that he touched and clasped with his hand both the sun and the moon; that he harnessed the chariot of the king; and that he saw ascetics, white elephants, geese, lions, a great rock, and mountains."[39] He is advised by a powerful ascetic *(ṛṣi)* that only the Buddha Dīpaṃkara can interpret his dreams; thus his dreams are the stimulus that makes him seek contact with this buddha who helps him to make the first step on the path to buddhahood. Although they are contained in texts composed in different times and places, the dream from a past life resonates with Queen Māyā's conception dream, King Śuddhodana's dream of the Buddha's departure from home, and the Buddha's five dreams—in all four cases dreams precipitate events in the Buddha's long journey toward enlightenment. Also, in the *Divyāvadāna* the ability to correctly interpret dreams is represented as a sign of superior spiritual ability or authority, since even a powerful ascetic cannot do it.

Returning to the *AN*, the interpretations of the third, fourth, and fifth of the Buddha's dreams address the after effects of the first two: the Buddha's awakening and the awakening of the Eightfold Path. It says the third dream (of white animals) refers to the white-robed householders who took refuge with the Buddha and that the fourth dream (of four birds) refers to members of the four castes who became nuns and monks.[40] These birds of four different colors (castes) become one color; that is, they lose their caste by entering the Buddhist order, where such distinctions are ignored. The fifth dream of walking on a mountain of dung refers to the Buddha receiving his requisites ("robes, alms, lodging, and medicines")[41] and yet not becoming attached to them—like the dung of his dream, they do not stick to him. Needless to say, these are also prophetic dreams in that many householders did take refuge with the Buddha, he did accept followers from the four castes, and he was not attached to the offerings made to him.

A third text that preserves the five dreams of the Buddha is the *Mahāvastu.* Somewhat like the *LV*, the *MV* presents the dreams of the Buddha's relatives along with those of the Buddha, and both the content and the meaning of his dreams resemble those in the *AN.* For instance, the second dream in both the *MV* and the *AN* has grass growing out of the Buddha's navel. In addition the *MV*, like the *AN*, contains an interpretation of these dreams. In this text it is the Buddha who tells his followers about his dreams and also interprets *(vyakaroti)* them. Thus, this is another text that attributes a positive value to dreams by having the Buddha narrate his dreams and interpret their meaning.[42] This is also the beginning of the tradition—more fully developed by Tibetan Buddhism—wherein only a master of dreams can correctly interpret dreams and where the successful interpretation of prophetic dreams is a sign of spiritual accomplishment.

The Buddha says that the prophecy contained in each dream was fulfilled *(vipāka)* by a later act of his,[43] a term that we shall see is used in the *Milindapañha* to mean the outcome or result of a dream.[44] Buddhaghosa, the great fifth-century C.E. scholar-monk who wrote voluminous commentaries on the Pali canon,[45] uses the word *vipāka* to discuss how prophetic dreams predict future events that have already matured, making it just a matter of time before they manifest in waking reality. The fulfillments of the *MV* are as follows: The first dream in which the Buddha rests, covering the whole earth, is fulfilled when he awakes to perfect enlightenment, as in the *AN.* The second dream, when *kṣīrikā* grass grows out of his navel and reaches the sky, is fulfilled when he turns the wheel of Dharma and teaches the Four Noble Truths.[46] The third dream is fulfilled by the many people who serve the Buddha, the householders of the *AN.* The fourth dream, as in the *AN*, is fulfilled by people from the four castes who follow the Buddha.[47] The fifth dream is fulfilled, as in the *AN*, when the Buddha receives the requisites and does not become attached to them.

A fourth text to preserve the five dreams of the Buddha is the *Mūlasarvāstivāda Vinaya (MSV)*. As in the *LV* and *MV*, the *MSV* presents these dreams within the context of dreams had by his relatives (his aunt Mahāprajāpatī and his wife) on the night of his departure from home.[48] The content of these dreams is the same as in the *MV* and *AN* in that the second dream is of grass *(tṛṇa)* growing out of his navel and, as in the *LV* and *MV*, the Buddha understands the meaning of his dream. He says: "From what I have seen in my dreams, it will not be long before I attain highest knowledge."[49]

In all the texts one of the most striking feature of these five dreams is the cosmic proportions of the Buddha's body: He can extend his hands and feet as far as the four oceans and needs a pillow the size of Mount Meru for his head. While this is suggestive of the theory that all buddhas actually have three bodies *(trikāya, sku gsum)*—the *dharmakāya*, the *saṃbhogakāya*, and the *nirmāṇakāya*—it also evokes other pervasive Indian stories, such as that of Puruṣa in which the body of a huge man is cut up to create the cosmos. Most especially, it evokes the sleeping god Viṣṇu, who dreamed the universe into existence as a "lotus that was the quintessence of the three worlds" growing out of his navel.[50] All four versions of the Buddha's dreams reflect this imagery. In the *LV* "a parasol comes out of the earth to shelter the three worlds," whereas in the *AN, MV,* and *MSV* grass grows from his navel up to the sky[51]—all symbols of a creative force rising up to the heavens. The "three worlds" refers to the three-tiered theory of the universe of ancient India: earth, atmosphere, and heavens. In interpreting the Buddha's dream both the *AN* and the *MV* connect this growth from his navel with the Four Noble Truths and the Eightfold Path—the Buddhist means of crossing over from the three worlds, bounded by time and space, to the freedom of enlightenment. Reduced to their simplest elements, both the Hindu and Buddhist stories describe the profound creative power of dreams and their ability to link the three worlds of the Indian universe and to break through the barriers that normally exist between these worlds in waking consciousness. Ultimately, these dream-stories attest to the power of beings such as the Buddha and Viṣṇu to exist in, and affect, all three worlds at once.[52] At the same time, both Viṣṇu's dream and the Buddha's second dream evoke birth metaphors; life comes out of their bellies. And while Viṣṇu's and Buddha's dreams have their obvious parallels, the Buddha's second dream once again harkens back to Māyā's conception dream, reversing the imagery of something entering her belly with something coming out of his: Māyā conceives the Buddha, the world savior, and the Buddha gives birth to the Dharma, which saves the world.

There is a problem, however, with the timing of the Buddha's dreams in these texts. Buddhaghosa, an important early source for a formal Buddhist dream theory, says the following in his commentary on this section of the *AN:* "When a Bodhisattva sees these dreams then the next day he will attain enlightenment *[buddho]*."[53] Indeed, Buddhaghosa actually has these dreams take place on the night of enlightenment, while the Buddha is sitting under the bodhi tree. He says: "Having gone to Bodhimanda [his seat under the Bodhi tree] in order to attain the highest enlightenment and while dwelling in Jetavana at the time of being a budding Buddha, the five great dreams were seen."[54] The *AN*, however, is not specific about the timing of these dreams, only saying that they occurred before the Buddha's full awakening or enlightenment (abhisambuddha). (The structure of the *AN* does not lend itself to chronology because it is a collection of brief sermons arranged into sections by number. For example, section 2 contains a sermon on the Two Things to be Avoided, section 4 the Four Noble Truths, and so on. The Five Great Dreams of the Buddha were placed in section 5.) The *LV, MV,* and the *MSV,* however, are linear biographical texts, and in them the position of the Buddha's dreams (relative to the dreams that his father, aunt, and wife have on the night before the Buddha leaves home) indicates that they occurred several years before his enlightenment.

Modern scholarship also lacks precision in its conclusions about the timing of these dreams. Har Dayal, even though he cites the *LV* and *MV*, also says the Buddha had these dreams the night before his enlightenment,[55] as does Roy Amore, who uses the *AN* and the *MV.*[56] E. M. Hare, in his notes to the *AN*, refers the reader to Edward Thomas, who, citing the *AN* and *MV*, also says that these dreams occurred the night before the Buddha's enlightenment.[57] In all probability these scholars were influenced by the term *abhisambuddha*, "wholly awakened," which indeed suggests that the dreams occurred during the night of enlightenment, although the *AN* is not clear about the exact time and the *MV* indicates they occurred before the Buddha's departure from home. The word *abhisambuddha* may also have influenced Buddhaghosa's interpretations of their timing. In Theravāda Buddhism enlightenment is not gradual—for these dreams to have awakened the Buddha means that they had to occur only moments before his enlightenment. Perhaps most significantly, the *LV, MSV,* and *MV*, which indicate that these dreams occurred before his departure from home, are, in their final forms, Mahāyāna texts,[58] while the *NK*, the standard Theravāda biography of the Buddha, contains neither the Buddha's dreams nor those of his relatives, except for the conception dream of his mother. Therefore, it is quite possible that Buddhaghosa was not familiar with the stories that connect the Buddha's dreams with his departure from home.

In writing his commentaries on the Pali canon, Buddhaghosa's main concern was to fashion a seamless whole in order to create an orthodox reading of the canon.[59] The fact that the Buddha does not sleep on the night of enlightenment is just one of many contradictions that were included. Buddhaghosa wants to make two points about dreams: first, enlightened beings, *arhats*, do not have them, and second, these particular dreams portend enlightenment. This is consistent with the evidence of the Theravāda texts of the Pali canon to be discussed in chapter 3, where only unenlightened people dream. Enlightenment completely transforms individuals, placing them beyond mundane concerns and disturbances, possibly including dreams. As we shall see, though, in Mahāyāna biographical texts this is not necessarily the case—indeed it is not always the case in Theravāda biographies.[60] With regard to the second point, dreams as portents, Buddhaghosa could just as easily, if not more easily, have placed these dreams at the night of the Buddha's departure from home. As for his two other examples of prophetic dreams, those of Queen Māyā and the king of Kosala, both prophecies are fulfilled at much later times: Kosala's in a future life and Māyā's when the Buddha achieves enlightenment, that is, becomes the world conqueror prophesied by her dream. What we are seeing here, in part, is a separation of the two traditions of Theravāda and Mahāyāna on the issue of dreams. Buddhaghosa's commentaries are not part of the Mahāyāna canon, and, as already mentioned, the *NK* does not contain the Buddha's dreams, while the biographical texts that become important to the Mahāyāna tradition do. One consequence is that the Buddha's dreams are more pervasive in Mahāyāna texts, where they proffer a positive model of dreaming.

In both traditions, though, the dreams of the Buddha serve a very important purpose. When O'Flaherty discusses these five dreams and their interpretation as they appear in the *AN* and the *LV*, she points out that they provide new meanings for dream interpretation by transferring traditional (Brahmanical) negative meanings into new, positive meanings within the Buddhist context.[61] By preserving the dreams of the Buddha and of his wife and father, along with their interpretations, these biographical texts do provide such new meanings. They are the beginnings of Buddhist dream theory.

Additionally, the fact that these dreams were preserved in various texts indicates that some importance was attached to them by several Buddhist authors in different times and places. Hirakawa makes a strong case that these authors were engaged in the work of creating the Mahāyāna school in conjunction with the stūpa builders who carved scenes from these stories on their encircling fences and gates.[62] He sees the main concern of the biographies as the explication of the causes and events leading up to the Buddha's enlightenment,[63] and dreams were part of that. Indeed, according to the *AN* they played an active part in his awakening. And, as stated in the *LV*, the Buddha's dreams provided a map to the dream world of an aspiring buddha; these are the dreams that tell one when the time has come to leave home. All of this suggests that dreams can act as guides in one's spiritual life, that dreams can provide sign posts along the path through this world of illusion to enlightenment. We will see many instances of this in what follows.

The crux is that although everyone can dream, not all dreams are significant; and some dreams—those that suggest the presence of other realms—need to be understood and incorporated into waking reality. Additionally, Buddhists need to understand dreams within a Buddhist context. Sacred biographies provided that context through dream narratives, beginning with the biographies of the Buddha and continuing until the present day.[64] These texts reassure the reader or hearer that all possible realms are encapsulated in the revelations of Buddhism. Moreover, as we shall see, the heroes of Mahāyāna Buddhism, the bodhisattvas, siddhas, and other adepts, have the ability to successfully pass back and forth between these realms. This suggests that they also have the power to protect and guide lesser beings through these realms and ultimately to salvation.

As stated above, the *LV* contains additional dreams of the Buddha from the night before his departure from home. They have a clear meaning for Buddhists: "He saw millions of beings carried away by the current of a river. He crossed this river and made a vessel to carry others across."[65] In this dream the river is saṃsāra, this world bounded by illusion, which the Buddha will cross over to reach the higher reality of enlightenment.[66] Therefore he can create a vessel, the doctrines of Buddhism, to carry others across. In the next dream "he saw many beings suffering from disease and he became a physician, giving them medicine and curing millions of beings."[67] The Buddha as physician, one who cures the sickness of ignorance, is a common theme from the earliest days of Buddhism.[68] He heals by bringing people to *nirvāṇa,* or salvation. In the last dream "he sat on Mount Meru as his throne, and saw disciples and gods bowing to him. He saw his victory in battle and heard the gods shout with joy."[69] The center of the world, Mount Meru,[70] provides him with the throne from which he sees both his human and divine disciples. The battle refers to his victory over the demon Māra on the night of his enlightenment.

Whether one looks at all the Buddha's dreams in the *LV* or just at the first five dreams preserved in various texts, they present a complex picture of religious innovation. These dreams offer new and radically different values for dream interpretation. For example, a Brahmanical Hindu who dreamed that he or she walked on a pile of dung might want to go through a purification ceremony.[71] Even though the opening lines of the Buddha's first dream in the *LV* make an appeal to the past by saying they are the dreams had by previous buddhas in other eons, this is done more to provide a unique lineage for his teachings than to appeal to the Brahmanical past. Jackson Steward Lincoln interprets the frequent dream appearance of an ancestor bringing an innovation (for instance, a new ritual) to the larger group as an appeal to the authority of the past.[72] He refers to these dreams as "culture initiating dreams,"[73] a term which is relevant to the Buddha's dreams because they make an appeal to a Buddhist past at the very moment the new religion is being created. There is a wonderful play on the concept of *sambuddha* (to be awakened or enlightened) in all this because the Buddha rejected the heritage of his waking life, both the benefits and the obligations of his position: he was no longer filial to his father (and consequently no longer filial to his father's religious tradition), nor would he be a dutiful husband and householder, but he accepted the heritage of his sleeping—but actually enlightened—life. This is a powerful intimation of the value placed on dream consciousness. The emphasis that the *AN,* and to a slightly lesser degree the *MV,* place on the causal effect of these five dreams in awakening the Buddha suggests that the origins of Buddhism can be attributed, at least partially, to these dreams. Given the widespread Indian belief that the whole universe originated in the dream of Viṣṇu, the origination of a new religious belief system in dreams poses no real break in Indian thinking.

THE DREAMS OF OTHERS

Dreams of the Buddha's Departure from Home

The Buddha's departure from home is a pivotal event in Buddhist history, marking his first step on the path to enlightenment. The significance of this event is continually evoked in the standard ordination practices of Buddhist nuns and monks, in which they imitate his actions by abandoning their homes, cutting off their hair, and changing from lay to monastic clothes.[74] In the Buddha's biographies the importance of this moment is signaled by the shared dreams various people have just before he leaves home.

In the *MV* the Buddha's father, aunt, and wife all have shared prophetic dreams that are interpreted by the god Brahmā to predict the Buddha's departure. King Śuddhodana dreams of an elephant covered in jewels that runs out of the city,[75] which calls to mind Queen Māyā's conception dream and its prediction that the Buddha may become an ascetic. The Buddha's aunt dreams of a noble bull that also runs out of the city,[76] and the Buddha's wife dreams that "a cloud surrounded Śuddhodana's palace and lightning accompanied by thunder and rain lit up the three worlds."[77] Brahmā interprets this last dream as follows: "Śuddhodana's son, like a cloud raining on the three worlds, will bring relief to those who are burned by the great fires of passion, by generating dharma and compassion beyond compare."[78]

In addition to predicting the Buddha's departure, these dreams and their interpretations contributed to the construction of the new, Buddhist system of dream interpretation. For instance, Śuddhodana's dream continues: "I was moved to great laughter and unrestrained weeping. My body trembled and was disturbed by torments and fevers."[79] Brahmā tells him, "By his going forth he will overcome the many forms of suffering—that is the meaning of laughing in your dream. Weeping in your dream means that those who listen to him will achieve unending bliss."[80] In Brahmanical dream theory unrestrained weeping and bodily torments would be taken as unfortunate omens.

Curiously, the three symbols used to represent the Buddha—the elephant, the bull, and the cloud—are interrelated symbols of male fertility. This symbolism is obvious and widespread in the case of elephants and bulls, whereas clouds, through their connection with rain, often symbolize semen.[81] And as was shown in the discussion of the elephant in Queen Māyā's dream, clouds are often seen as celestial elephants. The *MSV* voices a concern that some people would think the Buddha was impotent if he left home without consummating his marriage, and in this text he does so the night before he leaves home.[82] The use of such symbols and concerns about male fertility suggests the presence of similar issues in the *MV* as well as a spiritualization of those symbols that center on their might and power.

Though the images representing the Buddha in these three dreams differ, their symbolic and prophetic meaning is the same—the Buddha will leave home and achieve greatness. These shared dreams both add power to the story and stress the inevitability of what follows. The Buddha's desertion of his family and duties went against Indian practices and needed to be justified—three people having the same dream helped to do just that. And, in the *LV* and *MSV*, on the night of his departure from home the Buddha shared a dream with all the buddhas of the past. In both cases this is more than a dramatic device; all these texts are utilizing the belief that dreams can be shared and that shared dreams are inevitably truthful portents.

Quite similar dreams occur in another biographical text, the *Abhiniṣkramaṇasūtra* (hereafter the *AS*). Here, as in the *LV*, the dreams surrounding the Buddha's departure from home take place during the period in which he has the four visions that introduce him to life's realities and their solution. In the first vision the Buddha journeys out of the palace and sees, for the first time, an old man. His father then has seven dreams in one night, all signifying loss. He sees: a royal banner being carried out of the eastern gate of the city; the Buddha riding out the southern gate; the Buddha riding out the western gate; a flying disc leaving through the northern gate; the Buddha sitting in the road playing a large drum; the Buddha sitting in a tower throwing jewels to all kinds of living creatures; and, finally, six men outside the city weeping and pulling out their hair.[83] Since these dreams and the four visions of the Buddha are said to have been caused by a *devaputra* (a god),[84] they reflect early Buddhist and Hindu dream theory in which gods can be one of the causes of dreams. When Brahman priests are unable to interpret Śuddhodana's dreams, the devaputra disguises himself as a priest and interprets the dreams he caused. The text then continues with the Buddha again journeying out of the palace and having the last three of his four visions: of a sick man, a dead man, and a mendicant. After these visions the Buddha's aunt dreams of a great white ox leaving the city.[85] This resembles her dream of a white bull in the *MV*. King Śuddhodana then dreams that a bright light shines out from the royal banner, lighting up the whole world: "and then from the four quarters of heaven he thought he saw some clouds rising, and these, gathering together over the standard [the banner], distilled a soft rain above it, whilst flowers fell round it and soft voices sang sweetly, and a beautiful white umbrella with a golden handle appeared over it, and at last the four kings of heaven, with their retinues, appeared coming towards the city, and having taken the standard the gates opened and they went out."[86] This dream repeats the cloud imagery in the dream of the Buddha's wife in the *MV.*

The dreams of the Buddha's family complement his four visions: they are all *nimittam,* signs or portents, a part of Buddhist revelation. The four visions relate to the central teachings of Buddhism that life involves the suffering of old age, sickness and death and that there is a solution to suffering, which is to follow the path symbolized by the mendicant in the fourth vision. The shared dreams of the Buddha's family, however, also have their place in Buddhist revelation. While the Buddha's visions were presented to his open and awake eyes through the intervention of *devas* (gods), the devas also sent visions to the closed and sleeping eyes of the Buddha's family. As the four visions and his five dreams awaken the Buddha to what he must do, his family's dreams awaken them to the inevitability of the events that will follow—the Buddha's departure and eventual enlightenment.

Returning to the *LV,* on the night of the Buddha's departure from home, his wife, called Gopā in this text, has a long dream in which she sees danger for the whole world, then for herself, and finally for the king and her husband.

> She sees the whole earth, including oceans and mountain peaks, shaken, and trees broken by the wind. The sun, moon, and stars fall from the sky.
>
> She sees her hair cut off by her left hand and her crown fallen. Then her hands and feet cut off, and she is naked, her pearl necklaces and jewels broken and strewn about.
>
> She sees her bed broken, lying on the floor, the king's parasol broken and fallen ornaments carried away in a river. Her husband's ornaments, clothing, and crown are scattered in disorder on their bed.
>
> She sees light coming from the city, which is plunged in darkness. The beautiful nets made of precious materials are broken, and the pearl garlands have fallen. The great ocean is in turmoil, and Mount Meru is shaken to its foundations.[87]

This dream wakes Gopā up, and she asks the Buddha to interpret it for her. He answers her, in part, by saying:

> Be joyful, these dreams are not evil. Beings who have previously practiced good works *[kṛtapuṇyapūrvacaritā]* have such dreams. Miserable people have no such dreams.
>
> Seeing the earth shaken and the mountain peaks fallen to earth [means that] the gods, nāgas, rākṣasas, and bhutas will render you the greatest homage.
>
> Seeing trees uprooted, and your hair cut off with your left hand [means that] soon you will cut the nets of the passion and you will remove the veil of false views that obscures the conditioned world.
>
> Seeing the sun, moon, stars and planets fall [means that] soon, having conquered the passions, you will be praised and honored....
>
> Be joyful, not sad; be content and satisfied. Soon you will be delighted and content. Be patient, Gopā; the omens [nimittam] are auspicious.[88]

The Buddha's positive interpretation of this dream (one that Brahmanical Hindus would see as negative because of its images of a woman whose hair is shorn and who is naked and without jewelry), the length of the dream, and the repetition of its images in the interpretation suggest an attempt to establish a new dream terminology that reverses the world-affirming values of Brahmanical Hinduism.[89] It forms a pattern with the Buddha's own dream, which he also interprets in Buddhist terms. Actually, a Hindu interpretation of Gopā's dream would be appropriate here because the Buddha's desertion does wreck her life: Indian widows cut their hair and do not wear jewelry.[90] The positive interpretation of Gopā's dream helps gloss over the consequences of the Buddha's desertion of his duties as a householder. That the Buddhists were somewhat self-conscious about this abandonment of duty is shown in the *Buddhacarita*, in particular where there are long exchanges between the Buddha and various people on the subject of his departure from home.[91]

In the *AS* the Buddha has two wives, Yaśodharā and Gōtamī,[92] but only the dream of Yaśodharā is offered.[93] It is quite similar to Gopā's dream in the *LV* and is of the same length. Again, the Buddha understands the meaning of her dream, but he tells her to ignore it,[94] and, as in the *LV*, he then reveals his five dreams. In the *MSV* the Buddha has three wives: Yaśodharā, Gopā, and Mṛgajā, and once again it is Yaśodharā who dreams: "She saw her own maternal line broken, her marvelous couch broken, her bracelets broken, her teeth falling out,[95] the braid of her hair undone, happiness departed from her house, the moon eclipsed by Rāhu, and the sun rising in the east and then setting there again."[96] When she tells the Buddha her dreams, just as in the *LV*, he denies their prophetic meaning and explains them away through a piece of sophistry. He argues that everything she lost in her dreams is actually still there.[97]

The Jātakas

A third instance of the Buddha dismissing his wife's dream, even though he knows very well that it is significant, occurs in a past life story preserved in the *Vessantara Jātaka*. This tale of Gautama Buddha's life as Prince Vessantara is one of the most popular tales in South and Southeast Asia and exists in many literary and iconographic versions.[98] All the jātakas are said to have been told by the Buddha, who also explained the identity of the main characters in their present lives—usually the wife is his wife now, the enemy is his cousin Devadatta, and so on. It follows that the wife in this story, Maddi, is the Buddha's wife Yaśodharā in this life. She too has important, frightening, and ultimately prophetic dreams. While living in the forest with her husband Vessantara, who has become an ascetic, Queen Maddi has a dream and asks him to interpret it.

> A black man clothed in two yellow robes, with red flowers in his ears, came and entered the hut of leaves, grasped Maddi's hair and dragged her out, threw her down on the ground, and amidst her cries tore out her two eyes, cut off two arms, split her chest, and tearing out her heart dripping with blood went away. She woke up filled with fear, thinking, "I have seen an inauspicious dream; I will ask Vessantara to interpret my dream."...[Vessantara] understood the dream: "The perfection of my giving," he thought, "is to be fulfilled: tomorrow someone will come to beg for my children. I will console Maddi and let her go." So he said, "Your mind must have been agitated by uneasy sleep or by indigestion; do not be afraid." With this deceit he consoled her, and let her go. At daybreak, she did all that had to be done, embraced and kissed the children, and said, "Last night I saw a bad dream—be careful, my dears!"[99]

Even though Vessantara tries to distract Maddi from her intuitive understanding that this dream portends the loss of her children, whom her husband will give away later that day, she still warns her children to be careful. The dismissal of women's dreams becomes a leitmotif of Buddhist biography and suggests some anxiety about female dreamers. As we shall see in the next chapter, women can penetrate men's dreams, while here women's dreams help them intuit men's intentions. As we progress, we will see additional attempts on the part of males to harness female dream power.

Dreams occur in several other jātakas, and most of the dreamers are women. For instance, there are a series of tales in which various queens dream of the Buddha preaching in different animal incarnations: a golden goose, a golden peacock, and a golden deer.[100] In each case the queen convinces her husband to find the animals, which he does, and then the Buddha preaches to them in these forms. These three dreams echo the conception dream of the Buddha's mother, Queen Māyā, in that women bring forth the Buddha through dreaming.[101] However, a darker reflection of Māyā's dream is contained in the *Chaddanta Jātaka* (no. 514), in which the Buddha is incarnated as a six-tusked white elephant. Here a queen lies, saying she dreamed about the elephant, in order to have it hunted and killed.[102] So while Queen Māyā actually dreams of such an elephant and thereby conceives, thus bringing the Buddha to life, the queen in this jātaka does not really dream, but through her lie brings the Buddha to death. What remains consistent in all these stories is that dreams are taken seriously and acted upon.

Inauspicious dreams also appear in the collection. In the *Bhūridatta Jātaka* (no. 543) the Buddha is a *nāga* (a semidivine snake), and when he is captured by hunters his mother dreams: "that a black man with red eyes cut off her arm with a sword and carried it away with blood oozing."[103] In the *Vidhudrapaṇḍita Jātaka* (no. 545) a king dreams about the destruction of a precious tree, which he understands to symbolize a sage (the incarnation of the Buddha). Part of his dream echoes the previous dream: "Then a black man, dressed in a red cloth, wearing red flowers as earrings and with weapons in his hand came and cut down the tree."[104] Both dreams contain pan-Indian symbols of destruction—the colors red and black; at this popular level the Buddhists easily adopted the prevailing negative dream imagery that was familiar to their listeners or readers. However, three jātakas show some tension with Brahmanical dream interpretation. In the first example, the *Kuṇāla Jātaka* (no. 219), jealous co-queens bribe Brahman dream interpreters to say that the favorite queen's auspicious dream of a white elephant threatens the king's life. Here the culpability of the Brahmans is used to undercut their ability to understand dreams. In a second example from the *Vessantara Jātaka* (no. 547) Brahmans are represented as misinterpreting a king's dream.[105] Finally, in the *Mahāsupina Jātaka* (no. 77) the king of Kosala[106] has a series of sixteen dreams and wakes up terrified, thinking that they predict his death. Brahman priests advise him to offer many sacrifices and to perform rituals that will offset the danger these dreams predict. However, the king's wife, Queen Mallika, advises him to ask the Buddha, himself a Brahman priest in this life, to interpret these dreams, thus setting the scene for a contest. While the Buddha agrees with the Brahmans that the dreams foretell dire events, he says these events will occur in a distant future, when his teachings have declined and unrighteous kings rule. The Buddha then proceeds to interpret each of the sixteen dreams to describe the disorder and unruliness of that future age. The real point of this story, from the Buddhist perspective, is that Brahmans exploit the fear of dreams. Speaking to the king of Kosala about their interpretation, the Buddha says: "It was not truth, nor affection for you, that prompted the brahmans to explain [the dreams]. It was to get wealth, it was the insight of habitual greed that shaped their explanations."[107] What is at issue here is not the prophetic nature of dreams, which is accepted, but the ability to correctly interpret them.[108] This ability is linked specifically to the spiritual accomplishments of the Buddha in this jātaka. This is the beginning of a new, Buddhist interpretation of dreams.[109]

Māra's Dream

A final dream from the biographical literature of the Buddha is that of the god Māra, lord of the desire realm *(kāma loka)* whose name means death, and who is the main antagonist to the Buddha and his followers.[110] By achieving enlightenment the Buddha comes to understand the futility of desire, which not only challenges Māra's sovereignty but leads to the deathless state of enlightenment beyond Māra's realm. On the night of the Buddha's enlightenment Māra musters his army and provokes a prolonged battle with the Buddha. In the *LV*, on the night before this battle, Māra has a long nightmare.[111] In the first part he "saw his realm in darkness, his dwelling covered with dust and filled with sand and gravel. He saw himself running in all directions, overcome by fear and anger, without diadem or earrings, his lips, throat, and palate parched and dry, his heart tormented. His gardens were stripped of leaves, flowers, and fruits; the ponds were cracked and dry. He saw flocks of various birds with clipped wings."[112] When Māra tells one of his sons, Sārthavāha, about his terrible dream, the son advises him not to do battle with the Buddha.[113]

Although this dream is prophetic, Māra could follow its warning and not do battle. The opportunity to change course comes up again when the captain of Māra's army tells him to withdraw his army unless he wants his dream to come true.[114] This is one of two instances in these texts of a dream that offers an alternative outcome—the other is Māyā's conception dream, though of course, both dreams predict inevitable events.

It is instructive to compare Māra's dream to Gopā's dream, both of which are filled with images of distress and appear to be nightmares. We have already seen how the Buddha interprets Gopā's dream positively. Māra's dream is not interpreted, it is simply fulfilled. Yet line for line the imagery of loss and devastation contained in these two dreams is similar. Of course, nightmares do exist, but when interpreted in a Buddhist context that advocates abandoning the world and all its attributes, including the fearful events in these two dreams, there is nothing to fear: loss and devastation of worldly goods and position are what ascetic Buddhism prescribes. The text even strongly suggests that Māra's dream need not be fulfilled if only he changes his course of action—if he ceases to resist the revelation of Buddhism. In this sense Māra is the Buddhist Everyman, desperately clinging to a world that is ultimately unreal.

One important distinction between Māra's and Gopā's dreams is made when the Buddha says that Gopā had the dream of someone who has practiced good works in a former life *(kṛtapuṇyapūrvacaritā)*.[115] This is consistent with Buddhaghosa's commentary on the causes of prophetic dreams, which emphasizes the dreamer's merit *(puñña)* and demerit *(apuñña)*.[116] So, according to early Buddhist dream theory, Gopā's dream reveals the merit of her spiritual advancement, whereas Māra's demerit leads him to dream of impending doom.

Still, the imagery and mood in these two dreams is so strikingly similar as to reward a closer look. Actually, they share a continuum of meaning. In Buddhist literature women are often associated with saṃsāra, with this world of desire that is ruled by Māra's power; women are said to hold men back from spiritual advancement, at best entangling them in domestic affairs and at worst destroying their spiritual power *(tapas)* through sexuality. In this way women do Māra's work, a point made by his daughters' seductive attack on the Buddha on the night of his enlightenment.[117] As a woman, Gopā is one of Māra's snares that entangle men in his realm. Thus the similarities between these two dreams evoke the same message: Gopā and Māra, albeit in different ways, are both the losers when the Buddha achieves enlightenment. Both lose the power to attract the Buddha.

Several points can be drawn from the various dreams in the biographical literature of the Buddha. First, and most obviously, all the dreams are represented as accurate—they successfully predict events that follow—and, second, their interpretations are represented as being accurate. In addition to affirming the value of dreams, correct dream interpretation also suggests that other realms exist that are involved in the activities of the waking world. Not everyone has access to these realms through dreams, hence not all dreams are meaningful, and only unique individuals can successfully interpret dreams: for example, Brahmans (who interpret Māyā's dream), the Buddha (who interprets his wife's dream),[118] and the god Brahmā (who does the interpreting for everyone in the *MV*). In this context, it is significant that neither Māra nor his son actually interprets Māra's dream; both know only that it is filled with bad omens.

In these narratives the dream realm supports the Buddha's efforts and reveals the inevitability of his actions. This occurs most dramatically through shared dreams, such as those of the Buddha's father, wife, and aunt, all of which take place on the same night and have the same meaning. On the literary side, in Ong's terms, these dreams are "standardized themes," which were consistently chosen for inclusion by different biographers of the Buddha. As time went on, the audience for Buddhist biographies came to anticipate that dreams of various kinds, including conception and prophetic dreams, would appear in the biography of any important Buddhist, as would interpretations of those dreams.[119]

As mentioned in the introduction, all of this did not occur in an oneiric vacuum. While the early Buddhist community accepted and expanded upon prevailing Indian dream theories, it also questioned the meaning and implications of dreams in a variety of settings. It is to this material that we now turn.

3 Early Buddhist Dream Theory

THE DREAM NARRATIVES preserved in the biographical literature of the Buddha are deeply enmeshed in early Buddhist thinking and the dream beliefs of ancient South Asian culture. Alongside the biographical texts of the Buddha are several nonbiographical Buddhist texts that discuss the nature of dreams from a variety of angles: moral, philosophical, physiological, and so on. In this chapter I examine this literature in order to broaden our understanding of dreams in the Buddhist tradition. I also consider a dream narrative from the biography of Emperor Aśoka and a discussion of dream interpretation from the *Śārdūlakarṇāvadāna*. Both these texts add resonance to the dream narrations and interpretations we have just seen.

PALI TEXTS

The Vinaya

One of the earliest Buddhist discussions about dreams centers on whether people are morally responsible for them or not. While rationally it is possible to understand that a dream is only a dream, not reality, and that one is therefore not really responsible for what occurs in it, ideas about pollution and moral responsibility retain their emotional power whether one is awake or asleep.[1] Such an idea is not unique to India. Lincoln mentions various tribal people who attribute responsibility to the actions performed in dreams; when they awake, they behave as if the dream action had actually occurred.[2] The Pali *Vinaya*, the rules for Buddhist nuns and monks,[3] preserves some discussion about this issue because several rules were established in response to the dreaming experiences of the early Buddhist community. For example in *Vinaya* I.2.1 there is the case of a monk who emits semen during a dream. There, and in *Vinaya* IV.9.11, it is stated that the *intentional* emitting of semen *(sañcetanikaṃ sukkavisaṭṭhi)* is an offense requiring a formal meeting of the order, after which the offender is put on probation.[4] The Buddha ruled, however, that it is not an offense if he was dreaming.[5] In another *Vinaya* incident a monk dreams of having sex with his former wife. A senior monk tells him: "There is no offense since it was in a dream."[6] The notion that one is not morally responsible for what one does while dreaming is, in part, connected to the language of dreaming, in which one "sees"—not "has"—a dream: dreams are believed to come unbidden, from external forces.

At the same time the *Vinaya* evinces a lingering sense of the Vedic notion of responsibility for and possible pollution from dreams.[7] For instance, on three separate occasions one particular monk, Dabba the Mallian, is falsely accused of having sex with a woman. When the Buddha questions him, Dabba always answers: "Lord, since I was born, I never experienced sexual intercourse even in a dream, much less while awake."[8] A similar statement is made in the *LV,* which says, speaking of the woman who is to become the Buddha's wife: "May she not have a thought for another, even in dreams."[9] Both examples use dreaming as the outer limits of moral responsibility and purity.

A third incident in the *Vinaya* involving a monk emitting semen during a dream prompts the Buddha to elaborate on dreams and sleep. "Monks who mindfully *[sampajāna]* fall asleep do not emit impurities *[asuci na muccati],*" he says.[10] The Buddha then addresses the community of monks on this subject: "There are five disadvantages to falling asleep thoughtlessly, without mindfulness: sleeping uneasily, waking unhappily, seeing a bad *[pāpakaṃ]* dream, not being guarded by gods *[devatā]*, emitting impurity...five advantages come from mindfully falling asleep: sleeping easily, waking happily, not seeing a bad dream, being guarded by gods, not emitting impurity."[11] This is also one of the earliest references I have found to controlling consciousness before sleep in order to control dreams, a logical outcome for concerns about maintaining purity even while sleeping.

A dream experience of a different sort comes from *Vinaya* I.2.15, in which the Buddha tells the parable of a long-suffering man who successfully struggles against his anger. At a crucial point in the story his enemy, the source of his suffering, falls asleep with his head in his lap. The wronged man, thinking of revenge, draws his sword but then decides against it. He does so three times. After the sleeping man is awakened by a nightmare that he is being attacked, the two peacefully resolve their differences. The notion that the close proximity of someone to a dreamer causes him or her to dream in relation to that person seems to be fairly common in South Asia.[12] Of further significance, though, is that the dream is presented as a truthful indication of danger.

A catch-all of rules and their circumstances, the *Vinaya* presents some of the views of the early Buddhist community about dreams. Although dreams are morally neutral, it is better not to have dreams that compromise one's purity; hence they should be controlled. Dreams, too, as the last example shows, can have meaning. But the *Vinaya* has no consistent dream theory.

Buddhaghosa

An important early source for a formal Buddhist dream theory is the great scholar-monk Buddhaghosa.[13] Two of his works have similar detailed discussions of dreams: the *Samantapāsādikā* (his commentary on the *Vinaya*) and the *Manorathapūraṇī* (his commentary on the *Aṅguttara-Nikāya*).

In both texts Buddhaghosa creates a typology of dreams based on their four causes *(kāraṇa)*: (1) disturbances of the bodily elements *(dhātukkhobata)*, (2) previous experiences *(anubhūtapubbata)*, (3) influence of the gods *(devatoposaṃhārata)*, and (4) portents *(pubbanimittata)*.[14] He then elaborates on each of these causes and the value of the dreams they stimulate. Thus, poor bile leads to dreams about falling off mountains, flying through the air, being attacked by wild animals or thieves, and so on. Buddhaghosa says that such dreams are not true *(n'etaṃ saccaṃ hoti)*[15] and that they have no effect on waking life. Dreams of the second type, those caused by remembered objects and incidents, are also not true and are without effect. The third type is caused by the gods, and these dreams may be true *(saccaṃ)* or false *(alikaṃ)*. They affect waking life for good or ill since the gods may desire one's welfare or one's misery. The fourth type, the portent or prophetic dream, is caused by an individual's merit *(puñña)* or demerit *(apuñña)*—from acts committed in both the present life and in past lives. These dreams are true and have a good effect, as three examples show: the conception dream of the Buddha's mother Queen Māyā, the sixteen dreams of the king of Kosala (interpreted by the Buddha in the *Mahāsupina Jātaka*), and the five dreams of the Buddha.[16]

Buddhaghosa's separation of prophetic dreams from dreams stimulated by the body and from the recalled perceptions of waking life is significant.

As I will show, prophetic dreams are the product of pure consciousness, free of afflicted mundane sensory cognition and of impure consciousness. Prophetic dreams are perceived through a purified cognition.

Overall, Buddhaghosa believed that the maturation *(vipākaṃ)* potential of dreams is meager because dream mentation is fundamentally weak.[17] But prophetic dreams are a special case; they predict what has already matured and will inevitably manifest in waking reality; this is maturation in a karmic sense, due to the karma or merit accrued by one's previous actions.

Perhaps most significant is this general statement of Buddhaghosa's about dreams: "These four kinds of dreams are seen by ordinary people *[sekhaputhujjanā];* those who have perfected *[asekhā]* themselves do not see dreams."[18] Buddhaghosa's point is that Queen Māyā was not perfected, nor was the king of Kosala. Nor was the Buddha at the time of his five great dreams: these dreams were portents of his future perfection. This is the view of dreaming that continues today among the Theravāda[19]—it is a sign of not having reached enlightenment.[20]

The Milindapañha

An important philosophical text to discuss the meaning and function of dreams is the *Milindapañha (The Questions of King Milinda).*[21] In it King Milinda questions the Buddhist sage Nāgasena: "What is this that is called a dream and who sees it?"[22] Nāgasena answers that a dream is a nimittam, a portent, and he goes on to list six types of people who have dreams. The first three are based on the physical nature of the dreamer: those people of a windy nature *(vātiko),* a bilious one *(pittiko),* or a phlegmatic one *(semhiko).* T. W. Rhys Davids quotes the Sinhalese commentary to this text, which describes the dreams seen by each of these six types: "the first dreams of journeys through space, the second of fire and conflagrations, [and] the third of water."[23] These correspond to Buddhaghosa's category of dreams caused by bodily disturbances, and both are in agreement with the sixty-eighth appendix of the *Atharva Veda,* which also connects dreams to these three physical types.[24] Not surprisingly, we can see some common ground in Indian dream theory. The last three types are those who receive dreams from a god *(devatūpasaṁhārato),* those who indulge in dreams *(samudāciṇato),* and those who receive portents *(pubbanimittato).*[25] Nāgasena also says that only this last type of dream is true and that the others are false *(saccam, avasesaṁ micchā),*[26] which contrasts with Buddhaghosa's position that dreams sent by the gods may be true or false. Nāgasena does not, however, explain the source of dream portents, he merely says, "The portent appears in the mind,"[27] and adds that dreamers cannot interpret their own dreams; they need someone else to explain them. This is because the mind that sees the dream is not the mind that knows whether the dream will have a fearful or pleasurable outcome.[28] Of course, this makes the point that people are often puzzled by their dreams at one time or another. As we shall see, however, spiritually advanced beings are able to interpret their own dreams, although doing so may require some training.

Despite its intrinsic interest, the early Buddhist philosophical discussion of dreams has more in common with the medical literature on dreams[29] than with other contemporaneous discussions of dreams such as those in the *Vinaya* and the *Upaniṣads.* It is particularly surprising that neither Buddhaghosa nor the *Milindapañha* engages the *Vinaya* discussions that were prompted by the dream experiences of the early Buddhist community. Nor do they engage the discussions in the *Chāndogya* and *Māṇḍūkya Upaniṣads* that formulate four states of consciousness—waking, dreaming, deep sleep, and a fourth state that both transcends and encompasses all three.[30] In this context the *Chāndogya Upaniṣad* sets out two important epistemological points that endure in Indian thought today: (1) truth or knowledge is not apparent, it must be sought, and (2) the senses cannot be relied upon as a source of knowledge because nothing is as it appears, everything is clouded by *māyā,* illusion. Dreams and dreamlike states become one of the most frequent examples of māyā throughout the Hindu tradition, indeed throughout the Buddhist tradition as well.[31]

Another rich body of early Buddhist literature to present prominent dream experiences are various literary and folk texts that contain prophetic dreams, what Buddhaghosa and Nāgasena called portents,[32] to which we now turn our attention.

THE *AŚOKĀVADĀNA*

We have already seen several examples of dream narrations in the popular Buddhist collection of folk tales, the jātakas, discussed in chapter 2. The jātakas contain an assortment of dream types that continued into the later biographical literature: dreams are represented as predicting events such as conceptions and deaths and revealing the duplicity and inadequacy of Brahmanical dream interpreters. The jātakas also establish an ambiguous relationship between dreams and women, in which the latter figure both as liars and as boundaryless dreamers who experience the suffering of others in their own dream bodies. Several of these themes are brought together in the biography of Emperor Aśoka (third century B.C.E.), the *Aśokāvadāna.* This text, composed in Northwestern India during the second century C.E.,[33] is part of the *Divyāvadāna,* a Sanskrit collection of Buddhist tales and other writings. It contains a complex dream sequence involving Aśoka (the dreamer), Aśoka's son Kuṇāla (the subject of the dreams),[34] and Aśoka's wife Tiṣyarakṣitā (the stimulator of the dreams). Tiṣyarakṣitā, disappointed in her attempt to seduce Kuṇāla, has vowed to destroy him.[35] While Kuṇāla is visiting another city, she sends a letter—using Aśoka's name—that instructs the people of that city to blind him. I quote from the text at length because it demonstrates various stages of the dream process: the stimulus for the dream, the dream itself, the telling of the dream, its interpretation, and ritual attempts to ward off evil consequences.

> Now when Aśoka wanted something to be accomplished quickly, he always sealed the orders with his teeth. Therefore, that night, Tiṣyarakṣitā went to Aśoka, thinking she would get him to (bite the letter in his sleep and so) seal it with his teeth. But something startled the king, and he woke up.
>
> "What is it, my lord?" asked Tiṣyarakṣitā.
>
> "Oh, queen," Aśoka replied, "I have just had a nightmare! I saw two vultures trying to pluck out Kunāla's eyes!"
>
> "May the prince be well!" said Tiṣyarakṣitā (and the king went back to sleep).
>
> But then a second time he awoke, frightened, and said, "Queen, once again, I have not had a good dream."
>
> "What was it like?" she asked.
>
> "I saw Kunāla," he replied. "He was entering the city with a beard and long hair and long nails."
>
> "May the prince be well!" said Tiṣyarakṣitā (and again the king went back to sleep). This time, he did not awaken. Tiṣyarakṣitā managed to get the letter sealed with his teeth, and she sent it immediately to Takṣaśilā [the city where Kunāla was residing]. Aśoka, still asleep, dreamt that his teeth were falling out.
>
> When the night passed, the king called his soothsayers and asked them to interpret these dreams.
>
> "Your majesty," they replied, "one who sees such dreams will see the eyes of his son destroyed."

And they added:

One whose teeth decay
and fall out in a dream
will see his son's eyes destroyed
and the death of his son as well.

Hearing these words, Aśoka quickly got up from his seat, made añjalis [salutations of respect] in all four directions, and began to implore the deities:

May the gods who are well disposed
toward the Master [the Buddha], and toward the Dharma,
and toward the sangha, that most excellent assembly,
protect my son Kunāla!
And may all the best ṛṣis
in the world do likewise![36]

This dream sequence also contains elements of a dream manual—in its stock response to the meaning of teeth in dreams[37]—as well as a ritual response to offset the bad omen contained in the dream. In fact, the whole sequence portrays a popular understanding of dreams and has something to say about what causes dreams. Initially the text suggests that Tiṣyarakṣitā causes the dreams in two ways: (1) she orders the destruction of Kuṇāla's eyes, which is the subject of the dreams, and (2) she disturbs Aśoka's sleep, an act that prompts the telling of the dreams. Her reason for disturbing his sleep is to get his teeth marks on the letter about Kuṇāla; when she succeeds, Aśoka dreams his teeth are falling out. Teeth in this dream sequence symbolize Aśoka's power, which Tiṣyarakṣitā usurps, and Aśoka's son, whom she blinds; moreover, it is by touching Aśoka's teeth that Tiṣyarakṣitā prompts his dreams.

Later in the story, when he is reunited with Kuṇāla, Aśoka demands to know who blinded him. Kuṇāla answers:

The deeds of living beings never die.
The fruit of acts done in this world is one's own;

How then can I speak of this
as having been done by others?

> It is I, great king, who have committed an offense, and I who have to live with it. I am the one who did and caused to ripen the deeds that have generated my misfortune.[38]

Through Kuṇāla's answer the text emphasizes the inevitable law of karma: actions bear fruit that will ripen; prophetic dreams only predict inevitable consequences. In the same way that Tiṣyarakṣitā's role in causing Kuṇāla's suffering is secondary to his karma, so too is her part in inducing the dream. Kuṇāla's prior actions are coming to fruition and he will be blinded; the dreams in this text reveal a future event that is inevitable because of past karma. This is in accordance with Buddhaghosa's understanding of prophetic dreams caused by merit or demerit.

To emphasize these points about the relation of karma and dreams, the text then offers two stories about Kuṇāla's past lives. In the first he blinds many deer, an act that leads to him being blinded in many future lives; in the second he rebuilds a stūpa, and this leads to his being reborn a king's son.[39]

In her reading of this dream O'Flaherty emphasizes the way it contrasts illusion (māyā) and reality. She says:

> The truth of the dream is set against the falseness of waking life on several levels. On the level of the plot, it is set against the false queen (who says, "Long live Kunāla" when the king tells her his first two nightmares). On the philosophical level, the metaphor of the dream is absorbed into the larger metaphor of the seeing eye that is blind to the illusion of the world; Kunāla is grateful to the queen, he says, for by having him blinded she has enabled him to obtain true sight.[40]

O'Flaherty rightly points out that Aśoka's dream and the tragedy that befalls his son lead Aśoka to enlightenment, to a true vision of the world.

THE *ŚĀRDŪLAKARṆĀVADĀNA*

Like the *Aśokāvadāna*, the *Śārdūlakarṇāvadāna* is also contained in the *Divyāvadāna*. This story contains a discussion between a Brahman, Puṣkarasārin, and a Buddhist king, Triśaṅku, in which the Brahman tests the latter's knowledge of various matters, including dream interpretation.[41] By answering all the questions correctly the king wins the Brahman's daughter as a wife for his son. Thus, the story plays with the topic of Brahman dream interpreters that we have seen in the Buddha's biographies and especially in the jātakas. In this instance they are subsumed into the Buddhist dream tradition, an act confirmed by the Brahman's surrendering his daughter to a lower-caste marriage.

There are few surprises in the king's lengthy response, which contains common South Asian dream imagery. It begins with a list of dream images of prosperity: a god, Brahman, a cow, a blazing fire, an elephant, a horse, gold, various birds such as cranes, parrots, and geese, and flowers. It also contrasts the acquisition of tremendous power through riding a horse or elephant or traveling in a carriage with its loss by falling from any of these. Overall the images listed are consistent with those in Brahmanical texts, so much so that, rather surprisingly for a Buddhist text, it recommends making offerings and prayers to Brahmans in order to eliminate the effects of a bad dream![42] Another surprise is the warning that dreaming of a Buddhist nun wearing a stained robed (probably stained from menstrual blood, *kaṣāyaprāvṛtaṃ muṇḍāṃ nārīṃ malinanāsasam*) foretells trouble, though this is consistent with the usual dream association of women and death. It may also be a case where negative Brahmanical ideas about female ascetics complement Buddhist misogyny.[43] More to the point, this text shows that it is not the content that is important in these debates or contests of skill between Brahmans and Buddhists, but rather who commands knowledge of dream interpretation. In this case the king has proved his abilities as a dream interpreter.

BUDDHIST UNDERSTANDINGS OF THE SELF AND CONSCIOUSNESS

Early Buddhist ideas about dreams expressed in monastic rules, commentaries, philosophical texts, and folklore revolve around important and central tenets of early Buddhism, one of which is that there is no self, no abiding entity that defines who we are.[44] Through careful analysis the notion of an enduring and isolated self is shown to be a grave misreading of reality. The constituent parts of individual being, the five aggregates *(skandhas)*—body *(rūpa)*, sensation *(vedanā)*, perception *(saṃjñā)*, karmic predispositions *(saṃskāra)*, and consciousness *(vijñāna)*—are used to show that everything is momentary, that nothing inherently exists. Sensation and perception are dependent on the body and completely cease to exist at death. The transference of karmic predispositions and consciousness from one life to the next, the process of transmigration, is explained through the simile of the flame of one lamp used to light another: the flame is just energy, completely lacking in an inherent personality or individuality.[45] To use a material metaphor, the karmic predispositions are the woof and consciousness the warp of existence through the ceaseless round of birth, death, and rebirth, but the fabric they weave is without an enduring reality and without an enduring individuality. For Buddhists the self and the world it occupies possess only a conditional reality, which is to say that they participate in a reality that is conditioned by other factors, all of which are themselves conditioned.

Conditioned reality is described as dependent origination *(pratītya-samutpāda).* This doctrine formulates a twelve-part causal arising for all beings, beginning with ignorance and leading in turn to consciousness *(vijñāna),* which leads to form, or the body with its six organs of sense,[46] which give rise to desire, clinging, and so on, culminating in birth, old age, and death. By destroying ignorance through abandoning the false view of an enduring reality in self and phenomena, the primary cause of becoming is removed.[47] Correspondingly, Buddhists understand that there is both an ultimate and a conditional reality; advanced practitioners act "as if" this world were real but know that ultimately everything, ourselves and our world, is empty of an enduring reality.

Needless to say, this is a difficult existential position to keep in the forefront of one's mind on a day-to-day basis.[48] Most South Asian Buddhists tend to live their lives within the conditional understanding of the self, and, like other traditional peoples, South Asians experience the self situationally, as intrinsically part of a family, clan, and other cultural constructs (such as the idea of past lives and different kinds of visible and invisible beings).[49] As Anne Klein has said: "Persons do not spring to life in one individual form only, but are embedded in a series of lives, as well as in the social, spirit, and natural networks."[50] Hence, the Buddhist understanding of self includes (1) the notion of past lives and their influence on the present life as well as belief in future lives, (2) relationships with spiritual and natural beings of many different sorts, and (3) social arrangements that include family and clan members as an essential part of oneself.[51] This last point is dramatically demonstrated by the experience of shared dreams in which different individuals have the same dream, such as the dreams of the Buddha's family when he is about to abandon home and family for the ascetic life. This belief that one person can dream for another continues in the healing practices of Tibetan monks who dream about the cause of someone's illness.

The modern Western self-conscious notion of the self arises in large part out of a deep interiorization of literacy that is totally absent from the predominantly oral culture of early Buddhism in India and certainly remains absent in the living oral traditions of Tibetan Buddhism.[52] While Tibet wholeheartedly embraced literacy and went to great efforts to procure and translate Buddhist texts, it never abandoned the primacy of oral transmission. In Walter Ong's terms, Tibet maintained a residual oral state of consciousness.[53] One of the attributes of oral consciousness is a difficulty in articulating self-analysis, in large part because self-analysis requires undoing the situational thinking that predominates oral consciousness.[54] Consequently, the dreaming self of Buddhism, and of Buddhist heroes, is understood not in isolation but in a shared dream realm where individual dreamers and universal symbols meet and merge. Sometimes this happens quite literally, when different people have the same dream. In South Asia the boundaries between dreams and the waking state, humans and gods, ignorance and enlightenment, the self and others, are potentially all permeable. Understanding Buddhist dreaming requires understanding the possibilities that exist in their unbounded cognitive universe. In the West, many of us half-consciously participate in a similar, though in many ways distinctly different, unbounded universe when we attribute prophetic qualities to our dreams. The point is that while the Buddhist concept of dreaming may seem familiar to Western readers, its differences will be shown to be quite important.[55]

With this background in mind, we may turn to a later and fruitful period of Northern Indian Buddhism and its transmission into Tibet, where many of these ideas found a compatible home and also blended with indigenous practices.

4 Dreams in Indo-Tibetan Buddhism

DREAMS ARE PERVASIVE in Tibetan religious life. In biographies conception dreams are commonplace, while saints have dreams that come true, and they correctly interpret the dreams of others. Dreams are an important element in the discovery of *tulkus* (*sprul sku*, reincarnations)[1] and *termas* (*gter ma*, hidden texts),[2] are predictors of meetings with religious teachers—indeed they are a means of receiving teachings from the living and the dead, from humans and from divinities—and are accepted as clarifiers of religious teachings.[3] Before initiations disciples are often instructed to observe their dreams in order to ascertain whether the deity approves their initiation. Guiseppe Tucci explains that the purpose of seeking dreams during the initiation process is to receive a prognostication that confirms or denies the existence of *rten 'brel*, which he translates as "karma connection."[4] In other words, a sympathy must exist between the initiate and the realms she or he is seeking initiation into, or between the initiate and the deity of the initiation, and this sympathy can be revealed or denied through dreams. Some practitioners incorporate dreaming into their lives when they attempt to maintain a consistent stream of consciousness through waking life, the meditative state, sleeping, dreaming, and death. In these teachings dream consciousness is said to be similar to consciousness in the *bardo*, the period between death and rebirth. Consequently, adepts are trained in sleep and dream yogas in order to control their consciousness in the various states between waking, dreaming, meditating, and dying by maintaining a consistent state of awareness through all of them.

As we shall see shortly, running parallel to these beliefs and practices is the understanding that even in the waking state we are all asleep, that is unenlightened—dreaming our life away while immersed in illusion. We need to wake up, to recognize what is real and proceed toward the ultimate awakening, enlightenment. In this sense sleeping and dreaming are metaphors for the unenlightened state.

These seemingly contradictory views about the value of dreams reflect, on the one hand, the valorizations of dream practices going back to the time of the Buddha and, on the other hand, philosophical speculations about the nature of reality: a popular view of dreaming and an elite one, as explained in chapter 1. This situation is even more complicated in Tibet, where dreams were valued experiences long before the arrival of Buddhism.

INDIGENOUS PRACTICES

The religious practices of Tibet before the eighth century are somewhat elusive. Often they have been loosely referred to as a form of shamanism called Bon.[5] It is more accurate, however, to speak of two distinct though often intermingled sets of practices, Bon and folk religion, both of which show some distinctly shamanistic features and both of which intermingled with Buddhist practices.[6] Due to the great regional diversity that has always existed in Tibet, both Bon and the folk religion varied from area to area and underwent many changes.

Geoffrey Samuel makes an important argument for the enduring influence of indigenous shamanic beliefs and practices on the Tibetan Buddhism found among the mahāsiddhas and tantric lamas such as Milarepa's guru Marpa.[7] By shamanic he means both pre-Buddhist Bon and the folk religions of Tibet and Northern India. These are contrasted with what he calls "clerical" religion, which he associates with centralized political power.[8] In addition to figures such as the siddhas and tantrics, important examples of enduring indigenous practices can be found among the all-important bardo teachings and the oracles.

Among the pre-Buddhist Bon dreams were an accepted form of prognostication, most importantly as a means of identifying the god or demon who caused the trouble in someone's life.[9] This is quite similar to the practice of certain Buddhist lamas who dream for sick people in order to ascertain the demon causing their illness.[10] It also suggests that shamanic ideas and practices about dreams were incorporated into Tibetan "clerical" thinking, where they were elaborated upon, routinized, and rationalized through strict monastic disciplines. One has only to reflect on the many stories about the competition between Buddhism and shamanism in Tibet, especially those surrounding Padmasambhava—in which Buddhism always wins—to see the process of assimilation or co-optation.

Some early beliefs about dreams are presented in Tibetan folklore,[11] such as the ever popular epic of Gesar, which is pervaded with dreams. Gesar causes other people to dream,[12] and he himself has many dreams (particularly of deities who advise him),[13] as do several of the secondary characters.[14] This, of course, contrasts with the relative paucity of dreams in the Indian epics, especially those of primary characters.[15] Of some interest is the frequent use of *Mo* divination in this text to confirm the meaning of dreams,[16] and in one instance dreams are sought to confirm the meaning of other omens.[17] These otherworldly messages are believed to be interrelated, and therefore each should confirm the others.

René de Nebesky-Wojkowitz collected some dream interpretations during his field work in Sikkim between 1950 and 1953, most of which conform to those found in ancient Indian texts, both Hindu and Buddhist. He begins by listing some dreams that forebode good:

> to see oneself in a dream all clad in armour is a sign that there is no danger of one falling ill, and if seeing oneself carrying a weapon, then one will not suffer any harm from an enemy. To wear a magnificent dress in a dream is the sign that one will be praised and held in high esteem. Seeing oneself fording a river successfully, ascending the peak of a high mountain, or riding upward on a lion, tiger, a superb horse, or on a dragon are dreams indicating that one will attain great spiritual progress presently.[18]

It is particularly auspicious—foretelling happiness, wealth, and fame—

> to see the sun rising unobscured by any clouds, to hear the sound of drums and trumpets, to obtain rich food and splendid clothes, to see oneself sitting in a palatial building or on a throne. To see oneself wearing a beautiful hat is the sign that one can expect to receive favours from one's superiors. Dreaming that one drinks sweet-tasting water is an omen indicating that one will be blessed with a long life.[19]

A dream forebodes ill if one

> dreams about a storm, or if seeing oneself crossing a swamp or wearing an unclean, evil smelling garment, then such dreams are the fore-

> boding that one will suffer from some kind of pollution, as caused by illnesses or death. To see oneself hatless or gazing into a mirror are forebodings of sufferings, to see one's body covered with insects or to be bitten by a wolf are omens of approaching illnesses. To be hurt by weapons, see oneself pursued by a warrior, or descending into an abyss, to see a flood or a conflagration or lightning are dreams interpreted as an omen indicating the approach of dangers, such as are the outcome of inauspicious constellations of the stars. Signs that one stands under a curse or that an enemy tries to kill one by means of black magic are to see oneself in fetters, to be sinking into the earth, or to have one's body and head split in two. A foreboding that one's life is in danger is to see oneself riding naked on an ass which heads toward the South, to see red flowers, to sit amidst water, and to see rain falling from the clouds. Very evil omens, said to be the signs of approaching death, are to see one's bowels being torn out from the belly by a black woman, to be dressed in red clothes, pick red flowers, to wind a red turban around one's head, or to drink and dance with the dead.[20]

Nebesky-Wojkowitz concludes this sample with a list of the classes of deities that cause dreams, a list that incorporates the enlarged cosmos of Tibetan Buddhism, and which are best understood more broadly than his use of the term demon suggests as at least some of them were originally indigenous deities of Bon or the folk religion:

> If one saw a snowy mountain or a soaring white bird, then the *lha* [gods] caused this dream. When seeing an old temple, images of clay, a fox, or a small child, the dream was caused by the *'gong po* demons...snakes, frogs, girls with a pale-blue skin, and mountain-meadows are mirages caused by the *klu* [nāgas, snake and water deities]. The *btsan* [guardian deities] make one see rocks, trees, riders, and warriors, the *the'u rang* [demons] let appear ash-coloured children in one's dreams; if one sees the figures of Buddhist priests, of asses, monkeys, rats, horses, and dogs, those dreams were the work of the *rgyal po* [guardian deities] demons, and if one trembles with terror and fear in the sleep, this is due to the influence of the *bdud* [māras, demons].[21]

Of related interest are the interpretations of the dreams of weather-makers, a profession that had its origins in the Bon tradition and many of whom remain Bon practitioners:

> If the weather-maker sees in his dream a great river, a woman who pours out water or beer, cattle and wild animals grazing, or if he sees himself well-attired in a new dress, then a rainfall is soon to be expected. On the other hand dreaming about an empty house or tent, a huge fire, a bad harvest, or a destitute beggar are signs indicating drought.[22]

Norbu Chophel devotes a chapter of his study of Tibetan folk culture to dream interpretation in which he presents some of the oral tradition on this subject as well as excerpts from two dream interpretation books (Longdol Lama's *Sung-bum* and Karma Chakme's *The Mirror of Omens*).[23] The chapter also includes a section on the signs of death from a medical text, the *Ambrosia Heart Tantra.* On the one hand, Chophel's work reveals a bewildering array of dream beliefs and interpretations mixing popular and elite ideas. For instance, he defines *Zim-lam Tag-pa* (*gzim lam brtag pa,* the examination of sleep) as a faculty "reserved only for the high incarnate monks and Doctors of Divinity (Geshe)," in which you give such a monk a piece of your clothing to put under his pillow so that he will have a dream explaining the cause of your troubles.[24] On the other hand, his presentation of dream interpretations from the oral tradition sometimes involves indigenous deities and is often accompanied by advice on how to avoid their evil influence. For instance, to dream of a monkey means "being influenced or affected by curses from the local protective deity *[yul lha]*....Most Tibetans appease this deity every month with offerings and prayers to ensure good health, good harvest and prosperity."[25]

Dream practices that existed in Tibet prior to the arrival of Buddhism were absorbed by Buddhism, both at the elite and the popular levels, where they comfortably coexisted with the Buddhist belief in the prophetic value of dreams. Equally, dreams were, and still are, considered to be part of a vast network of prophecy, revelation, and visionary experience. Over time, the Tibetan Buddhist emphasis on iconography and the practice of visualization shaped and colored dream images, and sustained a fertile climate for dream experience.

BUDDHIST INFLUENCES IN TIBET

In the early days of Buddhism's spread into Tibet[26] the new faith was embraced by some members of the elite classes and strongly opposed by others. Some of this tension, as well as the indigenous belief in the importance

FIGURE 2

The Skar-cung pillar. Ninth-century edict by King Thride Songtsen declaring Buddhism was not to be abandoned even by reason of prognostications or dreams.

Photograph by Hugh E. Richardson.

FIGURE 3

Detail of the Skar-cung inscription.

Photograph by Hugh E. Richardson.

of dreams, is revealed in a ninth-century inscription that records King Thride Songtsen's (*Khri lde srong brtsan*, b. 774) renewal of his ancestors' vow "not to abandon or destroy the practice of the Buddhist religion [for any reason including]...prognostications or dreams."[27] (See figures 2 and 3.)

Over several generations many different Tibetan scholars went to India to collect texts from various Buddhist sources, while at the same time a mix of Indian, Central Asian, and Chinese teachers came to Tibet either bringing texts with them or elucidating those already known by the Tibetans. The teachings the Tibetans sought and received were those of Mahāyāna Buddhism, itself an eclectic movement without any central authority that ruled on the acceptability of texts. Consequently, once the Tibetans began formulating their canon, there was no authoritative model to follow, and over the centuries various editions, with attendant inconsistencies, were put together.[28]

Foundational to Tibetan philosophical thought,[29] and among the earliest Mahāyāna sūtras, are the *Prajñāpāramitā* (Perfection of Wisdom texts). Underlying the Prajñāpāramitā literature is the concept of *śūnyatā*, the emptiness of all existent beings and things.[30] Such thinking complements and elaborates upon the illusory nature of the world, and, indeed, dreams are frequently used to illustrate both emptiness[31] and illusion *(māyā, sgyu ma)*.[32] For instance, in the same way that, upon awakening, we are sometimes taken aback to find we were asleep and that our experience was an illusion, we realize that the dream was without substance, empty and void. In this sense awakening from a dream is not an awakening *from* the state of illusion to that of reality; it is an awakening *to* the unreality, the emptiness, of both states, because waking reality is believed to be as insubstantial, as empty, as a dream. Thus, awakening from a dream can provide an intimation of enlightenment itself.[33]

This discussion about the illusory and empty nature of dreams goes back to the earliest Buddhist articulations about the nature of the self, consciousness, reality and illusion discussed in chapter 3, and it remains pervasive in Tibetan thought. We shall meet up with these same philosophical ideas in chapters 8 and 9, which bring out the connections between dreams, emptiness, and illusion in Dream Yoga practices, in dream rituals preserved in the *Tangyur*, and in teachings given by Tsongkhapa and by the current Dalai Lama. Indeed, almost every conversation I have had with both scholarly and nonscholarly Tibetan monks about dreams began with them saying that dreams are an illusion and unimportant; then they would elaborate on the meanings of dreams with regard to prophecy, health, spiritual accomplishments, and so on.

Despite this, an important Prajñāpāramitā text, *The Large Sutra on Perfect Wisdom*, discusses dreams in yet other contexts. For example, it states that those pursuing the perfection of wisdom do not have evil dreams. Indeed, they have auspicious dreams in which they see and hear the Buddha or see other auspicious Buddhist symbols.[34] This is similar to the Buddha's assurances to his wife in the *LV* that she had the dream of someone who has practiced good works, and to Buddhaghosa's explanation that prophetic dreams are caused by one's merit or demerit. Even in their dreams, the text says, those on the bodhisattva path commit "no offence against the ten wholesome ways of acting";[35] in other words, they maintain their bodhisattva consciousness and behavior even while dreaming. This points toward the belief in the controllability of consciousness, at least throughout waking and sleeping. For instance, chapter 55 describes the dream life of bodhisattvas, adding that the content of their dreams and their awareness while in the dream state are "known as the irreversible mark of an irreversible Bodhisattva."[36] This implies, somewhat like the dreams of the Buddha, that certain dreams are a sign of not falling back from an advanced spiritual state.

The text also contains a passage that seems to be advocating the practice of Dream Yoga when it suggests changing the imagery while dreaming. If successful, this predicts the bodhisattva will win supreme enlightenment.[37] Another intimation of Dream Yoga is seen in chapter 52 in the dialogue between Śāriputra, a leading disciple of the Buddha associated with the Theravāda tradition, and Subhūti. Śāriputra asks if a bodhisattva can grow in wisdom while dreaming, and Subhūti answers:

> If...he grows through the development by day, then he also grows in a dream. And why? Because dream and waking are indiscriminate. If the Bodhisattva who courses by day in the perfection of wisdom has a development of the perfection of wisdom, then also the Bodhisattva, the great being, who dreams will have a development of perfection of wisdom.[38]

Here "bodhisattva" refers both to those rare beings, earthly and celestial, who have achieved the state of bodhisattvahood and to those earthly beings who aspire to bodhisattvahood, that is, the devotees of Mahāyāna who have taken the vow to become a bodhisattva.[39]

One of the ways in which Mahāyāna expanded the Buddhist cosmos was through the doctrine of the three bodies of the Buddha. This doctrine has several interpretations,[40] but it is generally understood as follows: The dharmakāya is the body of the Buddha's teachings, or the state of enlightenment itself; the saṃbhogakāya is the body of enjoyment, a celestial body such as the Buddha had while residing in Tuṣita heaven before incarnating on earth; and the nirmāṇakāya *(sprul sku)* is the earthly body of a buddha. It is this last body which is of interest here, since it is sometimes also referred to as the apparitional body—upon achieving buddhahood one's earthly body is immediately transformed into an apparitional body. The apparitional body is a magical body that can be transformed at will for the purpose of teaching all kinds of beings;[41] for instance, it can be used to enter someone's dream. This is helpful in trying to understand the later literature, which refers to and even valorizes dreams of and about not only the historical Buddha but also great saints who are understood to have become buddhas—through their apparitional bodies they too can enter one's dreams in order to teach or impart an important message.

Graeme McQueen has argued persuasively for the openness of Mahāyāna in certifying new revelation,[42] and he has pointed out the acceptability of dreams in this process.[43] He also brings out some of the dangers awaiting the bodhisattva, such as their requirement to undergo the journey of birth and death:[44] bodhisattvas need to pass successfully through the bardo, the intermediate state between death and rebirth, while maintaining their bodhisattva consciousness into their next incarnation. As will be seen in chapter 8, the mastery of dreaming is particularly useful in this journey.

Another potent influence on Tibetan Buddhism was the mahāsiddhas *(grub chen thob pa)*, wandering tantric yogis who flourished in Northern India between the eighth and twelfth centuries.[45] Their roots are readily found in the earliest sources of Buddhism, where the individual experience of enlightenment was valorized, but they also cleared a fresh path that sought enlightenment in one lifetime. This is the path of Vajrayāna, also referred to as Tantric Buddhism.[46] The mahāsiddhas were capable of extremely eccentric behavior, but even though they had access to vast stores of esoteric knowledge, they never lost touch with the common people. They blended the highest esoteric teachings of the elite tradition with the popular tradition of the people, especially the shamanic tradition.[47] Through their charismatic gifts and the example of their lives, they helped to invigorate Indian Buddhism and to establish Tibetan Buddhism as a vital religious system that was responsive to the popular traditions around it and open to innovation.[48] Each of the main orders of Tibetan Buddhism traces its lineage back to one of the mahāsiddhas. In the case of Milarepa's Kagyu order, their lineage goes back to Nāropa, an important formulator of Dream Yoga practices.

Indo-Tibetan Buddhism has both innovative tendencies (represented by the openness of Mahāyāna to new revelations and by tantric practitioners such as the mahāsiddhas, who emphasized personal experience and maintained connections to the earlier shamanic practices) and conservative tendencies (represented by monastic translators devoted to preserving the Buddhist scriptures as accurately as possible). These two tendencies can be seen as a continuation of the two earliest forms of spiritual authority in Buddhism, that of individual experience and that of faithfulness to scriptures preserved in the canon. This is not the whole picture, however, because new doctrines or scriptures were introduced by scholar monks who combined reason with scriptural justification and by yogis and mahāsiddhas who experienced visionary revelations. The spoken transmission *(bka' ma)*, an unbroken oral transmittal from teacher to disciple through the centuries, was often balanced by pure vision *(dag snang)*, a direct meeting with a celestial buddha or great teacher from the past during meditation, in the waking state, or through dreams.[49]

MEDICAL TEXTS

A final important element in the construction of Buddhist dream ideology came from medical practices that were imported into Tibet, where they influenced the development of indigenous medical texts and mixed with local practices. As Buddhism entered Tibetan life, it brought along other Indian and Chinese theories and practices, including those related to medicine.[50] The connections between Buddhism and medicine go back to early, frequent epithets of Buddha as the Great Physician[51] and of his teachings (Dharma) as the King of Medicine,[52] as well as to the practice of medicine by Buddhist monastics.[53] Buddhaghosa too showed familiarity with medical theory in his discussion of bodily disturbances as one of the causes of dreams. These epithets and activities proliferated in Mahāyāna Buddhism, where healing was valorized in pivotal works such as the *Lotus Sūtra*,[54] through the popularity of the Medicine Buddha, and in representations of the primordial buddhas as the first physicians and the first teachers of healing.[55]

Two ancient Indian medical texts composed in the early centuries of the Christian era, the *Caraka Saṃhitā* and *Suśruta Saṃhitā* (hereafter the *CS* and *SS*),[56] are still in use today as part of the Āyurvedic system of healing. Both texts show Brahmanic and sramanic, possibly Buddhist, influences and use dreams as a diagnostic tool. It is worth reviewing the use of dreams in these two texts, since they will surface in Tibetan medical texts.

Sudhir Kakar has written eloquently about the Āyurvedic approach to the "whole person in order to achieve an accurate diagnosis,"[57] and dreams are considered a significant revealer of the person. This idea is not unique to ancient India. Dreams were used as a diagnostic tool by such well-known ancient Greek doctors as Galen and Hippocrates, as well as by ancient Mesopotamian doctors.[58] Dream incubation, sleeping in a temple in order to dream a cure for an illness, was and remains a widespread practice throughout the Mediterranean,[59] including sleeping in the temple of Isis in ancient Egypt and the temple of Ptah at Memphis.[60] And, of course, shamanic dream techniques for healing are well documented throughout most of the world.[61]

The *CS* contains a classification system of seven kinds of dreams. The first three consist of dreams of objects that have been perceived previously through the three senses of seeing, hearing, and touching; the fourth consists dreams about objects that are desired; the fifth, dreams awakened by the imagination; the sixth, prophetic dreams; and the seventh, dreams caused by disturbances in the body.[62] The first five dream types are all connected to the senses through remembered perceptions, desired perceptions, or imagined perceptions. The sixth prophetic type of dream is not connected to the senses or the body and thus has an external quality—prophetic dreams are perceived to be free of the limits of sense perception and to be external to the individual. The seventh dream type, those stimulated by disorders in the body, is one of the most common explanations for dreams in all areas of the ancient world, and one commentary on the *CS* says that these dreams are the cause of disease.[63] We have already met with some of the images the *CS* lists for premonitory dreams of disease and death:

- traveling toward the south[64] riding a dog, a camel or an ass
- drinking in the company of ghosts, being dragged by dogs
- wearing red garlands and apparel and with a red body, laughing frequently and being dragged by a woman
- a growth from the chest
- anointed with ghee, offering oblations to the fire without flame, a lotus flower growing from the chest

- drinking in the company of *caṇḍalas* [a person born from a *sudra* father and a Brahmin mother]
- drowning in water, dancing with demons.[65]

The text continues with more dream images portending death or serious disease,[66] and it concludes with a statement about the importance of these dreams: "He who knows these frightful dream symptoms that lead to death does not, through ignorance, try to cure the incurable."[67] The inherent connection between symptom and omen is shown by the use of the word *pūrvarūpa,* which contains both meanings. Thus the dream can become a self-fulfilling prophecy because the attending physician will not treat a patient who has such dream, thereby allowing the disease to run its course until death.

The creative power of the mind to realize what it imagines (or dreams) can also bring on the predicted disease or death in a believing dreamer. The widespread belief in the ability of dreams to foretell death is easily understood when we recall the many connections between dreams, sleep, and death. People often dream of the dead, which can be very disturbing and even—for some believers—physically polluting: a sleeping body can easily be mistaken for a dead body, and many people believe that the soul leaves the body during sleep, which is why caution must be used in waking a sleeper.[68] Indeed, Hesiod says that Night is the mother of Sleep, Death, and Dreams,[69] and in Sanskrit all three words share the same root √svap. Sleep and dreams know death in a way waking consciousness does not: they have crossed a boundary into uncharted realms.[70] In like fashion, disease, which so often precedes death, can also be predicted.

The *CS* puts some parameters around dream experience when it separates meaningful dreams from meaningless ones based on when they occur:

> Dreams that tell a physician they will have no effect *[phala]* occur during the daytime, or are too short or too long.
>
> Those seen in the first part of the night have little effect. If one can not sleep [after a dream], then it will have a great effect.[71]

As the tradition develops, the most meaningful dreams are those that one has around dawn, in the last watch of the night.[72]

A slightly later medical text, the *SS,* also lists various dreams that indicate death in a patient, such as "dreams of going towards the south on the back of an elephant, or on that of any carnivorous animals, or of riding on a boar or on a buffalo or...carried towards the quarter by a dark woman with dishevelled hair and clad in a blood-red garment laughing and dancing.... [Or dreams] that members of vile castes have been drawing him southward, or that ghosts or anchorites have been embracing him, or that savage beasts with diabolical faces have been smelling his head."[73] In this text such dreams seem to be both caused by illness and to be symptoms of it, because the text adds that such dreams in a healthy person indicate the onset of illness—the dream is the first symptom of the illness to appear. Fortunately, it also has recommendations to avert their influence. It says that after having such a dream, one

> should get up in the morning and make a gift of Māsha-pulse, sesamum, iron and gold to the brahmans, and repeat the Tripāda Gāyatrī.
>
> Having dreamed a bad dream in the first watch of the night, a person should meditate upon a holy or auspicious subject, and then lie down again with all his senses fully controlled, and repeat the mantras sacred to the gods. An evil dream should not be told to another. The dreamer should reside in a holy temple for three nights, and worship the deity with the most fervent devotion, whereby its evil effects would become nullified.[74]

The recommendation of this text that "an evil dream should not be told to another" is challenged by the evidence of Indian literary texts we have surveyed. Here the detailed telling of dreams, especially those thought to be inauspicious, is a stock device. This does not, however, preclude someone from keeping silent about their dreams, and the recommendation itself would suggest that recounting the dream will contribute to or hasten its dreaded effect.

Of particular relevance to the study of dreams in Buddhism is the fact that actually neither the *CS* nor the *SS* fit as smoothly into the category of Brahmanical texts as had been previously supposed. Kenneth Zysk has persuasively argued for the early sramanic, especially Buddhist, influence on these texts. In part his argument is based on the polluting effects of practicing medicine, which led to the exclusion of medical practitioners from orthodox groups.[75] Instead, these doctors mingled with various ascetic groups, especially the Buddhists, whose Vinaya reveals a deep interest in medicine. By the mid-third century B.C.E. Buddhist monasteries were extending medical care to the population at large, and medicine was being taught in Buddhists monasteries.[76] In time, medical skill became an important part of Buddhist missionary activity in India and elsewhere.[77] For this reason Zysk argues that both the *CS* and the *SS* were formulated by sramanas who practiced medicine, especially Buddhists, and that with the decline of Buddhism in India these texts were Hinduized. Consequently, the dream theory in these texts is as Buddhist as it is Hindu.

One of the most important Tibetan medical texts is the *Four Treatises (rGyud bZhi)*, said to have been written in Sanskrit about 400 C.E. and which now exists only in Tibetan and Mongolian translations.[78] Actually it is a terma text, rediscovered in the eleventh century,[79] attributed to the historical Buddha (who is believed to have manifested as the Medicine Buddha in order to teach this text). It is, however, consistent with the earlier Indian medical texts, not only in accepting certain dreams as signs of illness and death, but in employing similar symbols—and sometimes even the same ones, such as the color red and the south—as in the following:

> Dreams of riding on a rat, monkey, tiger, jackal, or corpse is a sign of death. Dreams of riding naked toward the south on a buffalo, horse, pig, donkey, or camel means one will die. Dreams of tree branches with a bird's nest growing from one's forehead, or a tree with thorns growing out of one's chest, picking a lotus, falling into an abyss, sleeping in a cemetery; having a cracked head surrounded by crows and hungry ghosts with facial moles, having black skin that is falling off, entering the mother's womb (i.e., entering the afterlife state of the Bardo), being carried away by water, sinking in mud, being swallowed by fish, finding iron and gold and selling them, being defeated in battle, forcing people to pay taxes on dancing and getting married, sitting naked with shaven head and shaven moustache, drinking *chang* [beer] or being dragged by the dead who are wearing red clothes and red flower garlands, or dancing with the dead—these are omens of death. If the dreamer is sick, she or he will die. If one is not sick, the outcome is uncertain, so perform rituals [for protection].[80]

This text is also in agreement with other Buddhist texts that say the most relevant dreams are those that occur in the early morning.[81] Furthermore, it lists the contents of auspicious dreams:

> Seeing gods, great bulls, famous people, a blazing fire in a lake, bodies smeared with blood, people wearing white garments and carrying umbrellas, climbing mountains and trees having fruit, crossing rivers and lakes, climbing on high hills, riding on lions, elephants, horses or cows, going north and east, getting free of dangerous places, defeating enemies, being worshiped by parents and gods. To dream this means you will have a long life without sickness and you will obtain wealth.[82]

An important Tibetan commentary on the *Four Treatises* is *The Blue Beryl (Vaiḍūrya sngon po)*[83] of Sangye Gyatso (*sangs rgyas rgya mtsho*, 1653–1705),[84] regent of the great fifth Dalai Lama, which has been illustrated by a remarkable series of medical paintings.[85] Sangye Gyatso lists seven kinds of dreams: those corresponding to what one has seen, heard, intuitively sensed, aspired toward in the form of prayer, or mentally conceived; those that are prophetic, and those caused by disease.[86] The first five are of no consequence for medical diagnosis. Similarly, those caused by disease merely reflect the disposition of the patient and should be ignored by the doctor. It is the prophetic dreams of the patient that are useful to the doctor, and Gyatso uses the examples just quoted from the *Four Treatises.* He specifies that the most significant dreams are recurrent dreams (those that continue to be remembered) and those that occur toward dawn. The importance of dawn dreams is related to the different humors of the body, which influence dreams during different times of the night: phlegm in late evening, bile around midnight, and wind *(rlung, prāṇa)* toward dawn.[87]

Gyatso brings out the relationship between the wind humor and dreams in his analysis of the origin of dreams, during which he makes several other interesting points. (See plate 1, which shows the various dream images that originate from the heart center of the central figure.) He begins by saying that all the dreams of ordinary and healthy people begin in the *kun gshi rnam shes* (Skt.: *ālayavijñāna*): the seat of consciousness, which is the source of both normal perceptions as well as dream perceptions. "In healthy people dreams originate in the seat of consciousness situated in the heart center of the body, where the various sensory consciousnesses [perception and cognition] arise. When they are purified, then clarity manifests.... When, during sleep, the defiled mind rises with the impulsive movement of the life-sustaining breath *(srog rlung)* dreams arise."[88]

These dreams then spread from the heart center to various parts of the body, where different dreams are experienced. For example: "If the consciousness moves up to the crown of the head, it creates images of the gods and the sky.... If the consciousness descends to the lower part of the body, the dreamer moves through mountain slopes, forests and dark gorges, and so on."[89]

The life-sustaining breath *(srog rlung)*[90] is the most prominent of the five winds that travel along the various energy channels (Tib.: *rtsa;* Skt.: *nāḍī*) of the body.[91]

Given the influence of the physical body on dreams in this system, it is no wonder that they are accepted as a diagnostic tool; in dreams, it is believed, consciousness travels to different parts of the body, where it can reveal illness.

It is interesting to reflect upon the foregoing elite, elaborated theory of the relationships among the body, consciousness, and dreams in the context of the biography of Yuthog the Elder, a semi-legendary (traditionally eighth-century) Tibetan doctor and saint credited with spreading medical knowledge in Tibet, especially through the *Four Treatises.* In this text we find many dreams of the sort that is common in Buddhist biography. For instance, Yuthog's mother has a series of conception dreams, and Yuthog himself dreams, as do others.[92] What is curious is that even though dreams have a clearly articulated value in medical diagnosis, and this biography describes many encounters with sick people, there is not one example of a medical dream—there are no interpretations of patients' dreams by physicians. Instead the text presents the prophetic dreams that are typical of Buddhist sacred biography. However, the absence of medical dreams in the presence of so many other prophetic dreams does not belie the importance of medical dreams as much as it indicates the extent to which the popular ideology about dreams dominates the elite medical ideology. The biography is first and foremost that of a saint, one who happens to manifest his saintliness through medical skill. As the biography of a saint, it calls for biographical dreams in order to underscore the inevitability and cosmic significance of events in a way that even the best medical diagnosis cannot. At the same time it suggests that the elaborate dream ideology of the medical texts and their commentaries was quite possibly not generally used by doctors.[93]

Another biography shows dreams being used to diagnose and cure illness in a very different way. The monk Paldan Lodo (1527–96), a master of Dream Yoga, used his own dreams to locate the source of someone else's illness. The source was often found to be a demon, whom he then battled on behalf of the sick person,[94] a practice common among shamans throughout this region as well as other parts of the world.[95] In one instance, the headman of a village went to him to complain about an epidemic that had struck his village and to ask if it could be stopped. In a long dream sequence Paldan Lodo transformed himself into a fierce protective deity, visited the village, and met up with the local deity/demon who, in turn, complained that he had been defiled by the dead bodies in the village and therefore had punished them with an epidemic. Then Paldan Lodo "brought the god to account. He was terrified and cried: 'O Great Wrathful One, I beg you to be patient. I will do what you say.'"[96] With the epidemic over, Paldan Lodo changed his form and gave the demon religious teachings. Then he woke up.

Despite their differences, these two biographies of Buddhist healers show the incorporation and enduring legacy of both imported and indigenous dream practices. Yuthog's biography emphasizes the *Four Treatises* yet is rich in mythological incidents and shamanistic practices, while Paldan Lodo's biography, even though it makes references to instruction in Dream Yoga,[97] records distinctly shamanistic dream experiences.

PART TWO

Continuity of Dream Material

FIGURE 4

Queen Māyās Dream. Gandhara Style.

Asian Art Museum, San Francisco. Photograph by Mary Storm.

5 *Conception Dreams*

IN PART TWO OF THIS BOOK I examine dream narrations in Tibetan biographies that demonstrate continuity with the dream material in the early Indian biographies of the Buddha.

Emphasizing continuities between the Indian and Tibetan biographies conforms with Charles Keyes's point that the life of a Buddhist hero must reflect the life of the historical Buddha:

> A man can be recognized as a Buddhist saint only insofar as his actions are seen to have been movements along the path first exemplified in the life of the Buddha himself.... In some instances the biographer of a Buddhist saint may find the evidence of Buddhist holiness in the actual or historical events of his subject, since the saint himself is often well aware of the need to model his behavior on that of the Buddha. His life may become, at least in some instances, what has been termed "enacted biography" by Reynolds and Capps *[The Biographical Process]*. But there can never be an exact repetition or imitation in fact of previous events for the whole course of a human life. Even consciously copied patterns of the model may manifest themselves quite differently, since the stage—the social conditions in which the life takes place—is invariably radically different to that first stage in the sixth century B.C. The biographer is always faced, then, with the problem of showing that surface appearances (that is, actual events) notwithstanding, the underlying structure of the life is that found in the path of Buddha.[1]

In the next three chapters I argue that specific types of dreams persist in Buddhist biographies from the earliest texts into the present, even in the different cultural contexts of India and Tibet, and that they remain a significant part of the structure of Buddhist sacred biography.

Conception dreams are found in the stories of heroes and religious figures from around the world. As examples, Jackson Lincoln offers the stories of Alexander, Zoroaster, and Jesus.[2] Stories about the birth of Christian and Muslim saints are also rich in such dreams.[3] In general, conception dreams are believed to be a sign of divine involvement, and in some cases actual divine fathering. In the Bible, even though divine or angelic annunciations often take the place of conception dreams, most notably in the case of Mary's conception of Jesus (Luke 1: 31–33),[4] a variant of this process does occur in a dream, that of Joseph, the stepfather of Jesus: "An angel of the Lord appeared to him in a dream, saying, 'Joseph, son of David, do not fear to take Mary your wife, for that which is conceived in her is of the Holy Spirit'" (Matt. 1: 20–21). This dream proclaims Mary's sexual innocence and Jesus' divine origin so that Joseph will marry her and accept her child.

As we have seen, Queen Māyā's conception dream is pervasive throughout Buddhist art and literature, where, like most dreams, it has multiple meanings. It utilizes the powerful and pure image of a white elephant to delineate the nature of the Buddha; it suggests a miraculous conception; and it establishes a precedent for the parents of Buddhist heroes. It is this last point that is of interest here. Since this dream is so well known, it is not surprising that conception dreams should figure in the biographical literature of highly revered Tibetans,[5] as well as in the folk literature such as the epic of Gesar[6] and in the folk opera *Drowa Sangmo.*[7] Conception dreams actually became a standard part of the biographies of significant Buddhist leaders; they are the most common category of dreams in these biographies, and they are an important sign that the child will be extraordinary. They simultaneously predict the future child's religious authority and confer it on him.[8] In the texts that follow, however, it is not just mothers who have conception dreams, Buddhists fathers also have such dreams. In the case of men it is sometimes a way of extending their paternity or confirming it. Compare, for instance, the just-quoted dream of Jesus' stepfather Joseph with that of Padmasambhava's stepfather King Indrabhūti.

Padmasambhava is a semi-legendary figure who helped the spread of Buddhism in eighth-century Tibet. His stepfather has a variation on a conception dream because, as Padmasambhava's name means, he is born *(sambhava)* from a lotus *(padma)*,[9] not a human mother.[10] Nonetheless, King

Indrabhūti, who eventually adopts him, dreams before he learns of the wondrous child lying in a giant lotus in the middle of a lake: "In a dream a radiant golden dorje with nine points appeared from the sky and came into my hand. And, I [the king] dreamed that the sun was rising in my heart."[11] As we have seen in the *Mahāvastu*, the sun is a symbol for a buddha. *Vajra* or *dorje* refers mainly to the ritual object representing the male aspect of tantric practice,[12] though here it also symbolizes a male practitioner. It is a preeminent symbol for the active force or energy of universal compassion and one that frequently appears in other Tibetan dreams.

By virtue of having had this dream, King Indrabhūti presumes a unique relationship to Padmasambhava, that of an adopted parent. He publicly affirms this relationship when he relates his dream and names Padmasambhava "the lake-born *vajra*,"[13] thus making explicit the connection between the child of the lake lotus and the *vajra* (ritual implement) of his dream. We will see several other instances of a private dream becoming part of a public event.

Padmasambhava's biography is relevant to this study because he is an important transitional figure between Indian and Tibetan Buddhism—he is the great Indian mahāsiddha who journeyed to Tibet in order to subdue the demons obstructing the spread of Buddhism. Furthermore, his biography contains a remarkable number of conception dreams. In addition to King Indrabhūti's two dreams, there are five more conception dreams, bringing the total to more than one-third of the dreams in the text (fifteen in all). Some patterns from these dreams resonate with the conception dream of Padmasambhava. All the children born from such conception dreams are or become royal. With one exception, King Thrisong Detsen, all the children predicted by conception dreams have miraculous powers, undergo trials of a tantric nature, and convert many people to Buddhism—all attributes of Padmasambhava's story. One dream actually occurs through the agency of Padmasambhava, when a young girl falls asleep in a cave and dreams Padmasambhava blesses her. "Upon awakening she remembered the dream and thought it had been like experiencing the pleasure of a husband."[14] She later gives birth to a son who becomes king of Bodhgayā.

The celestial buddha Mañjuśrī is involved in a conception when he causes the dream of King Thrisong Detsen's mother. Thrisong is the Tibetan king who invited Padmasambhava to Tibet, so it is a particularly meaningful dream in the tradition:

> While the king and queen were asleep Mañjuśrī sent a ray that sprang from his heart to the womb of the queen. She then dreamed that the sun rose and that she conceived a beautiful child and that the earth was covered in light and that miraculous gems rained down. When the king heard about the dream he rejoiced and performed a ceremony.[15]

Two other conception dreams involve nectar *(bdud rtsi)*, a mystical substance that transforms consciousness through conferring insight. The mother of Garab Dorje dreams that she drinks nectar poured from a stone vessel,[16] and the princess Dharmabhitti dreams that "she saw a handsome white man (a daka), / who poured nectar from a vessel onto her head."[17] When Dharmabhitti's child grows up, he converts Kashmir to Buddhism.

Some of the conception dreams are presented as the actual *cause* of pregnancy. For instance, another version of Garab Dorje's conception emphasizes that it takes place while his mother is living as a nun completely away from men; she conceives him through a dream about a beautiful white man (a *daka*) who "held a crystal vessel in his hand which had the letters *oṃ ā hūṃ svāhā* engraved upon it. Three times he set the vessel upon the crown of her head, and light then shone from it. While this happened, she beheld the threefold world perfectly and clearly."[18] Garab Dorje is said to have been the first Dzogchen master. Like the Buddha, he brought a liberating teaching, and, like the Buddha, he was conceived purely, through a dream.

The last example of a conception dream in this text is one that leads to the birth of Mandāravā, one of Padmasambhava's two Tibetan consorts and among his chief disciples. Her mother dreamed that "a turquoise stūpa came out of her head and that the kingdom of Zahor was burned by eight suns rising together. She told the dream to the king, and he performed a great ceremony."[19]

These dreams pointedly identify the children as significant contributors to Buddhism, an identification strengthened by the use of specifically Buddhist objects such as vajras and stūpas (structures that enclose relics). The sun is a frequent symbol for a buddha or Buddhism; nectar *(dudtsi)*, the transforming potion of insight, symbolizes the doctrines of the Buddha,[20] while the vessels *(bumpa)* symbolize the disciples who will internalize and transmit the doctrine[21]—both are used in tantric rituals.[22]

Some additionally meaningful symbols appear in the conception dream of Padmasambhava's other Tibetan consort and biographer, Yeshe Tsogyel. Her father dreams first of an eight-petaled lotus pouring out light, then of a coral stūpa, and finally of a lute that plays by itself. This dream utilizes the symbol of the lotus (standing for a buddha or bodhisattva), while the stūpa establishes her as someone who carries Buddhist teachings, and the lute playing by itself suggests that she will be listened to by many people. Her mother dreams that she receives a rosary made of coral and conch shell beads; the coral beads pour forth blood and the conch shell beads pour forth milk.[23] In tantric symbolism the color red (coral) signifies blood and women, while white signifies semen and men. In the mother's dream the meaning of red is stated, but sperm is conflated with milk.[24]

I have quoted from these dreams in order to familiarize the reader with some of the most frequently found images in Tibetan dreams—images that also figure prominently in the conception dreams of the parents of the great founder of the Gelugpa order, Tsongkhapa (1357–1419). For instance, the colors red and white also predominate in two of the three dreams Tsongkhapa's mother had before his birth:

> His mother dreamt that she and one thousand other women were in a flower garden to which a boy dressed in white and carrying a vessel came from the east while a girl dressed in red and holding peacock feathers in her right hand and a large mirror in her left came from the west. The boy went to each of the women in turn and asked the girl if she would be suitable. The girl repeatedly rejected them until the boy pointed to Tsong Khapa's mother, whom she indicated as the perfect choice. The boy and girl then purified Tsong Khapa's mother by bathing her and when she awoke the next day she felt very light.[25]

Tsongkhapa's father also has dreams before his birth:

> His father dreamt of a monk who came to him from the Five-peaked Mountain (Wu-tai-shan) in China, a place particularly associated with Manjushri. This monk required shelter for nine months which, in the dream, his father gave by accommodating him in their shrine room for that length of time.[26]

Both parents also have conception dreams:

> His mother saw monks coming with many different ritual objects, saying that they were going to invoke the statue of Avalokiteshvara. When the statue appeared, it was as big as a mountain yet, as it

> approached her, it diminished in size, finally entering her body through her crown aperture.
>
> Tsong Khapa's father dreamt of Vajrapani, who, from his own pure realm, threw down a vajra, which landed on his wife.[27]

Tsongkhapa's mother has yet another dream before his birth. In this dream she saw:

> many monks arriving with offerings. When she inquired about their purpose they replied that they had come to pay their respects and gain an audience. Simultaneously, the boy in white from her previous dream appeared and pointed to her womb. With key in hand he entered it and opened a box, from which came the golden statue of Avalokiteshvara. This statue was stained, and a girl in red appeared and cleaned it with a peacock feather.[28]

Her dreams are as rich in tantric male and female imagery as those in the dreams of Yeshe Tsogyel's parents. The boy is dressed in white, the color associated with semen in tantric texts, while the girl is dressed in red, the color of (menstrual) blood. This imagery is also a reversal of the negative connotation of red—and of its direct or oblique association with women—in the medical literature. Furthermore, these gendered images are suggestive of *upāya* (skillful means) and *prajñā* (insight), the male and female aspects of practice, the mastery of which are necessary for enlightenment.[29]

Returning to the dreams of Tsongkhapa's parents, Geshe Ngawang Dhargey underscores their relevance when he says that they—and other dream images such as being born without causing any pain to the mother and the appearance of an auspicious star at birth—were portents "of the birth of someone remarkable. In this respect Je Rinpoche's [Tsongkhapa's] birth resembled that of the Buddha."[30]

The dreams of Tsongkhapa's parents maintain continuity in the tradition by evoking Queen Māyā's conception dream, especially through his mother's dreams. In both cases, the future mothers first see an object in their dreams (a statue, an elephant), and then this object enters their bodies. This echoing of Māyā's dream continues in the third dream of Tsongkhapa's mother, where he is symbolically understood to be in a box in his mother's womb, just as the Buddha is surrounded by a jeweled sanctum *(paribhoga)*[31] in his mother's womb. The vajra in his father's dream is another sign of the continuities that were established in Tibetan sacred biographies, such as the vajra in the conception dream of Padmasambhava's adopted father. The first dream of Tsongkhapa's father also establishes Tsongkhapa's spiritual lineage. The monk in his dream is associated with Mañjuśrī, the celestial bodhisattva of wisdom,[32] an obvious symbol for Tsongkhapa, who became a monk known for his wisdom and who had visionary experiences of Mañjuśrī throughout his life. Indeed, this dream suggests that Mañjuśrī is involved in Tsongkhapa's conception and somewhat distances the father from having actually sired the child.

The parents' second set of dreams add to Tsongkhapa's spiritual lineage. First, his mother dreams of a statue of the celestial bodhisattva Avalokiteśvara, who is known for his compassion and is considered the protector of Tibet.[33] Second, his father dreams of Vajrapāṇi[34] who, along with Avalokiteśvara and Mañjuśrī, is one of the best-known guardian deities of the Buddhist doctrine. This spiritual lineage is often invoked by what is regarded as Tsongkhapa's prayer:

> Avalokiteśvara, mighty treasure of immaculate love,
> Mañjuśrī, Lord of stainless knowledge,
> Vajrapāṇi, destroyer of all demonic forces,
> O Je Tsong Khapa, Losang Drakpa,
> Crown jewel of the sages of the Land of Snow,
> Humbly I request your blessing![35]

The symbols of these dreams are rich with meanings about both the child's future and his importance to Buddhism.

In contrast to the Buddha, Tsongkhapa, and Padmasambhava, whose conceptions and births are preceded by auspicious dreams and wondrous portents, no dreams or portents precede or occur at the birth of Milarepa (1040–1123).[36] Even though throughout his life Milarepa will have supernormal abilities, the important point of his biography is that he is born as an ordinary human; his human birth is a testament to what can be achieved in one lifetime *with* the guidance of a guru. Given this emphasis on the guru—the relationship between Milarepa and his guru Marpa is at the heart of the biography—appropriately it is Marpa and his wife Dakmema who have dreams the night before Milarepa arrives seeking teachings. Their dreams, which are rich in gendered symbolism, establish a sacred mother-son and father-son relationship. Marpa dreams that his guru Nāropa

> gave him a slightly tarnished five-pronged vajra...and a golden vase filled with nectar saying "With the water in this vase wash the dirt from the vajra, then mount it on top of the banner-of-victory." When Marpa did this the brilliance of the vajra lit up the whole universe and the six classes of beings were freed from sorrow and filled with happiness. They prostrated themselves and paid reverence to the Venerable Marpa and his banner-of-victory.[37]

The next morning Dakmema tells Marpa about the dream she had the night before.

> Two women from Urgyan [*ḍākinīs*, semidivine women] were carrying a crystal stūpa [that] had some impurities on its surface. They said, "Nāropa commands the lama [Marpa] to consecrate this stūpa and to place it on the summit of a mountain."...And you washed the stūpa with the water in the vase and performed the consecration. Then you placed it on the mountaintop, where it radiated a great light and projected numerous replicas of itself upon the mountaintops. The two women watched over these stūpas.[38]

Marpa remains silent about his own dream, though he thinks to himself that their dreams are in agreement;[39] instead, he disparages dreams: "'I do not know what dreams are, they have no origin.'"[40] Later in the text, however, Marpa once again refers to these dreams and partly explains their meaning to Milarepa when he says:

> From the very first moment I knew you were a disciple capable of receiving the teaching. The night before you came here I learned from a dream that you were destined to serve the teaching of Buddha. Dakmema, in a similar but even more remarkable dream, saw two women guarding a stūpa, indicating that the ḍākinīs will protect the teaching of our lineage. In this way, my lama and the ḍākinīs sent you to me as a disciple.[41]

These two dreams complement each other and make some important points. We are by now familiar with the rich meanings of nectar in vessels, while the impurities of the stūpa and the tarnishing of the vajra represent Milarepa's bad karma accumulated from harming the relatives who cheated him of his inheritance. In their separate ways, Marpa and Dakmema will help Milarepa to work off this karma.

Dakmema's dream of a crystal stūpa carried by two ḍākinīs parallels another dream of a crystal stūpa that appears later in the biography, after Milarepa's death, when his disciple Rechungpa dreams of ḍākinīs carrying Milarepa away in a crystal stūpa. In Dakmema's dream this imagery is reversed: the stūpa comes *to* them, indicating that Milarepa is being brought to life, the opposite of death. We have already seen that stūpas also figured prominently in the conception dreams of two female saints, Mandāravā and Yeshe Tsogyel. Stūpas are womblike receptacles[42] most often containing the relics of Buddhist saints, but they also contain sacred texts and religious implements. Essentially, they are memorials, not tombs. They are there to remind people of the Buddha and his teachings;[43] indeed, a consecrated *(rab gnas)* stūpa is considered an emanation of the Buddha's mind.[44] Also, a saint such as Milarepa is thought to be a living buddha. Consequently, there is a continuity of meaning among stūpas, buddhas, saints, and teachings;[45] the appearance of a stūpa in a dream evokes these related ideas and is an appropriate symbol to represent a Buddhist hero. At the same time, these dreams elegantly suggest the continuum of birth, death, and rebirth. It is particularly interesting that Dakmema should have received such female imagery from two women in her dream, while Marpa received the masculine imagery of a vajra from his male guru. These dreams establish Dakmema as Milarepa's true mother and Marpa as his true father. This is appropriate symbolism because the guru-disciple relationship is often referred to as a father-son relationship.[46] Indeed, Marpa and Milarepa often refer to each other as father and son throughout the biography, while Dakmema and Milarepa refer to each other as mother and son.

Since conception dreams are a prominent feature in other biographies, we would expect to find a conception dream in Milarepa's, and must assume it has been left out for a reason. One possible reason is that, structurally, conception dreams occur at the beginning of biographies, and this place is already occupied by the dreams of Rechungpa, Milarepa's disciple. The most persuasive reason, however, is that the dreams of Marpa and Dakmema—the spiritual parents of Milarepa—function as conception dreams. The point of the biography is that Milarepa was truly born, or at least spiritually reborn, when he met Marpa—it is one of the great guru-disciple stories in Buddhist literature. In this context it is worth noting that Dakmema also plays a vital role in Milarepa's discipleship. It is she who comforts and advises Milarepa in the face of Marpa's harshness and indeed, in one instance, gives Milarepa spiritual teachings.[47] She is the gentle mother, while Marpa is the demanding father. They are Milarepa's true parents,[48] especially given his biological mother's negative influence (she directed him toward the study of black magic) and his biological father's absence (he died when Milarepa was young).

The vajra in Marpa's dream also evokes the vajra in the conception dream of Padmasambhava's adopted father, further suggesting parenthood as well as the existence of a common source and a continuity between Milarepa and Padmasambhava. Later in the tradition, Tsongkhapa's father also sees a vajra in a conception dream, which in turn evokes these earlier dreams. As one of the preeminent symbols of Tantric Buddhism, the vajra is an appropriate symbol for each of these heroes; it is a way of saying that they are the essence of the tantric teachings clothed in human form. Additionally, Dakmema's dream of a stūpa evokes the inner sanctum mentioned in the *LV*, the receptacle that encircled the Buddha while he resided in his mother's womb,[49] and the box in the dream of Tsongkhapa's mother.[50] The masculine imagery of the vajra combined with the feminine imagery of the stūpa are quite suggestive of pregnancy, particularly in this context of a conception dream.

Be that as it may, a conception dream still belongs at the beginning of a biography, or at least at that part of the biography that tells of the hero's birth. Instead, Rechungpa has parallel dreams that both begin and end the biography. Rechungpa interprets his first dream to mean he should ask Milarepa to tell his life story, and in this way the biography begins. This is yet another use of dreams: they set the biography in sacred time. Rechungpa's first dream does this particularly well because he dreams he is in the abode of the ḍākinīs, a setting reminiscent of the celestial beginning of the *LV*. Here, a woman dressed in red robes guides him to the celestial buddha Akṣobhya,[51] who is preaching to an assembly about the lives of the Buddha and various bodhisattvas.[52] Akṣobhya concludes his discourse with the life of Marpa, saying: "The teaching is ended. In the morning I shall tell the story of Milarepa. Come to hear it."[53] Rechungpa understands this dream to mean he should ask Milarepa to tell his life story, and then he sees five ḍākinīs[54] who encourage him to ask Milarepa for his life story.[55] At the end of the biography Rechungpa again dreams of these five ḍākinīs, who now carry away the relics from Milarepa's cremation cell. This series of dreams brings out the significance of a female presence in Tibetan men's dreams and demonstrates the reversal of Indian female dream imagery. The ḍākinīs, through their gender and the dream symbol of the stūpa, evoke both conception dreams and dreams of death portended by the appearance of women. This reversal of dream imagery is made all the more apparent by Rechungpa's dream guide, a woman wearing red clothing, which in Indian texts signals death. The function of the ḍākinīs is to instigate the telling of the biography, to bring it to life, and to end it. An echo of the life-giving function is the appearance of two ḍākinīs in Dakmema's dream, which portends Milarepa's arrival and consequently his rebirth into the spiritual life.

Conception dreams express the belief that Buddhist heroes first manifest on the dream level, long before they take on an earthly form. This parallels the idea that dreams are a sign of things to come, of things coming to fruition, which we saw as early as the five dreams of the Buddha, and which we will see more of in the later tantric tradition.

In the biographies, conception dreams are pretty much the only women's dreams there are. The fact that they are an essential part of the beginning of most biographies suggests that they are stereotypical; and indeed, they all follow a similar pattern of impregnation and other sexual imagery. The male-dominated textual tradition of Tibetan Buddhism is not the place to look for women's dreams, and the dreams found there reveal more about the tradition's affirmation of dream consciousness than about women's consciousness, though the rich gendered imagery is consistent with regard to color (in the dreams about Yeshe Tsogyel and Tsongkhapa—the imagery is somewhat more slippery in the case of stūpas). Most obviously, the impregnating deities are all male. We will encounter a few women's dreams in the next chapter, and in chapter 10 we will return to the topic of gendered dream imagery and women dreamers.

6 Shared Dreams

SHARED DREAMS OCCUR when two or more people have a dream with the same meaning, although the content may differ, on the same night. The dreamers can be either in the same place or far apart. While examples of such dreams can be found in other cultures,[1] South Asia is an especially rich source for them. Part of O'Flaherty's study of South Asian dreams focuses on the shared dreams of total strangers living far apart who fall in love in their dreams and then find each other in waking reality.[2] Such a romantic type of shared dream does not appear in the biographies of Buddhist saints, though other types do.

Shared dreams neatly encapsulate the permeability of the South Asian sense of self, a self that overlaps with the divine (the source of prophetic dreams) and with other people. In Buddhist biographies shared dreams also suggest that the events they symbolize are of such cosmic importance that they affect both the dreaming life of the community and its conscious life.

One of the most dramatic examples of this in Buddhist literature occurs in stories about the Buddha's departure from home, when he and various members of his family all have shared dreams. As we have already seen, they all dream on the same night, but their dreams contain different symbols. For instance, in the *Mahāvastu* the Buddha's father dreams of an elephant leaving the city, his aunt dreams of a white bull leaving city, and his wife dreams of a great cloud that pours rain.[3] That the rich symbolism of the shared dream appealed to various compilers is shown by similar groups of shared dreams from this night preserved in other biographies of the Buddha: in the *Lalitavistara* the Buddha, his father and wife all dream;[4] in the *Abhiniṣkramaṇasūtra*, it is also the Buddha, his father and wife who dream;[5] and in the *Mūlasarvāstivāda Vinaya*, it is the Buddha, his wife, and his aunt.[6]

A variant of the shared dream is one that transcends time, as do the five dreams of the Buddha, which are said to be the same dreams had by buddhas of the past.[7] Another example of this type is Queen Māyā's conception dream of a white elephant which is said to be the same dream as that had by the mother of the preceding buddha Dīpaṁkara.[8] Additional examples of such transtemporal shared dreams are contained in the *Lotus Sūtra* and the *Ārya Svapna Nirdeśa Sūtra,*[9] which describe the dreams had by all bodhisattvas. According to the *Lotus Sūtra* a bodhisattva begins these dreams as follows:

> In his sleep he sees visions in the shape of Buddha; he sees monks and nuns appearing on thrones and proclaiming the many-sided law.
>
> He sees in his dream gods and goblins, (numerous) as the sands of the Ganges, as well as demons and Nāgas of many kinds, who lift their joined hands and to whom he expounds the eminent law.
>
> He sees in his dream the Tathāgata preaching the law to many kotis of being with lovely voice, the Lord with golden colour.
>
> And he stands there with joined hands glorifying the Seer, the highest of men, whilst the Gina, the great physician, is expounding the law to the four classes.
>
> And he, glad to have heard the law, joyfully pays his worship, and after having soon reached the knowledge which never slides back, he obtains, in dreams, magical spells.[10]

The bodhisattva then receives a prophecy that she or he will achieve buddhahood, after which the following dreams occur:

> And after seeing in his dream the gold-coloured one [the Buddha], him who displays a hundred hallowed signs, he hears the law, whereafter he preaches it in the assembly. Such is his dream.
>
> And in his dream he also forsakes his whole realm, harem, and numerous kinfolk; renouncing all pleasures he leaves home (to become an ascetic), and betakes himself to the place of the terrace of enlightenment."[11]

Shared dreams of this type serve to dramatize the essential sameness of all Buddhist heroes and to highlight their notion of the self as transtemporal. They dream communal dreams, dreams that transcend individuality as well as time.

Some intriguing evidence of transtemporal shared dreams survives from other ancient Indian sramanic groups. For instance, the *Sāmañña-phala Sutta* of the ancient Ājīvikas lists "seven and seven hundred dreams" that Basham suggests are "dreams of great psychic significance, supposed to occur just before the final emancipation of the soul."[12] And one of the major texts of the Jain canon, the *Bhagavatī Sūtra,* lists the dreams that Mahāvīra (the Jain founder) had before his final enlightenment. He saw the following ten things:

> (1) One big frightful and spirited Tāla-Piśāca (devil) defeated in dream, (2) One big white-feathered male cuckoo, (3) One big variously coloured-feathered male cuckoo, (4) One large pair of garlands endowed with all jewels, (5) One big udder of a white cow, (6) lotus-lake furnished with flowers from all sides and on all sides, (7) One large sea murmuring with [a] thousand ripples of waves crossed by swimming with arms, (8) One big sun shining with rays, (9) One great Manusottara mountain covered with and surrounded by its own green and blue rays of colour, (10) One soul seated on a best throne on the peak of one great Mandara-mountain (Sumeru).[13]

This text also offers a detailed interpretation of these dreams. For example, the first dream indicated that obstructing karma "is uprooted by Śramaṇa Lord Mahāvīra."[14] And the eighth dream "indicated the attainment of the infinite highest, coverless, pure, unobstructed complete omniscience (Kevalajñāna) and self-awareness or intuition (Darśana) by the Master."[15] These are prophetic dreams in that they predict the spiritual attainments of the dreamer. In fact, the *Bhagavatī Sūtra* offers several examples of dreams that are indications of liberation:

> If a man or a woman beholds a big row of horses or a flock of elephants or a herd of oxen in a dream and thinks himself or herself mounted by mounting them or he or she beholds one long rope stretching eastward and westward touching both the seas, contracts himself or herself by contracting (it), thinks himself or herself contracted, or he or she beholds one long rope stretching to the east and west and touching both the borders of the Universe, cuts it and thinks himself

> or herself cut thus, then he or she will attain liberation and put an end to all miseries just at the present moment.[16]

The *Bhagavatī Sūtra* actually begins its discussion of dreams by expressing the belief that the mothers of Jain heroes have particular dreams when they conceive.[17] Queen Triśalā, the mother of Mahāvīra (c. 549–477 B.C.E.), the founder of Jainism, had such a dream. Before looking at her dream, though, it is helpful to know that the two sects of Jainism, the Digambaras ("sky-clad") and the Śvetāmbaras ("white-clad"), differ on at least one important point regarding Mahāvīra's biography: In the Śvetāmbara scriptures the god Indra transplants Mahāvīra, while an embryo, from the womb of a Brahman woman to that of Queen Triśalā, a *kṣatriya.*[18] *Yet both women then have exactly the same dream* when they, so to speak, conceive Mahāvīra.[19] In fact, Queen Triśalā's dream and its interpretation take up approximately one-third of Mahāvīra's biography, and quite a bit of space is also devoted to the Brahman woman's dream and its interpretation.[20] The Digambaras, on the other hand, do not accept the transplanting of Mahāvīra, but they do accept Triśalā's dream as foretelling Mahāvīra's conception. Both sects frequently describe these dreams in their literature, and they are repeated daily by devout laymen and laywomen at their morning devotions.[21] Their images are reproduced in manuscripts and in temples.[22]

According to the *Kalpa Sūtra* (composed sometime before the first century B.C.E.), on the night that Mahāvīra entered Queen Triśalā's womb she had fourteen sequential dreams[23] in which she saw fourteen different things: a white elephant, a white bull, a lion, the goddess Śrī, a garland, the moon, the sun, a large flag, a vase, a lake, the milk ocean, a celestial abode, a heap of jewels, and a fire.[24] When Queen Triśalā tells her dreams to her husband and asks him to interpret it, he says it means they will have a son who will be a great king. The next day, however, the king sends for the official dream interpreters, who make several interesting points. First, they say the dreams mean the child will either be a universal emperor or a *jina* (a Jain hero).[25] Second, the interpreters cite dream books which explain that there are thirty great dreams: The mothers of jinas or of universal monarchs have fourteen of these dreams, the mothers of lesser, though still important beings, have fewer of these dreams, the mothers of *vasudevas* (the helpers of the monarchs and, one assumes, of the jinas) have seven dreams, the mothers of *baladevas* (the half-brothers and helpers of the helpers) have four dreams, and the mothers of *mandalikas* have only one dream.[26] These dreams are a set formula that repeats whenever exemplars are born.

A Jain example of a shared dream occurring on the same night comes from Hemacandra's *Triṣaṣṭiśalāpuruṣacarita* and involves the arrival of a great teacher:

> In this city [Hastināpura] Prince Śreyānsa, heir to King Somaprabha, saw in a dream: [Mount] Meru, entirely dark, was made extremely brilliant by sprinkling it with pitchers of water. The merchant Subuddhi saw a thousand-rays fallen from the sun; replaced in it by Śreyānsa, then the sun too was very bright. King Somaprabha saw one man completely surrounded by many enemies gain the victory with the assistance of Śreyānsa.
>
> These three told each other their dreams in the assembly and, not knowing their interpretation, went back to their own houses. Just then, as if to make apparent the meaning of the dreams, the Master entered the town of Hastināpura for alms.[27]

Tibetan Buddhist biographies also contain examples of shared dreams that are used to announce similar important religious events. One group of such dreams center on Padmasambhava's departure from home. First, the king, like the Buddha's father, has a dream: "Now Indrabhūti had a dream of bad omens. He dreamed that the sun and moon set at the same time, and he dreamed that they would weep in the palace."[28] Then Padmasambhava's wife, Bhāsadharā, like the Buddha's wife, has the following dream: that the mountains and earth shook, a great dead tree was uprooted, heaven and earth spun around, her hair was cut, and a tooth pulled out."[29] As the Buddha's wife did, Bhāsadharā also asks Padmasambhava to interpret the dream for her. But he dismisses it: "Bhāsadharā, you have a happy mind, not an evil one, so sleep silently with good dream omens."[30]

These dreams, along with other motifs from the life of the Buddha, are incorporated into Padmasambhava's biography in order to establish him as a second Buddha, one of his most frequent titles. While Padmasambhava's biography is a unique literary work, it takes its model from the life of the Buddha and has duplicated some of the external, public events from the Buddha's life such as abandoning wealth, position, and family in order to pursue the spiritual life. It also duplicates some of the internal, private events, such as these shared dreams and the conception dreams of King Indrabhūti, in order to establish an even more profound connection between the Buddha and Padmasambhava.

Other shared dreams in Padmasambhava's biography also have to do with departures, such as when a great spiritual master leaves for another country. For instance, after Padmasambhava has stayed in Nepal for three months, he continues his journey to Tibet. Then, "the pandits of India and Nepal had dreams with bad omens: that the sun and moon rose together in Tibet, that all the Dharma went to Tibet, and that the barbarian region was filled with temples."[31]

The next dream in this group concerns a translator *(lotsawa)*. These men are greatly revered in the Tibetan tradition for the many sacred books they translated from Sanskrit into Tibetan. When one of these, Vairotsana, departs for Tibet the king, his ministers, and the pandits all have "dreams of ill omen."[32] One dreams that two bodhisattvas, who have yakṣa heads and are free of faults, are carrying the sun away with them.[33] The dreams of others have a vivid imagery of loss: the gems of Mañjuśrī are carried away; the eye from the Mother Substance is torn out and carried away; the heart from Śrī Siṃha is torn out and carried away; and the Tree of the Awakening (the Bodhi tree under which the Buddha achieved enlightenment) is being carried away to Tibet.[34]

A final shared dream in this text concerns the Indian pandit Vimalamitra who accepts an invitation to go to Tibet:

> Everyone's dreams were agitated, the ḍākinīs shed tears, and there was an error in the king's clock. In the morning the king had everyone compare their dreams, and they all agreed that they were unusual signs. Then a woman possessed by gods asked, "Has the king's dharma teacher gone to Tibet?" The king replied, "Yes, the scholar Vimalamitra has left for Tibet."[35]

The shared dreams in Padmasambhava's biography are similar to the dreams of the Buddha's wife, aunt, and father that occur on the night the Buddha departs from home, and they reflect the psychic as well as the tangible loss caused by the departure of such spiritual masters.[36] In continuing this motif of a shared dream Padmasambhava's biographer is suggesting not only that shared dreams occur and that they have a great Buddhist hero as their subject but that the departure of Padmasambhava and these two gurus—who are living embodiments of the Buddha, who manifest his teachings, and whose inner lives (dreams) and external lives (actions) reflect the Buddha's—is an equal loss.

The biographical literature of Milarepa and his disciples also contain several incidents of shared dreams. In the *Mi la'i mgur 'bum* (hereafter the *Mgur 'bum*), popularly known as the *Hundred Thousand Songs of Milarepa,* before Milarepa and his disciple Gampopa (sGam po pa, 1079–1153) actually meet and even though they are far apart, each dreams of the other. While these dreams do not occur simultaneously, they are shared dreams in that they are represented as taking place in close proximity, perhaps within thirty-six hours of each other, and are related by their content. The dream sequence begins when Milarepa's disciples ask who will continue his teachings after he is dead. Milarepa answers that he knows someone and that he will find out more about him by studying the dream he will have that night. The next morning Milarepa, based on his dream, describes a monk he calls "the Physician" (this is Gampopa, who, like his father before him, was a doctor), saying he will soon join them and have the ability to spread Milarepa's spiritual instruction in the ten directions. Milarepa says: "Last night I dreamed of his coming with an empty crystal vase, which I filled with nectar from my silver vase."[37] Almost simultaneously, though far away, Gampopa dreams that a green yogi (Milarepa) puts his hand on Gampopa's head and spits.[38]

These two dreams go further than just showing the prophetic value of dreams. First, they demonstrate the ability of a guru and disciple to connect on the level of dream consciousness, on an otherworldly level, even before they actually meet on a waking level. Second, Gampopa's dream shows that teachings can be transmitted through dreams. (When he awoke his meditation was improved because of his dream, and he had a realization of insight.) Third, Milarepa's whole performance vividly demonstrates the importance of dreams: he announces that he will use dreams to observe where this future disciple lives; then, after his dream, he reports Gampopa's whereabouts and successfully predicts his coming. In this incident Milarepa demonstrated the dreams of an accomplished master of Dream Yoga. He displayed his control of dreams by announcing that he will seek information by means of dreams and by stating, afterward, that a dream provided this information.

At the same time this dream cycle evokes another set of shared dreams, the dreams Marpa and his wife had the night before Milarepa went to them for teachings, dreams in which nectar, symbolizing the Buddhist doctrine that confers enlightenment, and vases, symbolizing the aspiring disciple, also formed the content. This lineage especially uses dreams to emphasize the spiritual connections between its members, both those living concurrently, and those from other times.

Though the individual dreamers, the content of the dreams, and their outcomes all vary, in each case the shared dream focuses on the biographical subject.[39] Several meanings can be extracted from this type of dream. The first and most obvious one is that shared dreams both demonstrate the validity of dreams and signify the importance of the individual in the dreams. When the dreams of two or more people have the same meaning, the dreams gain importance; the fact of being shared adds weight to their meaning. Since shared dreams about the same individual are actually quite rare, they mark the uniqueness of that person, and they confer religious authority on him. Finally, the events symbolized in these shared dreams suggest that significant spiritual events are enacted first on the dream level and only later take place in waking life.

7 Dreams as Signs of Spiritual Accomplishment

THE DREAMS OF TIBETAN SAINTS differ from the prophetic dreams of secondary characters (parents, wives, disciples) in two ways: First, saints are portrayed as masters of dreams because they are capable of interpreting their own as well as other people's dreams. Second, in many cases their dreams are a sign of spiritual accomplishment in that they confer spiritual powers and are proofs of charisma. (The dreams of their parents and disciples, in contrast, remain oblique prophecies.) The spiritual accomplishments that are revealed in such dreams can either manifest simultaneously with the dream (the dreamer wakes up with a new ability or understanding) or later in their life. Examples of both types are seen in the Buddha's five dreams: the first and second dreams awaken him; the remaining three are fulfilled later in his life.

Similar notions appear in many cultures, as evidenced by the studies of Lincoln, Eliade, and La Barre, who all found that the first signs of shamanic power often follow dreams.[1] Such power is a fair equivalent for the *siddhi*, the spiritual power, that often initially manifests in Buddhist dreams. The *Āryā-Tārā-Kurukulle-kalpa* offers one example of this: "When the sign appears in the dream, the siddhi arise automatically." The sign is most often that of the tutelary deity *(yi dam)*.[2] Deities of various kinds have always been part of the basic structure of the Buddhist cosmos, and they are present in Buddhist dream material beginning with Brahmā interpreting the dreams of the Buddha's family in the *Mahāvastu*.[3] Particularly active in tantric dreams are *ḍākinīs*, the ubiquitous female deities of Tantric Buddhism, as is attested by their frequent appearances in Milarepa's dreams and by Nāropa's allusion to "the place of dreams, the mysterious home of the dakinis."[4] Geshe Kelsang Gyatso quotes the *Vajradaka Tantra* while discussing their tendency toward nocturnal appearances:

> The Ladies [dakinis] of these Places
> Bestow siddhis upon practitioners.
> They always come at night,
> They always go at night.[5]

Dream appearances of the Buddha and other well-known saints from the past are also well attested to in Buddhist biographies, especially those of advanced practitioners. The Venerable Deshung Rinpoche describes the dreams of a successful tantric meditator as follows: "Your mind is so purified that the Buddha appears in dreams and teaches you, you have auspicious dreams of turtles and the like, you dream that you see the sun and the moon, that you take a bath, that you color white cloths, and so forth."[6]

In Tibetan biographies the dreams of an aspirant mark the stages of her or his development from disciple to saint , and in some cases adepts achieve the power to enter the dream life of others. Significantly, dreaming is not necessarily separate from waking spiritual practice but can actually provide an additional dimension in which teaching and the conferring of siddhi occurs. As we shall see, this is especially so in the case of Milarepa and several of his disciples, mainly Rechungpa and Gampopa, though I also refer to examples from biographies associated with other orders of Tibetan Buddhism in order to avoid the idea that this only occurs in Kagyu biographies.

THE BUDDHA

In the *Lalitavistara* the Buddha explains to his wife that all the buddhas of the past, present, and future repeat the same pattern: when it is time for them to leave home they have the same dreams.[7] These dreams are signs of spiritual accomplishment because they awaken a buddha's spiritual awareness. They are the dreams one *should* have when such awareness comes to fruition, and their content symbolizes the dreamer's conquest of the world and all its creatures. These points are elaborated upon most clearly in the *Aṅguttara-Nikāya*'s interpretation of the Buddha's five dreams. The text specifies that, in the first dream, having the world as his bed awakens the spiritual consciousness of the Buddha; in the second, the grass growing out of his navel is the awakening of the Eightfold Path, the Middle Way practices that become the foundation of Buddhism; in the third and fourth, the animals refer to his followers; and, in the fifth, walking on dung refers to his unattached attitude.[8] In other words, these dreams reveal the spiritual accomplishments of the Buddha, some of which are activated by his dreams and others of which will be fulfilled in the future.

Here, at the beginnings of Buddhism, in the life of the Buddha, there is an emphasis on dreaming that is, in large part, attributable to the milieu of the time, which was receptive to dream revelations. While later texts do not specifically refer back to these dreams of the Buddha as a template for dreaming, the presence of meaningful dreams in the later texts does suggest an enduring tradition of dream revelation from the time of the Buddha up to the present. The later efflorescence of dreaming in Mahāyāna and Tantric Buddhism has already been examined in chapter 4. A second, equally important factor is the sudden proliferation in Tibet of sacred biographies marking the stages of spiritual development that lead to enlightenment. In these texts the active involvement of dreams comes to the fore. Clearly, from the earliest days of Buddhism dreams were part of the study of consciousness, which is the key to enlightenment, and dreams received a full, though informal,[9] treatment in the biographies.

MILAREPA AND HIS DISCIPLES

Milarepa's biography records his dreams not just from one night, as in the biographies of the Buddha, but from his entire life. This suggests that by Milarepa's time, at least in the Kagyu lineage, dreams had increased in importance in Buddhist biographical literature and practice. This thesis is further supported by Milarepa's emphasis on the practice of Dream Yoga, to be discussed more fully in the next chapter.

The most notable example of a dream revealing Milarepa's spiritual accomplishment is his four pillars dream. Structurally, this dream is at the center of the biography and marks the beginning of his transition from youth and discipleship to spiritual accomplishment. The context for this dream is the small community of spiritual disciples that have gathered around Marpa, a married landowner who was an irascible, unpredictable, independent, and powerful teacher and translator of Indian Buddhism. Though Marpa had many accomplished students, it was expected that his biological son would succeed him. The untimely death of this son created a spiritual crisis to which Marpa responded by calling upon a teaching he had received from his guru, Nāropa. He does not elaborate on this teaching, he merely says: "I, and the [spiritual] descendants of the Master Nāropa, received the power to prophesy through dreams. Nāropa's prophecy for the Kagyu doctrine was good. Chief disciples, go and wait for your dreams."[10]

Only Milarepa's dream is preserved in the text because it was the only dream to contain a prophecy *(luṅ bstan)*,[11] which Marpa interprets as a prediction for the future of the Kagyu teachings. At the center of the dream is Tibet, symbolized by a snow-covered mountain. Surrounding it, marking the four cardinal directions, are four great pillars, each one with an animal on top (see plate 4).[12] Marpa interprets these animals to symbolize the individual natures of Milarepa and three other advanced disciples as well as providing details about their spiritual accomplishments. For instance, Marpa says that each one had "realized secret instruction [tantric teachings]"[13] and predicts that all four will arrive "in the realm of liberation."[14] However, it is the pillar representing Milarepa that contains the prediction for the propagation of the Kagyu lineage. Milarepa describes it as follows:

> I dreamed that to the North a great pillar was raised.
> At the top of this pillar soared a vulture *[rgod po]*,
> Its pointed wings were spread,
> Its nest perched on a crag.
> This vulture had a fledgling
> And the sky was full of little birds.
> The vulture gazed upward
> And impelled itself through space.[15]

Marpa interprets this to mean:

> The great pillar rising to the North
> Is Milarepa of Gungthang.
> The vulture which hovered over the pillar
> Means that Mila is like unto the vulture.
> Its pointed wings outspread
> Are the realization of the secret instruction.
> Its eyrie in the cliff
> Means that his life will be harder than the rock.
> The fledgling born of this vulture

Means that he will be without rival.
The small birds filling space
Signify the propagation of the Kagyü Doctrine.
Its gaze turned toward the heights
Is a parting from the world of birth and death.
Its flight toward the immensity of space
Is the arrival in the realm of liberation.
The dream of the North is not ill-fated. It is favorable,
O monks and disciples assembled in this place.[16]

Marpa's lengthy and detailed interpretation of this dream is a demonstration of its importance not only to Milarepa, but to Marpa's whole spiritual lineage, the Kagyu order.

This dream and its interpretation by Marpa is also referred to in the short biography of Gampopa, Milarepa's famous disciple, contained in *Mi la'i mgur 'bum* (the so-called *Hundred Thousand Songs*),[17] which adds that the four pillars dream also foretold the appearance of Gampopa.[18] This reminder of Milarepa's dream at the beginning of Gampopa's biography serves to acknowledge and affirm the importance of dreams in the transmission of teachings and consequently in the continuation of the lineage. Indeed the circumstances surrounding that dream continue to be echoed in the rest of Gampopa's story. Of course, placing a dream, or at least a reference to a dream, at the opening of a biography evokes the opening dream of Milarepa's biography and, indeed, the conception dreams in most Buddhist biographies.

Gampopa's short biography is filled with significant dreams. Near its end Milarepa has a dream containing a prophecy about the future of his teachings. He tells the dream and his interpretation of it to his disciples in the following words:

> Last night I dreamed that a vulture *[bya rgod po]* flew from here to Weu and descended on the top of a great mountain where many geese gathered around it. After a short while, they dispersed in different directions, each goose gathering five hundred more companions, filling the valleys with geese. This dream means that although I am a yogi, many [of my] followers will be monks. I rejoice that I have done my duty to the Buddha's teachings.[19]

This dream echoes both Milarepa's dream of the four pillars through the continuing symbolic repetition of Milarepa as a vulture—in a Tibetan context meaning a wild, strong bird—and Marpa's interpretation of it: the continuation of his spiritual lineage. Here, the prophecy contained in Milarepa's four pillars dream is fulfilled, in part, by Gampopa's eventual success as a spiritual teacher, for it is Gampopa who promulgated the Kagyu order through his main disciples, who developed its various schools.[20]

The way Milarepa's four pillars dream and its fulfillment echo through Kagyu biographies—it is also contained in Marpa's biography[21]—accomplishes several things. First, it assures the preservation of the dream, its interpretation, and its fulfillment. Second, it demonstrates the spiritual advancement of the dreamers (Milarepa and Gampopa) and the accuracy of its interpreters (Marpa and Milarepa). Third, it allows the reader/hearer to recognize the dream's fulfillment in the success of the Kagyu lineage. It also affirms dreaming as an acceptable means of spiritual transmission.

Several other dreams in Gampopa's biography reveal achievements of spiritual accomplishment, a point emphasized by Milarepa's interpretation of them. First, there is Gampopa's dream that anticipates his meeting with Milarepa, which is preceded by a statement to the effect that dreams reveal signs of spiritual accomplishment: "in his dream Gampopa had the premonitions *[snga-ltas]* which precede achieving the tenth stage"[22] of a bodhisattva. In fact, though, Gampopa's dream actually transforms his spiritual consciousness. The entire text of the dream and its result is as follows. Gampopa saw "a greenish yogi [Milarepa is often depicted as having green skin due to only having eaten nettles at one point in his life] with a large body wearing cotton rags and carrying a cane stick. The yogi put a hand upon his head and spit. This improved Gampopa's concentration *[zhi gnas kyi ting 'dzin]*, and he had the realization of insight *[lhag mthong]*."[23] In other words, the signs of an improved meditation first appeared on the dream level and then manifested on the waking level.

Later in the text Gampopa has another dream that Milarepa interprets in great detail, each aspect of which reveals Gampopa's spiritual accomplishments,[24] and which causes Milarepa to give a detailed teaching regarding the meaning of dreams. The first few verses of Gampopa's dream are as follows.

> I dreamt I wore a hat with silken brim
> Beautified by fur along its edge;
> Above it was the image of an eagle.

I dreamt I wore a pair of greenish boots
Well cut, embossed with brass
And fastened by silver buckles.

I dreamt I wore a white silk robe,
Red-spotted and adorned
With pearls and golden threads.[25]

Milarepa answers Gampopa's request that he interpret this dream by first making the point that most dreams are meaningless, but he then continues with a detailed interpretation that is twice as long as the dream:

Dreams are unreal and deceptive, as was taught
By Buddha Himself, in the Final Truth of Pāramitā.[26]
To collect, supply, and study them
Will bring little profit.
So the Buddha used dream as one of the Eight Parables[27]
To show the illusory nature of all beings.
Surely you remember these injunctions?
And yet, your dreams were marvelous—
Wondrous omens foretelling things to come.
I, the Yogi, have mastered the art of dreams,
And will explain their magic to you.

The white hat on your head indicates
That your view will go beyond the "high" and "low."
The fair trimming on the brim is a sign
That you will demonstrate the Dharma
Essence, subtle yet profound.
The lovely colors of the fur imply
That you will explain the various teachings
Of the Schools without mixing them.
The flying eagle [vulture] on the top means that you
Will gain Mahāmudrā, the foremost view—
And will see the Essence of the Unborn.

The Mongol boots that you dreamt of wearing
Portray your climbing from the lower to the higher Vehicles.
Their green color and adorning bosses

Meant that you will attain Buddha's Four Bodies.
The "pair" shows increase of the Two Provisions.
The silver ring-strap on the boots
Is the absence of wrong practices;
Also it foretells that you
Will be like a son of Buddha—
Humble and self-restraining,
The exemplar of all Buddhist acts.

The silk robe you dreamt of wearing
Indicates that you will not be sullied
By any vice. The threads of gold
Symbolize a worthy and stable
Mind. The red spots foretell
Compassion and altruism.[28]

Milarepa's interpretation continues along these lines and leads into a further speech about the place of dreams within the overall scheme of life. He begins with the familiar warning that most dreams are as illusory as existence itself, but then tells Gampopa and two other disciples, Shiwa 'Od and Rechungpa, to remember their dreams that night.[29] This parallels Marpa's instructions to his disciples that led to predictions about their future spiritual accomplishments, as do these dreams of Milarepa's disciples.

In song no. 57/54, "Rechungpa's Departure," Rechungpa has a series of four dreams, each one revealing a spiritual accomplishment, until the last one, which Milarepa interprets as meaning it is time for Rechungpa to go and teach others. In the first of the four dreams Rechungpa is shouting, which Milarepa equates with speaking the doctrine. He dreamed "he loaded wool on a dog and shouted, 'Write the letters!' Together they reached a mountain pass and from one side came eighty-eight people to greet them while from the other came another eighty-eight people to meet them."

When Rechungpa asked what the dream meant, Milarepa sang an interpretation: "The dog means you will have friends, the wool that your mind will be smoother than wool, 'Write the letters' means that you will be skilled in practice, shouting that you will sing from experience, the eighty-eight means that people will greet and welcome you."[30]

Rechungpa's second dream and Milarepa's interpretation of it reads:

> Rechungpa dreamed he threw off his clothes and washed his body with water. He then became a bird that flew away onto a tree. Then he looked into a mirror. [Milarepa's interpretation is]: "Removing your clothes [represents removing] the eight dharmas.[31] Washing with water [represents receiving] the stainless instructions. [Becoming] a bird [represents the attainment of] kindness and compassion. The [bird's] wings [represent] the two accumulations [merit and wisdom]. Descending on the tree [indicates you will sit on] the tree of enlightenment. The mirror represents signs of the ḍākinīs."[32]

Rechungpa's third dream and Milarepa's interpretation of it are as follows: "he rode backward on a donkey, wearing a robe called 'Hope.' [Milarepa's interpretation is]: 'Riding the donkey of Mahāyāna you turn away from Saṃsāra and face Nirvāṇa the source of all hope.'"[33]

In his fourth and final dream Rechungpa saw

> that he put a jewel on the top of his head and wore a spotless robe. Then he looked into a clear mirror. In the right hand he held a dorje, in the left a skull full of food. He sat cross-legged on a lotus seat while light coiled around his back and his body was ablaze with a great fire. In front of him a fountain sprang up and the sun and moon rose in his heart. On his left stood many men and women; on his right was a lamb and a group of kids. That one lamb became many.[34]

This dream depicts Rechungpa as a powerfully centered spiritual master surrounded by his disciples. In his interpretation Milarepa makes explicit connections between the dream images and Rechungpa's spirituality, so much so that it leads Milarepa to send Rechungpa forth to become a teacher himself. It also provides an opportunity for an elaboration of Buddhist dream imagery.

> "The jewel means that you contemplate your Guru upon your head; the pure white robe means the Kagyu; looking into the mirror means the introduction of the oral teachings; holding the dorje in the right hand means you will destroy thought constructions; [the skull in your] left hand means you will experience emptiness and bliss; the lotus seat means you will not be soiled with the faults of defilements; sitting cross-legged means you will abide in samādhi: the luminous aura coiling around your back means that you will achieve Bodhi (true perception).

> The fountain springing forth means that you will experience portents; the blaze like fire in your body means you will have gtu mo (mystic heat); the sun and moon means you will abide in the state of realization; the men and women standing on your left means that heroes and heroines will invite you; the kids and lamb on your right means you will raise up your disciples; the increasing of the lambs means the spreading of the oral teachings.
>
> "Accordingly, it is now suitable that you no longer stay with me. The time has come for you to have your own disciples and to benefit others on a grand scale."[35]

Milarepa also had dreams that revealed his spiritual accomplishments before he left his guru, and this tradition continues with Rechungpa and, as we shall see below, with Gampopa as well. In all three instances dreams revealed the spiritual accomplishments to both the master and the disciple and thus transformed the lives of the dreamers: they ceased being disciples and became masters.

Returning to Milarepa's biography, his dream experiences continued after he left Marpa, and they continued to reveal his further spiritual accomplishments. Once, when he was in a spiritual quandary, he dreamed that he "was plowing his field. Since the earth was so hard I wondered whether I should give it up. Then Marpa appeared in the sky and said, 'My son, strengthen your will, have courage, and work; you will furrow the hard and dry earth.' Thus, Marpa guided me and I plowed my field. Immediately a thick and abundant harvest sprang up."[36]

When Milarepa woke up he thought to himself: "dreams are insubstantial and mistaken, not even fools grasp at them,"[37] but as usual, he contradicted his disparaging remarks. First, he interpreted this dream to mean he should persevere in his meditation.[38] Second, he composed a song about this dream and his interpretation of it. The first few lines of this song illustrate the way Milarepa develops the agricultural imagery of his dream into spiritual metaphors.

> I cultivate the field of fundamentally non-discriminatory mind
> With the manure and water of faith,
> And sow the seed of a pure heart.
> The powerful thunder of my invocations reverberates,
> And the rain of your blessings falls effortlessly.

Upon the oxen of a mind free from doubt
I put the yoke and plow of skillful means and wisdom.
Steadfastly I hold the reins without distraction.
Cracking the whip of effort, I break up the clods of the five poisons.
I cast away the stones of a defiled heart,
And weed out all hypocrisy.
I cut the stalks and reap the fruit of action
Leading to liberation.[39]

It is worth noting that in this dream it is now Milarepa who is plowing a field, a reference to the first time he saw Marpa. Marpa knew that Milarepa was coming to see him because both he and his wife had premonitory dreams. By choosing to plow his field and be thus engaged when Milarepa first sees him, Marpa establishes a powerful and an enduring visual impact. As Milarepa's song shows, plowing is an apt metaphor for the hard work that leads to spiritual accomplishment,[40] and it suggests transformation (of seed to crop). But this dream also plays with transference; not only has Milarepa internalized Marpa—which is exactly what a disciple should do—he has become Marpa: the disciple has become the guru.

The *Mgur 'bum* records two additional dreams of Milarepa in which ḍākinīs give him information about his spiritual life. In song 19 he dreams of "a beautiful woman adorned with jewels and bone ornaments. She says to him: 'Yogi Milarepa, follow the instructions of your guru and go to Mt. Kailasa and meditate. On the road you will meet a karmically connected person, be kind to him.'"[41] When he awakes he thinks to himself: "This prophecy is sent by the tutelary deity and the ḍākinī through the grace of the guru to induce me to renew my efforts. I will go there."[42] And indeed, Milarepa meets Dampa Gyagpu, who becomes his disciple. In song 17, Milarepa dreams about another ḍākinī who offers veiled predictions about future disciples. He dreams that "a bluish woman with golden hair and eyebrows was leading a youth of about twenty years old. She said, 'Milarepa, you will have eight pieces from your heart. This is one of them, therefore teach him.'"[43] Reflecting on this dream Milarepa thinks: "the woman seems to have been a ḍākinī and I will have eight successful disciples, each like my own heart. Today, I shall meet a karmically awakened man."[44] Once again Milarepa accepts the authority of his dream and the next day he meets his future disciple, Shiwa 'Od. These two dreams demonstrate Milarepa's spiritual accomplishment by showing his ability to interpret accurately his own dreams and by revealing his connection to the realm of the ḍākinīs.

The foregoing examples can be multiplied by a quick perusal of other important Tibetan biographical texts. For instance, Tsongkhapa (1357–1419), the founder of the Gelug order, had many dreams that revealed signs of his spiritual accomplishment. One of the most explicit and well known refers to his enlightenment through a dream. Thurman's comments on this dream provide a temporal and spatial frame for it and reveal its impact on Tsongkhapa: "In an autumn predawn stillness in the year 1398, Tsoṅ-kha-pa achieved perfect enlightenment at O-de-gun-rgyal in Ol-kha. He awoke, joyous and invigorated, from a prophetic dream in which he had received blessings from the great Indian masters Nāgārjuna and Buddhapālita."[45] The point is that Tsongkhapa's meditative practices transformed his dreams until he achieved a continuous, unbroken, and enlightened stream of consciousness throughout his waking and sleeping life.

A second of Tsongkhapa's dreams preserved by Jamyang Choje also portends his spiritual accomplishments:

> While contemplating the principal mandala
> Of Manjushrivajra, Guhyasamaja,
> You dreamed that Maitreya and Manjushri,
> Who were speaking of Dharma, passed down to you
> A jewelled vase brimming with water,
> Portending that you would master all teachings.[46]

Tsongkhapa was able to receive teachings and blessings in his dreams, and both he and others accepted such dreams as signs of what he had accomplished spiritually.

Tsongkhapa also had three dreams that anticipated his meetings with earthly teachers. Each dream revealed particular details about the teachers, details that Tsongkhapa confirmed when he met them.[47] This is similar to Gampopa's dream before meeting Milarepa, and they are also a variation on gurus' dreams of future students. For example, Marpa dreams of Milarepa,[48] and Milarepa dreams of Gampopa,[49] Dampa Gyagpu,[50] and Shiwa 'Od.[51] These reversals, in which Tsongkhapa dreams of gurus, rather than gurus dreaming of disciples, is one indication of the mutuality Tsongkhapa was able to establish with his various teachers: he both taught them and was taught by them. The first of these dreams is about the Lama Chokyi Pel. In his dream, Tsongkhapa asked him how many times he had received Kālachakra teachings from Buton Rinpoche. The Lama's answer was seventeen. Subsequently, when Tsongkhapa met him he was able to substantiate this number.[52]

PLATE I

Medical painting based on the Rgyud bzhi *showing dreams and dream images originating in the heart center of the central figure.*

From a recent set of paintings by Romeo Shrestha and his atelier.
Collection of the Museum of Natural History, New York.
Photograph © by J. Beckett and D. Finnin.

PLATE 2

Lineage of the Kagyu order. Above the central figure of Milarepa are Vajradhara and Marpa, and the Five Sisters protective goddesses are below. To his right: Nāropa above Gampopa. To his left: Tilopa above Rechung.

PLATE 3

From a set of biographical tangkas of Milarepa. To the left of Milarepa's arm is a scene showing details of Rechung's dream in the realm of Aksobhya. The scene above and to the right shows Rechung being urged by a sign to ask Milarepa to relate his life story.

PLATE 4

From a set of biographical tangkas of Milarepa.
Below central figure is shown the four pillar dream.

PLATE 5

Scenes from the life of the historical Buddha. Central Tibet.
In the upper right is the representation of the dream of Queen Māyā.

Private collection. Photograph © by Hughes Dubois.

PLATE 6

Vajrayoginī in the form of Khecarī according to the school of Nāropa.

Museum of Natural History, New York. Photograph © by J. Beckett and D. Finnin.

PLATE 7

Wheel of the transmigratory realms of existence.

Museum of Natural History, New York. Photograph © by Lee Boltin.

PLATE 8

From a set of biographical tangkas of Milarepa. The lower right depicts Gampopa's dream. Above, the dream is related to Milarepa. The upper left shows details of other dreams of disciples.

The second and third dreams are as follows:

> One night...Tsong Khapa dreamt of the Nyingma Lama Kyungpo Lhaypa, seated on a great throne, a crown on his head and bell and dorje in hand, repeating the word "karmavajra," the Sanskrit form of Tsong Khapa's mystic name. Je Rinpoche was overjoyed and determined to go to Zhalu where this lama lived. Another night, he dreamt of the same Lama who had at his heart many circles of mantras. The image was so vivid that Tsong Khapa could read them all individually. Consequently he journeyed to Zhalu to meet this Lama, who proved to be identical to the figure in his dreams.[53]

The crowned lama seated on a throne is an indication of spiritual mastery, while the bell and vajra symbolize the path of Vajrayāna. By noting the accuracy of Tsongkhapa's dreams, the biography demonstrates his advanced spiritual abilities; Tsongkhapa is able to commune on a dream level with teachers—both living and dead—who are or will be important to his spiritual advancement.

The tradition of meeting teachers in and through dreams is not limited to Tibetan Buddhism. Atīśa (982–1054), the Indian teacher who had such a tremendous influence on Tibetan Buddhism, also had several such dreams when he was studying with various Vajrayāna teachers. In one the *paṇḍita* Vagīśvarakīrti gave him many tantras, and in another a ḍākinī gave him several more.[54] On another occasion he dreamed that the goddess and celestial buddha Tārā told him where to find a female ascetic who "could tell him all that he wished to know."[55] So there is some evidence that the tradition of receiving specific teachings through dreams, or being told where to go and who to meet to receive teachings, existed in India as well. In support of this, when Tucci discussed the essential role of the lama in the transmission of doctrine to the disciple, he noted that this transmission can occur through a dream.[56] The contemporary teacher Namkhai Norbu also affirms the validity of the transmission of teachings through dreams; he says that a teacher can enter his or her disciple's dreams, and he offers frequent examples from his own life.[57] Similar dreams occur in the Karmapa lineage as well.[58] When I queried the Venerable Thinley about the wealth of dreams in the biographies of the Karmapas he explained that "the Karmapas are special, they are incarnations (tulkus) and therefore can meet with the ḍākinīs. Their dreams come true, and they have discourse with deities [in their dreams.] This is not the ability of regular people."[59]

Two final biographical examples will suffice. One comes from the biography of Drukpa Kunley (1455–1570), who dreamed that a ḍākinī both instructed him to go to Bhutan to spread Buddhism and also predicted the success of his mission.[60] The second comes from the biography of Buton (1290–1364, one of the great codifiers of the Tibetan canon). Shortly before his death, Buton had a dream that predicted his ultimate spiritual success, rebirth in Tuṣita heaven. He described his dream as follows: "Last night I had a very auspicious dream. There were three long ladders stretching from the Tuṣita; on the middle one Maitreya was to be seen while I was ascending on one side. When it was asked who was going on that side, it was established that I was certainly going to the Tuṣita."[61]

This wonderful imagery of ascending to heaven on three ladders is reminiscent of the three ladders in the Buddha's miraculous descent from Trāyastrimśa heaven after preaching to his mother,[62] and it recalls another dream Buton had in which he ascended to Tuṣita heaven and other worlds by becoming lucid in his dream—that is, conscious that he was dreaming—and holding onto a moonbeam.[63]

Just as all the foregoing dreams are a way of helping the dreamers to realize their spiritual accomplishments, their presence in the biographies also reveals these attainments to the reader. Dreams of spiritual accomplishment validate both the dream experience and the charisma of the dreamer.

THE ABILITY TO INTERPRET DREAMS

A second way in which dreams reveal the spiritual accomplishment of saints and thus validate their charisma is through their ability to interpret dreams, both their own and those of others. We have already seen several examples, and this is consistent with the findings of La Barre and others who have listed the interpretation of dreams not only as a function of the shaman but as a sign of his or her power.[64] Ordinary people are not believed capable of accurately interpreting dreams, and the need for an interpreter indicates the dreamer's lack of spiritual awareness. Those who are connected to other realms do not need an interpreter; they understand the spiritual messages in their own dreams and in the dreams of others.

Underlying the belief in the interpretability of dreams is the notion that dreams are a form of cognition, another way of thinking. Of course, dreams are part of the cognitive, linguistic, and symbolic tools of any culture, but not everyone understands their meaning. This is what makes dream interpreters spiritually powerful; they have a larger grasp of reality; they comprehend and function in both the waking realm and the realm of sleeping and dreaming with equal facility. Furthermore, a dream interpreter is able to connect with individuals in a deeply personal way and can give them greater access to their own experience of the divine.

The first dream to be interpreted in the biographical literature of Buddhism is Māyā's conception dream, where the interpreters are Brahman priests. Focusing on these dream specialists enables us to observe an important element in the Buddhist view of dream interpretation. Here traditional Indian (Brahmanical) dream interpretation is represented as both adequate and accurate. As an adult, however, the Buddha turns Brahmanical interpretations upside down when he interprets his wife's and his own dreams in a new, Buddhist light.[65] We have seen other Buddhist texts that explicitly use dream interpretation as an opportunity to denigrate Brahmanical dream interpretation and by extension the whole Brahmanical religious system. For instance, in the *Mahāvastu* the god Brahmā challenged the Brahmanical interpretation of Māyā's dream by stating unequivocally that the child will be a Buddha.[66] Other examples occur in the Pali jātakas. In the *Kuṇāla Jātaka* Brahman dream interpreters are shown accepting bribes to alter their interpretations; in the *Mahāsupina-Jātaka* Brahman interpreters are accused of greed and said to be incapable of true dream interpretations; while in the *Vessantara Jātaka* Brahmans are shown misinterpreting another king's dream.[67] The *Lalitavistara* lists dream interpretation as one of the Buddha's many accomplishments, and in a different context the Buddha reveals his deep understanding of dreams in a story he tells about the reconciliation of two enemies through dreams.[68] Even in one of his past lives—when he himself is, ironically, a Brahman priest—the Buddha is represented as a superior dream interpreter, correctly interpreting the king of Kosala's dreams in the *Mahāsupina-Jātaka*. In this instance the Buddha is even a better dream interpreter within a Brahmanical context. At issue in these examples is not the prophetic nature of dreams, which is accepted, but the ability to correctly interpret them. At the same time, these challenges to Brahmanical authority are also the beginning of a new Buddhist interpretation of dreams.

We can trace Milarepa's development as a dream interpreter through four of his own dreams. We have already looked at most of these dreams, so I will only briefly summarize them here. The first occurs early in the biography and indicates that Milarepa cannot yet interpret dreams. This is the dream in which a ḍākinī appears and tells him to seek teachings on the transference of consciousness to dead bodies,[69] but he needs to ask Marpa what the dream means. The second dream occurs after his four pillars dream, which Milarepa is able to interpret for himself. This dream actually ends his days as a student because he dreams that his mother is dead,[70] a fact he confirms upon returning to his former home. Once there, Milarepa has a third dream, which he does not describe, saying only that it predicts a happy event if he remains where he is for a few days, which he does. This dream is explained when the woman he had been betrothed to in his youth comes to see him.[71] Later Milarepa has an elaborate dream about Marpa, one rich in agricultural images that he interprets with ease.[72] These dreams reveal Milarepa's evolving abilities in dream interpretation in much the same way that all his recorded dreams mark his progress from disciple to master.

Milarepa's biographies particularly reward the study of dreams in their many dimensions. As we have seen, the *Mgur 'bum*, in contrast to the biography, focuses on Milarepa's later life as an accomplished yogi; he always appears as a confident and competent dream interpreter. Further analysis of these texts, though, reveals another dimension in Tibetan dream interpretation—one that is particularly evident in Milarepa's four pillars dream as it relates to establishing charisma both for the dreamer and the interpreter. Upon scrutiny the dream's seemingly unmediated voicing of divine or cosmic will is shown to have been carefully orchestrated by Marpa. As mentioned above, the stimulus for this dream was the presumption that Marpa's son would continue his lineage—he would become a highly valued guru who receives expensive gifts in exchange for esoteric teachings. Then the son dies quite suddenly. When Marpa's chief disciples ask who will succeed him, Marpa briefly instructs them in the practice of obtaining sought dreams by telling them to observe their dreams that night. The next morning all the disciples gather together to tell their dreams to Marpa. One can imagine the tension, the anticipation, produced by such a public means of divination, but the outcome is actually completely in the hands of Marpa, who not only decides whose dreams are significant but then interprets the dreams exactly as he chooses. Only Milarepa's dream and its interpretation are preserved—Milarepa is the winner in this dream contest—and he is shown to be such a powerful dreamer that his dream accurately predicts the spiritual accomplishments of his fellow disciples. By affirming the validity of his dream, Marpa both names him as heir and confers the charisma necessary for continuing his lineage. At the same time the entire scene, from Marpa's initial instructions telling his disciples to observe their dreams to their interpretation, enhances Marpa's own charisma. Through this incident Marpa not only displays his charisma but has it confirmed by the obedience of his disciples, by his ability to distinguish meaningful from meaningless dreams and his ability to interpret them, and by Milarepa's having a prophetic dream. Marpa is then in the perfect position to confer some of his charisma on Milarepa.

Other studies of the cultural limitations placed on dreaming are relevant to this discussion. Studies by Jackson Lincoln, E. R. Dodds, A. D. Nock, and others point out that despite the sometimes profound feeling of otherness experienced in dreams, they occur within a cultural milieu that shapes their content. Furthermore, in narrating often incoherent dream imagery the dreamer attempts to make it coherent and relevant to her or his experience, as does the interpreter: there is a constant sifting and sorting of dream imagery on the part of the dreamer and the interpreter.

Although there are various kinds of dream lists and dream manuals,[73] there is no consistent system of dream interpretation in Tibetan dream material. Dream lists are inconsistent and do not seem to have any relationship to the dream interpretations contained in the biographies. Disciples relate to their gurus dreams they consider significant or disturbing and seek their interpretation. They do not necessarily consult dreams lists or dream manuals. But the scene between Milarepa and Marpa is important for its detailed exchanges between a guru and his disciple regarding the dynamics of dream interpretation. The point is that disciples cede control of their consciousness to the guru. Through the process of training disciples, the guru breaks down all their preexisting ideas in order to present them with an alternate understanding of reality that will lead to their spiritual enlightenment. The guru thereby directs spontaneous dream experiences into prescribed channels. Though dreams can be an opening for religious innovation, we need to pay careful attention to the years of teachings that condition the disciple's consciousness and to the controlling factor of the guru's interpretation. How much of this interpreting is done consciously by the guru and how much unconsciously will have to remain speculative.

In this regard it is of interest to observe Milarepa's use of dreams in relation to his disciples. Apropos, in the short *Mgur 'bum* biography of Gampopa (song no. 41/38), Milarepa's disciples ask him who will continue the lineage after he dies. He answers them by saying he will seek an answer in his dreams,[74] which prompts his dream of Gampopa. This is an interesting inversion of his own experience with Marpa, where the guru tells the disciples to dream. In Milarepa's case his control of dream prophecy regarding his lineage is complete: he himself has the dream, shapes its narration, and interprets it. Later, perhaps when he believes his disciples are more advanced, he instructs three of them—Gampopa, Shiwa 'Od, and Rechungpa—to seek dreams in order to know what their own future spiritual accomplishment will be.[75] A review of their dreams and Milarepa's interpretations reveals how free-wheeling dream interpretation can be.

Gampopa is upset because he thinks he had a very evil dream *(rmi lam shin tu ngan):* "I killed many beings of different races and stifled their breath."[76] This dream flies in the face of the Buddhist emphasis on non-injury, yet Milarepa gives it a very positive interpretation: "Son, you are not deprived of your hope. Many sentient beings will ask for their deliverance from you, and you will be their hope."[77] Shiwa 'Od dreams that "from the East a warm sun was absorbed into the center of my heart."[78] In his interpretation Milarepa says that it "was a middling dream. Your commitment was small so you will not be able to benefit many living creatures, but you will be able to go to the Pure Land."[79] Despite the exalted meaning of the sun in other Tibetan biographical dreams, such as the conception dreams surrounding the births of Mandāravā, King Thrisong, and Padmasambhava (where it indicates he is a second Buddha),[80] and Shiwa 'Od's own impression that it is a good dream, Milarepa all but dismisses it.[81] Rechungpa dreams "I arrived at three big valleys and shouted in a loud voice."[82] This dream is similar to a later dream Rechungpa has, discussed above. Actually it is the first in a series of four dreams that culminate in Rechungpa going forth to teach others.[83] In his interpretation Milarepa continues to equate shouting with speaking the doctrine: "Rechungpa, because you are stubborn and disobeyed my word three times you will be born three times as a famous scholar in three different valleys."[84] Rechungpa is one of Milarepa's best-known disciples, but one particular area of disagreement between them was Rechungpa's love of scholarship, an activity that Milarepa valued less than practice.[85] Taking all three dreams at face value, it seems obvious that Milarepa's interpretations favor Gampopa. Of course, this could also be a literary device to retroactively explain Gampopa's inheritance of many of Milarepa's teaching lineages, for shortly after this dream he is said to have left Milarepa and begun to gather his own disciples. Nevertheless, these interpretations remain amazingly discordant.

Significantly, Milarepa, through his personal charisma, his tremendous spiritual authority as the guru, and his insightful understanding of his disciples, controls the interpretation and thus controls their spiritual futures. So although these dreams that reveal future lineage holders and the spiritual accomplishments of disciples point to the innovative potential of dreams, in fact they can also be read as carefully orchestrated events with prescribed outcomes.

From the time of the earliest biographies, those of the Buddha, dream interpretation has been shown to be contested ground. I will return to the issue of dream interpretation in chapters 9 and 10. For now, we have seen that successful interpretations of dreams are not isolated events within individual biographies; they are central to the main purpose of the text, namely, to demonstrate spiritual accomplishments and confer charisma.

PART THREE

Innovations in Dream Material

FIGURE 5

Viṣṇu dreaming the universe into existence. Cambodian.

Samuel Eilenberg Collection, Metropolitan Museum of Art.

8 Dream Yoga

THUS FAR the discussion has focused on continuities in dream material from the time of the Buddha to that of Milarepa, but in this section the focus shifts to innovations found in the biographical dream material of Milarepa and his disciples. Several factors contributed to these innovations. First, many more dreams are recorded for Milarepa than for the Buddha, thus providing more dreams for analysis. Second, all the dreams in the biographies of the Buddha are spontaneous, while in Milarepa's biographies some dreams are sought or induced. Third, and of relevance to sought dreams, there are frequent references to the practice of Dream Yoga. Finally, there is a virtual explosion of positive female dream imagery. The first three of these factors offer evidence that dreaming was increasingly incorporated into spiritual practice (further evidence for this will be presented in chapter 9). Although Milarepa's biographies are the focus of this final section, relevant materials from nonbiographical sources are introduced to provide a context for these dream innovations.

DREAMS AND RELIGIOUS INNOVATION

Dreaming as a source of religious innovation has a long history in world religion. The anthropologist Edward Tylor was one of the first modern scholars to argue for dreams being the source of many religious beliefs including the concept of the soul.[1] A later, important anthropological study of the innovative function of dreams in religion was that of Jackson Steward Lincoln. Writing in 1935 primarily about Native American dreams, Lincoln offers examples of specific cultural items that have originated in dreams: religious ceremonies, songs, crafts, cures, tribal totems, guardian spirits, secret societies, and so on.[2] Obviously, many things can be attributed to dreams, but Lincoln is careful to delineate what he means by this idea: "'Originating in dreams' does not mean that the dream is the ultimate origin of a culture item, but, that it is merely the continuation of previous mental and cultural experiences which are given form in dream. The dream is regarded as an intermediate stage between the initial mental process and the cultural result, where such result is indicated."[3]

Lincoln is saying that dreams are one way of thinking and consequently one way of organizing knowledge. This notion survives in Western and other cultures through the expression "to sleep on an idea" and its attendant implication that sleep and dreams are necessary aids to thinking and understanding, a point also brought out by Freud.[4]

Eliade, too, emphasizes the cognitive function of dreams in his discussion of how shamans learns their craft.

> The shaman's instruction often takes place in dreams. It is in dreams that the pure sacred life is entered and direct relations with the gods, spirits, and ancestral souls are re-established. It is always in dreams that historical time is abolished and the mythical time regained—which allows the future shaman to witness the beginning of the world and hence to become contemporary not only with the cosmogony but also with the primordial mythical revelations. Sometimes initiatory dreams are involuntary and begin even in childhood, as, for example, among the Great Basin tribes. Even if they do not follow a strict scenario, the dreams are nevertheless stereotyped; the candidate dreams of spirits and ancestors, or hears their voices (songs and teaching). It is always in dream that the candidate receives the initiatory regulations (regime, taboos, etc.) and learns what objects he will need in shamanic cures.[5]

Examples of such initiations and instruction through dream are also found among Tibetan shamans.[6]

Through dream experiences shamans are thought to gain power over the dream world—they understand that world in ways not available to others—consequently they are able to mediate between the dream and the waking worlds. One expression of this idea is found in the frequency with which shamans are called upon to act as dream interpreters.[7] As will become clear in my discussion of Dream Yoga, some of the innovations in Tibetan dream practices came about through the mingling of pre-Buddhist indigenous shamanic practices and beliefs about dreams with the Buddhist goal of enlightenment.

Of course, dreams can be conservative as well as innovative, a point brought out by Lincoln's formulation that people dream within a pattern established by their culture.[8] For instance, Hindus who have not been exposed to Christianity will not dream of the Christian idea of heaven; they will dream within the Hindu cultural pattern. E. R. Dodds, in his study of the ancient Greeks, develops this idea: "In many primitive societies there are types of dream-structure which depend on a socially transmitted pattern of belief, and cease to occur when that belief ceases to be entertained. Not only the choice of this or that symbol, but the nature of the dream itself, seems to conform to a rigid traditional pattern."[9] As we will see, especially in Tibetan dream ritual texts, dreamers receive highly detailed instructions on exactly what they should see. In other words, dreaming is incorporated into institutional attempts to model practice.

Despite this conservative streak, for almost everyone dreams can interrupt the mundane reality of the waking world by positing an alternative reality that needs, somehow, to be incorporated into waking life.[10] When contact with this alternative reality is sought and achieved through spiritual discipline, as it is in Indo-Tibetan Buddhism and various forms of shamanism, mundane reality can never be the same for the practitioner. Hans Peter Duerr describes the experience of one who has crossed between these realities: "His home will have lost much of its homeliness. But just as a world *taken for granted* is not a world *understood*, he will *now* understand much of his own world for the first time, even if from then on he will at times experience what it is like to tell the blind what 'red' is."[11] Dreams can reveal to an individual insights so powerful that the concerns or realities of waking life are lost in the blinding light of this new awareness. Such a dream shapes their reality, shapes their understanding of the waking world. In the same way, when an individual's dreams—or dreams in general—are granted religious authority, they can have powerful consequences in the public life of a culture. This occurs when the private dream experience is believed to hold significance for others, when the dream becomes a cultural item. Two leading examples are the dream origins of Melanesian cargo cults and the Ghost Dance of Native Americans.[12] The role of dreams in these two movements hinges on the connections between dreams and political/religious authority, about which the anthropologist Michael Brown makes two points. First, "through a special sensitivity to the meaning of dreams, a leader may be able to give voice to unconscious concerns that his followers are unable to articulate. This adeptness ultimately contributes to his ability to mobilize the support of others." In other words, the dream of the leader will become the doctrine of the future. Second, such dreams can become a subversive force.[13]

The mahāsiddhas and isolated yogis such as Milarepa lived on the fringes of society where they pursued highly individualistic spiritual paths that often purposely conflicted with social values. They were at the forefront of religious innovations because they were willing to utilize anything in their search for the most direct and rapid route to enlightenment. In this sense, their religious innovations were not actual breaks with the past as much as insights into what they believed were the primary teachings of Buddhism. Of particular interest here, they accepted the earlier Mahāyāna notion that dreams were a means to access those teachings, and dreams became an important part of their spiritual practice. Indeed, among them dreaming became a formalized practice known as Dream Yoga, to which we now turn.

THE SIX YOGAS

Dream Yoga, a practice promising mastery over dreams,[14] is a term that covers many different practices. On the one hand there are simple traditions, such as someone whispering in your ear while you sleep: "This is only a dream. What you are experiencing is only a dream." This is meant to encourage the dreamer, without awakening, to become lucid in the dream.[15] On the other hand there are philosophically rich and experientially detailed studies of esoteric practices such as Nāropa's Six Yogas *(na' ro'i chos drug)* and the Six Yogas of Niguma.[16] Niguma is usually described as Nāropa's sister, occasionally as his consort. These two elaborate systems are designed to harness human consciousness and direct it toward enlightenment. Milarepa's biographies frequently refer to the Dream Yoga lineage he received from Marpa, who was one of Nāropa's disciples.

It seems fairly certain that the Six Yogas were brought together and systematized by the Indian mahāsiddha Nāropa (1016–1100) from earlier, mostly oral teachings.[17] Though these Six Yogas enjoy a special fame among all the orders of Tibetan Buddhism, they are particularly prominent in the Kagyu and Nyingma orders.[18]

The Six Yogas are:

1. *Tummo (gtum mo)*—Inner Heat
2. *Gyulus (sgyu lus)*—Illusory Body

3. *Milam (rmi lam)*—Dream
4. *Odsal ('od gsal)*—Light
5. *Phowa ('pho ba)*—Transference of Consciousness
6. *Bardo (bar do)*—Intermediate State[19]

Each yoga involves meditation and other disciplines that are designed to achieve various ends. Inner Heat Yoga begins with the transformation of the practitioner's physical and subtle bodies through intense forms of meditation—a useful ability for those practicing in caves during the winter, and a practice in which Milarepa is said to have excelled.[20] Illusory Body, Dream, and Light yogas bring the illusory nature of all existence to the forefront of the practitioner's consciousness, while the Transference of Consciousness Yoga (in which Milarepa's guru, Marpa, is said to have been proficient)[21] and Bardo Yoga prepare the practitioner for utilizing death as a means of salvation. All six of these yogas point to the integral connections believed to exist between the body and consciousness, and they are among the many tantric practices designed to transform both the body and consciousness as a means of hastening enlightenment.

Through *gyulus*, the illusory body, one is able to roam freely in various states of existence that require the other yogas: *milam*, to control the dream state; *odsal*, a state where one experiences being absorbed into the Clear Light of the Void; *phowa*, transferring consciousness out of one's own body into other bodies or places; and *bardo*, entering the intermediate state between death and rebirth while alive. Success in these yogas enables practitioners to control their consciousness after death by directing it toward enlightenment rather than incarnating into another body.

In order for the illusory body to appear, the body of form (the coarse human body) must be separated from the subtle body (the mental body of channels and winds).[22] This occurs naturally at death, when the illusory body breaks free to roam the bardo, and while dreaming. A third way to separate them is through meditational practices such as phowa.

Several points need to be kept in mind about these yogas. First, they are not theories but highly complicated and actual yogic practices that are performed under the supervision of a guru. Second, these yogas are undertaken by advanced practitioners who have received training in other, equally advanced practices.[23] For instance,

> To purify worldly clingings and to lay a good foundation for the advanced practice of the Six Yogas, the disciple should first obtain the four complete Initiations of Demchog [a tantric deity], and practice

> the Arising Yoga until he has reached a fairly stabilized stage. To conquer inertia and laziness, he should meditate more on death; to overcome his hindrances, he should pray to the Buddhas and arouse the Bodhi-Mind; to prepare sufficient provisions for the Path of Dharma, he should give alms and make the Mandala offerings; to cleanse himself from sins and transgressions, he should repent and recite the Mantra of Vajrasattava; to attain the blessings, he should practice the Guru Yoga.[24]

Arising Yoga, the preparatory practice for the Six Yogas, stresses the generation and dissolution of elaborate visualizations—for instance, visualizing the world as dissolving into the great void.[25] These preliminary practices suggest that deep commitment is involved in practicing the Six Yogas. Garma Chang emphasizes that the these yogas are interrelated; they are to be practiced in conjunction with one another. Mastery of *tummo* in particular is a necessary prerequisite for Dream and Bardo yogas.[26] As if this were not daunting enough, the Venerable Thrangu Rinpoche adds that among the Kagyu (and other serious practitioners) the practice of Dream Yoga involves a three-year retreat.[27]

The control of consciousness is a central issue of the Six Yogas. Through their practice one can maintain consciousness all along the continuum of the waking, dreaming, and death states, thereby mastering illusion rather than being mastered by it. Tucci explains:

> If our daily conduct of life does not conform to the precepts of the teacher then the karma accumulated in us in the past ensnares us in the illusions it awakens, while we add new illusions to those already stored up. Such illusions also affect the images in dreams, which are contaminated by them. Being perpetuated in this way, this state affects also the state of intermediate existence after death. The effect of impure apparent reality thus spreads over three realms: illusion as action of karma, the extending of such illusion into dream life, and the influence of the impure illusory states on the mental body *(yid lus)* when it seeks a new incarnation at the moment of death. Against this triple realm of "impure" illusion can be opposed a triple realm of "pure" illusion, which is created through meditation on one's own body as the divine body—into which one's own body can be transformed through the prescribed methods because of its lack of real substance. This "pure" illusion guards the dream state against the images caused by impure concepts. In the intermediate existence which takes place between death and new reincarnation the *yid lus* is transformed.[28]

Significantly, the transformation of one's coarse physical body into a divine body is accomplished through elaborate visualizations performed during intense meditation states. Such visualization practices inevitably influence the content and quality of dreams.

All this is a strikingly new element in the role of dreams in Indo-Tibetan Buddhism. In early Indian Buddhism meaningful dreams were primarily a source of prophecy and a way of being connected to other, divine realms (as well as a way of demonstrating that connection). While Indo-Tibetan Buddhist dreams remain connected to prophecy, they are also *actively* incorporated into salvational teachings that require the practitioner to have profound and immediate experiences of the illusory nature of all reality, both while awake and while asleep. Experiencing the impossibility of actually taking hold, when awake, of a physical object perceived in a dream comes to describe a higher reality: In grasping the objects of our daily life we think we are in contact with the real, but in fact it is just another form of dreaming. The belief that the components of waking life and the insubstantial material of dreams are equally illusory comes to mean that just as practitioners are able to transform their consciousness during the day, so they can also transform dream consciousness. Ultimately this means that they will be able to transform consciousness during the all-important bardo state (the in-between state of death and rebirth), which leads to either rebirth or liberation. Thus one's practice, which is essentially the awareness and control of consciousness, should be extended throughout the continuum of consciousness: waking, sleeping, and death.[29] One should practice throughout the twenty-four hours of the day, making every circumstance an action for practice.[30] The following diagram may prove helpful:

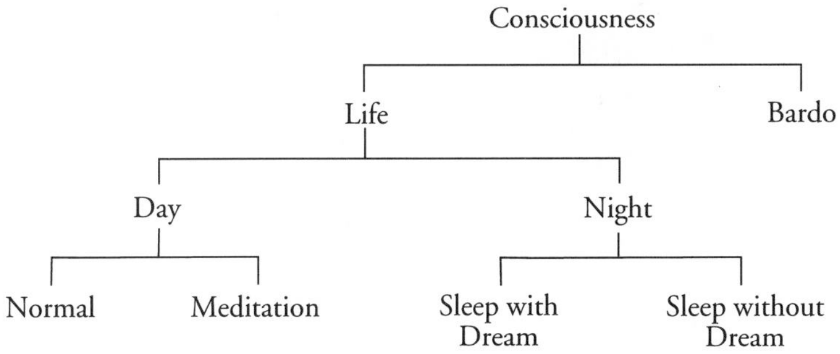

The state of meditation is closely related to the dream and bardo states; it is also a key to the continuum of consciousness through the different states. Meditation is believed capable of controlling and then freeing consciousness to roam beyond this earthly realm not only into the bardo but into other realms as well. Changing consciousness is the ultimate Buddhist goal, and meditation is the definitive practice toward that end. Since dreaming is also a form of consciousness, we can begin to see why dream *consciousness* became a matter of crucial interest, somewhat to the detriment of dream *content.*

Waking consciousness, dreaming, and death are all equally illusory states that need to be transcended in order to achieve enlightenment. This transcendence can be achieved through the Six Yogas by utilizing three periods of practice. During the day, focus on waking consciousness by reminding yourself that you are really dreaming, that everything you are experiencing is a dream, is as unreal or empty as a dream. At night, practice Dream Yoga, first by apprehending your dreams, being conscious that you are dreaming, then by transforming the dream into whatever you wish, such as going to one of the heavens and receiving teachings from a celestial Buddha. The third period is the after-death state, the bardo, which is just as unreal as waking and sleeping life and can be entered at will.[31] Failure to control these states, especially the after-death state, leads to another birth in saṃsāra without any choice over its conditions and the possible loss of all the spiritual knowledge gained in this life. On the other hand, dying with control means maintaining one's spiritual knowledge and, in the case of advanced adepts, becoming enlightened.

The final goal is control of the after-death state, the first step of which is the ability to know when you are in it, rather than experiencing the disorientation that is the fate of non-yogis. In this practice sleep is taken as more than a metaphor for death, it is the training ground for death and consequently for enlightenment. As Geshe Kelsang Gyatso explains it: "If we have gained proficiency in recognizing sleep as sleep and dreams as dreams, we will also be able to recognize the intermediate [after-death] state for what it is."[32]

Actually, these teachings, which link dreams and death, take us back to some of the earliest religious ideas about dreams, such as the belief that dreams can carry one to the realm of the dead, thereby providing information on the afterlife. At the same time, the persistent and seemingly contradictory Buddhist views of dreams—as powerful forms of cognition and also as the primary example of the illusory nature of the world—are resolved because conscious dreaming is one of the best cognitive means for understanding illusion.

PRACTICE IN TIBET

One of the ways the Six Yogas came to Tibet was through Marpa, who had studied them in India with Nāropa[33] and Niguma (fl. eleventh century).[34] Marpa, in turn, passed them on to his disciples. Appropriately, part of this transmission is through a dream Milarepa has shortly after his long-awaited initiation by Marpa but before he himself has mastered Dream Yoga. He dreams that

> a beautiful ḍākinī with blue skin and wearing a brocade dress and bone ornaments appeared. Her eye-brows and lashes sparkled with light. She said, "Son, you already have the teaching Mahāmudra and instruction in the six yogas. These lead to enlightenment through continuous meditation, but you do not have the teaching concerning the transference of consciousness to other bodies that leads to Buddhahood in one moment of meditation. Ask for it."[35]

Phowa, the transference of consciousness to other bodies, is one of the Six Yogas, and this dream would seem to indicate that so far Milarepa had received only preliminary instruction in them. This is further suggested by the fact that Milarepa does not know what to make of the dream. "Is it a warning from the gods? Is it a demon's trick?" he asks.[36] While Milarepa may have studied these techniques, he had not yet mastered them. Nonetheless, Marpa is so impressed by Milarepa's dream that he goes to India get these teachings from Nāropa.[37]

The *Mgur 'bum* presents evidence of Milarepa's eventual success in mastering Dream Yoga: Milarepa instructs his disciples in Dream Yoga[38] and makes frequent and pointed references to the Six Yogas. In song 1, for instance, Milarepa longs for Marpa and he sings a song in which he imagines him teaching the Six Yogas to his disciples.[39] In song 23 Rechungpa asks Milarepa what Marpa taught him, and Milarepa answers: "If in this life you long for Buddhahood, examine your mind without agitation and meditate on the Six Yogas which are the essence of all the Tantras."[40] These are the only specific teachings Milarepa mentions, and they are referred to as the highest teaching. In song 25 a group of women who are seeking teachings from Milarepa ask him for his life story. Milarepa sums up the major events of his life in a few verses, including the teachings he received from Marpa. He says he learned "to contemplate the Mahāmudrā, which is the introduction of the profound, natural state of all things, and the Six Yogas of Nāropa."[41] In the Kagyu order Mahāmudrā is a fast path to enlightenment (in one lifetime), whereby, through meditation, the practitioner has a direct, personal realization of the nature of mind.[42] Song 32/29 also gives a prominent place to the Six Yogas and again links them with the practice of Mahāmudrā, the aim of which is to alter the practitioner's consciousness so that she or he can recognize the true nature of reality. In this sense, the Six Yogas are utilized as an extended form of Mahāmudrā practice.

Another story in which Milarepa teaches the Six Yogas is song 26, a much loved story that has been popularized through monastic dance performances.[43] One day, while Milarepa is sitting outside his cave, a deer, a hunter's dog, and the hunter appear before him. These three arrive separately, thereby affording Milarepa the opportunity to offer an appropriate sermon to each. The last two lines of his three sermons are the same: "I will give you instruction in the Six Yogas of Nāropa and show you how to practice Mahāmudrā."[44] These two, along with the injunction to meditate in solitary places, are the essence of Milarepa's teachings.[45]

A final reference to Dream Yoga occurs in song 30/27, which points out the connections between Dream Yoga and the bardo state. Here Milarepa is instructing the goddess Tseringma on how to prepare for death, in the course of which he describes the bardo and tells her to practice Dream Yoga.[46] As we see, Milarepa instructed all classes of beings—humans, animals, and deities—in teachings that involve dreaming.

Other well-known Tibetan religious figures pursued these practices, such as Gampopa's student, the first Karmapa Dusum Khyenpa (1110–1193), who attributes his enlightenment at the age of fifty to Dream Yoga.[47] The biography of Buton (1290–1364) makes frequent reference to his practice of the Six Yogas,[48] and in it he records some of his experiences with Dream Yoga:

> On another occasion, intending to go to the Tuṣita [heaven], he proceeded on the way holding on to a moon-beam. Then having awakened, he said that he had not seen the Tuṣita itself. Proceeding to the Abhirati world [a heaven] in the east, he said that a thousand Buddhas were seated in ranks in a palace of jewels. He stated that one would see this if, looking at a Pure Land one conceived of going anywhere riding on

> the sun and moon or holding on to a shaft of light or soaring on a garuḍa, and so forth.[49]

In describing his own dreams, Buton is teaching his disciples how they too travel on such auspicious vehicles to various heavens once they are lucid in the dream state.

Tsongkhapa studied the Six Yogas of Nāropa at Gdan-sa[50] and Drikung monasteries,[51] and shortly before his death he gave a discourse on them at Drepung. Most significantly, he wrote a commentary on the Six Yogas,[52] that gives detailed instructions on their practice, though, of course, he strongly recommends relying on a guru "who possesses the unmistakable experience of Dream Yoga."[53] His instructions on Dream Yoga presume preparatory spiritual practices and are divided into two parts: practice during the day, such as developing a strong intention to have a dream, and practice during the night. "If no dream whatsoever appears, there is then no way for the yogi to practice the Dream Yoga; therefore, he must use all methods to produce a dream as given in the Tantric instructions.[54] If the dream takes place but is not clear, it will still be difficult for the yogi to practice Dream Yoga. Therefore, it is necessary to have a clear dream—clear to the point that the yogi can relate it when he awakes."[55] During the dream itself, the yogi should aspire to become lucid in order to purify and develop the dream, which will enable her or him to travel to Buddhist heavens to hear teachings from celestial buddhas. In this regard Tsongkhapa, like Buton, describes the dreamer as riding on the rays of the sun and moon.[56] For Tsongkhapa, however, the final practice is that the yogi, while in the dream state, visualizes that his or her body is the yidam, the tutelary deity, and sees the seed syllable *hūṃ* appear in the heart emanating "rays of light that gather all the visions in the dream and draw them back" into itself.[57] In this way they will experience the emptiness *(śūnyatā)* of all existence, the realization of which leads to enlightenment.

As this instruction suggests, and as we have seen in Milarepa's biographies, both advanced practitioners and struggling disciples find prophecies in sought dreams, to which we now turn our attention.

9 Ritual Dreaming

As we saw in the preceding chapter, having a dream is a necessary component of Dream Yoga, and various means were used to achieve this end: performing a ritual, going to sleep in a sacred place, praying for a dream, or simply concentrating the mind on having a dream before going to sleep. Such dreams are referred to as sought dreams, and they have been documented among the ancient Greeks, Native Americans, Christians, and shamanic people around the world.[1] The progression from spontaneous dream to sought dream is a reasonable development. If one accepts the prophetic value of dreams in general, then whether the dreams occur spontaneously or as the result of consciously setting out to have a dream, one still has received a prophecy. This chapter surveys the literary evidence for sought dreams (and for rituals to offset the negative effects of dreams) in ancient and medieval India and Tibet; it then introduces some Tibetan dream rituals taken from the canonical literature. As with Dream Yoga, this chapter documents the increase of dream practices in Indo-Tibetan Buddhism during and after the periods of the mahāsiddhas.

SOUGHT DREAMS

Evidence for the sought dream in South Asia before the period of the mahāsiddhas (eighth to twelfth centuries) is slim, although we have seen one possible example in the Buddha's advice to fall asleep in the state of mindfulness (*sampajāna*, *Vinaya* I.295). A clearer example of a sought dream comes from an early *Upaniṣad*, the *Chāndogya* (circa ninth to seventh century B.C.E.), where a ritual to attain greatness includes the practice of dream incubation.[2] In the *Upaniṣads* one attains greatness (power, fame, prosperity, immortality) through knowledge of the hidden connections that exist between the human body, especially the vital powers, and the cosmos.[3] The ritual lasts for a fortnight, and it invokes the increasing power of the waxing moon by beginning with a sacrificial consecration on the night of the new moon and ending on the night of the full moon. On the last night the officiant drinks a mixture of herbs, honey and curd. Then he

> cleans the goblet or cup and lies down behind the fire either on a skin or the bare ground, remaining silent and unresistant.[4] If he sees a woman [in a dream], he should know that this rite has been successful. In this connection, there is this verse:
>
> When a man sees a woman in his dreams,
> During a rite to obtain a wish;
> He should recognize its success,
> In that dream vision *[svapnanidarśane]*.[5]

The dream predicts the ritual's success or failure, and it is a particularly intriguing example when compared to later Buddhist dream practices carried out before an initiation, which seek the approval of dream women (especially ḍākinīs).

Pantañjali's *Yogasūtra* (second century C.E.) connects a primary ascetic practice, *prāṇāyāma* (breath control), with dreams: it defines knowledge of dreams and sleep as prāṇāyāma's object of study.[6] Mircea Eliade's commentary on this passage brings out an important function of prāṇāyāma, which is to be an aid in penetrating all four Upaniṣadic states of consciousness with perfect lucidity (waking, dreaming, dreamless sleep, and the fourth state of consciousness that both transcends and encompasses the other three).[7] Consequently, the advanced yogi can be lucid while dreaming and therefore maintain a unified consciousness between all four states.[8] The control of dream consciousness through ascetic practices is similar to the advice the Buddha gave to his nuns and monks, and they point toward later, more fully developed practices. Correspondingly, in Indian and Tibetan medical literature, some dreams are caused by bodily disorders, and they travel on the winds (Skt: *prāṇa*; Tib.: *rlung*) of the body,[9] so it follows that control of breath, which is part of the control of consciousness, can affect dreams and, it is argued, in the case of advanced practitioners can lead to actual control of dreams.

In the later *Upaniṣads*, dating from the early centuries of the Common

Era, we find similar notions as well as a new approach to dreaming. The *Nāradaparivrājaka Upaniṣad* says, "A man who is as much in control of himself when he dreams as when he is awake is said to be the very best, the foremost of all who follow the Vedānta."[10] Several of these *Upaniṣads* refer to an ascetic's ability not to dream, "for he always remains the same during day and night,"[11] and not to be attached to dreams.[12]

Two other early examples of the practice of sought dreams come from the *Sāmavidhāna Brāhmaṇa*, a ritual text of the *Sāma Veda*.[13] In order to have a prophetic dream the text recommends the following:

> 1. Place the deity who dwells in the dung *(Saṣkarevāsinīm)*[14] in a basket along with unhusked grains, incense and flowers, and put it on the head. Then lay down in a pure place with the head toward the east and sing the hymn [from the *Sāma Veda*] that begins *"imam uhuvu."* After this one should remain silent while falling asleep and he or she will see[15] in a dream the fruit *(phala)* of what will come.[16]
>
> 2. Alternatively, place a poison pill *(garagolikaṃ)* in a box and sing the hymn that begins "*āyāhi susamā hi ta.*" Then one should remain silent while falling asleep and he or she will see.[17]

In the first ritual, the unhusked grain stands for the dormant potential of dreaming within us all. As a birth metaphor it contrasts sharply to the death imagery of the poison pill in the second ritual. The latter ritual may very well be connected to the widespread South Asian belief that through dreams one can access the realm of the dead in order to learn the secrets of the future.

In elucidating this text the commentary introduces some intriguing terms related to sought dream practices. For instance, it begins with "Now we will see what is not seen" *(athāto 'dṛṣṭadarśanānām)*, which it glosses by saying that "what is unseeable" is subject to "dream consciousness" *(svapnajāgaritavishayā)* and that the means to this are "dream methods" *(svapnavishayaprayogam)*.[18] These scant remains of dream practices, when put together with others that we will turn to shortly, appear to be similar to the practice of dream incubation in the Hellenistic world during the same period.

Overshadowing all these practices is the well-known myth, so frequently depicted in South Asian art, that we are all participating in God's dream of creation. One version is contained in the *Kūrma Purāṇa*, which describes the beginning of this *kalpa*, or eon, when nothing existed but a vast ocean and Lord Nārāyaṇa (Viṣṇu), who slept on the coils of a great snake. As he sleeps he dreams, and out of his navel grows a wonderful lotus, from which arises the universe:[19] God's dream is the basis of all that exists, including waking reality.[20] Thus, by entering into the dream state one can possibly enter into direct relationship with God and his creative powers. Indeed, we all do just this whenever we dream, in that we create whole worlds out of nothing.[21]

Given this blend of philosophical analysis and mythical imaginings, it is not surprising to find two stories in Somadeva's *Kathāsaritsāgara* that revolve around sought dreams. This eleventh-century collection of stories is based on an earlier (c. first century C.E.) and now lost collection,[22] which was Buddhist or at least heavily influenced by Buddhism, and traces of that influence remain in Somadeva's collection.[23] For instance, in one story, a king loses a debate with a Buddhist monk and converts to Buddhism. Later in the story he asks the monk to teach him how to become a bodhisattva. The monk replies that one must first be free of all sin, and there is but one method to be sure of that: doing a *svapna māṇavaka*—seeking a dream. When the king does this and dreams, he is reminded of a minor sin he committed and told how to expiate it.[24] In this story a *svapna māṇavaka* is a Buddhist technique for producing dreams; yet, another story in this collection uses the same term in a Hindu context when it has a Kṣatriya pandit do a *svapna māṇavaka* in order to have a dream for his king.[25] Examples such as these show how easily ideas about dreams flowed between different South Asian religions as part of the common culture.[26]

The term *svapna māṇavaka* also appears in a twelfth-century Indian text on constructing mandalas that was translated into Tibetan and widely used, the *Vajrāvalīnāmamaṇḍalapāyikā* of Abhayākaragupta. This text recommends seeking and examining a dream (Skt.: *svapna māṇavaka*; Tib.: *rmi-lam brtagpa*) in order to establish that the deities approve the proposed location of the mandala. One should put on clean clothes, recite the mantra *Oṃ mucili svāhā / oṃ mohin svāhā / oṃ dantini svāhā,* twenty-one times, and make offerings to

> Bhagavan Lokeśvara and lie down comfortably on a clean place with the crown of the head to the south and facing the east [i.e., on one's right side]. If one has a bad dream, recite the mantras of Amṛtakunṭali, or think that in ultimate reality all phenomena lack self-nature. Other-

> wise, examine your dreams once again. [If in the dream] the site is granted by the deities or not objected to [by them] one should perform those [rituals] which will be shown below. [The ritual] is absolutely not [to be done] if [they] object.[27]

This compilation of sought dreams from various Indian texts indicates that dreaming was perceived as a way of communicating with deities, both by Buddhists and Hindus, and a way of knowing the future. Tibetan literary sources show that these beliefs flourished in Tibet. We have seen several examples of sought dreams in Milarepa's biographies. Marpa teaches him and his other disciples to prophesy through sought dreams (which prompts Milarepa's important four pillars dream with its prediction about the future of the lineage),[28] and Milarepa continues the tradition in his own practice[29] and instructs his disciples in Dream Yoga.[30] Additional examples were shown to exist in Buton's and Tsongkhapa's biographies, which describe personal experiences of sought dreams and instructions for disciples in their practice.

This tradition continues today. During the week-long Kālachakra ceremony held at Madison, Wisconsin, in 1981 His Holiness the Dalai Lama was very clear about the how and why of dreams in this initiation. He distributed *kusha* grass among those seeking initiation saying, this "kusha grass is given for the sake of having unmistaken, clear dreams. It is also for the sake of clearing away pollutants and uncleanliness so that your mind will be clear."[31] The kusha grass was to be placed under both the mattresses and the pillows of the initiates' beds,[32] the heads of which were to be pointed in the direction of the ritual site. Further instructions were to sleep on the "right side in the lion posture,"[33] to "engage in techniques so that you fall asleep within a virtuous attitude," and to pay attention only to the dreams that occurred around dawn.[34]

Since these dreams are believed to portend the effect of the initiation on the individual dreamer, in order to assure a beneficial effect, they have to be dealt with ritually. The Dalai Lama offered the following methods of dealing with bad dreams:

> the main technique is to meditate on emptiness, but also, in situations of fright and discomfort, it is important to take specific cognizance of the object—the person or being who is the source of the fright or displeasure—and then cultivate compassion and love....

> Now as an additional means to overcome bad dreams, I will scatter water, simultaneously reciting the mantra oṃ āh hūṃ hoḥ haṃ kṣhaḥ. During this, visualize that all bad effects are cast away by the force of the mantra and the wisdom understanding emptiness.[35]

Two points need to be made about these instructions. First, given the large number of people who participated in this initiation, the Dalai Lama himself could not be available to interpret all their dreams. People were free to consult many of the teachers participating in the ceremony, or they could utilize the Dalai Lama's general instructions if they had a frightening dream. Second, while the Dalai Lama's comments demonstrate the continuing importance of sought dreams in Tibetan Buddhism, they point to the necessity of being able to deal with such dreams if they are judged to be inauspicious. As we will see in the *Tangyur* texts discussed below, although a practitioner may seek a dream for spiritual purposes, this does not guarantee a good dream, and rituals have existed from ancient times to avoid the evil effects of bad dreams. These so-called bad dreams may only be dreams that the guru interprets as being inappropriate; thus the rituals designed to dispel any lingering effects can also be seen as a form of reshaping consciousness. Of course, if one has an extremely disturbing dream, such ritual means of expiation would be welcomed by the dreamer.

The Dalai Lama's suggestion that one should meditate on emptiness to dispel bad dreams reminds us of the importance of māyā (illusion) in the South Asian understanding of dreams: like reality itself, dreams can be products of māyā. Dream experience is used to teach that experience, both waking and sleeping, arises in our consciousness—neither one is more real because both are māyā. From the point of view of Mahāyāna, all reality is empty, void of enduring reality; this truth is veiled by māyā. Thus the importance of māyā's influence on dreams reins in the destabilizing possibilities of unorthodox prophetic dreams—they could easily be dismissed as illusions. As we move through the Tibetan canonical materials, we will see that the detailed instructions on how to dream and what to see keep dream experience running through carefully designed channels. Of course, more often than not dreaming broke free of its philosophical and instructional cubbyhole into the open spaces of human experience—people continued to have dream experiences, both sought and unbidden. Continuing references to dream rituals designed to ward off the effects of bad dreams testify to the pervasive belief of dreams as an important, indeed sometimes terrifying, source of prophecy. So uncomfortable or inauspicious dreams, in addition to being dismissed because of their illusory nature, could also be formally discharged through rituals. As we shall see shortly, several such rituals occur among the instructions for sought dreams contained in the Tibetan canon.

The foregoing shows that the sought dream was and remains a fairly common practice in Tibetan Buddhism, both informally or as part of elaborate esoteric practices. What remains consistent in all these practices is that dreams are recognized as part of the cognitive process of progressing along the spiritual path. In the same way as one learns from the guru while awake, one can learn from dreams while asleep. Both require disciplined attention. The instructions to remain aware while dreaming, to think "this is a dream" while dreaming, are similar to the instructions for daily practice, which is to remain aware, to pay attention to your mental activities and bring them under control. Dreaming teaches one that dream experience and waking experience both arise in our consciousness—neither is more real than the other.[36]

RITUALS TO COUNTERACT BAD DREAMS

Some of the earliest recorded dream rituals of South Asia are designed to ward off the effects of bad dreams. These rituals indicate the two-way traffic believed to exist between the states of waking and dreaming: what happens in one affects the other. The dream may predict a future waking event, but equally a waking event, a ritual, can subvert the dream event. The *Vedas*, which are concerned about the possibly polluting effects of dreams as well as their negative consequences, contain several hymns and rituals to dispel their effects.[37] Ancient medical texts, such as the *Suśruta Saṃhitā*, offer the recommendation to recite mantras, or spend the night in a temple, and caution against telling a bad dream to anyone else.[38]

Another remedy to avert the effects of bad dreams is a short ritual that accompanies an appeal to Viṣṇu, the god whose dream created the world: "Twigs of red sandal, smeared with clarified butter, are to be offered into the fire along with a thousand mutterings of the Gāyatrī (Sāvitrī) *mantra* (*RV* III.62.10); one may utter the eight names of Viṣṇu—Acyuta, Viṣṇu, Keśava, Hari, Satya, Janārdana, Hamsa, and Nārāyaṇa—after bath, facing the east."[39]

All these ideas are absorbed into Indian Buddhism and later into Tibetan Buddhism, where they mixed with indigenous ideas about dreams. One ritual from the time of the Buddha involved King Ajātaśatru, whose ministers protected him from the effects of a bad dream by placing him in a tank "filled with the four sweetnesses."[40] Such a bath blends Vedic ideas about pollution through dreams with the notion that purification through bathing breaks any connection to the dream by washing away its residual effect and thus preventing its fulfillment. Other examples occur in the *Aśokāvadāna,* where King Aśoka ritually saluted the four directions and implored the gods to prevent the evil effects of his bad dream about his son,[41] and in the *Mahāsupina Jātaka,* where Brahman priests attempted to offset the effect of the king of Kosala's bad dreams with an elaborate sacrifice at a crossroads.[42] The Tibetan medical text entitled the *Four Treatises (Rgyud bzhi)*[43] says that the effects of bad dreams can be overcome by prayer, meditation, acts of charity, and so on,[44] while Jamgon Kongtrul recommended reciting mantras and visualizing a protective enclosure *(srung 'khor)* to avoid their negative influences.[45] And, of course, amulets can be worn to avert their predicted effects.[46]

An example of assuring the outcome of a good dream occurs in the *Kalpa Sūtra.* When Queen Triśalā, Mahāvīra's mother, has her conception dream, she says:

> "These my excellent and pre-eminent dreams shall not be counteracted by other bad dreams."

Accordingly she remained awake to save her dreams by means of (hearing) good, auspicious, pious, agreeable stories about gods and religious men.[47]

Additional dream rituals contained in this text involve the dream interpreters before they answer the king's call to interpret the dreams. "Then the interpreters of dreams, being called...bathed, made the offering (to the house-gods) *[balikarman],* performed auspicious rites and expiatory acts,[48] put on excellent, lucky, pure courtdress, adorned their persons with small but costly ornaments, and put, for the sake of auspiciousness, white mustard and Dūrvā grass on their heads."[49]

This quote adds some intriguing details to the lore about ancient Indian dream interpreters, especially the purificatory use of grasses, which, in the event of an inauspicious dream, may have been used to cleanse the dreamer and to carry away any negative effects from the dream.[50]

A Tun-huang manuscript written in Old Tibetan contains rituals for both assuring the outcome of good dreams and expiating bad ones. The first involves elementary purifications and honoring the gods, while the second transfers the bad dream to inanimate objects like pieces of wood or bits of earth and then destroys or discards them.[51]

Thus prayer, silence, wakefulness, amulets, charity, transfer of dream influences to objects, and washing them away are actions that are believed to counteract the effects of bad dreams. But, such rituals are rare in Buddhist biographical texts because the vast majority of dreams contained in them are positive and therefore do not require rituals to deflect their effect. If anything, Tibetan biographies describe rituals that stimulate rather than counteract dreaming. Details about both aspects of dream rituals, however, are found in the Tibetan canon.

DREAM RITUALS FROM THE *KANGYUR* AND *TANGYUR*

The huge Tibetan canon has a long history of compilation beginning in the fourteenth century[52] and is divided into two parts: (1) the *Kangyur (bka' 'gyur)*, meaning "translation of Buddha's word" and referring to the teachings attributed to the Buddha, and (2) the *Tangyur (bstan 'gyur)*, meaning "translation of the treatises" and referring to discourses by famous Buddhist teachers, commentaries, and other works. Both parts contain dream rituals involving sought dreams, although they are somewhat disjointed, incomplete, and presented without context. In contrast, Milarepa's biographies are all context but contain very little actual dream teachings. In this section I argue that the canonical practices complement the dream instructions found in the biographies. The biographies reveal settings in which the rituals could have been utilized, and, reciprocally, the canonical texts provide detailed examples of dream practices that were only alluded to in the biographies.

A *Tangyur* text entitled *Milam Tagpa* (*rMi lam brTagpa*, The Examination of Dreams)[53] is a translation of the Sanskrit composition of an Indian scholar named Glorious Advaya (dPal lDan gNyis su med), collected from the writings of Nāgārjuna.[54] This short text gives a set of instructions for obtaining two kinds of dreams, those that will generate the thought of enlightenment and those that will bestow empowerments or initiations *(dbang)*. It begins with instructions on how to have such dreams, provides five lists of example dreams containing both good and bad predictions, and concludes with instructions for avoiding the ill effects of inauspicious dreams.

The first set of instructions to obtain dreams are as follows: "On a seat of Kuśa grass prepare a pillow of fragrant grasses and put on a garland of *(jatapa)* flowers. Recite mantras[55] [in order to consecrate] milk from a young girl,[56] and then use it to anoint the eyes."[57] This is an esoteric text and therefore it does not offer explanations of all its details; those would be given in the oral teachings; however, a few comments may be ventured about this eye ointment. As discussed above, South Asian and other ancient people say that they *see* (Skt.: √*dṛś*, Tib.: *mthong ba*) a dream rather than *have* a dream. Such language expresses the fact that dreams are experienced as given to individuals rather than created by them. This use of language emphasizes the external rather than the internal origin of the dream, thereby lending them a divine or demonic authority. To say one has seen rather than had a dream is to suggest that the dreamer is the passive recipient of an objective vision.[58] Putting on eye ointment—in other words, ritually preparing the eyes—demonstrates how literally they were thinking of dreams in terms of seeing. All around the world it is believed that the application of magical ointments empowers, transforms, and protects the body, and that is the case here. Milk is widely used in Indian rituals—and this was originally an Indian text—because of its positive qualities: unlike any other food, milk can be obtained without causing harm to any living creature, animal or vegetable; from churning the Milk Ocean the gods derived *amṛta*, the nectar of immortality; and, of course, a mother's milk is the ultimate symbol of nurturance. I will take up the gendered dimension of this passage in the next chapter.

The *Milam Tagpa* emphasizes that dreams occurring around dawn are the most important: "In the first part of the night habitual propensities *(bag chags)*[59] are agitated; in the second part of the night ghosts are active; so examine the dream that comes in the third part of the night."[60] This emphasis on the relevance of dreams that occur in the last part of the night is frequently made in other Tibetan texts.[61] The *Milam Tagpa* then presents a small dream manual in the form of four short lists of dreams which predict four different good futures.

1. Dreams that predict becoming one who possesses compassion: "In a dream [seeing yourself] holding a mirror in hand, seeing the crescent moon, riding in a chariot, wearing white clothes and white ornaments, subduing an elephant with an iron goad."

2. Dreams that predict being able to explain Dharma with compassion: You see yourself "finding gold, wetting one's body, putting a vessel on top of one's head, governing other lands, riding a horse to a jeweled island, being lifted up in a palanquin by humans, gathering lotus flowers, holding books in one's hands, blowing a conch, putting on garlands of flowers and also catching peacocks with a net."

3. Dreams that predict becoming one who is worthy of offerings by all: "Carrying a whip and being victorious in battle, being such a [powerful] king that other kings are in your retinue, converting an army into doing peaceful work, sending messenger birds, burning forests with fire, swimming in water without sinking, moving in the sky and floating there using the sun and moon as ornaments, sitting on the Lion Throne, spreading a white umbrella and erecting a victorious flag."

4. Dreams that predict things will happen according to one's wishes: Seeing "blister water flowing [from one's skin], seeing a crashing heap of fire without being afraid, eating snakes and scorpions, holding vajra and bell, reaching the top of a mountain, your hand surrounding a city, worshipping the *lamas* [monks] and tutelary deities, writing books and building stūpas, walking naked, dancing and singing, associating with the community of monks, putting on good clothes and eating fruits, saying the benedictions of the *tathāgatagarba*, making prophecies, filling up a big pond, and building high mansions."[62]

There is also a list of bad dreams that predict one will have mental torments: Seeing "an enemy take your ornaments, seeing a young lady who is worried, being confined in a dungeon, being robbed of one's wealth and property, being put in iron [shackles], being crushed by bad beings, wild animals striking your body, your body wrapped with rags and covered with stains, eating polluted food, drinking polluted water, running away when you see your lama, teacher, friends and parents, seeing a deep gorge without human beings in it or a very wild place where one suffers because you cannot find food and drink, saying 'Alas, I am suffering,' taking off armor and then being struck by weapons, walking in a very thick forest being attacked by tigers, wolves, and other animals."[63] The text advises that in the event of such inauspicious dreams one should make an offering by burning sesame seeds.[64]

Tibetan literature contains many lists of dreams that predict good, evil, or indifferent outcomes, but there are very few consistencies between the lists or even within them.[65] For instance, a text from the *Ratnakūṭa* section of the *Kangyur*, the *Ārya Svapna Nirdeśa Sūtra*, lists 108 auspicious dream images that appear to one pursuing the bodhisattva path. Mainly they see the *Tathāgata* doing various auspicious things such as preaching, sitting, and walking, or they see his robe or umbrella or bowl, and so on. But some of them are frightening images: "an earthquake [the earth spinning]; among an army about to give battle [walking among wolves and jackals]; being sick; falling from a precipice; meeting death [being bound and awaiting execution]; sitting among enemies [walking through knives and swords]."[66] These are not the positive dream images that we would expect, and some of the images that predict desirable things seem strange: seeing "blister water flowing [from one's skin], eating snakes and scorpions, walking naked." In contrast, the images predicting mental torments seem appropriate: seeing "an enemy take your ornaments, being confined in a dungeon, being robbed of one's wealth and property, being put in iron [shackles], being crushed by bad beings, wild animals striking your body," and so on.

At least five points can be made about these lists. First, they appear in collected materials from various sources that never aimed at consistency in or between texts. For instance, the translator of the *Milam Tagpa* (from Sanskrit to Tibetan) said he compiled it from the writings of Nāgārjuna, about whom there are many legends associated with magic, which explains both its piecemeal quality and its magical elements. Second, these lists are similar to, and indeed some contain, directed visualizations: they are guides for those who want to train their consciousness. Third, their lack of consistency requires the disciple to rely on her or his guru for an interpretation of whether a dream is good or evil. Fourth, as we have seen, and will continue to see, these texts are not necessarily complete; things are left out to be filled in by oral instructions from the guru. In the *Milam Tagpa* the mantra for the preparatory rituals is missing, and the final instructions for having an auspicious dream are explained in another text, the *Ratnamudrā.* Fifth, the last two points, as well as the preceding instructions and those that follow, suggest both the esoteric element in these practices and the influence of the guru on the disciple's dream life. When combined with the evidence of the biographies, it seems safe to assume that the disciples' dreams were affected, indeed shaped, by the expectations and instructions of their gurus. Disciples relate dreams they consider significant or disturbing to their gurus and seek their interpretation. They do not consult dream lists. Consequently, disciples both attempt to dream of appropriate images and surrender interpretation to the guru because they rely on their gurus to bend their consciousness toward enlightenment. In this sense, Tibetan dream practices enhance institutional attempts to model practice on the deepest levels of one's being, as do meditational practices that rigidly define visualization experiences. Here "institutional" refers to the monastic hierarchy in which disciples slowly prove themselves in order to gain access to esoteric teachings such as these. Whereas the disciple seeks instruction in the control of consciousness, the guru has control over the instructions on how to "see" a dream, what one should see, and how to interpret it. Theoretically, Tibetan Buddhism breaks out of this authoritarian model if and when the disciple goes on to formal practices of Dream Yoga, which lead to self-control of dream images and events, but such control continues to undercut the spontaneous experience of dreams.

The *Milam Tagpa* also displays some of the ways in which the Tibetan dream tradition blended earlier, possibly shamanic, dream practices, such as seeking dreams and dispelling their negative influence, with later philosophical notions about māyā and emptiness. Despite its detailed instructions on how to have a dream and its dream lists, the text never loses sight of the essentially illusory nature of dreams and of all existence: "upon analysis there is no [independent] origination, therefore one should keep in mind the secret mantra of Dependent Origination."[67] An important lesson to be drawn from dreaming is that waking reality is insubstantial in the same way that dreams are, and that both can be manipulated. In the same way, inappropriate dreams—those that wander outside prescribed channels—can easily be dismissed as mere illusions.

A similar blending of sources can be seen in the Six Yogas of Nāropa, including Dream Yoga. It seems fairly certain that these practices were first systematized by Nāropa based on his study of earlier, mostly oral teachings. In other words, Nāropa, and his guru Tilopa before him, were influenced by popular and possibly shamanic dream techniques, as were most of the mahāsiddhas. Like most shamans, the mahāsiddhas were notoriously independent practitioners, and while some practitioners maintained their independence, the *Milam Tagpa* and other canonical texts (to be discussed shortly) suggest institutional attempts to control the practices they describe. There is a constant tension in Tibetan Buddhism between uniform and independent practice, which is understandable given the influence of the structuring goals of a monastic elite[68] and the highly individualistic nature of shamanic practices.

Two points need to be made here. First, as in any other religious tradition there was diversity of practice and belief in Buddhism, especially between ordained monastics and wandering yogi practitioners.[69] Second, the lack of a central authority in Buddhism both allows the freedom for innovation among practitioners and creates anxiety about orthodoxy.[70] For instance, we have seen a complexity of practices categorized under the term Dream Yoga, ranging from philosophically detailed studies of the Six Yogas to simply having someone whisper in your ear while you sleep: "What you are experiencing is only a dream."

Another *Tangyur* text offers instructions on a form of Dream Yoga that leads to realizing emptiness, and it also blends sought dream practices with directed visualizations.[71] The text advises: first, bow down to Avalokiteś-vara, take refuge in the Three Jewels, generate the thought of enlightenment, and control oneself; then enter a meditation cell and meditate on dreams. The text gives detailed instructions on visualizing Avalokiteśvara and then visualizing "the letter *hrīḥ* as the actual embodiment of mind [and placing it] in the center of one's heart."[72] One should then go to sleep like the King of Yogis, in other words with an aware mind and possessing virtue and compassion. It probably also refers to the sleeping lion's posture, lying on one's right side. The text goes on to give further instructions involving the syllable *hrīḥ*. "When very close to falling asleep the syllable *hrīḥ* should be condensed into two drops, then gradually the lower drop should be condensed into the upper drop, then all the various appearances gather into one body. Then place the single drop in the center of a lotus, and as if placing water into water [they all become one] one's mind becomes like the stainless mind purified of all the entities and non-entities. One should hold firmly, without moving, in this state of great clarity."[73]

The goal here is to perceive all phenomena as illusions, without any intrinsic nature. If you are successful,

> One will see in the sky, like a heap of clouds, the mandala of the Conquerors surrounded by the divine assembly of Buddhas, Bodhisattvas, Śrāvakas and Pratyeka Buddhas. Then, without taking much time, one will achieve clarity. Like a lotus rising from the mud, the pure will [separates from] the mind which is polluted by the ignorance of intoxicating duality, isolates itself and like the sun in the sky, spontaneously, independently, and luminously rises.
>
> When the dreamer is in the city of dream he should hold both pleasure and sorrow as mere thought, as being like appearances reflected in a mirror, as neither existent nor non-existent, nor both existent and non-existent, as like a rainbow in the sky, or the sound of thunder, or perceiving being born and ceasing. The person who remains in clarity understands [that all things are like] this. For instance, the flow of the stream of mirage is not coming from any direction such as the east and it is not going anywhere. When one understands dreams in this way one realizes [the nature of illusion]. Like the sound of a bell, or a guitar, or an echo and so forth, the dreamer understands all these composite phenomena through the three doors of liberation [emptiness, wishlessness, and signlessness]....

When one awakes from sleep one is able to remove one's mind from all cravings. Then one can realize the teaching of this doctrine [emptiness].[74]

This text utilizes sought dreams not only to control consciousness but to reshape it permanently, to achieve an altered understanding of reality that continues into waking consciousness.

A final *Tangyur* text I want to discuss is entitled *rMi lam sGrol ma'i sGrub thabs* (Skt.: *Svapna Tārā Sādhana*), a text devoted to the female buddha Tārā that promises to produce prophetic dreams. The title of this text defines it as a *sādhana (sgrub thabs)*, a meditative visualization technique through which one attempts to accomplish identification with a particular deity, in effect to become the deity.[75] Through correctly seeing and identifying with the characteristics of the deity, the adept is able to transform into the deity. This is accomplished by envisioning oneself as looking like the deity, sounding like the deity through chanting their particular mantra, and assuming the deity's mental state[76]—one must, however, be initiated into such practice in order for it to be effective. In this text success in such visualization/identification paves the way for clear dreams, suggesting that in large part the emphasis on dreaming in Tibetan tantric practice goes hand-in-hand with the tantric emphasis on visualization as a necessary component of practice.

The text begins with a detailed visualization practice for seeing Tārā and instructions on how to make preparatory offerings and mantras. Tārā is perhaps the most popular deity in Tibetan Buddhism. She is known as the Savioress, one who can protect her devotees from physical and psychic dangers, and she can also lead the way to enlightenment. Thus she is the perfect guide through the possibly treacherous dream realm. As alluded to in the text, in popular practice Tārā is represented as having twenty-one forms. I have translated the text in its entirety in order to give a sense of its intricacy.

I bow down to the noble dream Tārā.

Tārā has a form like the full moon in the middle of a cloudless sky, possessing a cool, perfect ray of white light.

In order to have a clear dream I bow my head to Tārā's feet and explain each propitiation.

Get up very early with a virtuous mind, clean your face and scent your body. Use beautiful offerings to adorn the image of Reverend Tārā, whose mind is beneficial to all sentient beings, and take refuge in the Three Jewels and in the goddess Tārā. Possessing a virtuous mind and accumulating merit, in order to dispel obstacles to dreams, say the following mantra: *Oṃ amṛta kuṇḍali hanahana sarva vighāṃ taḍadi taḍaḥ sarva pā paṃ hūṃ phat svāhā.* Then one should meditate on the exalted goddess in the sky like the stainless Vaidurya.

The beautiful *paṃ* syllables are very smooth, moist and clear, and they develop golden petals upon which there appears a white and cool moon disk that is called the holder of the rabbit. In the center of it is the syllable *tāṃ* dispelling all darkness in the three realms through its superb ray of light, which is like that of the King of the Constellations (the moon).

The Reverend Dream Tārā, the peaceful one, the virtuous one, has the form of perfectly developed youth, a face, two hands, and the gesture of bestowing excellence. She is holding a blue lotus, elegant, charming; all the directions are filled up by this incomparable one. Her hair is very fragrant and curled and adorned with many divine jewels. She has upper garments of blue silk and a multicolored lower garment; her girdle is a garland of pearls all of equal beauty tied with sacred thread. Her crown is adorned by Amoghasiddhi and she sits cross-legged, with the right leg drawn up, the left leg is extended. She remains neither in saṃsāra nor nirvāṇa. From her hair emanates an assembly of buddhas and bodhisattvas who are exactly like this Wisdom Goddess. Invite them to partake of the offering and then absorb them into your own being, blessing them with the dorje of body, speech, and mind. Then Tārā is praised by the buddhas of the ten directions.

After that make an offering of the mandala of the world and, with an undistracted mind while holding a precious rosary, respectfully offer supplication to the Noble Lady (Tārā) through offerings of flowers and good food and drink: the three whites—yogurt, milk, and butter—and the three sweets—sugar, honey, and molasses. Concentrate one-pointedly on Noble Tārā and recite this excellent secret mantra 2,400,000 times: *Oṃ svapna Tāre svāhā.* Then, without regarding worldly things, for the benefit of oneself and others, examine the dream signs.

On the holy days one should worship Tārā as a female virgin who is not contaminated by worldly phenomena. Wash oneself with sweet-smelling water and put on decorated clothes. Use flowers, incense, butter lamps, scented water, food, and cymbals to make a preliminary offering. Give white foods of yogurt and milk and so forth, cowry shells and silk; be courteous and so forth. Scatter water with a conch shell and then comfortably disperse the deities. In the evening, in the house of a celibate yogi, hold a bell and remain on a pillow smeared with the scent of flowers and draw a mandala with five offerings, especially *gugul* (an incense that drives away evil spirits) and light butter lamps. Then with bits of round clay measured to the size of peas, recite seven times *Oṃ kundali hūṃ phat.* Scatter twenty-one of the clay peas in the ten directions to remove any obstacles and visualize jewel offerings on the mandala which has been drawn on your seat. Then pray for whatever you want to see in the dream and go to sleep saying this mantra: *Oṃ svapna Tārā svapna avalokini trailokya nirdarshani trailokya vajrirani bhutam bhavaṃ bhavasi shama shubha shuta satyekathaya svāhā* (*Oṃ* Dream Tārā Dream Avalokini, Shower of the Three Worlds, Vajra Queen, the who confers auspicious goodness, tell me the truth). One should recite this mantra either 108 or 21 or 7 times, while making supplication. Even if you recite this mantra one time it will be accomplished. From the sky the Noble Lady will spread a cool ray of light rising from her heart and eliminate all the obscurations from one's tormented heart so that it becomes pure like a cloudless sky. Her hands and arms are strong like an elephant's trunk, spreading nectar and pouring down streams of nectar which fill up one's heart. Through this power one's body becomes very pure like a crystal vessel, cleansed and very beautiful. With a one-pointed and undisturbed mind one should recite the eight syllable mantra *Oṃ Tāre Tu Tāre Ture* to the superb excellent goddess until one falls asleep in the posture of the sleeping lion.

Then, not lacking mindfulness and remembrance, one will see either auspicious or inauspicious dreams, sometimes actually or sometimes through a symbol or through words.

This tantra which was spoken by the Buddha in order to accomplish various activities is called the Great Goddess Examination Accomplishing All Purposes, which you can also call the Dream Tārā. The sādhana of the Dream Tārā was compiled by Chandra Mitra.[77]

These last two rituals attempt to transform one's mind and waking body in order to clear the way for spiritual realization and prophecies through dreams. Both texts emphasize that such dreams are not a given, one must ritually prepare to receive them. Their detailed and elaborate instructions complement the simple dream instructions found in the biographies, and together they confirm a rich legacy of practices and teachings pertaining to dreams in Tibetan Buddhism, a legacy that flourished during the independent period of Buddhist practice typified by the mahāsiddhas and that was later incorporated into institutional practices as well. The presence of dream rituals in both types of Buddhist organizations, independent and institutional, is a testament to the power ascribed to dreams as an aid to spiritual development.

10 *Gender in Indo-Tibetan Dreaming*

THE PRECEDING CHAPTERS have shown that throughout the centuries dreams remained a significant element in Buddhist biographies in a variety of ways. They are often a *deus ex machina*, a revealer of the inevitability of karma, and an important element in shaping the plot line. Dreams reveal an alternative dimension of time and space, one that crosses into the main story in much the same way that dreams cross from sleeping life into waking life. Access to this dimension is a source of spiritual power, either through having significant dreams or being able to accurately interpret dreams, and power is always contested. We have seen several examples of contested dream power between Buddhists and Hindus in folk tales, where each challenges the other's ability to interpret or control dreams (e.g., *Kathāsaritsāgara*, *Jātakas*, *Śārdūlakarṇāvadāna*). A more subtle contest, though, also takes place in terms of gender.

Since the vast majority of Indo-Tibetan biographies are written by and are about men, there is an abundance of material on men's dreams and very little on women's dreams. Within male dream experience, though, we have seen frequent and significant appearances by various females, usually divine ones, and occasionally the dreams of certain women were recorded. These two sources of dream data, men's and women's, reveal some important things about Buddhist perceptions of women's power and powerlessness, and about the male co-optation of that power for male ends and to render women irrelevant. In short, women are free to be powerful in men's imaginations or psychic experiences, but not in social reality.[1] We have seen that when men dream of women they are usually frightening, awe-inspiring, and powerful—for example, the disheveled women who signify death in the epics and medical texts, or the siddhi-bestowing ḍākinīs of the biographies. When women dream they subtly voice a connection to these powerful and possibly dangerous dream women of the male imagination. In several of the texts surveyed here, women's dreams are often a form of protest against something their husbands want to do, something that the men have not actually articulated but which the women are capable of perceiving. Despite the fact that husbands frequently dismiss and denigrate their wives' dreams (the Buddha, Prince Vessantara, Padmasambhava, and Marpa all do so) subsequent events prove women's dreams to be accurate prophecies. Another powerful literary means of denigrating women's dreams is the presentation of women who lie about their dreams in order to achieve their own, usually evil, ends (e.g., jātakas). Briefly stated, there is a pattern in Buddhist biographies of women's true dreams being ignored and their false dreams being acted upon. At the same time, men have positive and empowering dreams about imaginary, often divine women.

WOMEN AND FEMALE DEITIES IN MEN'S DREAMS

A gendered dimension to dreams recorded in Indian texts has existed from the earliest period. This flows naturally out of Vedic cosmology, wherein goddesses are connected with natural elements such as the forests and—of relevance here—the night; thus goddesses are associated with the mysterious and dangerous, darkness, and sleep. This mythology was given a negative turn in the medical texts of ancient India, which interpreted the appearance of women in dreams—particularly women who are disheveled, dressed in red, or dark skinned—as portents of illness and even death.[2] Goddesses such as Durgā and Kālī personify these dream women, as do the many female ghouls, ogresses, and wrathful yoginis of South Asian literature; they are usually depicted as disheveled, with dark skin, and adorned with bloodied body parts, and they have great power, are frightening and unpredictable.[3] Examples of such frightening dream women are found in popular literature as well, such as Valmiki's *Rāmāyaṇa* (composed circa second century B.C.E.), where Trijaṭā, a demoness who is guarding Sītā, has a dream that foretells Rāma's victory over the demons. It is a rather long dream, and one filled with violent imagery, as shown by the following excerpt: "Then, proceeding towards the south, he [Rāvaṇa, the villain] entered a lake where even the mud had dried up and a dark woman clad in red, besmeared with mud, placed a rope round the neck of Dashagiva [Rāvaṇa] dragging him to the region of death."[4] Another dream in the

Rāmāyaṇa is that of Bharata (Rāma's brother), which he has after Rāma has been exiled and his father has died. Part of his dream is as follows: "Thereafter that virtuous monarch [his father], adorned with red garlands, his body daubed with sandal-paste, seated in a chariot drawn by asses, proceeded towards the south. Finally I beheld a woman dressed in red, a female demon of hideous aspect, who, as if in play, was bearing the king away."[5]

These dreams share images of women, the color red, mud, and being dragged toward the south, images that also appear in the *Kathāsaritsāgara* (a famous eleventh-century collection of stories),[6] where King Naravāhanadatta dreams that "he saw his father being dragged away by a black female toward the southern quarter,"[7] and in the *Mahābhārata* (composed circa fifth century B.C.E. to fourth century C.E.), where the dark-skinned goddess Kālī appears in a dream to lead the Pāṇḍava warriors away to their death.[8] I will return to the theme of women and death at the end of this chapter.

In contrast to these frightening dream women, the *Chāndogya Upaniṣad* (circa eighth to sixth century B.C.E.), which is overall a rather favorable text toward women, says seeing a woman in a dream after performing a ritual portends the success of the ritual, suggesting that not all dream images of women are negative.[9] This may represent a more positive view of women held by some early sramanic groups, a view that surfaces in later goddess movements, and especially in Tantra.

The Tibetan tradition also contains negative female images in its medical texts, but, by and large, women (human or divine) and female images (such as the color red)[10] appear frequently in dreams and have a positive connotation, whether as a singular female image or coupled with reciprocal male imagery. A fertile climate for such dreams was created by tantric practices that recommend using the things of this world to achieve enlightenment, including the participation of actual women in rituals as well as female imagery, both benign and frightening. However, real women are for the most part passive and silent participants in the male-centered rituals that are conducted in a covert and secretive fashion.[11] In contrast to these real women, Tantra emphasizes the iconography and visualization of active and powerful ḍākinīs[12] and other female deities, some of whom are distinctly fierce in appearance, dancing wildly and wearing necklaces of human skulls.

The term *ḍākinī* refers to a range of female beings who can be spirit women or historical women who achieved tremendous spiritual power. On rare occasions the term is used to describe a highly advanced living female practitioner. *Ḍākinī* was translated into Tibetan as *mkha' 'gro ma*, which means "sky-goer"—they cross over between realms, that of saṃsāra and nirvāṇa and that of the living and the dead. Consequently, ḍākinīs can confer enlightenment, they can take one beyond death. As we have seen, ḍākinīs frequently appear in dreams of Buddhist heroes, and Nāropa referred to "the place of dreams [as] the mysterious home of the dakinis,"[13] while Geshe Kelsang Gyatso quotes the *Vajradaka Tantra* when discussing their tendency to appear at night:

> The Ladies [ḍākinīs] of these Places
> Bestow siddhis upon practitioners.
> They always come at night,
> They always go at night.[14]

In their oracular dream function they may well be sisters in spirit to the female oracles that were prevalent in pre-Buddhist Tibet.[15]

Ḍākinīs frequently appear in the dreams of Milarepa and his male disciples. Notably, Rechungpa has parallel dreams at the beginning and end of Milarepa's biography in which five ḍākinīs figure prominently. In the beginning of the biography they evoke conception dreams, and at the end they evoke dreams of death portended by the appearance of women. Rechungpa's first dream begins with a woman dressed in red who guides him to the realm of the Buddha Akṣobhya, where he sees "five beautiful young women [wearing] white, blue, yellow, red, and green."[16] These rainbow colors symbolize the ḍākinī's role as a bridge between heavenly and earthly realms. In the first dream the ḍākinīs encourage Rechungpa to ask Milarepa for his life story and at the end of the biography Rechungpa dreams they carry away Milarepa's relics from his cremation cell.[17] These five ḍākinīs refer to the goddess Tseringma, who was converted by Milarepa, and the four female companions who usually accompany her. Tseringma and her companions became protectors of the Buddhist religion, and they made frequent appearances in Milarepa's life.[18] Their role of protecting Buddhist teachings (Milarepa's biography is considered a teaching) requires that they guard or frame the borders of the biography, where they help both to instigate the telling of the biography and to end it.

Ḍākinīs can also be life givers. Tseringma is connected to healing practices—she and her companions are referred to as "the five long-lived sisters."[19] Structurally Rechungpa's first dream occupies the place of conception dreams that usually open Tibetan biographies. In this sense, these five ḍākinīs conceive the biography, at least in Rechungpa's mind.

Similarly, two ḍākinīs appear in another pseudo-conception dream, Dakmema's dream portending Milarepa's arrival to begin his spiritual studies.

In one of Milarepa's dreams he sees "a beautiful ḍākinī"[20] who tells him to ask for teachings on the transference of consciousness to dead bodies (phowa), one of the Six Yogas that prepares adepts to utilize death as a means of salvation. In medieval Tibetan culture there is a continuum of birth, dreaming, death, rebirth, salvation, and women; a continuum that incorporates and yet recasts earlier Indian theories in which seeing a woman in a dream predicts death. And, of course, this continuum is connected to the ḍākinī Niguma, herself a promulgator of the Six Yogas, and probably the ḍākinī in this dream. Indeed, she initiated her most famous disciple, Khyungpo Naljor, into these yogas by appearing in his dreams.[21]

More broadly, ḍākinīs have an important salvational role in that they can bestow siddhis, the supernormal powers that lead to enlightenment. Like Niguma, quite often they bestow these through dreams, as in Marpa's biography. In one dream a ḍākinī appears holding a vase in her hand and says she is a messenger from Maitrīpa, one of Marpa's gurus. She then places the vase on Marpa's head. Marpa awakens from this initiatory dream filled with great joy.[22] In another dream three ḍākinīs appear to Marpa and elaborate on Nāropa's teachings.[23] Marpa's biography also repeats Milarepa's ḍākinī dream about the transference of consciousness, making explicit connections between these two dreams and between these two biographies.

Other examples occur in the life of the great treasure finder Pemalingpa (1450–1521), who was assisted in his work by the many ḍākinīs who appeared to him in dreams[24] as well as by Yeshe Tsogyel, Padmasambhava's consort, who through dreams taught him ritual songs and dances.[25] Additionally, Gampopa's student, Dusum Khyenpa (1110–1193), the first Karmapa, also dreamed of five ḍākinīs, all dressed in red, who on three separate nights warned him to be careful about teaching Dream Yoga.[26]

Appropriately, ḍākinīs, both human and divine, are protectors and teachers of Dream Yoga. In addition to Niguma's lineage of these teachings there is Sukasiddhī, who is sometimes conflated with Niguma.[27] Another important female practitioner and teacher of Dream Yoga was Machig Lapdron (1055–1153).[28]

Vajrayoginī, a female celestial buddha whose pure land is called Ḍākinī Land, is also deeply connected to night and dreams. Her highest yoga tantric practices *(anuttarayoga)* begin at night, with the yoga of sleep, during which practitioners attempt to control their consciousness, to remain alert and mindful during sleep so that, on the one hand, no negative influences will affect their consciousness and, on the other, that ḍākinīs will appear in their dreams to help them with their practice.[29]

Vajrayoginī is the embodiment of transcendent wisdom. She appears to her devotees in dreams and visions in various guises, sometimes as a beautiful young girl, sometimes as an ugly old woman. She appeared to Tilopa[30] and to Nāropa in order to teach them the practices that can lead to enlightenment in one lifetime,[31] part of which involved Dream Yoga. Her appearances can be sudden, wild, and shocking. While Tilopa was studying she appeared in front of him as a dark-skinned, bald woman with a grey mustache, in order to elucidate a text for him.[32]

Other divine females appear as teachers in the dream life of male Buddhist saints: Through a dream the celestial buddha and goddess Tārā instructed Atīśa to go to Tibet, where he had a tremendous influence on the development of Buddhism.[33] In a similar dream, the goddess Palden Lhamo instructed Drukpa Kunley to go to Bhutan and convert the people to Buddhism.[34] Additionally, these divine woman can be actively sought, as in the *Tangyur* dream ritual that invokes the dream presence of Tārā.

These examples point to the theme—well known in world religion and mythology—of male dependence on a female guide[35] in order to complete their quests, win their goal, or achieve enlightenment. Wisdom and insight (prajñā) are feminine terms in South Asian as well as other religious traditions, and they are frequently personified by goddesses or semidivine women whose aid must be won in order to succeed in gaining spiritual knowledge or power.

WOMEN DREAMERS

The dreams of women, however, present a totally different pattern from those of men. To begin with, the most frequently preserved women's dreams in Buddhist biographies are conception dreams.[36] Given that the conception dream of the Buddha's mother, Queen Māyā, is so well known, it is not surprising that such dreams figure prominently in Buddhist biographical literature; indeed they are stereotypical. Overall, conception dreams are a mixed metaphor of passivity and power. In most cases the women are the passive recipients of fetuses—they are after all sound asleep at the time. This passivity is further emphasized by devices such as the "boxes" that are believed to surround the fetuses placed in the wombs of Queen Māyā[37] and Tsongkhapa's mother, thus protecting their male fetuses from the polluting effects of a woman's body. Even so, conception dreams also bespeak primal female powers of generation, suggesting that women do not require men—or at least not human men—in order to conceive. I will return to the theme of maternal power at the end of this chapter.

We have also seen a fairly wide if somewhat ambiguous range of women dreamers. In early Indian literature, whether Buddhist, Hindu, or Jain, an astonishing number of women have prophetic dreams. In some literary texts women are the only dreamers, and they are shown to be important dreamers because their dreams come true. For the most part women are otherwise silent in these texts, so when they are given voice, either by appearing in dreams or by relating their own dreams, it is particularly striking. Although the texts privilege this voice—women's oracular speech is the only female speech given pride of place—their prophetic words are inevitably ignored or manipulated by the men around them.[38]

The second-century C.E. South Indian epic the *Shilappadikaram* is a good example of a text in which the only dreamers are women and they are helpless to prevent the events predicted by their dreams. All the action in this story pivots around the dreams of two women, that of the heroine Kannaki and that of the queen of the city that Kannaki will eventually destroy. In book 1, Kannaki's husband has left her for a beautiful courtesan. When someone expresses the hope that her husband will return Kannaki answers: "He may come back, but my trials will not end. I had a fearful dream. The two of us were walking hand in hand toward a vast city. Some people told a lie, so that Kovalan [her husband] was accused of a crime. When I heard it, I felt as if I had been bitten by a scorpion. I ran to the king, and threatened him and his city with disaster."[39]

Shortly after the recital of this dream, Kannaki's husband returns, and they move to another city, "impelled by fate that had devised for ages past their final destiny."[40] This fate, or karma, was revealed in Kannaki's dream. In book 2 tragedy has struck and, due to a misunderstanding, Kannaki's husband has been executed. Now the queen of the city where his execution took place also has a frightening dream: "Alas! I saw, in a dream, a scepter bent, a fallen parasol. The bell at the gate moved of itself and rang loudly. Alas! I also saw...I saw the eight directions of space wavering, the night devouring the sun. Alas! I also saw...I saw the rainbow shining in the night, a glittering star falling by day. Alas!"[41]

The queen interprets the dream herself and says that what she has seen "are portents of a fearful danger at hand." As soon as she relates this dream to her husband the king, Kannaki shows up. As the king listens to her dream, its fulfillment begins: "He [the king] felt his parasol fallen, his scepter bent."[42] In the end, both the king and the queen die and their city is destroyed.

In this text the power of dreams to affect waking life is dramatically presented. When these two prophetic dreamers meet, the connections between their dreams are made explicit and the dire consequences they predict are confirmed and begin to manifest in the waking realm.

This is a very dramatic presentation of the power of two female dreamers, a power that completely contrasts with their more usual lack of power in waking life. In several other texts we have considered, many women have the psychic power (through dreaming) to predict what will happen, and yet they remain helpless to avert disaster. Indeed, when they voice their concerns and fears by telling their dreams, men often dismiss the dreams outright or deny the woman's ability to interpret them. While it is true that in literary texts certain dreams can be useful plot devices, especially because certain dreams are believed to reveal the inevitable unfolding of karma, the consistent use of women as passive dreamers and men as active interpreters reveals a familiar gender ideology.

As mentioned, in several texts the authority to interpret dreams was shown to be contested ground between Buddhists and Hindus, most obviously in the Pali jātakas, where Brahmans are portrayed as inadequate and even corruptible interpreters; in the *Śārdūlakarṇāvadāna,* where a Brahman tests a Buddhist king's knowledge of dream interpretation; and in the *Kathāsaritsāgara,* where authoritative knowledge of dream consciousness shifts between Buddhist and Hindu religious experts. Similarly, in many biographical texts dream interpretation is contested in terms of gender: women dream, but men interpret.[43] As we have seen, the ability to correctly interpret dreams is a tremendous source of spiritual and temporal power because while everyone can dream, only a few people truly understand their dreams. What sets dream interpreters apart is their ability to grasp the whole of reality; they can understand and function within the waking and sleeping worlds, within the real and the illusory. Men acknowledge women's power to access dream realms when they listen to their dreams, but through their interpretations men subvert that power and make sure that it does not translate into the waking world.[44]

For the most part the dreams we have just seen are preserved in literary texts; often they function to shift the action, to set the stage for an inevitable outcome. In them dreaming is a passive, unheroic form of acting, that is best performed by a woman (or a junior male), and it is a way to harness female power and keep it and women in their place.[45] When Buddhist heroes dream, however, they reveal their internalization of this female power and at the same time maintain their power as dream interpreters. In all the South Asian texts I have surveyed, the authoritative voice of dream interpretation is a male one.[46]

In Buddhism the pattern of men interpreting the dreams of their wives begins with the Buddha's biography. In the *LV* the Buddha's wife Gopā awakens from a nightmare and asks the Buddha what it means. It is a long dream, and the Buddha gives it an equally long and detailed interpretation before telling her his own dream and its interpretation. Several things are going on in this exchange, not the least of which is the Buddha affirming male access to the dream realm both as dreamer and interpreter. As already noted above, it is also an important moment in the development of Buddhist dream interpretation in that he rejects prevailing Brahmanical interpretations. At the same time the Buddha must reject the obvious meaning of the dream, Gopā's loss of her husband and the kingdom's loss of an heir, if he is to go forth into the religious life. Gopā's dream accurately describes the emotional consequences of his desertion; she sees the whole earth shaken and herself naked, with her hair, hands, and feet cut off. The Buddha's dismissal of her fears and his interpretation undermine her prophetic powers and silence her protest: "Be joyful, these dreams are not evil. Beings who have previously practiced good works have such dreams. Miserable people have no such dreams.... The omens are auspicious." Yet, when compared to the only nightmare in the same text (Māra's), line for line the imagery is the same.[47]

The Buddha's dismissal of his wife's dream is repeated in the *AS* and the *MSV*, the other main texts in which it appears. In fact, in the *MSV* his wife extracts a promise from him to take her wherever he goes. Of course, he does not take her with him, and the text glosses this as meaning he promised to take her along to nirvāṇa.[48] This process is even repeated in the very popular *Vessantara Jātaka*, a past life story in which the Buddha and Gopā are called Vessantara and Maddi. In this tale Maddi has a prophetic dream that reveals her husband will give their children away. When she asks him to interpret it, he dismisses it, attributing it to indigestion, and the text goes so far as to say: "with this deceit *[mohetvā]* he consoled her." Of course, the next day he gives the children away.[49]

In both these dream narrations the wives fearfully present their dreams—they know they bode ill. In speaking their fears these women are attempting to deflect the dream's influence and protesting (at least intuitively) their husbands' power to bring disaster upon them. Even though we have seen many examples of rituals to offset the harmful effects of dreams, in these scenarios they are not used because the men want the dreams to be fulfilled. In this way the texts present women as powerful dreamers, as capable of receiving prophetic dreams, but at the same time the texts underline their actual powerlessness: the women cannot avert the fulfillment of their dreams. They do not even resort to widely available ritual means to do so.

It is clear that these women know what is going on, what is going to happen, and they voice their fears and their protest in the only acceptable way they can, through their dreams. Like women in trance, they are not ultimately responsible for their words; dream narrations are a safe way to protest male authority over their lives.[50] Hence the consistent pattern of women who dream, who fully understand the meaning of their dreams, and yet who ask their husbands to interpret them is shown to be a way of obliquely having direct discourse with their husbands. For instance, this pattern is also maintained around conception dreams when the wife who dreams asks her husband what it means. This is actually a roundabout way of getting their husbands to affirm paternity or to approve the pregnancy. However, when the men dismiss their dreams, or interpret them in ways favorable to what they want, women are ultimately silenced and returned to the background of male drama.

Two Tibetan texts parallel this theme. In Padmasambhava's biography, the early parts of which are carefully modeled on the life of the Buddha, his wife, Bhāśadharā, also has prophetic dreams before he too deserts her to become a monk. She dreams that the earth shook, her hair was shorn, and she lost a tooth. When she asks him to interpret it, he too dismisses it, saying, "sleep silently *[kha rog nyol]*."[51] The same pattern occurs in Milarepa's biography, albeit in a dream about an arrival rather than a departure. This is when Dakmema dreams that Milarepa is coming to study with Marpa. Here the pattern is similar to the Buddha's in that Marpa dismisses his wife's dream, although he later admits (to Milarepa, not to Dakmema) it was a true one, and Marpa himself has a prophetic dream. So, like the Buddha, Marpa takes over his wife's dream powers, and he himself dreams. Marpa can afford to remain silent about his own dream because he does not need indirect means of communication; he is in full command of his life, his wife's life, and the lives of his disciples.

Dakmema and Marpa's dreams, as well as those of Gopā and the Buddha, also suggest a gendered pattern to shared dreaming. As we saw in chapter 6, the shared dream in South Asia is most often that of a man and a woman each dreaming of the other, usually in a romantic context. I have not found such romantic tales in a Buddhist context, but shared dreams between men and women do exist, as in these two examples. Though the content of the dreams is different, they are understood to be about the same event, and they occur on the same night. Marpa's and Dakmema's shared dreams are gendered both in terms of the dream images and the gender of the dreamers. It is Dakmema who dreams of two females (the ḍākinīs) carrying a stūpa, while Marpa dreams of his male guru, who gives him a vajra.

This pattern of female-male dream-sharing falls away in the rest of the biographies I have looked at, in the main because they have been about celibate men, though sometimes mothers and fathers of a saint will have conception dreams or dreams of their child before birth. And, while female dreamers continue to appear, mainly as mothers having conception dreams, it is male dreamers who come to the fore. This suggests a pattern of Tibetan men gradually internalizing female dreaming abilities, which is shown in part by the frequent and powerfully transformative appearances of women and female deities in male dreams. In large part the biographies of tantric practitioners focus on receiving spiritual instruction and initiations from living male gurus and from nonliving female deities through dreams and visions. Tibetan Buddhism created an environment that valorized such experiences through its vivid works of art depicting ḍākinīs and other female deities, through visualization practices focused on female deities, and through stories about past masters who had received such visitations. In these and other ways, male practitioners rejected or at least limited their contact with actual women while they actively pursued wish-fulfilling female phantoms.

Returning to the texts in which women dream, in all the examples discussed thus far, women dreamers possess the ability to prophesy, which is a kind of power, and one deemed important and acceptable enough to provide major plot shifts. But both the male denial of the dreams and their eventual fulfillment (to the frustration of the female dreamer) totally coopts this female power, thus representing woman as powerless dreamers and interpreters. Despite all this, these incidents tacitly acknowledge women's power to invade men's dreams as well as women's ability to intuit men's intentions through their own dreams, and to voice that intuition without fear of repercussion. That dreams are believed to be a special female weapon against men is demonstrated by stories of women lying about their dreams or using dreams for deceptive and manipulative ends. Examples of this have been seen in the *Kuṇala Jātaka,* where a co-queen bribes a Brahman dream interpreter to deny the auspiciousness of the favorite queen's dream, and in the *Chaddanta Jātaka,* where the queen lies about having a dream in order to harm the Buddha.

A particularly chilling example of a woman's destructive manipulation of dreaming occurs in the *Aśokāvadāna,* discussed in chapter 3, in which Emperor Aśoka's dream about the blinding of his son is physically stimulated by his ill-intentioned wife, Queen Tiṣyarakṣitā. Since Aśoka sealed all his urgent orders by biting down on them, Tiṣyarakṣitā needs the imprint of his teeth on the letter that will doom his son. Here, in very evil guise, we see woman's role as stimulator of male dreams, but in this case the woman is outside the dream, even though she all too clearly symbolizes women as evil portents within a dream. While such passages represent women as powerless and silent in waking life, in the dream world, when men are asleep and defenseless, women are perceived as all powerful. This inversion of social reality contrasts with the inability of women dreamers to act effectively to prevent the outcome of their dreams and accentuates the perniciousness of Queen Tiṣyarakṣitā's ability to act effectively, as she repeatedly tries to get Aśoka to bite down on the letter while he sleeps. The truth is that women have uncontrolled access to sleeping men, both physically and psychically—an idea captured iconographically in sculptures of Viṣṇu dreaming, which show his devoted wife massaging his feet while he sleeps (see figure 5).

During dreams boundaries between time and space, reality and illusion, sleeping and waking, all shift and even melt away, as does the individual integrity of the dreamer. Indeed we have even seen several dramatic examples of shared dreams in which two or more people have the same dream on the same night. We already know that traditional South Asians, both women and men, have a broad sense of self that includes family members, past lives, invisible beings, and so on. From the dream material we have examined so far, however, it appears that when women dream their personal boundaries include others, whereas men, for the most part, retain sharper dream boundaries. When a women sees herself in a dream, the self that she sees often represents someone else, for example, her child or husband. One example of this is found by contrasting Maddi's dream about the loss of her children with that of Aśoka. Two of Aśoka's three dreams are about injuries to his son, and only the third dream is about injury to Aśoka himself, while Maddi's dream in the *Vessantara Jātaka* is entirely about violence done to her person. Similarly, in the *Bhūridatta Jātaka* a mother dreams about the destruction of her own body when her son is captured by hunters. Other examples include all the dreaming wives we have touched upon: the Buddha's wife, Padmasambhava's wife, and the two women in the *Shilappadikaram.* That women were understood to have more porous dream boundaries than men no doubt reflects their waking social roles, especially the usual marriage arrangement in India whereby a woman marries out of her natal home and village into that of strangers: the home of her husband's family. Several scholars have noted Indian women's sense of being split between two homes,[52] of having their boundaries challenged and being spread thin by the need to intuit the wishes of two families, one of which is unfamiliar to them. It is this porousness, though—this weakness of boundaries, if you will—that becomes the source of women's power in dreams, both to penetrate other people's dreams (mainly men's) by appearing in them and to be penetrated in their own dreams by men's intentions.

Before going further, two related points about the Indo-Tibetan Buddhist biographical tradition need to be restated. First, it is dominated by men as subjects and as authors. Thus all representations of women are filtered through male experience.[53] Second, they do not strive to be factual representations of someone's life; rather, they present (and interpret) the events that lead to an individual's enlightenment, including visions and dreams. Whether or not the dreams actually occurred is unknowable. What we can know about these dreams is that they are examples of what male Buddhists thought about dreams and, of relevance to this chapter, what they thought about women. These ideas then seeped into the general consciousness of the societies where these stories were read, recited, and retold.

At the same time, at root here is the male dismissal of actual, living women, especially from the lives of monastics, and the internalization of imaginary women, including the co-optation of women's imaginary process in dreaming. This goes back to Tantra's incorporation of female imagery and female deities and the distancing of actual women. Some women were participants in tantric rites, but these practices do not represent a union of equals; for the most part they were marginal women, who were silent participants and sworn to secrecy. The few exceptions, such as the biography of Yeshe Tsogyel, a document of questionable historical accuracy, only serve to emphasize the rarity of biographies about female practitioners when compared to the innumerable biographies of male practitioners.

The biographies we have examined admit the dreams of women when they are deceptive and dismiss them when they are truthful, yet at the same time they report many male dreams in which women grant men spiritual power. In other words, male Buddhists render actual women irrelevant, meaningless and powerless, while they empower the imaginary women of their dreams. In effect, in one motion, male Buddhists both co-opt women's subjectivity for themselves and deny the subjectivity of real women.[54]

DREAMS, DEATH, AND WOMEN

Perhaps the most inauspicious imaging of women is in relation to death, a topic also connected to dreaming. Until fairly recent times there was an almost universal belief in the ability of dreams to predict death, a notion that persists among a great variety of people. In South Asia this connection is easily understood when we recall that certain dreams were an accepted sign of death in both medical texts and in epic literature. As we have seen, language itself conflates dreams, sleep, and death in the Sanskrit root √*svap*, which can mean "to sleep" and "to be dead" and is also the root for the noun "dream." In Tibet, the practice of Dream Yoga is said to give one entry into the bardo state between death and rebirth. And, of course, people around the world often dream about the dead, leading to the idea that through dreams we can access the realm of the dead and conversely that death can access us through dreams. Additionally, many people believe that the soul leaves the body during sleep as it does in death, which is why caution must be used in waking a sleeper,[55] and a sleeping body can just as easily be mistaken for a dead body. A famous Buddhist example that plays with this idea is found in the biographies of the Buddha where, on the night of his departure from home, he observes the sleeping women of the harem, leading him to the reflection that he is living in the middle of a cremation ground *(śmaśana).*[56]

As already mentioned above, Hesiod says that Night is the mother of all three: Sleep, Death, and Dreams.[57] Sleep and dreams know death in a way that waking consciousness does not because in crossing over the boundaries of waking consciousness, they are believed to draw close to the netherworld. This point is brought out in the *Bṛhadāraṇyaka Upaniṣad* where the discussion of dreams and sleep inevitably leads to the discussion of death (4.3.13–38 and 4.4).

Examples of women's association with death abound in early Buddhist literature,[58] and we have seen many examples, both in ancient Indian medical texts and in Indian epics and folk tales, where women figure prominently in dreams that predict death, especially women who are dark skinned, who wear red or carry red flowers, who are wild in appearance, or who are strong enough to drag someone away to the south, to the land of the dead. This is actually a description of the goddess of death, Mṛtyu, "a black woman with red garments and red eyes,"[59] as well as of Kālī.

Some of these negative images survive in Tibetan dream narrations,[60] but for the most part they were incorporated into tantric practices that purposely utilized death imagery—for instance, the frequent recommendation to live and meditate in cremation grounds. In earlier dream interpretation death imagery was to be feared. In Tantric Buddhism, confronting and overcoming the fear of death is part of the practice leading to enlightenment. Once the tantric adept has truly realized the impermanence of all existence, the essential emptiness of all phenomena, there is nothing more to fear. In this way the tantric incorporation of female imaging of death can be seen as a positive valuing of the feminine, in that women, through their connection to death, can lead one to enlightenment.[61] Yet, this heroic co-optation of frightening female imagery never really leaves the control of men, nor ever really advances the lives of actual women. These dream women may terrify male practitioners, but the men are being trained to overcome that fear. In effect, female imagery is used to conquer a fear of female power.[62]

There are many complicated ideas about, and associations between, women, death, and enlightenment in Indo-Tibetan literature. The goal of Tantric Buddhism is to achieve liberation from the endless cycle of being born and dying through ritual techniques and practices that utilize the human body. However, it appears that the female body, at least when utilized by men through actual or symbolic practices, is particularly useful in achieving this end. At the same time, different types of literature gender dreams differently. The ritual texts of the *Tangyur* and *Kangyur*, except for the one dedicated to Tārā, emphasize seeing the male body of the buddhas, while the biographies have no such dreams of buddhas—instead they have frequent dreams of female bodies in the form of ḍākinīs. A third genre of literature, medical texts, holds that dreams about women and the color red predict death. This association of women and death exists in many cultures through women's biological connection to birth, which inevitably leads to death; through menstruation, where the shedding of blood does not kill the menstruating woman but can threaten men with its power, usually its polluting power; and through the dominant role of women in death rituals.[63] On the positive side, associating the female with death frequently means associating females with immortality. This is to suggest that female forces have control over life and death to such a degree that they can free one from death. Some symbolical examples of this thinking are reflected in the skull necklaces of ḍākinīs and the word *padmabhājana* (lotus vessel), which is used, for example in the *Hevajra Tantra*, for both vaginas and skulls.[64] Either actually or symbolically, vaginas and skulls, the feminine and death, are essential for the tantric rituals that lead to enlightenment.

Returning to women's ability to give birth, women are also seen as the source of their husband's immortality because they provide the sons so essential to the continuation of ancestor worship.[65] This complex of related ideas reveals the connection between the negative appearances of dream women in medical texts and the positive conception dreams of real women in the biographical literature: women can dream us all into existence and when we dream of them they call us back to death. Tantric dream practices obliquely acknowledge these beliefs when they transform such female dream imagery into siddhi-conferring ḍākinīs, women who call one to enlightenment. Examples of this can be seen in the presence of the five ḍākinīs who begin and end Milarepa's biography, as well as in Dakmema's dream and in Milarepa's dream of a ḍākinī telling him to learn more about death. It also brings us back to the *Tangyur* text that used the consecrated milk of a nursing mother as an eye ointment to procure dreams. Mother's milk is the most positive, life-enhancing female image imaginable in a climate that associates women with death.[66] The use of this milk affirms the need for a female guide through the dream realm that hovers between life and death, because it is women who successfully traverse this realm *for others* biologically, and by extension spiritually. Putting a mother's milk on the eyelids enables one to see with the eyes of this primal female power and assures one's return to waking life.

Conclusions

In this study of dreams in Indo-Tibetan Buddhist biographies I have traced several themes over almost two thousand years of Buddhist history: (1) dreams are a significant part of Buddhist belief; (2) they are an accepted mode of cognition in Indo-Tibetan Buddhism; (3) control of dream cognition establishes religious authority; (4) some dreams, mainly those of and about heroes, confer charisma; and (5) dreams, through their prophetic role in Buddhist sacred biography, maintain continuity with the early Indian tradition while also contributing innovations in belief and practice. For the most part, I have let the biographies speak for themselves, though I have supplied corroborating evidence from a variety of philosophical, medical, ritual, and other texts. I have also tried to suggest some of the intricacies of the innovative function of dreams in terms of the routinization and genderization of Buddhist dream narratives. The inclusion of nonbiographical texts in this study has served both to broaden it and to allow an analysis of both elite and popular views about dreaming.

I have presented an assortment of textual evidence for Buddhism's incorporation of indigenous dream practices. The elite tradition accepted popular beliefs about dreams and dream practices because these assist believers along the path to enlightenment—and because the illusory nature of dreams serves as a prime example of emptiness. In Tantric Buddhism, whatever works is incorporated into practice, and dreams work in these various ways.

From a historical perspective, the new religious movements of Buddhism and Jainism brought about a shift away from early Indian dream theory mainly because they had founders about whom they wrote biographies in which the founders had dreams and others dreamed about them. In contrast to these two movements, Brahmanical Hinduism had no founders, did not emphasize biography, and dreams do not play a primary role in the lives of its later heroes. In Buddhism, from the biographies of the Buddha onward, the persistent focus on the life of an individual as both a model for the Buddhist experience and a source of inspiration led to the valorization of their internal and external experiences, including their dreams and the dreams of the major people in their lives.

Dream interpretation is usually part of any dream narrative, so it was included in the biographies. I have highlighted some of the issues concerning the religious authority to interpret dreams. For instance, Buddhist dream interpretation begins with the biographical literature of the Buddha—the Buddha interpreted his own and his wife's dreams, and the dreams that his family members had on the night of his departure are also interpreted. We have also seen examples of Buddhists contesting the views of Brahmanical dream interpreters. Within the Buddhist community, dream interpretation was also found to be a loaded issue, when husbands (such as the Buddha and Prince Vessantara) deceived their wives about the meaning of their dreams. Truthful dreams were purposely *mis*interpreted so the men could achieve their ends. This tradition of misinterpretation or dismissal of important dreams continued in the Tibetan biographies—for example, in the account of Dakmema's dream and Marpa's dismissal of it. We have also seen instances of gurus attempting to control the dream life of their disciples through their interpretations. Granted that the goals pursued by the means of disinforming through dreams, in the case of women, or reshaping the unconscious minds of disciples, have a fine end in sight—that of enlightenment, they also demonstrate a very inconsistent pattern of dream interpretation in Buddhism. We have also found other inconsistencies in the canonical dream manuals, as well as inconsistencies between the manuals and the dream interpretations preserved in the biographies. Although Tibetan Buddhism has a science of consciousness in relation to dreams, especially in the various practices of Dream Yoga, it remains wide open in terms of interpretation. Clearly Indo-Tibetan dream interpretation was and remains as subjective as dreaming itself.

Despite these inconsistencies, and despite the fact that dreams never fully escaped their role as a significant example of the illusory nature of reality, Tibetan Buddhism enhanced and developed the dream beliefs and practices of early Indian Buddhism. It accepted the prophetic possibilities of dreams and the belief that dreams can give the dreamer access to other realms and confer spiritual accomplishments, but it also actively explored the spiritual potential of the dream realm—culminating in Dream Yoga—

and it created copious literary records of the prophetic value of dreams and of various rituals to stimulate or counteract dreams. With the development of Mahāyāna and Vajrayāna, in other words, dream experience became increasingly incorporated into Buddhist spiritual practice. Correspondingly, given the increased role of females in the rhetoric of Vajrayāna as well as in its iconography and visualization practices, there is a marked increase of females and female imagery in male dreams. These last two points surface in the work of and the stories surrounding the great mahāsiddha Nāropa, whose teachings were spread by the Kagyu order.

This study has demonstrated the persistence and elaboration of dreams in Indo-Tibetan Buddhism as a source of prophecy, spiritual instruction, and religious innovation along with attempts to routinize their innovative function. I have demonstrated my general thesis, that dream practices increased during and after the period of the mahāsiddhas, by dividing the dream narratives of the Indian and Tibetan biographies into the categories of continuities and innovations. By doing so I have shown that dream narratives became more frequent and took on new functions, even though the basic types of dreams remained constant.

My task was made somewhat easier due to the proliferation of sacred biography as a genre of Tibetan literature. As has been shown, these texts foreground dreams and give them a full, though informal, treatment. For instance, I have shown that dream narratives are essential to the overall structure of Milarepa's main biography and they also play an important part in several of the stories contained in the *Mgur 'bum*, especially those relating to the transmission and continuation of the Kagyu lineage. All the elements of dream narratives found in the Buddha's biographies are present here: conception dreams and shared dreams, dreams revealing spiritual accomplishments, and formidable dream interpretation—despite the fact that Milarepa's biography differs significantly from the Buddha's in at least two important ways: it pointedly emphasizes Milarepa's human origins, and, second, it emphasizes the guru-disciple relationship (which is completely absent from the Buddha's biography).

The Milarepa texts also delineate innovations in dream narratives and attribute some of them directly to Nāropa. First, in various circumstances but especially when a prophecy is required, dreams are *sought*. Of course, the spontaneous dream persists, but the sequence of events in the earlier tradition was that someone dreams, then the dream is interpreted, and later events fulfill the dreams. In the sought dreams, however, the sequence of events is that first an issue develops, then the dreamer announces the intention to dream in order to resolve the issue, then he relates and interprets his dream, and, finally, later events fulfill the dream. The progression from spontaneous dream to sought dream is a reasonable development: If one accepts the prophetic value of dreams in general, then whether the dreams occur spontaneously or as the result of consciously setting out to have a dream, one still receives a prophecy. Obviously, the sought dream received additional stimulation from the second innovation, Dream Yoga, a practice that advocates the purposeful control of the dreaming consciousness to further spiritual awareness. The practitioner of this yoga must consciously seek to have dreams—not just wait for the spontaneous appearance of a dream—in order to have the dream experiences that are essential to this practice. This led me to explore more formal dream practices as they were presented in philosophical and ritual texts. The third innovation in dream material is the dream in which the hero receives spiritual instructions from a ḍākinī, which was shown to be part of an ideology of gender in Buddhist dreaming. Dream narratives of this kind are not found in the biographical literature of the Buddha.

Some early biographies say that the Buddha fathered himself by choosing to generate himself into his mother's womb through a dream, and they assert that his five great dreams generated the Buddhist path by awakening his consciousness and the Eightfold Path within him. As I suggested in my discussion of his dreams—and of Queen Māyā's dream, so prominent in textual and iconographic representations of the life of the Buddha—there would be no Buddha and no Buddhism without dreams.

Appendix: Lucid Dreaming

TODAY MANY WESTERNERS are interested in the Tibetan practice of Dream Yoga, and I have often been asked if it is like lucid dreaming. My answer is yes and no, in large part depending on what is meant by lucid dreaming and what is meant by Dream Yoga. In the broadest sense—the control of dreams—the two are similar, in the same way that they are similar to the incubation dreams of the ancient world and the consciously sought dreams of shamans. To consciously choose to dream before going to sleep, and to attempt to shape the events and content of the dream, are elements of both modern lucid dreaming as described by Stephen LaBerge[1] and Dream Yoga. The context, content, method, and aim of these two practices remain totally different, however.[2] And they certainly have very different histories.[3]

One of the most interesting sources for lucid dreaming is Kilton Stewart,[4] a colorful American from a Mormon family who first made an appearance in Southeast Asia in the 1930s as an attractive, personable, and engaging young man. Casting around for a future, he decided to become an anthropologist, the high point of his studies being the Senoi, an aboriginal people of northern Malaysia. He did not know their language, though he probably had an able translator in a government field ethnographer, H. D. Noone, who arranged his first visit. This took place in 1934 and lasted about sixteen days. Returning to Europe, he underwent a brief Rankian psychoanalysis in Paris and reinvented himself as a psychoanalyst. In 1938 he made a second trip to the Senoi, this time lasting seven weeks. Once again he was accompanied by Noone, who was himself working on Senoi dreams. The information collected on this trip later provided the data for his dissertation in anthropology, "Magico-Religious Beliefs and Practices in

Primitive Society—a Sociological Interpretation of Their Therapeutic Aspects." Before he completed his degree, however, World War II intervened, and he was shipped back to the United States where he set himself up as a psychoanalyst in New York City. In 1946 he returned to Europe and registered at the London School of Economics, where he was awarded a Ph.D. in 1948.

Stewart's claims in his dissertation are markedly more modest than those he made in his later articles, which describe Senoi teachings on the control of dreams and discussions of dreams at tribal councils and informal morning groups—none of which has been corroborated by other, more professionally trained, anthropologists.[5] Stewart's methods of collecting dream data were not consistent, and those collected under the influence of hypnosis are particularly questionable. Significantly, several of the claims of his later articles are not to be found anywhere in the dissertation, and he made no later trips among the Senoi. In all fairness, he may have had field material he did not put into his dissertation, but this seems unlikely especially in the face of other deceptions. For instance, in his later articles he exaggerated his professional status and the amount of time he spent among the Senoi. He also altered his data, emphasizing how children are guided by adults to change fearful dreams of falling into joyful dreams of flying—yet only four of the 228 Senoi dreams he collected are flying dreams, and three of these are fearful dreams. He presented data that not only do not exist in the dissertation but actually fly in the face of the dreams he recorded in the 1930s. In other words, Stewart made it up.

In his later articles Stewart described how the Senoi publicly tell their dreams every morning, taking the time to resolve any dream conflicts that occurred with tribal members before setting about the day's business.[6] He represented the Senoi as a conflict-free society and attributed this to (1) their daily dream sharing and (2) their ability to become lucid in their dreams, which enabled them to control dream events and contents in ways that enhance self esteem and promote social harmony.

Stewart was an idealistic advocate for individual human development leading to a utopian harmony.[7] In the 1960s the Esalen Institute in California, one of the more influential institutions of the human potential movement, picked up Stewart's theories and incorporated them into its program. From there Stewart's ideas were promulgated in a series of influential books and articles that captured the imagination and hopes of a generation dissatisfied with Western values.[8] Corroboration of Stewart's findings were proffered by Patricia Garfield, who said she had studied Senoi dream practices and interviewed tribal members. In fact, she spent two days in Malaysia and interviewed a few Senoi employees at a hospital far from any real tribal life, and these interviews were conducted through a chain of interpreters speaking English to Malay, and then Malay to Senoi. However, her bald claims of expertise were accepted.[9]

William Domhoff summarizes the appeal of this theory:

> Paradoxical as it may sound, I think that Senoi dream theory had a deep appeal for Americans at this time because it was a new application of our deepest and most ingrained beliefs about human nature presented in the context of an allegorical story about community and authenticity. Very simply, the "Senoi way of dreaming" actually rests on the unquestioned American belief in the possibility of shaping and controlling both the environment and human nature. For Americans, but not for most people, and certainly not for the Senoi, human nature is malleable and perfectible. We are what we make ourselves. We can do it if we try. Senoi dream theory is an extension of that basic precept to the world of dreams. The fact that it is unwittingly presented in a mystique of the primitive only makes it all the more attractive. It is independent evidence for our convictions.[10]

I would like to add that the "wisdom and mystery of the East" plays as effective a role in Western self-deception as does Domhoff's "mystique of the primitive," and that it is equally wrongheaded to look to Tibetan Buddhism for confirmation of American idealism. Having said this, I would like to elaborate upon the ways that Dream Yoga and lucid dreaming differ in their context, content, method and aim.

Context. Dream Yoga: spiritual advancement takes place in a culturally and religiously supportive environment with at least a thousand-year history of such practice. Lucid dreaming: practitioners work in isolation or in recently formed dream groups, sometimes under the supervision of a trained psychologist, often not.

Content. Dream Yoga: practitioners share Buddhist imagery with very specific meaning. Lucid dreaming: dream content and meaning are often highly individualized.

Method. Dream Yoga: practitioners work with a guru and radically alter their lifestyle by taking religious vows, forming an intention to achieve the religious goal of enlightenment, and, often, living apart from others for years. Lucid dreaming: practitioners work with an experienced lucid dreamer or simply read a book on the subject.[11] As mentioned, the methods of Dream Yoga and lucid dreaming are similar in their use of self-suggestion. In both, an attempt is made to control dream content by concentrating on what one wants to dream about before going to sleep, and, once asleep and in a dream state, one attempts to remain lucid and maintain something like a waking consciousness in order to control the events of the dream. For instance, in lucid dreaming, if you dream you are being chased by a bear, you may want to stop running and confront the bear in order to conquer your fear. (This example points to the fact that often one becomes lucid during nightmares or anxiety dreams, dreams that are excluded from traditional Dream Yoga practices.)[12] Two final methodological differences are that lucid dreaming may begin when awake, and in Buddhism the time of nights one dreams is important.[13]

Aim. Dream Yoga: the goal is spiritual advancement, reduction of attachment to earthly pleasures, and, ultimately, dissolution of the notion of an enduring self or world. Lucid dreaming: the goal is realizing earthly pleasures and maintaining attachment to them—for instance, achieving sexual orgasm[14]—or attaining other psychological or practical benefits that enhance the sense of self. Although lucid dreaming can be used for spiritual practice, its broad usage and its existential base set it apart from Dream Yoga.

In the same year that Domhoff published *The Mystique of Dreams* (1985) the psychophysiologist Stephen LaBerge published his influential book, *Lucid Dreaming.*[15] Of course, nothing in LaBerge's training really prepared him for understanding religious phenomena with the same professionalism that he brings to his own field, nor does he seem to have been trained in textual analysis or the languages of the cultures he combs for evidence of lucid dreaming. Unfortunately, his enthusiasm leads him to misconstrue much of the nonscientific evidence he uncovers. For instance, he assumes the dream activities of eighth-century Tibetans are exactly the same as his.[16] They are not. We have already seen the importance of understanding the dreamer's cultural context,[17] and certainly knowing the language of the dreamer is essential to any understanding of dreams. As has been shown in the discussion of "seeing" a dream versus "having" a dream, linguistic clues are quite important for what they reveal about the dreamer's understanding of and relationship to dreams.

LaBerge not only describes lucid dreaming but advocates its practice; his book is a "how to" guide. He utilizes whatever comes to hand, though he seems to be particularly attracted to Buddhist practices. But he seems to belong in the direct line of idealistic teachings about dreams that starts with

Stewart and passes through the Esalen Institute and its heirs. "What is needed [he says] is unprecedented vision: both to avoid the abysmal catastrophe of nuclear war, and to find the path to true humanity. With the future to gain, and nothing to lose, we shouldn't fear to take our heads out of the sand and into the dream, for dreams may have much to contribute here (for example, novel and creative solutions not thought of during waking life)."[18]

One might wish for more direct action in coping with modern social problems, but there is certainly nothing reprehensible in this idealism. However, his combination of wholesale co-optation and trivialization of Asian religious teachings is disturbing. Of course, LaBerge is on unfamiliar ground when it comes to esoteric Asian thought, but mockery is a poor substitute for his scholarship. For instance, after describing Bhagwan Shree Rajneesh as "an unworldly guru with sixty-two Rolls-Royces," he lists three of Rajneesh's techniques for lucid dreaming. He says the last one

> is simple enough if you happen to be the obsessive type. [Rajneesh] advises the would-be lucid dreamer to 'try to remember for three weeks continuously that whatsoever you are doing is just a dream.' In my view, anyone who could remember anything at all for three weeks continuously ought to be able to do practically [sic] anything! For such a talented person, lucid dreaming should present little difficulty.[19]

I have no interest in defending Rajneesh or his automobiles or the purported obsessiveness of his or any other spiritual discipline. The purpose of such a jocular tone is to have us all share a laugh instead of trying to understand Asian dream practices. When these practices are seriously studied, they reveal significant differences to lucid dreaming.

Notes

Chapter 1

1 See, for instance, Barbara Tedlock, ed., *Dreaming: Anthropological and Psychological Interpretations* (Cambridge: Cambridge University Press, 1987); and G. E. von Grunebaum and Robert Caillois, eds., *The Dream and Human Societies* (Berkeley: University of California Press, 1966).

2 See the classical study of Native American dreaming by Jackson Steward Lincoln, *The Dream in Primitive Cultures* (1935; New York: Johnson Reprint, 1970); and the more recent typology of Native American dreams, Lee Irwin, *The Dream Seekers: Native American Visionary Traditions of the Great Plains* (Norman: University of Oklahoma Press, 1994).

3 For more examples of conception dreams see Otto Rank, *The Myth of the Birth of the Hero,* reprinted in *In Quest of the Hero,* ed. Robert A. Segal (Princeton: Princeton University Press, 1990); for some Christian examples see Lisa M. Bitel, "*In Visu Noctis:* Dreams in European Hagiography and Histories, 450–900," *History of Religion* 31, no. 1 (August 1991): 52.

4 For example, see C. G. Jung, "The Practical Use of Dream-Analysis," reprinted in C. G. Jung, *Dreams,* trans. R. F. C. Hull (Princeton: Princeton University Press, 1990), pp. 89–90, 98–99, 106–8.

5 Ibn Hisham 'Abd al-Malik, *The Life of Muhammad,* trans. A. Guillaume (Karachi: Oxford University Press, 1955), pp. 105, 106.

6 There have been several important studies of dreams in recent years, but few of these works dealt with dreams as they are preserved in texts, least of all in sacred biographies. See, for instance, Tedlock, *Dreaming,* and von Grunebaum and Caillois, *The Dream and Human Societies.* For a fine collection of essays on literary dreams see Carol Schreier Rupprecht, ed., *The Dream and the Text: Essays on*

Literature and Language (Albany: State University of New York Press, 1993). The only major work devoted to South Asian dreams has been Wendy Doniger O'Flaherty's *Dreams, Illusion, and Other Realities* (Chicago: University of Chicago Press, 1984), but it deals primarily with the Hindu religious tradition.

7 See Bitel, *"In Visu Noctis,"* p. 55, for this process in Christian hagiography.

8 There is a growing scholarship on South and Southeast Asian Buddhist biography. John S. Strong's two studies, *The Legend of King Aśoka: A Study and Translation of the Aśokāvadāna* (Princeton: Princeton University Press, 1983) and *The Legend and Cult of Upagupta: Sanskrit Buddhism in North India and Southeast Asia* (Princeton: Princeton University Press, 1992), reveal the richness of these sources and offer a review of scholarly opinions. A useful survey of French scholarship on this topic can be found in André Couture, "A Survey of French Literature on Ancient Indian Buddhist Hagiography," in *Monks and Magicians: Religious Biographies in Asia*, ed. Phyllis Granoff and Koichi Shinohara (1988; Delhi: Motilal Banarsidass, 1994), pp. 9–44. See also Stanley Jeyaraja Tambiah, *The Buddhist Saints of the Forest and the Cult of Amulets* (Cambridge: Cambridge University Press, 1984), especially for his discussion of the biographies of the Buddha as *dhamma*, pp. 113, 119; and Juliane Schober, ed., *Sacred Biography in the Buddhist Traditions of South and Southeast Asia* (Honolulu: University of Hawai'i Press, 1997).

9 Matthew Kapstein captures this idea when he suggests translating the Tibetan word for sacred biography, *namtar*, as "soteriography"; "The Illusion of Spiritual Progress: Remarks on Indo-Tibetan Buddhist Soteriology," in *Paths to Liberation: The Mārga and Its Transformations in Buddhist Thought*, ed. Robert E. Buswell, Jr., and Robert M. Gimello (Honolulu: University of Hawai'i Press, 1992), p. 195. See also Janice D. Willis, "On the Nature of Rnam-Thar: Early Dge-Lugs-Pa *Siddha* Biographies," in *Soundings in Tibetan Civilization*, ed. Barbara Aziz and Matthew Kapstein (New Delhi: Manohar, 1985), pp. 304–19. For their being allegorical accounts of specific paths of yogic practice see "Translator's Introduction," in Dudjom Rinpoche, *The Nyingma School of Tibetan Buddhism: Its Fundamentals and History*, trans. Gyurme Dorje and Matthew Kapstein (London: Wisdom Publications, 1990), vol. 1, bk. 2.

10 See Benjamin Kilborne, "Dreams," in *Encyclopedia of Religion*, ed. Mircea Eliade (New York: Macmillian, 1987), hereafter *EOR*, 4: 483, for more on this point.

11 See E. R. Dodds, *The Greeks and the Irrational* (Berkeley: University of California Press, 1951, 1973), p. 105, for his discussion of this concept among the ancient Greeks.

12 Tanjur. *Rgyud 'grel: The Corpus of Indian Commentaries on Vajrayana Buddhist Literature translated into Tibetan* (Delhi: Delhi Karmapae Chodhey, Gyalwae Sungrab Partun Khang, 1982–1985), vol. 48 *(tshi),* f. 130a.

13 This topic is discussed at length in Diana L. Eck, *Darśan: Seeing the Divine Image in India* (Chambersburg: Anima, 1981). For the importance of the eye in Buddhism see the definitions under *cakkhu* in T. W. Rhys Davids and William Stede, *Pali-English Dictionary* (1921–1925; Delhi: Motilal Banarsidass, 1993), pp. 259–60.

14 Eck, *Darśan*, especially pp. 5–7.

15 For these and some other definitions see Monier Monier-Williams, *Sanskrit-English Dictionary* (1899; Oxford: Oxford University Press, 1976), pp. 470–71. One instance of *darśana* being used in the sense of dreams comes from the ancient Indian medical text, the *Suśrutasamhitā*, xxix.23, discussed below.

16 Reginald Ray discusses the medium of *seeing* in two different Buddhist contexts. The first is as a continuity of transmission. For instance, when King Aśoka sees the monk Piṇḍola, who had actually seen the living Buddha, Aśoka believes he is thereby more directly connected to the Buddha. Reginald A. Ray, *Buddhist Saints in India: A Study in Buddhist Values and Orientations* (New York: Oxford University Press, 1994), p. 156. (A similar, though more convoluted, transmission through seeing occurs when the monk Upagupta asks the god Māra, who had seen the Buddha, to use his divine powers to manifest as the Buddha so that Upagupta can see him. Strong, *Upagupta*, pp. 105–11.) Ray's second context for seeing relates to the cult of Buddhist saints who are seen iconographically not only in human form but in stūpas and other symbols, thereby allowing devotees to "participate in their enlightened charisma." Ray, *Buddhist Saints*, p. 369. See also Gregory Schopen, "Burial *Ad Sanctos* and the Physical Presence of the Buddha in Early Indian Buddhism: A Study in the Archaeology of Religion," *Religion*, no. 17 (1987): 195, where he discusses the recommendation of the Mahāparinibbāna Sutta to *see* the pilgrimage sites of the Buddha.

17 For recent discussions on dating the Buddha see Frank Reynolds and Charles Hallisey, "Buddha," in *EOR*, 2: 321; Heinz Bechert, ed., *The Dating of the Historical Buddha*, 2 vols (Göttingen: Vandenhoeck and Ruprecht, 1991–92); and Akira Hirakawa, *A History of Indian Buddhism: From Śākyamuni to Early Mahāyāna*, trans. and ed. Paul Groner (1990; Delhi: Motilal Banarsidass, 1993), pp. 22–23.

18 I will be using two biographical texts for Milarepa: Gtsaṅ smyon He ru ka, *Mi la ras pa'i rnam thar*, ed. J. W. de Jong ('s-Gravenhage: Mouton, 1959), hereafter Gtsaṅ smyon, *Mi la;* and Gtsaṅ smyon He ru ka, comp., *Mi la'i mgur 'bum* (Delhi: Sherab Gyaltsen, 1983), hereafter Gtsaṅ smyon, *Mgur 'bum*. The latter is popularly known as the hundred-thousand songs of Milarepa.

19 These texts were composed over a thousand-year period, and they also underwent the transition from oral to written forms of presentation. Walter Ong has

demonstrated the influence of orality on characterization and plot details in *Orality and Literacy: The Technologizing of the Word* (London: Methuen, 1982), p. 70. That the dreams in these texts, particularly those in the Buddha's biographies, have survived from the oral levels of the texts is one indication of their importance in Buddhist belief and practices. Though she does not specifically discuss biographies, Anne Klein's presentation of the range of written and oral philosophical texts is highly suggestive of the complex relation that exists between these two modes of communication in Tibetan culture. Her comments on Ong are also pertinent. Klein, *Path to the Middle: Oral Mādhyamika Philosophy in Tibet* (Albany: State University of New York Press, 1994), esp. pp. 1–12.

20 I am indebted to Dr. Antonella Crescenzi for helping me to clarify my thoughts on this distinction; conversation, Dharamsala, April 23, 1995. See also Antonella Crescenzi and Fabrizio Torricelli, "A Tun-huang Text on Dreams: Ms Pelliot tibétain 55 1 IX," *Tibet Journal* 20.2 (summer 1995): 3–17.

21 See Ray, *Buddhist Saints*, pp. 44–68, where he argues that the historical Buddha represents a paradigm of Buddhist sainthood. Ray, however, overlooks dreams, in the main because he develops his paradigm almost exclusively from the *Buddhacarita,* which plays down the role of dreams. See also Tambiah, "The Buddha's Life as Paradigm," in *Buddhist Saints of the Forest*, pp. 113–31.

22 See, for instance, *Lalitavistara*, ed. P. L. Vaidya (Darbhanga: Mithila Institute, 1958), 142.29–143.3, hereafter *LV,* Vaidya, discussed below in chapter 2; and Reynolds and Hallisey, "Buddha," pp. 327–28.

23 *Le Mahāvastu*, ed. É. Senart, 3 vols. (Paris: L'Imprimerie nationale, 1890), I.201–5, hereafter *MV,* Senart.

24 See Reginald A. Ray, "Buddhism: Sacred Text Written and Realized," in *The Holy Book in Comparative Perspective,* ed. Frederick M. Denny and Rodney L. Taylor (Columbia: University of South Carolina Press, 1985), pp. 76–77 n. 5, which quotes examples of this from the *Milindapañha*, the *Laṅkāvatāra Sūtra*, and the *Mahāvadānasūtra.*

25 One of the most common Buddhist notions of various realms is represented by the Wheel of Becoming or Rebirth (Skt.: *bhavacakra*; Tib.: *Srid pa'i 'khor lo*), a frequent subject of Buddhist art (see plate 7), which has the five or six realms or destinies *(gatis)* of the gods, humans, asuras, hungry ghosts, hell beings, and animals, usually all held in the grasp of Impermanence or the wrathful deity Yama, the god of Death, or Māra, Lord of the Realm of Desire, and archenemy of enlightenment. All sentient beings transmigrate through these six realms according to their karma. The goal is to get off this wheel by achieving enlightenment. They were painted in the entrance-halls of monasteries from the earliest times. See

Étienne Lamotte, *History of Indian Buddhism: From the Origins to the Śaka Era* (1958; Louvain-La-Neuve: Institut orientalist, 1988), p. 77.

A later elaboration is the division into the threefold realms of desire, form, and formlessness; the gatis take place in the desire realm. Richard F. Gombrich, "Ancient Indian Cosmology," in *Ancient Cosmologies*, ed. Carmen Blacker and Michael Loewe (London: George Allen and Unwin, 1975), pp. 110–42. Overall, see Louis de La Vallée Poussin, "Cosmogony and Cosmology (Buddhist)," in *Encyclopaedia of Religion and Ethics*, ed. James Hastings (New York: Charles Scribner's Sons, 1914), 4: 129–38. Steven Collins has a short discussion of these realms in relation to human consciousness in *Selfless Persons: Imagery and Thought in Theravāda Buddhism* (Cambridge: Cambridge University Press, 1982), pp. 213–18.

Finally, Mahāyāna introduced innumerable buddhafields *(buddhakṣetra)*, referred to as "pure lands" or heavens, presided over by celestial buddhas, one of the best known being Buddha Amitābha and his Western Paradise.

26 Collins, *Selfless Persons*, pp. 41–52; Gombrich, "Ancient Indian Cosmology," pp. 110–11; and *Upaniṣads*, trans. Patrick Olivelle (Oxford: Oxford University Press, 1996), pp. xlv–xlix.

27 For instance, Eva Dargyay's work on the Buddhist biographies of ancient Tibetan political leaders reveals a contrast to commonly held Buddhist cosmological concepts regarding the inevitability of karma and the emphasis on individual effort. In these texts "History...is seen as the outflow of a divine plan carefully crafted in a *buddhakṣetra* [Buddha field or heaven], eons before mankind [sic] emerged on this planet....Historical events are neither random happenings nor the fruits of previous acts (*karma*), but mirror a divine plan of salvation which was crafted in the past." "Srong-Btsan Sgam-Po of Tibet: Bodhisattva and King," in *Monks and Magicians,* p. 111. I have found a similar emphasis in the biographical literature of the Buddha, particularly in connection with the buddhas of the past and the future. See also Reginald Ray's introduction to *The History of the Sixteen Karmapas of Tibet,* by Karma Thinley (Boulder: Prajñā, 1980), pp. 3–4, where Ray argues, to my mind unsatisfactorily, that the dream and vision states described by Tibetan masters are essentially statements about mundane reality.

28 See Collins, *Selfless Persons*, pp. 57–60, for his elaboration on the ancient Indian idea that knowledge is power, and pp. 150–54 for the dichotomous views of the self that contribute to inconsistencies in the formulation of cosmologies.

29 These realms can also be visited through meditational trances, for example, the Buddha experienced various of these realms on his night of enlightenment; e.g., see Aśvaghoṣa, *Buddhacarita*, ed. and trans. E. H. Johnston (1936; Delhi: Motilal Banarsidass, 1984), XIV.1 ff, hereafter the *BC*.

30 As will become clear, I am using the term "charisma" as it was formulated by

Max Weber, primarily from his *The Sociology of Religion*, trans. Ephraim Fischoff (Boston: Beacon, 1964), chaps. 1, 5, 7; and *From Max Weber: Essays in Sociology*, trans. and ed. H. H. Gerth and C. Wright Mills (New York: Oxford University Press, 1946), esp. "Bureaucracy and Charisma: a Philosophy of History," pp. 51–54, and "The Sociology of Charismatic Authority," pp. 245–50. For the working through of his thesis in Buddhism see Max Weber, *The Religion of India: The Sociology of Hinduism and Buddhism*, trans. and ed. Hans H. Gerth and Don Martindale (New York: Free Press, 1958), pp. 204–56. For an excellent survey of the various types of religious authority and their relation to charisma, see Joachim Wach, *Sociology of Religion* (Chicago: University of Chicago Press, 1962), pp. 331–74.

31 Literary dream material often contains a fourth stage, the fulfillment of the dream.

32 For some examples of the influence of dreams on new religious movements and their relation to charisma see Kelly Bulkeley, *The Wilderness of Dreams* (Albany: State University of New York Press, 1994), pp. 6, 232. See also Bitel, *"In Visu Noctis,"* pp. 39–59, for a discussion of the medieval Christian understanding of the need to control dreams and their interpretations in order to control dissent and/or heresy; and Richard L. Kagan, *Lucrecia's Dreams: Politics and Prophecy in Sixteenth-Century Spain* (Berkeley: University of California Press, 1990).

33 Weber's fullest definition is in Gerth and Mills, *From Max Weber*, p. 55.

34 In order to facilitate discussion of a wide range of studies of different cultures, I will be using the frustratingly imprecise word *shaman* as a transreligional term to describe a religious virtuoso who functions most often among tribal peoples. See the discussion of the geography of this term in Carmen Blacker, *The Catalpa Bow: A Study of Shamanistic Practices in Japan* (London: Unwin Paperbacks, 1982), pp. 23–24.

35 A. Leo Oppenheim, in his comments on Pharaoh's dream and other dreams in ancient Near Eastern literature, suggests that the need for a dream interpreter indicates a lack of power on the part of the dreamer; those who are connected to the divine or the sacred do not need a lesser person to interpret for them, they understand the spiritual messages in their own dreams and in the dreams of others. "Mantic Dreams in the Ancient Near East," in von Grunebaum and Caillois, *The Dream and Human Societies*, pp. 341–50.

36 Quoted in Ninian Smart and Richard D. Hecht, *Sacred Texts of the World* (New York: Crossroad, 1982), p. 131.

37 *Majjhima Nikāya*, ed. V. Trenckner (1888; London: Routledge and Kegan Paul, 1979), 1.171.

38 For a recent thoroughgoing discussion of dreams and cognition in Western

thought see Harry T. Hunt, *The Multiplicity of Dreams: Memory, Imagination, and Consciousness* (New Haven: Yale University Press, 1989).

39 See Dodds, *The Greeks and the Irrational*, p. 102. But see also Tedlock's important discussion, which points out that such concepts have cultural limitations in "Dreaming and Dream Research," *Dreaming*, pp. 1–8. In either case, the tension between reality and illusion brought out by dreams is extremely relevant to the Indo-Tibetan dream experience. For a brief overview of how Western philosophy has dealt with the reality value of dreams and an outline of the continuing discussion, see A. R. Manser, "Dreams," in *Encyclopedia of Philosophy*, ed. Paul Edwards (New York: Macmillan, 1967), 1: 414–17.

40 The anthropologist Edward B. Tylor (1832–1917) was so impressed by pervasive beliefs in the external, or objective, quality of dreams in earlier periods of history that he argued for dreams being the source of many religious beliefs, such as the concept of the soul. He postulated that ancient people believed the soul experienced the dream while the body slept; that is, the soul actually journeyed in dreams to other times and places. Tylor contended further that these dream experiences led to the notion that the soul survives after death. This idea of an afterlife was supported, somewhat circularly, by dream experiences that pictured the dead as alive and existing in an alternate, enduring reality (*Primitive Culture: Researches into the Development of Mythology, Philosophy, Religion, Language, Art, and Custom* [New York: Henry Holt and Company, 1865], 2: 24, 49, 75 ff.) His main argument is that archaic people granted dreams a reality equal to that of the waking world (2: 440–44); they experienced dreams as a window onto another world, a world as real as the waking world. For these people, dreams had cognitive force. They allowed them to apprehend and learn about worlds not available to them during normal waking consciousness and gave them insights into waking reality. In short, dreams were regarded by many early people as powerful and significant sources of information about the whole of reality, not just waking reality. But most of them distinguished between significant and insignificant dreams. For some examples, see G. William Domhoff, *The Mystique of Dreams: A Search for Utopia through Senoi Dream Theory* (Berkeley: University of California Press, 1985), pp. 24–32. Domhoff also provides a readable account of important issues in the study of dreams, such as the limits of what we can know about dreams versus what we want to believe about dreams.

Tylor's purpose in writing this book was to contribute to our understanding of the origins of culture and religion. Weston La Barre is also concerned with the origins of religion, and he too grants dreams a vital role in that process. See Weston La Barre, *The Ghost Dance: Origins of Religion* (New York: Dell, 1972), pp. 13, 19, 26, as well as his discussion of related ideas in the works of Jane Harrison, W. H. R. Rivers, Karl Abraham, and Geza Roheim on pp. 60 and 68 n. 37. A Buddhist example of how a dream contributes to the origin of a religion can be seen in the five great dreams of the Buddha, discussed below.

41 Patricia Cox Miller found ample evidence to support the cognitive function of dreams. Significantly, even though most of her evidence was gathered from Christian dreamers, she found it cut across sectarian lines: Pagans, Christians, and Jews were all intellectually and spiritually engaged by dreams and dream theory as a means of mediating their reality. *Dreams in Late Antiquity: Studies in the Imagination of a Culture* (Princeton: Princeton University Press, 1994), pp. 3–10. See also G. E. von Grunebaum, "Introduction: The Cultural Function of the Dream as Illustrated by Classical Islam," in von Grunebaum and Caillois, *The Dream and Human Societies*, pp. 3–21.

42 See Tambiah for more on the sources of religious charisma, *Buddhist Saints of the Forest*, p. 325.

In another context, the anthropologist Michael Brown has expressed the first and third of my theses as follows: "If dreaming is a kind of thinking, then it might profitably be studied in terms of its place in the total knowledge system of a culture. What role do dreams play in the acquisition, validation, modification, and transmission of knowledge?...what can dreams tell us about 'principles that recur in the active processes of sense making?'...Finally, what connections are there between the symbolic force of dreams and processes of personal empowerment in the waking world?" (Brown, "Ropes of Sand: Order and Imagery in Aguaruna Dreams," in Tedlock, *Dreaming*, p. 156.) The biographies under study here amply demonstrate the role of dreams in acquiring knowledge and in the achievement of personal empowerment, or religious authority.

With pointed relevance to the South Asian materials under study here, Gananath Obeyesekere argues that "this mode of knowledge...is one of the most powerful and ancient forms of knowing....I believe that hypnomantic knowledge [derived from dreams, trances, and other ecstatic experiences] also lies at the base of most South Asian religions; on it are superimposed the ratiocinative speculations of the great historical religions of this region." (*Medusa's Hair: An Essay on Personal Symbols and Religious Experience* [Chicago: University of Chicago Press, 1981], p. 180.) See also Kilborne, "Dreams," pp. 482–92; one of his main points is that dreams are a theory of knowledge in world religion.

43 On this point I am influenced by Lee Irwin's subtle analysis of Native American dream experience, though the social integration of Buddhist dreamers is generally more limited than that of tribal people. However, Irwin also distinguishes between "master dreamers" (shamans) and less experienced dreamers. See *The Dream Seekers*, pp. 118–38, 168–74.

44 Charles Keyes emphasizes the necessity that later saints' biographies maintain

continuities with the biography of the founder. "Death of Two Buddhist Saints in Thailand," in *Charisma and Sacred Biography*, ed. Michael A. Williams (Chambersburg: American Academy of Religion, 1982), p. 152. Frank Reynolds and Donald Capps highlight differences that exist between the biographies of founders and their followers in *The Biographical Process: Studies in the History and Psychology of Religion* (The Hague: Mouton, 1976), pp. 4–5. See also Richard Kieckhefer, "Sainthood," in *Sainthood: Its Manifestation in World Religions*, ed. Richard Kieckhefer and George D. Bond (Berkeley: University of California Press, 1988), esp. pp. 29–33, for his discussion of similar issues of continuity and discontinuity in Christian hagiography.

45 Bearing in mind that most sacred biographies, especially those just cited, began as oral presentations in oral societies, see also Ong's discussion of conservatism and originality in such societies, *Orality and Literacy*, pp. 41–42.

46 Ray, *Buddhist Saints*, p. 8. See also p. 14 n. 17.

47 Donald Weinstein and Rudolph M. Bell, *Saints and Society: The Two Worlds of Western Christendom, 1000–1700* (Chicago: University of Chicago Press, 1982), p. 17.

48 This goes back to teachings on the Eightfold Path. See Lamotte, *History of Indian Buddhism*, pp. 26–53; Hirakawa, *History of Indian Buddhism*, pp. 39–42, 210–13.

49 *Mahā-parinibbānasuttanta*, 6.1. David Snellgrove has translated this passage from the Tibetan edition, which is the same in spirit as the Pali. See his "Śākyamuni's Final Nirvāṇa," *Bulletin of the School of Oriental and African Studies* 36 (1973): 401–2. Donald Lopez discusses the Buddha's last words as a problem of spiritual authority in relation to hermeneutical endeavors practiced in a variety of Buddhist cultures over several centuries in his introduction to *Buddhist Hermeneutics*, ed. Donald S. Lopez, Jr. (1988; Delhi: Motilal Banarsidass: 1993), pp. 1–10. For further discussion of the paradoxical relationship of these two aspects of religious authority in Buddhism, see Ray, "Buddhism: Sacred Text Written and Realized," pp. 148–60, and Ray, *Buddhist Saints*, pp. 365–66. Lamotte also briefly discusses the absence of authority in Buddhism in *History of Indian Buddhism*, pp. 62–65. He also discusses the development of canons by differents sects, pp. 133–91. See also K.N. Jayatilleke, *Early Buddhist Theory of Knowledge* (London: George Allen and Unwin, 1963), who discusses authority in early Buddhism, pp. 171–205, 382–401 and 416–21, and Nathan Katz's discussion, which includes a critique of Jayatilleke, in *Buddhist Images of Human Perfection* (Delhi: Motilal Banarsidass, 1982), pp. 205–14.

Robert Thurman's examination of these two sources of authority in early Buddhism leads him to argue that reason has more authority than scripture, "Buddhist Hermeneutics," *Journal of the American Academy of Religion* 46, no. 1 (1978): 20.

50 For the issue of the Buddha's words as revelation, see Graeme MacQueen, "Inspired Speech in Early Mahāyāna Buddhism," pts. 1 and 2, *Religion* 11, no. 4 (1981): 303–19; 12, no. 2 (1982): 49–65. These two articles are also helpful for their discussion of revelation in a later period.

51 In this context we have to acknowledge the enormous influence of the bodhisattva doctrine, in which spiritually advanced beings, both human and divine, vow to help others achieve enlightenment. In the end, though, with all the help in this and any other world, enlightenment still must be achieved by the individual. The same holds true for the celestial buddhas who can grant rebirth in one of their heavens, which helps one toward enlightenment, but does not grant it. For more on bodhisattvas see Har Dayal, *The Bodhisattva Doctrine in Buddhist Sanskrit Literature* (1932; Delhi: Motilal Banarsidass, 1970), and Donald S. Lopez, Jr., "Sanctification on the Bodhisattva Path," in Kieckhefer and Bond, *Sainthood*, pp. 172–217. For celestial buddhas see David Snellgrove, "Celestial Buddhas and Bodhisattvas," in *EOR*, 3: 133–43.

52 See Tambiah's discussion of the Buddha's biography as a source of religious authority in the Buddhist community, *Buddhist Saints of the Forest*, p. 119.

53 Buddhist biographies reflect both elite and popular ideas in a variety of ways that are hard to disentangle. Usually they were initially oral texts, some of which portrayed the lives of saints who were influenced by popular practices, such as Milarepa, that were later written down, preserved, and thus somewhat controlled by literate monastics. At the same time, the elite religious tradition itself was inevitably influenced by indigenous, non-Buddhist practices.

This point will be discussed in chapter 4 in terms of shamanic influences on Buddhist practice, but see also Robert A. F. Thurman, whose discussion of Buddhist missionary activity highlights some of the ways the elite Buddhist tradition merged and blended with the indigenous folk traditions, "Worship and Cultic Life: Buddhist Cultic Life in Tibet," in *EOR*, 15: 472–75. Dargyay finds the influence of the religious expectations of the common people (her term) in political biographies ("Srong-Btsan," p. 111), and Ramesh Chandra Tewari finds the incorporation of a popular and indigenous oracle into mainstream Buddhist practice ("Pre-Buddhist Elements in Himalayan Buddhism: The Institution of the Oracles," *Journal of the International Association of Buddhist Studies* 10, no. 1 [1987]: 135–55).

Hirakawa highlights two streams in the biographies of the Buddha, that of the laity with their salvational issues and that of the monastics with their doctrinal issues (*History of Indian Buddhism*, pp. 260, 264, 270–74), and it seems reasonable to suppose that similar lay and monastic influences also shaped Tibetan biographies. Following Collins (*Selfless Persons*, pp. 147–54) and Ray (*Buddhist Saints*, pp. 31–36), though, I would modify Hirakawa's argument in order to distinguish elite, literate and educated monastics from monastics who were/are closer to the views of the popular tradition.

Collins describes central topics in Southeast Asian Buddhism in terms of two different types of discourse. Sliced one way, they reveal the great/little tradition distinction; sliced another way, they reveal the conventional/ultimate truth distinction (*Selfless Persons,* pp. 147–54).

Ray, *Buddhist Saints,* pp. 31–36, following Frauwallner, distinguishes between literate monks living in monasteries, who pursued the time-consuming task of textual study, and forest monks, who spent their time on meditation. Though, see also Tambiah, *Buddhist Saints of the Forest,* pp. 11–77, who stresses the fluidity of these two types of early Buddhist monks. A similar division occurs in Tibetan Buddhism between ordained monastics and wandering yogi practitioners. The important point is that there was diversity of practice and belief in Buddhism, as in any other religious tradition.

54 Dreams have been an important philosophical example of the human inability to know what is real and what is not in many schools of thought. For instance, after dreaming he was a butterfly, the Taoist sage Chuang Tzu (c. 369–286 B.C.E.) awoke and wondered whether he was now a butterfly dreaming he was a man. Chuang-tzu, *Chuang Tzu: Basic Writings,* trans. Burton Watson (New York: Columbia University Press, 1964), p. 45. For a discussion of this and another passage on dreams as examples of Chuang Tzu's skepticism see Philip J. Ivanhoe, "Zhuangzi on Skepticism, Skill, and the Ineffable Dao," *Journal of the American Academy of Religion* 61, no. 4 (winter 1993): 640–43. Plato raises the same issue in the *Theatetus* when he has Socrates ask how one determines whether we are at the moment asleep and dreaming or awake. *The Dialogues of Plato,* trans. B. Jowett (1892; New York: Random House, 1937), 2: 160. This topic continues to engage Western philosophical thought, see Manser, "Dream," 1: 414–17. Bold skeptics throughout history have voiced their opinion that dreams are lacking in any real meaning (Cicero) or arise because of bodily disturbances (Aristotle). (For these and other critics from the ancient world, see Miller, *Dreams in Late Antiquity,* pp. 42–46.) And, on the religious side, Martin Luther is often quoted as saying, "God protect me from my dreams!" indicating his belief that dreams were not sent by God but by the devil. These are minority voices, though. The great majority of humankind is fascinated by dreams and seeks to extract meaning from them, primarily because we tend to experience dreams as given, rather than as our own creations.

55 Most South Asian Buddhist texts are meant to be chanted, not read in solitude. See Paul Williams, *Mahāyāna Buddhism: The Doctrinal Foundations* (London: Routledge, 1989), pp. 37–38. See also Gregory Schopen, "The Phrase 'sa pṛthivipradeśaś caityabhūto bhavet' in the Vajracchedikā: Notes on the Cult of the Book in Mahāyāna," *Indo-Iranian Journal* 17, nos. 3/4 (November/December 1975):

147–81. In Tibet, reciters of biographies and other texts were called *manipas*, according to Giuseppe Tucci, *The Religions of Tibet*, trans. Geoffrey Samuel (Berkeley: University of California Press, 1980), pp. 207–8. These were itinerant monks who illustrated their stories with religious scrolls; D. L. Snellgrove and Hugh Richardson, *A Cultural History of Tibet* (Boston: Shambhala, 1986), p. 258. In East Asia, of course, the copying of texts was and remains a popular form of devotion, see e.g., Miriam Levering, "Scripture and Its Reception: A Buddhist Case," in Miriam Levering, ed., *Rethinking Scripture: Essays from a Comparative Perspective* (Albany: State University of New York Press, 1989), pp. 58–101.

56 For a discussion of such distinctions in both Theravāda and Mahāyāna Buddhism, see Collins, *Selfless Persons*, pp. 13–26, 147–54; for this distinction in pre-Buddhist India, see pp. 30–32; in Tibet see Tucci, *Religions of Tibet*, pp. 163–248; and overall see Donald K. Swearer, "Folk Religion: Folk Buddhism," in *EOR*, 5: 374. For the Tibetan situation see the illustration and short discussion in Richard H. Robinson and Willard L. Johnson, *The Buddhist Religion: A Historical Introduction*, 3d ed. (Belmont, CA: Wadsworth, 1982), pp. 145–46. See also Melvyn Goldstein's discussion of the monastic population in the great monastery of Drepung in Melvyn C. Goldstein and Matthew T. Kapstein, eds., *Buddhism in Contemporary Tibet: Religious Revival and Cultural Identity* (Berkeley: University of California Press, 1998), esp. pp. 15–22; and Tucci, *Religions of Tibet*, pp. 125–46.

57 See Bitel, *"In Visu Noctis,"* for her discussion of the relationship between Christian and indigenous European ideas about dreams, and for the Christian limitation of significant dreams to an elite of saints and kings, pp. 41–59.

58 From *Islam Observed*, pp. 2–3, quoted by Collins, *Selfless Persons*, p. 262. See ibid., pp. 262–66, for the working through of Geertz's ideas in a Theravāda context.

Ray has argued persuasively for a distinction and a tension in ancient and medieval India between the charismatic Buddhism of the forest saints, or virtuoso meditators, and the scholastic Buddhism of an elite, settled monasticism, which pursued textual studies. He stresses the innovative nature of the former and the conservative tendencies of the latter. In other words, elite Buddhists (conservative and scholastic) see a need to question the claims of charismatic authority, part of which entails limiting the innovative function of dream experience. This is not a wholly unreasonable position given the historically documented power of charismatics to initiate religious innovations. The presence of controls are a mark of how seriously the tradition takes dreams. See Ray, *Buddhist Saints*, e.g. pp. 379–80 and passim, though he softens this argument somewhat on pp. 413–14 and 438–47, which include relevant comments on Tibetan Buddhism. See also Tambiah's important discussion of this distinction in twentieth century Thailand, *Buddhist Saints of the Forest*, and especially pp. 321–34. Geoffrey Samuel has a closely related discussion in the Tibetan context in "Early Buddhism in Tibet: Some Anthropological Perspectives," in Barbara Aziz and Matthew Kapstein, eds., *Soundings in Tibetan Civilization* (New Delhi: Manohar, 1985), pp. 383–97.

59 Williams, *Mahāyāna Buddhism,* pp. 24–25.

60 Ibid., pp. 1–33. On this point see also Schopen, "The Phrase 'sa pṛthivipradeśaś caityabhūto bhavet,'" passim.

61 Snellgrove and Richardson, *Cultural History of Tibet,* pp. 247–48; Tucci, *Religions of Tibet,* pp. 125–46.

62 Almost every conversation I have had with Tibetan monks about dreams began by their saying that dreams are an illusion and unimportant; then they would elaborate on the meanings of dreams with regard to prophecy, health, spiritual accomplishments, and so on. More specifically, this is especially a Mahāyāna point of view; as discussed below, Theravādins have other issues with regard to dreaming.

For an example of the Mahāyāna view see the *Aṣṭasāhasrikā Prajñāpāramitā,* one of the most ancient Mahāyāna sūtras, which contains a long passage equating magical illusion and dreams and then lists a variety of beings and ideas which are like both of these, e.g., all beings, all objective facts, the various classes of saints (including buddhas), buddhahood itself, and even nirvāṇa. Quoted by MacQueen, "Inspired Speech," pt. 2, p. 57. Yet, this text also affirms the revelatory importance of dreams, ibid., p. 52.

63 Sigmund Freud, *The Interpretation of Dreams,* trans. and ed. James Strachey (New York: Avon, 1965), chap. 3.

64 See, for instance, E. R. Dodds, who acknowledges Freud's influence but chooses a different course, one that I found helpful in developing a methodology to examine the dreams contained in Buddhist biographical literature: "There are two ways of looking at the recorded dream-experience of a past culture: we may try to see it through the eyes of the dreamers themselves, and thus reconstruct as far as may be what it meant to their waking consciousness; or we may attempt, by applying principles derived from modern dream-analysis, to penetrate from its manifest to its latent content. The latter procedure is plainly hazardous: it rests on an unproved assumption about the universality of dream-symbols which we cannot control by obtaining the dreamer's associations. That in skilled and cautious hands it might nevertheless yield interesting results, I am willing to believe; but I must not be beguiled into essaying it. My main concern is not with the dream-experience of the Greeks, but with the Greek attitude to dream-experience" (*The Greeks and the Irrational,* p. 103).

65 Freud says in the his preface to the first edition of *The Interpretation of Dreams* "none of the dreams already reported in the literature of the subject [of dreams] or collected from unknown sources could be of any use for my purposes. The

only dreams open to my choice were my own and those of my patients undergoing psychoanalytic treatment" (p. xxiii; see also p. 137). Carl Jung echoes this position in "On the Nature of Dreams," Jung, *Dreams*, p. 69. Freud, of course, understood dreams to carry repressed or at least hidden meanings, while Jung agreed that people often needed help in interpreting them. For a succinct summary of basic psychoanalytic theories about dreams see Domhoff, *The Mystique of Dreams*, pp. 110–14.

66 Quoted by La Barre, *Ghost Dance*, p. 38, from W. H. Auden, *The Collected Poetry of W. H. Auden*, p. 166.

67 See, for example, Jung, "On the Nature of Dreams," pp. 70–71, and "The Analysis of Dreams," in *Dreams*, pp. 9–11.

68 Jung, "On the Nature of Dreams," *Dreams*, p. 76.

69 Ibid., pp. 77–79.

70 Such readers are directed to Jung's wonderful memoir, *Memories, Dreams and Reflections*, trans. Richard and Clara Winston (New York: Vintage, 1965), which offers many details about Jung's use of dream analysis in his own and in his patient's lives.

71 The works of Sudhir Kakar, an Indian trained in Western psychoanalytic theory, are insightful about the psychological life of South Asians. See, especially, *Shamans, Mystics, and Doctors: A Psychological Inquiry into India and Its Healing Traditions* (Delhi: Oxford University Press, 1982).

72 To cite just one example, "On the Nature of Dreams," *Dreams*, p. 73. However, this is a constant refrain in Jung's writing on dreams.

73 Robert A. Paul and Lee Siegel have both done psychoanalytic studies of the biographical literature of the Buddha, though they jump between the various biographical sources, picking and choosing details from different texts as it suits their needs. This approach is problematic because each biography has its own point of view and therefore needs to be examined in its entirety before comparing it to other texts. See Robert A. Paul, *The Tibetan Symbolic World: Psychoanalytic Explorations* (Chicago: University of Chicago Press, 1982); Lee Siegel, "Out of the Palace of Pleasure: A Study of Psychoanalytic Implications of the Biographical Legends of Gautama the Buddha," in *Dream-Symbolism in the Śrāmaṇic Tradition: Two Psychoanalytical Studies in Jinist and Buddhist Dream Legends*, ed. Jagdish Sharma and Lee Siegel (Calcutta: Firma KLM, 1980).

Chapter 2

1 For some of the earliest representations of this dream, which may even occur in the Aśokan Rock Edicts, see Karl Khandalavala, "Heralds in Stone: Early

Buddhist Iconography in the Aśokan Pillars and Related Problems," pp. 21–22; and Biswanarayan Shastri, "The Philosophical Concepts and the Buddhist Pantheon," p. 56, both in *Buddhist Iconography* (Delhi: Tibet House, 1989; papers presented at an international seminar organized by Tibet House). The dream may also be represented at pre-Aśokan sites in Andhra Pradesh, see D. Sridhara Babu, "Reflections on Andra Buddhist Sculptures and Buddha Biography," in *Buddhist Iconography*, pp. 100–101.

2 Early iconographic representations of this dream and its interpretation are briefly discussed in Patricia Eichenbaum Karetzky, *The Life of the Buddha: Ancient Scriptural and Pictorial Traditions* (Lanham: University Press of America, 1992), pp. 11–15. See also her dissertation, Patricia D. Eichenbaum, "The Development of a Narrative Cycle Based on the Life of the Buddha in India, Central Asia, and the Far East: Literary and Pictorial Evidence" (Ph.D. diss., 1980), and the list in Dieter Schlingloff, *Studies in the Ajanta Paintings: Identifications and Interpretations* (Delhi: Ajanta Publications, 1987), pp. 17–18, 37–38 nn. 30, 32, and 33. See also the important discussion of iconographic representations of the life of the Buddha in John C. Huntington, "Pilgrimage as Image: The Cult of the Aṣṭamahāprātihārya," pt. 1, *Orientations* 18, no. 4 (April 1987): 55–63.

3 See H. Lüders, ed. *Bhārhut Inscriptions*, rev. ed. (Ootacamund: Government Epigraphist for India, 1963), pp. 89–90, for a brief discussion of some of these texts as well as some of the texts that do not include it. For the early Chinese biographies, see Karetzky, *Life of the Buddha*, p. 4.

4 The *Lalitavistara* is available in a Sanskrit edition, edited by P. L. Vaidya (hereafter *LV*, Vaidya); an English edition is available through Gwendolyn Bays' translation (*The Voice of the Buddha: The Beauty of Compassion* [Oakland: Dharma Press, 1983], hereafter *LV*, Bays) made from Edouard Foucaux's French translation from the Sanskrit. It was composed anonymously around the beginning of the Common Era, although it contains much earlier material from the oral tradition.

5 The *Abhiniṣkramaṇasūtra*, trans. by Samuel Beal from the Chinese edition as *The Romantic Legend of Śākya Buddha* (1875; Delhi: Motilal Banarsidass, 1985), pp. 37–39, hereafter the *AS*. This text, whose Sanskrit version has been lost, was probably composed among the Dharmaguptakas, a Hīnayāna school of early Buddhism (see Hirakawa, *History of Indian Buddhism*, p. 265).

6 Aśvaghoṣa. *Buddhacarita*, ed. and trans. E.H. Johnson (1936; Delhi Motilal Banarsidass, 1984, I.4, hereafter *BC*). It was composed around the beginning of the Common Era, and Johnston's edition contains the extant early chapters in Sanskrit, which are translated into English along with an English translation of the later chapters which are available in Tibetan.

7 *MV,* Senart, II.12. English translation by J.J. Jones, *Mahāvastu,* 3 vol. (London: Pali Text Society, 1949–56); the dream is in vol. II.11. Jones argues that its long compilation period began in the second century B.C.E. and continued into the third or fourth century C.E. (*MV,* Jones, I.xi–xii).

8 *The Gilgit Manuscript of the Saṅghabhedavastu, Being the 17th and Last Section of the Vinaya of the Mūlasarvāstivādin,* ed. Raniero Gnoli (Rome: Istituto italiano per il medio ed estremo oriente, 1977), 1: 40, hereafter *MSV.* This text comes from the Sarvāstivāda school of early Buddhism, which spread into Central Asia, Tibet and China and was completed around the third century C.E.; *Mūlasarvāstivāda-vinayavastu,* ed. S. Bagchi (Darbhanga: Mithila Institute, 1967), p. xiii.

9 Cited by W. W. Rockhill, *The Life of the Buddha* (Varanasi: Orientalia Indica, 1972), p. 15. The Tibetan historian Bu ston, though, quotes the dream from the *LV.* Bu ston Rin chen grub, *The History of Buddhism in India and Tibet,* trans. E. Obermiller (1932; Delhi: Sri Satguru, 1986), pp. 10–11.

10 Both references occur in the context of the subjects Padmasambhava (traditionally dated to the eighth century) studies. One reference says that during his study of astrology he learns about the year when "the six-tusked white elephant was incarnated" *(glang-pa thal kar mche drug sprul),* an obvious reference to Māyā's dream; *Padma bka' thang shel brag ma* (Leh, 1968), at 65b.1, hereafter *Padma.* The other says that Padma "was taught all about the year of the conception of the Buddha, the year in which the mother of the Buddha dreamt that a white elephant entered her womb, the year of the Buddha's birth, and how these esoterically significant periods have correspondence with the Tibetan calendar"; W. Y. Evans-Wentz, *The Tibetan Book of the Great Liberation* (1954; New York: Oxford University Press, 1968), p. 122.

11 *Nidānakathā,* in *The Jātaka Together with Its Commentary,* ed. V. Fausbøll (London: Trübner, 1877), I.50, hereafter *NK.* This text began as an introduction to the jātakas but rapidly became the standard Theravāda biography of the Buddha. The dream and its interpretation are translated by T. W. Rhys Davids as *Buddhist Birth Stories* (1880; New York: E. P. Dutton, 1925), pp. 149–51, hereafter Rhys Davids, *Buddhist Birth Stories*).

12 *NK,* I.51. The *LV* has essentially the same interpretation, pp. 45, 11–140.

13 The only other dream I have found that allows for a possible alternative outcome is Māra's dream, discussed below. Of course, there were various rituals to offset the negative effects of dreams and/or to ensure their positive effects, some of which will be discussed below, especially in chapter 9.

14 *NK,* I.58. Rhys Davids, *Buddhist Birth Stories,* pp. 166–67; *LV,* Vaidya, 136–38. Since even the gods are doomed to eventually reincarnate, probably into lower

existences, they too are in need of the Buddha's teachings on how to get off the Wheel of Becoming. Consequently, they make frequent appearances in the Buddha's life in order to assist him in his salvational goal.

15 *MV*, Senart, has *vaipañcanika*, II.12. See emendation to *vaipañcika* in Franklin Edgerton, *Buddhist Hybrid Sanskrit Grammar and Dictionary* (1953; Delhi: Motilal Banarsidass, 1985), p. 510.

16 Brahmā is the highest god in the Pali canon.

17 *So bhavati buddho. MV*, Senart, II.11–14; for English translation, see *MV*, Jones, II.11–13.

18 *MV*, Senart, II.13. This speech is quite similar to the one preserved in the *AS*, but there it is attributed to the Brahman dream interpreters. See *AS*, pp. 38–39.

19 For further discussion of the symbolical use of elephants in India see Heinrich Zimmer, *Myths and Symbols in Indian Art and Civilization*, ed. Joseph Campbell (1946; New York: Harper, 1962), pp. 102–9; Paul B. Courtright, *Gaṇeśa: Lord of Obstacles, Lord of Reason* (New York: Oxford University Press, 1985), pp. 21–31; and Jagdish Sharma, "Symbolism in the Jinist Dream World," in Sharma and Siegel, *Dream-Symbolism in the Śrāmaṇic Tradition*, pp. 27–28. Dayal summarizes the major Western scholarship on the various meanings attributed to the elephant in Māyā's dream in *The Bodhisattva Doctrine in Buddhist Sanskrit Literature*, pp. 295–96; but see also P. Banerjee, "The Story of the Birth of Gautama Buddha and its Vedic Parallel," in *Buddhist Iconography*, p. 4, who refers to the elephant as a fertility symbol, especially in its connection to the early Indra cult.

20 The *MV's* association of the sun with royalty contrasts with most of the dreams in later Buddhist biographies, where the sun clearly represents the Buddha and/or Buddhism. This is one among many signs of the flexibility of dream symbolism in Buddhist literature. Compare, for instance, Gopā's dream in the *LV* and many of the dreams in Padmasambhava's and Milarepa's biographies, discussed below. See also James R. Russell, "The Dream Vision of Anania Sirakac'i," *Revue des études arméniennes, nouvelle serie* 21 (1988): 159–70, for a discussion of the sun's association with divinity in various dream experiences. Lincoln also discusses the sun as a dream symbol for kings and fathers in *The Dream in Primitive Cultures*, pp. 115–16. For a brief discussion of the sun and moon in Buddhist art, see D. C. Bhattacharyya, "Metamorphosis of a Central Asian Symbolism," in *Buddhist Iconography*, pp. 149–53.

21 S. K. Gupta suggests some of these associations may be connected to the elephant's usefulness in war, for which there are references dating to the 326 B.C.E. battle against Alexander; Gupta, *The Elephant in Indian Art and Mythology* (New Delhi: Abhinav Publications, 1983), p. 5.

22 See Zimmer, *Myths and Symbols*, pp. 104–9; and Courtright, *Gaṇeśa*, pp. 21–31, for more on the elephant's association with clouds and rain.

23 See the comparative discussion of the views of various texts in Lüders, *Bhārhut Inscriptions*, pp. 89–91.

24 See, e.g., Ernest Jones, *On the Nightmare* (New York: Liveright, 1951), pp. 82–83.

25 Ibid., pp. 92 ff. A seventh-century Indian text, the *Kādambarī* by Bāṇabhaṭṭa describes various acts performed by Queen Vilāsavatī in order to conceive a son, including sleeping in the temples of the goddess Caṇḍikā and telling her dreams to Brahmans; quoted by David N. Lorenzen, *The Kāpālikas and Kālāmukhas: Two Lost Saivite Sects*, 2d ed. (Delhi: Motilal Banarsidass, 1991), pp. 16–17.

26 H. W. Schumann, *The Historical Buddha*, trans. M. O'C. Walshe (London: Penguin, 1989), p. 7. *MV*, Senart, I.355–57 and II.3.1 ff., says she was the youngest of the seven sisters that Śuddhodana married, and that she was in the prime of life when she gave birth twelve years later. In general, see Telwatte Rahula, *A Critical Study of the Mahāvastu* (Delhi: Motilal Banarsidass, 1978), pp. 187–202, for his lengthy discussion of Māyā.

27 *MV*, Senart, I.145–46, II.5–6. In the *MV* all these events are repeated in the life of the preceding Buddha Dīpaṃkara: his mother also sleeps apart from her husband for one night and dreams of an elephant entering her womb (I.201–5).

28 *Bodhisattva...rajñah śuddhodanasyemaṃ svapnamupadarśayati sma.... LV*, Vaidya, 135.1–2. King Śuddhodana understands this to be a prophetic dream, one that reflects the predictions made at the Buddha's birth, and he does all he can to prevent its fulfillment. First, he tries to distract the Buddha by building palaces for him and instructing the harem women to continuously sing and play musical instruments. Later, he builds walls around the palace and increases the number of guards. This chapter is translated in Bays, *The Voice of the Buddha*, pp. 283–98.

29 *LV*, Vaidya, 140.16–141.2, 143.2.

30 *LV*, Vaidya, 143.1. See Ray's brief discussion and notes on the earliest sources for the idea of previous Buddhas in "Buddhism: Sacred Text Written and Realized," pp. 149–50, 176–77 nn. 5–8. Gombrich makes the point that this seems to be an idea copied from the Jain notion of the *tīrthaṅkaras*; Richard Gombrich, "The Significance of Former Buddhas in the Theravādin Tradition," in *Buddhist Studies in Honour of Walpola Rahula*, ed. Somaratna Balasooriya et al. (London: Gordon Fraser, 1980), pp. 62–72, esp. pp. 64 and 68. The biographies of previous buddhas are contained in the *Mahāpadāna Sutta* and the *Buddhavaṃsa;* see ibid. for more on these two texts. See also A. G. S. Kariyawasam, "Buddha Nature," in *The Encyclopedia of Buddhism*, ed. G. P. Malalasekera (Ceylon: Government of

Ceylon, 1961–1979), 1: 435–38, for his discussion of previous buddhas; and Frank Reynolds, "Rebirth Traditions and the Lineages of Gotama: A Study in Theravāda Buddhology," in Schober, *Sacred Biography*, pp. 24–30, for his discussion of them as a biographical source.

31 Additionally, the *Lotus Sūtra* has a speech attributed to the Buddha in which he describes the dreams of those who aspire to enlightenment; *Saddharma-puṇḍarīka or the Lotus of the True Law*, trans. H. Kern (1884; New York: Dover 1963), pp. 278–79. The *Ārya Svapna Nirdeśa Sūtra* from the Tibetan canon lists 108 auspicious dream images that appear to one pursuing the bodhisattva path; *Kanjur*, Sde dge edition (Reprinted Oakland: Dharma, 1980), vol. *ka*. Similar evidence survives from other ancient Indian sramanic groups.

32 In other texts, such as the *Aṅguttara Nikāya*, it is a sacred grass that grows out of his navel up to the sky, which is reminiscent of the lotus growing out of Viṣṇu's navel.

33 *LV*, Vaidya, 142.29–143.14. Numbers have been added as an aid for discussion.

34 *Aṅguttara Nikāya*, ed. E. Hardy (London: Pali Text Society, 1896), iii.196.1, hereafter *AN*, Hardy; English translation by E. M. Hare, *The Book of the Gradual Sayings*, (London: Pali Text Society, 1934), hereafter Hare, *Book of Gradual Sayings*. The dreams and their interpretations are translated in 3: 175–77.

35 *AN*, Hardy, iii.196.7. Similarly, the *Bhagavatī Sūtra* says Mahāvīra dreamed while still in the state of only having finite knowledge *(chadmasthakāla)*, i.e., before his final enlightenment; Jogendra Chandra Sikdar, *Studies in the Bhagawatīsūtra* (Muzaffarpur, Bihar: Research Institute of Prakrit, Jainology, and Ahimsa, 1964), p. 197.

36 *AN*, Hardy, iii.196.7.

37 Ibid., iii.196.3.

38 Ibid., iii.196.8.

39 *Divyāvadāna*, ed. E. B. Cowell and R. A. Neil (Cambridge: Cambridge University Press, 1886), pp. 247–48. John Strong has translated this part of the story in *The Experience of Buddhism* (Belmont, WA: Wadsworth, 1995), p. 19–23.

40 *AN*, Hardy, iii.196.9.

41 Ibid., iii.196.11.

42 He also interprets his dream in the *MSV*, 1: 83, discussed below.

43 *MV*, Senart, 137.18. These dreams and their interpretations are translated in *MV*, Jones, II.132–34.

44 *Milindapañha*, ed. V. Trenckner (London: Williams and Norgate, 1880), bk. 4, dilemma 75, p. 298. Translated by T. W. Rhys Davids as *The Questions of King Milinda* (1894; Delhi: Motilal Banarsidass, 1965), pp. 157 ff.

45 He may have based his work on earlier, now lost, sources. Hirakawa, *History of Indian Buddhism*, pp. 125, 133–34. See also John Ross Carter, "Buddhaghosa," in *EOR*, 2: 332–33.

46 The Fourth Noble Truth states that the cessation of suffering is to be found in following the Eightfold Path, so this interpretation is connected to that of the *AN*.

47 *MV*, Senart, ii.138–39.

48 *MSV*, 1: 82.

49 Ibid., 1: 83.

50 The story of Puruṣa is in *Rig Veda* X.10. Viṣṇu's dream is in *Kūrma Purāṇa*, I.9.10. The *Matsya Purāṇa* says that to see grass sprouting from any other part of the body than the navel is an evil dream. Cited in Sadashiv Ambadas Dange, ed., *Encyclopaedia of Puranic Beliefs and Practices* (New Delhi: Navrang, 1987), 2: 448. On this point see also *Caraka Saṃhitā*, ed. and trans. Ram Karan Sharma and Vaidya Bhagwan Das (Varanasi: Chowkhamba Sanskrit Series, 1977), hereafter the *CS*, 2: 546 (dreams about growths from the chest), 549 (growths from the head).

51 *AS*, Beal, also has a plant, p. 129. For the religious meaning of grasses in ancient India, see Jan Gonda's excellent study, in which he makes this general point in relation to Vedic ritualism: "The vital power inherent in grasses, which are a part or constituent element of nature, brings the one who uses or wears them or has them ritually spread into contact with nature's energy and vitality, transfers it to him, makes him participate in it, purifies, wards off evil, or makes a place, a rite or other event auspicious."

All these elements are present in the grass symbolism of the Buddha's dream. Jan Gonda, *The Ritual Functions and Significance of Grasses in the Religion of the Veda* (Amsterdam: North-Holland Publishing, 1985), p. 6.

52 See A.K. Coomaraswamy, *Elements of Buddhist Iconography* (1935; Delhi: Munshiram Manoharlal, 1972), p. 17, for his discussion of this symbolism in terms of the tree of life. See also a slightly different interpretation of these dreams by Roy C. Amore, "Comparative Study of Buddha's Pre-enlightenment Dreams: Implications for Religion," in *The Notion of "Religion" in Comparative Research*, ed. Ugo Bianchi (Selected Proceedings of the Sixteenth Congress of the International Association for the History of Religions, Rome, 1990), pp. 541–46.

53 *Bodhisatto kadā ime supine pasi ti sve buddho bhavissāmi ti.* Buddhaghosa, *Manorathapūraṇī*, ed. Hermann Kopp, vol. 3 (London: Pali Text Society, 1936),

v.xx.6. This becomes important in the Theravāda tradition, which insists that arhats (enlightened beings) no longer dream.

54 *Bodhimaṇḍaṃ āruyha sambodhiṃ patvā anukkamena Jetavane viharanto attano makulabuddhakale diṭṭhe pañca mahāsupine.* Ibid., v.xx.6.

55 Dayal, *The Bodhisattva Doctrine*, p. 306.

56 Amore, "Comparative Study of Buddha's Pre-enlightenment Dreams," p. 541.

57 Edward J. Thomas, *The Life of Buddha as Legend and History* (London: Routledge and Kegan Paul, 1969), p. 70 n. 4.

58 The *LV*, while originally a work of the Sarvāstivāda sect (forerunners of the Theravāda), is in its current redaction a thoroughly Mahāyāna text, while the *MV* is attributed to the Lokattaravāda and the Mahāsaṅghika, also forerunners of Mahāyāna. Hirakawa, *History of Indian Buddhism*, pp. 262–65. The *MSV* is the Sanskrit and northern vinaya that became the basis for the Tibetan vinaya. For discussions of the various schools of early Buddhism see ibid., pp. 105–23; Lamotte, *History of Indian Buddhism*, pp. 517–48; and André Bareau, "Buddhism, Schools of: Hīnayāna," in *EOR*, 2: 444–57, particularly noteworthy for its clear table on p. 447.

59 I am grateful to Dr. Grace Burford for helping me to clarify my thoughts on Buddhaghosa.

60 Although contemporary Theravāda monks are quite clear that *arhats* do not dream, in Tambiah's study of a modern *arhat*, Archan Mun of Thailand, he dreams both before and after his enlightenment. The study of dreams in Buddhism is fraught with such contradictions. See Tambiah, *Buddhist Saints of the Forest*, pp. 83–84, 100–101. See also Michael Carrithers's brief study of the dreams of Sinhalese monks, who basically follow Buddhaghosa's and the *Milindapañha*'s theory of dreams, "Hell-Fire and Urinal Stones: An Essay on Buddhist Purity and Authority," *Contributions to South Asian Studies* 2, ed. Gopal Krishna (Delhi: Oxford University Press, 1982), pp. 25–52.

61 O'Flaherty, *Dreams*, p. 153. Similarly, medieval Christian theologians made an effort to take charge of the dream life of Christians by becoming the authoritative interpreters of dreams; see Bitel, *"In Visu Noctis,"* pp. 39–59.

62 Hirakawa, *History of Indian Buddhism*, p. 273.

63 Ibid., pp. 264–67.

64 A parallel situation can be found in medieval Christianity's understandings of dreams; see Bitel, *"In Visu Noctis,"* esp. pp. 52–55.

65 *LV*, Vaidya, 143.15–18.

66 For the pervasiveness of this imagery in early Buddhism see Collins, *Selfless Persons*, p. 250 and notes on p. 306.

67 *LV*, Vaidya, 143.19–22.

68 See the discussion of the Buddha's relationship to healing in chapter 5.

69 *LV*, Vaidya, 143.23–26.

70 For more information on the meaning of Mount Meru in Buddhism and Hinduism see Stephen Schuhmacher and Gert Woerner, eds., *The Encyclopaedia of Eastern Philosophy and Religion* (Boston: Shambhala, 1989), p. 225; for a discussion of Mount Meru as well as the overall significance of mountains in world religion, see Diana Eck, "Mountains," in *EOR*, 10: 130–34.

71 G. M. Bolling, "Dreams and Sleep (Vedic)," in *The Encyclopaedia of Religion and Ethics*, ed. James Hastings (New York: Charles Scribner, 1913), 5: 38 ff.

72 Lincoln, *The Dream in Primitive Cultures*, pp. 93–98.

73 Ibid., p. 98.

74 See Collins, *Selfless Persons*, pp. 165–76, for his thoughtful analysis of abandoning home in Buddhist theory and practice.

75 *MV*, Senart, ii.133.15. Jones translates these dreams and their interpretations, *MV*, Jones, 2: 129–31.

76 Ibid., ii.134.15–22.

77 Ibid., ii.135.18–21.

78 Ibid., ii.136.7–12.

79 Ibid., ii.133.19–21.

80 Ibid., ii.134.2–13.

81 See, for instance, O'Flaherty, *Dreams*, p. 18 and passim. In addition to Yaśodharā's dream and Brahmā's interpretation of it, the Buddha is linked with clouds in two jātaka tales. In some versions of the *Dīpaṃkara Jātaka* the Buddha's name is Megha, meaning "cloud," and in the *Vessantara Jātaka* the action of the story is precipitated when the Buddha, known as Prince Vessantara, gives away a magnificent white elephant that ensures adequate rainfall, suggesting the continuum of elephant-rain-cloud. Additionally, an early Mahāyāna text, the *Ratnaguṇasaṃcayagāthā* uses the simile of a cloud to express the uniqueness and ineffability of a bodhisattva: "He becomes one who, like a cloud, stands in the sky without anywhere to stand on." Quoted by Ray, *Buddhist Saints*, p. 258.

82 *MSV*, 1: 81. See John Strong's discussion in "A Family Quest: The Buddha, Yaśodharā, and Rāhula in the *Mūlasarvāstivāda Vinaya*," in Schober, *Sacred Biography*, pp. 113–28.

83 *AS*, pp. 111–12.

84 Called "T'so Ping," ibid., pp. 107 ff.

85 Ibid., p. 126.

86 Ibid., pp. 126–27.

87 *LV*, Vaidya, 140.16–141.2. A.-M. Esnoul considers this one of the oldest passages in the text. See "Les songes et leur interprétation dans l'Inde," in *Les songes et leur interprétation*, ed. A.-M. Esnoul. (Paris: Éditions du Seuil, 1959), p. 238. Bays translates this dream and its interpretation in *The Voice of the Buddha*, pp. 293–96.

88 *LV*, Vaidya, 141.9–142.28.

89 This is a point made by O'Flaherty in her discussion of this dream (*Dreams*, p. 153), and the same point can be made about Brahmā's interpretation of dream imagery in the *MV*.

90 See A. L. Basham, *The Wonder That Was India: A Survey of the Culture of the Indian Sub-continent Before the Coming of the Muslims* (New York: Grove, 1959), pp. 186–87. For a modern study of widowhood see Susan S. Wadley, "No Longer a Wife: Widows in Rural North India," in *From the Margins of Hindu Marriage: Essays on Gender, Religion, and Culture*, ed. Lindsey Harlan and Paul B. Courtright (New York: Oxford University Press, 1995), pp. 92–118. See also a wife's (Maddi's) long lament, which has the refrain "the life of a widow is a bitter fate in this world," and in which she emphasizes that even if her husband is abusive, it is worse to be a widow. This text also enumerates a widow's sorrows and bad treatment; Margaret Cone and Richard Gombrich, *The Perfect Generosity of Prince Vessantara: A Buddhist Epic* (Oxford: Oxford University Press, 1977), pp. 29–30. Significantly, Maddi is the Buddha's wife in an earlier incarnation.

91 See, for example, *BC*, chaps. 9 and 10.

92 In *The Blue Annals* the Buddha also has two wives, though they are called Yaśodharā and Gopā; 'Gos Lo tsa ba Gźon nu dpal, *The Blue Annals*, trans. George N. Roerich (1949; Delhi: Motilal Banarsidass, 1976), p. 18, hereafter 'Gos Lo tsa ba, *Blue Annals*. For some comments on the Buddha's wives see *AS*, pp. 101–2 n. 1. See also André Bareau, "Un personnage bien mysterieux: l'épouse du Buddha," in *Indological and Buddhist Studies, Volume in Honour of Professor J. W. de Jong on His Sixtieth Birthday*, ed. L. A. Hercus et al. (Canberra: Australian National University, 1982), pp. 31–59.

93 *AS*, pp. 127–28.

94 Ibid., p. 128.

95 For Freud, as discussed below in chapter 3 in relation to Aśoka's dream, a woman's dream of her teeth falling out means giving birth; *Interpretation of Dreams*, p. 423 n. 1. Indeed, in the *MSV* this is the night Yaśodharā conceives Rāhula.

96 *MSV*, 1: 82. As Strong points out in "Family Quest," the Buddha and Yaśodharā have a much more interesting relationship in this text than in any of the other biographies. For early iconographic representations of Yaśodharā's dream see Karetzky, *Life of the Buddha*, p. 66.

97 *MSV*, 1: 83.

98 See Cone and Gombrich, *Perfect Generosity*, pp. xxxv–xliv, for the diffusion of this story and pp. 109–10 for a list of versions in other languages; see pp. xxxv–xxxvii for its iconographic representations. The Pali version contains the oldest surviving material. See also Forrest McGill, "Painting the 'Great Life,'" in Schober, *Sacred Biography*, pp. 195–217. For more on the jātakas in general see Maurice Winternitz, *A History of Indian Literature*, 3 vols. (1927; Delhi: Oriental Books Reprint, 1977), 2: 113–56; and Frank Reynolds, "Rebirth Traditions and the Lineages of Gotama: A Study in Theravāda Buddhology," pp. 20–24.

99 No. 547, *The Jātaka Together with Its Commentary*, ed. Fausbøll, 6: 540–41; hereafter *Jātaka*, Fausbøll. English translation, *The Jātaka*, ed. E. B. Cowell, 6 vols. (1895; London: Pali Text Society, 1973), hereafter *Jātaka*, Cowell.

100 See, respectively, the *Mahāhaṃsa*, the *Mora*, and the *Ruru Jātakas*, nos. 534, 159, and 482, *Jātaka*, Fausbøll. The *Ruru Jātaka* also occurs as tale no. 26 in the Sanskrit collection, the *Jātakamālā*, trans. J. S. Speyer (1895; New Delhi: Motilal Banarsidass, 1971), pp. 234–44. See also Schlingloff, *Ajanta Paintings*.

101 In this collection the only dream connected to conception is contained in the *Mahā Ummagga Jātaka* (no. 546)—when the Buddha's mother conceives, the local king dreams of a huge flame that illuminates the whole world. *Jātaka*, Fausbøll, 6: 331.

102 Ibid., 5: 42–43.

103 Ibid., 6: 186.

104 Ibid., 6: 324.

105 Ibid., 4: 295.

106 During the lifetime of the Buddha, Kosala was one of the four major independent states of northern India, though it was later absorbed by the state of

Magadha. Balkrishna Govind Gokhale, *Buddhism in Maharashtra: A History* (Bombay: Popular Prakashan, 1976), pp. 19, 22.

107 *Jātaka*, Fausbøll, 1: 342–43.

108 Another dream interpretation contest is contained in the *Śārdūlakarṇāvadāna*, discussed in chapter 3, and similar dream practices float between Buddhists and Hindus in the *Kathāsaritsāgara*, discussed in chapter 9.

109 More will be said about the Buddha as an innovative dream interpreter in the next chapter.

110 For more on Māra see Patricia Eichenbaum Karetzky, "Māra, Buddhist Deity of Death and Desire," *East and West*, no. 32 (1982): 75–92; Ernst Windisch, *Māra und Buddha* (Leipzig: S. Hirzel, 1895); and chapter 4 of the *Saṃyuttanikāya* (trans. as *The Book of Kindred Sayings* by C. A. F. Rhys Davids and F. L. Woodward, 5 vols. [London: Pali Text Society, 1917–30]), which contains various confrontations between the Buddha and Māra.

111 O'Flaherty, *Dreams*, p. 31, briefly discusses instances from the *Mahābhārata* and the *Rāmāyaṇa* in which those who will be defeated have nightmares before a battle.

112 *LV*, Vaidya, 219.4–8. Bays translates this dream in *The Voice of the Buddha*, 2: 459–61.

113 *LV*, Vaidya, 220.21–221.18. Māra's dream and his conversation with his son afterwards are essentially the same in the *AS*, pp. 199–203.

114 *LV*, Vaidya, 230.30.

115 Ibid., 141.9.

116 Buddhaghosa, *Manorathapūraṇī*, v.xx.6. See also Buddhaghosa's *Samantapāsādikā*, ed. J. Takakusu and M. Nagai (London: Pali Text Society, 1930), 3: 520.

117 Liz Wilson is particularly helpful on these points. See *Charming Cadavers: Horrific Figurations of the Feminine in Indian Buddhist Hagiographic Literature* (Chicago: University of Chicago Press, 1996), pp. 70–76.

118 The Buddha also interprets the King of Kosala's dream and the *LV* lists dream interpretation as one of his accomplishments (156.17). See also *Vinaya* I.x.2.15 where the Buddha includes a meaningful dream in a story he tells, one which reveals his deep understanding of dreams.

119 Ong, *Orality and Literacy*, pp. 23, 34. See also Norman N. Holland, foreword to *The Dream and the Text*, ed. Rupprecht, p. xviii.

Chapter 3

1 Kakar's recent work in India shows the persistence of these ancient ideas; see *Shamans, Mystics, and Doctors,* e.g., pp. 51, 84.

2 Lincoln, *The Dream in Primitive Cultures,* p. 26. Freud discusses some of the European arguments that have been offered both for and against taking moral responsibility for our dreams. See, for example, *Interpretation of Dreams,* pp. 101, 658–59. O'Flaherty discusses a folktale with a similar theme in *Dreams,* p. 67.

3 For discussion of the structure of the Pali *Vinaya* see Hermann Oldenberg's introductions to the Pali edition, *Vinaya Piṭaka,* vol. 1 (1879; London: Pali Text Society, 1969), hereafter *Vinaya,* Oldenberg; and I. B. Horner's introduction to her translation entitled *The Book of the Discipline* (London: Oxford University Press, 1938). For a thorough discussion of this and other Buddhist vinayas see Lamotte, *History of Indian Buddhism,* pp. 165–79.

4 *Vinaya,* Oldenberg, respectively, III.112 and IV.30–31.

5 Ibid., III.112. This point is upheld by the *Kathāvatthu,* a compilation of controversial points among the various schools of early Buddhism, which cites the Buddha as having said "what is done in a dream is not really done." *Sabbaṃ supinagatassa cittaṃ abyākatan. Kathāvatthu,* ed. Arnold C. Taylor (1894; London: Pali Text Society, 1979), XXII.6. A later Mahāyāna text, *The Large Sūtra on Perfect Wisdom,* trans. Edward Conze (Berkeley: University of California Press, 1975), p. 415, makes the point that while a dream itself is without karmic accumulation, when the dreamer wakes up and thinks it over her or his reaction to the dream may have a karmic accumulation. For instance, if one dreams of killing someone and then wakes up thinking that was the right thing to do, this is said to be equivalent to the conscious notion of wanting to kill someone.

6 *Vinaya,* Oldenberg, III.39.

7 See Bolling, "Dreams and Sleep," pp. 38–40. See also *Ṛgveda,* 10.164.3.

8 E.g., *Vinaya,* Oldenberg, II.125.

9 *LV,* Vaidya, 97.26.

10 *Vinaya,* Oldenberg, I.295.

11 Ibid.

12 The Sanskrit dramatist Bhāsa used such a dream for the title of his play, the *Svapnavāsavadatta,* and we will see another example in the *Aśokāvadāna,* to be discussed shortly.

13 He may have based his work on earlier, now lost, sources. Hirakawa, *History of Indian Buddhism,* pp. 125, 133–34. See also Carter, "Buddhaghosa," 2: 332–33.

14 Buddhaghosa, *Manorathapūraṇī* v.xx.6, 3: 316; Buddhaghosa, *Samantapāsādikā,* 3: 520.

15 This primary division of dreams into true and false is the usual first step in any dream theory. See Freud, *Interpretation of Dreams,* p. 37; and Dodds, *The Greeks and the Irrational,* pp. 106–7, who refers to them as significant and non-significant dreams.

16 Buddhaghosa, *Manorathapūraṇī* v.xx.6, p. 316. An analogous idea existed in ancient Greece; see John J. Winkler, *The Constraints of Desire: The Anthropology of Sex and Gender in Ancient Greece* (New York: Routledge, 1990), p. 33, where he cites Artemidorous's view that "a few persons of perfect virtue are said to have mainly or only predictive dreams" and notes a similar view in Plato.

17 He also makes this point in the *Samantapāsādikā,* 3: 521.

18 *Tañ ca pan' etaṃ catubbidham pi supinaṃ sekhaputhujjanā va passanti appahīnavipallāsatta, asekhā na passanti pahīnavipallāsattā.* Buddhaghosa, *Manorathapūraṇī* v.xx.6, p. 317. Despite its rich tradition of dream practice, this may hold true for the Mahāyāna tradition as well. According to Thrangu Rinpoche, at a certain point realized beings will cease to dream; personal communication, Sarnath, India, March 14, 1995. See also Namkhai Norbu, *Dream Yoga and the Practice of Natural Light* (Ithaca: Snow Lion, 1992), pp. 29, 59, 64, 110.

19 Carrithers, in "Hell-Fire and Urinal Stones," briefly alludes to the continuing use of these dream theories by present day Sri Lankan Buddhist monks, pp. 26–28 and passim. In the spring of 1995 I lived in the Thai Monastery at Sarnath, India, where I was able to discuss the dream process with many visiting Theravāda monks, all of whom espoused this view. A similar position is ascribed to the early Mahāsāṅghika sect by Vasumitra in the *Samayabhedoparacanacakra,* which states their belief that the Buddha never slept or dreamed; quoted by Strong, *Experience of Buddhism,* p. 131.

20 See the dream of a modern Thai monk in Tambiah, *Buddhist Saints of the Forest,* p. 83, which is taken seriously as a sign of future enlightenment and, consequently, also as a sign of his not yet being enlightened. This same monk, however, also dreams *after* his enlightenment (pp. 100–101). The study of dreams in Buddhism is fraught with such contradictions.

21 Though parts of this text were composed in the first century B.C.E. in northwestern India, book 4, the subject of discussion here, was added in Sri Lanka perhaps as early as the second century C.E.; T. Pobozniak, "Genesis of the

Milindapañha," in *Sanskrit and World Culture,* Schriften zur Geschichte und Kultur des Alten Orients, no. 18 (Berlin: Akademie Verlag, 1986), p. 508. See also Lamotte's older, but still useful, discussion of this text and the historicity of King Menander (Milinda), *History of Indian Buddhism,* pp. 419–26.

22 *Kin c' etaṁ supinaṁ nāma, ko c' etaṁ passatīti. Milindapañha,* Trenckner, bk. 4, dilemma 75, p. 298; Rhys Davids, *Questions of King Milinda,* pp. 157 ff.

23 Rhys Davids, *Questions of King Milinda,* pp. 157–58 n. 3.

24 This text also lists other causes as bodily disturbances and messages from the gods. Though composed at a later date than the rest of the *Vedas* (sixth century C.E.), this text contains ideas from earlier periods. Indeed, Anne-Marie Esnoul refers to it as the most ancient Indian text on dreams for which some of the sources remain unknown; "Les songes," p. 215. It also contains examples of both good and bad dreams as well as ways to cancel out the harmful effects of bad dreams through festivals and offerings (pp. 217–20). See also Bolling, "Dreams and Sleep," p. 38; and O'Flaherty, *Dreams,* pp. 19, 24, where she summarizes some of the ideas contained in this text.

25 *Milindapañha,* Trenckner, p. 298.

26 Ibid., p. 298.

27 *Nimittaṁ āgantvā cittassa āpātham upagacchati.* Ibid., p. 298.

28 *Taṁ cittaṁ supinaṁ passati na taṁ cittaṁ jānāti: evaṁ nāma vipāko bhavissati khemaṁ vā bhayaṁ vā ti.* Ibid., p. 299.

29 See the discussion of dreams in Indian and Tibetan medical literature in chapter 4.

30 *Chāndogya Upaniṣad,* in A. N. Bhattacharya, *One Hundred and Twelve Upaniṣads and Their Philosophy,* Parimal Sanskrit Series, no. 26 (Delhi: Parimal Publications, 1987), 8.7–12; *Māṇḍūkya Upaniṣad,* in ibid., 1–12.

31 Jan Gonda cites several examples of dreams or dreamlike states that have been used as examples of māyā's power both in its negative and positive aspects in the *Upaniṣads* (p. 171), in the Vedānta philosopher Gauḍapāda (pp. 176, 180–81), in Śaṅkara (p. 185), in Rāmānuja (pp. 188–89), in the Vedānta sūtras generally (p. 180), in Sarvajñātma Muni (p. 185) as well as in the Buddhist Mādhyamika school (p. 178); Gonda, *Change and Continuity in Indian Religion* (The Hague: Mouton, 1965), chap. 6, "Māyā." Mircea Eliade adds Patañjali to this list; *Yoga: Immortality and Freedom,* trans. Willard R. Trask (Princeton: Princeton University Press, 1958), pp. 36, 89. See also O'Flaherty, *Dreams,* pp. 114 ff., for her survey of māyā in Indian thought and the relation of māyā to dreams.

32 Similarly, one can find many tales involving dream narrations in Brahmanical literature. For further discussion of dreams in South Asian folklore and literary texts, see Serinity Young, "Dreams," in *South Asian Folklore: An Encyclopedia,* ed. Peter J. Claus and Margaret A. Mills (New York: Garland, forthcoming).

33 The *Divyāvadāna* was popular in Northwest India, Central Asia, and Tibet; John S. Strong, *The Legend of King Aśoka,* pp. 16–28. According to Strong it is, however, clearly a Hīnayānā text of that region (p. 164).

34 The Pali version of the Aśoka legend, preserved in the *Mahāvaṃsa* and other texts, does not mention a son called Kuṇāla; rather, it focuses on a son called Mahinda, who is said to have been the first Buddhist missionary to Sri Lanka. For a comparison of these two versions see Strong, *The Legend of King Aśoka,* pp. 18–26, and for various versions of Kuṇāla's story in Northern Buddhist countries see p. 151 n. 32.

35 This chapter was translated into Tibetan in the eleventh century by Padmākaravarman and Rinchen bZangpo, ibid., p. 171.

36 Strong, *The Legend of King Aśoka,* pp. 274–75.

37 Freud has some interesting things to say about what he calls dreams "with a dental stimulus" (p. 420). For instance, if a man dreams his teeth are removed, Freud takes it to symbolize castration (*Interpretation of Dreams,* pp. 392, 422 n. 1.) Whether there is a connection in the early Indian context, with its emphasis on ancestor worship, between castration and the death (or blinding) of an only son will have to remain an open question. See also the *CS* v.35, 2: 549–50, which lists dreaming about the loss of teeth as one of the premonitory symptoms of death or serious disease, but for the dreamer, not the dreamer's son. For Freud, when a woman has such a dream it means giving birth (*Interpretation of Dreams,* p. 423 n. 1). Interestingly, in the *Mūlasarvāstivāda Vinaya* the Buddha's wife dreams, among other things, that her teeth fell out. She has this dream on the night she conceives her son Rāhula. This dream imagery and its dismissal are also found in the dream of Padmasambhava's wife on the night before he, too, leaves home, *Padma,* f. 57b 4–6.

38 Strong, *The Legend of King Aśoka,* p. 283.

39 Ibid., pp. 285–86.

40 O'Flaherty, *Dreams,* p. 36.

41 *Divyāvadāna,* ed. P. L. Vaidya (Darbhanga: Mithila Institute, 1959), 33.617–732. For a loose translation of this section of the text see Sharmishta Sharma, *Astrological Lore in the Buddhist Śārdūlakarṇāvadāna* (Delhi: Eastern Book Linkers, 1992), pp. 57–60.

42 *Divyāvadāna,* ed. Vaidya, pp. 617–20, 624–25, 697.

43 Ibid., 648. For more on female asceticism in ancient India, both Brahmanical and Buddhist, see Serinity Young, "Gendered Politics in Ancient Indian Asceticism," *Union Seminary Quarterly Review* 48, nos. 3–4 (1994): 73–92. These and other notions about women and dreaming will be discussed in chapter 10.

44 The doctrine of no self is perhaps most famously formulated in Nāgasena's simile of the chariot in the *Milindapañha,* Trenckner, pp. 25–28. A helpful presentation of various theories of consciousness in Buddhist thought is D. J. Kalupahana, "Consciousness," in *Encyclopedia of Buddhism,* 4: 230–42; and Nakamura Hajime, "Buddhism, Schools of: Mahāyāna Buddhism," in *EOR,* esp. 2: 466–71.

45 *Milindapañha,* Trenckner, p. 40. See also Collins, *Selfless Persons,* pp. 213–18, for his discussion of the transmigration of consciousness, and pp. 242–48 for consciousness in the death and rebirth process.

46 The five sense organs—eyes, ears, nose, tongue, and form—lead to sight, hearing, smell, taste, and touch; the mind *(manas)* is taken as the sixth organ, leading to perception and consciousness *(vijñāna).*

47 This doctrine appears throughout early Buddhist literature, including the *BC,* XIV.53 ff., and the *LV,* chap. 22. See Collins, *Selfless Persons,* pp. 116–43 and passim for a more thorough exposition of the self and reality in relation to epistemology in early Buddhism. But see also Patrick Olivelle's discussion of the "new" individualism of the sixth century B.C.E. sramanic movements in contrast to the Vedic model of self; *Saṃnyāsa Upaniṣads: Hindu Scriptures on Asceticism and Renunciation* (New York: Oxford University Press, 1992), pp. 32–36, 42–51.

48 This is perhaps seen most clearly in Buddhism's involvement in the death ceremony anniversaries of South and East Asia. See Swearer, "Folk Religion," p. 376. See also Gregory Schopen, "Archaeology and Protestant Presuppositions in the Study of Indian Buddhism," *History of Religions* 31 (August 1991–May 1992): 13–15, for archaeological and epigraphic evidence of Buddhist belief in a continuing self after death.

49 Sudhir Kakar has wonderfully captured the East-West distinction when he says, "The Indian injunction 'Know Thyself' *(atmanamvidhi)* is related to a Self other than the one referred to by Socrates. It is a self uncontaminated by time and space and thus without the life-historical dimension which is the focus of psychoanalysis and of Western romantic literature." *Shamans, Mystics, and Doctors,* pp. 7–8. See also Alan Roland, *In Search of Self in India and Japan: Toward a Cross-Cultural Psychology* (Princeton: Princeton University Press, 1988), pp. 7–10 and passim, who distinguishes between the "I-self" of the West and the "we-self" of Asia.

50 Anne C. Klein, *Meeting the Great Bliss Queen: Buddhists, Feminists and the Art of the Self* (Boston: Beacon Press, 1995), p. 44. In chapter 2 Klein offers an interesting comparative discussion of the notions of the self in Western and Buddhist thought. See also the dialog between His Holiness the Dalai Lama and the philosopher Charles Taylor in *Sleeping, Dreaming, and Dying: An Exploration of Consciousness with The Dalai Lama*, ed. Francisco J. Varela (Boston: Wisdom, 1997), pp. 11–21, and the more general discussion of consciousness and the self on pp. 86–98 and 111–26.

51 Collins arrives at similar conclusions, but his analysis is based on what he sees as the dichotomous discourses about the self of the little and great traditions; *Selfless Persons*, esp. pp. 147–54 and passim.

52 See, for example, Klein, *Path to the Middle*, and Janice D. Willis, *Enlightened Beings: Life Stories from the Ganden Oral Tradition* (Boston: Wisdom, 1995), both of which are based on the oral tradition, and the editors' introduction to *Tibetan Literature: Studies in Genre*, ed. José Ignacio Cabezón and Roger R. Jackson (Ithaca: Snow Lion, 1996), p. 14.

53 Ong, *Orality and Literacy*, p. 29. I would suggest that some strong evidence for this can be found in the way Tibetans have almost "fetishized" writing in the ubiquitous use of prayer flags, prayer wheels, mani stones, amulets, and so on. Writing maintains a "magical" quality that eludes those who have interiorized literacy and possess a literate consciousness rather than an oral one.

54 Ibid., p. 54.

55 For a thoughtful essay on the importance of such differences, particularly in relation to the notion of a self, see Collins, *Selfless Persons*, pp. 1–26.

Chapter 4

1 Sogyal Rinpoche, *The Tibetan Book of Living and Dying* (San Francisco: HarperSanFrancisco, 1993), pp. 98–99. For additional examples see Karma Thinley, *The History of the Sixteen Karmapas*, pp. 47, 110, 117, 119, etc.; and Michael Aris, *Hidden Treasures and Secret Lives: A Study of Pemalingpa (1450–1521) and the Sixth Dalai Lama (1683–1706)* (Shimla: Indian Institute of Advanced Study, 1988), p. 128, who summarizes some of the dreams connected with finding the Sixth Dalai Lama.

2 See the brief discussion in Janet Gyatso, "Drawn from the Tibetan Treasury: The *gTer ma* Literature," in Cabezón and Jackson, *Tibetan Literature*, p. 153, for her important argument that *termas* are an indigenous Tibetan practice, pp. 154–55.

3 One of the best known *tertons* (discoverers of *termas*), Pemalingpa (1450–1521), only accepted as authoritative what he learned from Padmasambhava and the

ḍākinīs (semidivine women) through his dreams and visions. His autobiography is uniquely free of teachers or spiritual training of any sort other than through such dreams and visions. For some of his dreams and visions see Aris, *Hidden Treasures*, pp. 27–28, 37, 54–55, 79–80.

4 Giuseppe Tucci, *The Theory and Practice of the Mandala*, trans. Alan Houghton Brodrick (New York: Samuel Weiser, 1973), p. 91. Tucci actually records his own Hevajra initiation experiences of 1939, in which he was given a leaf to put under his pillow and told to recall his dreams. Fortunately, his dreams of mountain peaks were deemed auspicious and the initiation was confirmed (pp. 91–92). Such instructions might suggest to students of psychology that the teacher, through sought dreams, learns whether the student's subconscious is ready for initiation, but Tibetan Buddhists do not understand dreams in this way. Rather they emphasize that dream consciousness can be purer and more authoritative than waking consciousness and that it allows various deities to manifest in dreams either actually or symbolically in ways that can be interpreted as approving or denying the initiation.

5 Before the eighth century the word *bon* referred to a class of priests who invoked deities as distinct from those who offered sacrifices. For more information on Bon see Namkhai Norbu, *Drung, Deu, and Bon: Narrations, Symbolical Languages and the Bon Tradition in Ancient Tibet* (1982; Dharamsala: Library of Tibetan works and Archives, 1995); David L. Snellgrove, *The Nine Ways of Bon: Excerpts from gZi brjid* (London: Oxford University Press, 1967); and Per Kvaerne, *The Bon Religion of Tibet* (Boston: Shambhala, 1996).

6 Tucci, *Religions of Tibet*, pp. 163–212, 241. See also Samuel, "Early Buddhism in Tibet," pp. 383–94; and David Snellgrove, *Indo-Tibetan Buddhism: Indian Buddhists and Their Tibetan Successors* (London: Serindia, 1987), pp. 386–407.

7 Samuel, "Early Buddhism in Tibet," pp. 390–94.

8 Ibid., pp. 383–88. He elaborates on this thesis in *Civilized Shamans: Buddhism in Tibetan Societies* (Washington, DC: Smithsonian Institution Press, 1993). Shamanism is most often found among loosely organized social groups. This is similar to Padmanabh S. Jaini's discussion of ancient Indian religion through contrasting sramanic and Brahmanic movements; Padmanabh S. Jaini, "*Śramaṇas:* Their Conflict with Brāhmaṇical Society," in *Chapters in Indian Civilization*, ed. Joseph W. Elder (Dubuque: Kendall/Hunt, 1970), 1: 39–82. Samuel is not alone, however, in referring to this enduring legacy among Tibetan lamas and monks today. For instance, see Kapstein, "The Illusion of Spiritual Progress," pp. 197–98; Barbara Aziz, "Reincarnation Reconsidered: Or the Reincarnate Lama as Shaman," in *Spirit Possession in the Nepal Himalayas*, ed. John T. Hitchock and Rex L. Jones (1976; New Delhi: Vikas Publishing House, 1996), pp. 343–60; William Stablein, "Mahākāla the Neo-shaman Master of the Ritual," in ibid., pp. 361–75; and Robert

A. Paul, "Some Observations on Sherpa Shamanism," in ibid., esp. pp. 150–51, which contain fairly recent examples of shamanism losing ground to Buddhism.

9 Snellgrove and Richardson, *Cultural History of Tibet*, p. 55.

10 See the discussion of these lamas in the section on medical texts at the end of this chapter.

11 For a short but useful discussion of Buddhism's adaptation of pre-Buddhist Tibetan folklore to explain Buddhist doctrine to a wide audience see Michael J. Sweet "Mental Purification *(Blo sbyong):* A Native Tibetan Genre of Religious Literature," in Cabezón and Jackson, *Tibetan Literature*, pp. 246–47.

12 Alexandra David-Neel and Lama Yongden, eds. and trans., *The Superhuman Life of Gesar of Ling* (Boston: Shambhala, 1981), pp. 194, 216–17. Given the great number of versions of the Gesar epic that exist, I have accepted this readily available translation, not as authoritative but rather as richly suggestive of the pervasiveness of dreams in this epic. For a discussion of the versions in East Tibet, see Geoffrey Samuel, "The Gesar Epic of East Tibet," in Cabezón and Jackson, *Tibetan Literature*, pp. 358–67.

13 David-Neel and Yongden, *The Superhuman Life of Gesar of Ling*, pp. 99, 107–8, 213, 219, 222, 234, 235, and 251.

14 Ibid., pp. 71–72, 75, 113–14, 171, 211, and 233.

15 Serinity Young, "Dreams," in *South Asian Folklore: An Encyclopedia* (forthcoming).

16 David-Neel and Yongden, *The Superhuman Life of Gesar of Ling*, pp. 68, 129, 180–84, 188–89.

17 Ibid., pp. 107–8.

18 René de Nebesky-Wojkowitz, *Oracles and Demons of Tibet: The Cult and Iconography of the Tibetan Protective Deities* (1956; Graz, Austria: Akademische Drück- u.Verlagsanstalt, 1975), p. 465.

19 Ibid., p. 465.

20 Ibid., pp. 465–66.

21 Ibid., p. 466.

22 Ibid., p. 472.

23 Norbu Chophel, *The Folk Culture of Tibet* (Dharamsala: Library of Tibetan Works and Archives, 1983), pp. 89–104.

24 Ibid., p. 94.

25 Ibid., p. 92.

26 Some indigenous sources for the early history of Buddhism in Tibet are: Sa skya pa Bla ma Dam pa Bsod nams rgyal mtshan, *Rgyal rabs gsal ba'i me loṅ*, trans. as *The Clear Mirror: A Traditional Account of Tibet's Golden Age* by McComas Taylor and Lama Choedak Yuthok (Ithaca: Snow Lion, 1996); Bu ston, *The History of Buddhism in India and Tibet;* 'Gos Lo tsa ba, *Blue Annals.* Western sources include Tucci, *Religions of Tibet;* and Snellgrove, *Indo-Tibetan Buddhism.*

27 Translated in Snellgrove and Richardson, *Cultural History of Tibet*, p. 38. The inscription appears on the Skar-cung stone pillar at Ra mo sgang near Lhasa (see figures 2 and 3).

28 For a brief discussion of some of these editions see *Encyclopedia Tibetica: The Collected Works of Bo-doṅ Paṇ-chen Phyogs-las-rnam-rgyal* (New Delhi: Tibet House Library, 1969), 2: 1–7.

29 A succinct summary of the four main philosophical schools of Buddhism in relation to the illusory nature of reality is contained in Geshe Wangyal, *The Door of Liberation: Essential Teachings of the Tibetan Buddhist Tradition* (New York: Maurice Girodias, 1972), pp. 16–18. See also Hajime Nakamura, "Buddhism, Schools of: Mahāyāna," especially pp. 466–71; and Yoshinori Takeuchi and John P. Keenan, "Buddhist Philosophy," pp. 540–47, both in *EOR;* and Paul Williams, *Mahāyāna Buddhism*, chaps. 3–5.

30 For a full philosophical discussion of this notion see Frederick J. Streng, *Emptiness: A Study in Religious Meaning* (Nashville: Abingdon Press, 1967). See also Paul, *Tibetan Symbolic World*, esp. pp. 43–80, for an anthropological and psychoanalytic discussion of this topic, and Collins, *Selfless Persons*, pp. 147–54.

31 Actually there are eight, sometimes twelve, similes for reality, understood as phenomena (dharmas), used to illustrate emptiness. In the list of eight, the dharmas are said "to be like an illusion, a mirage, a reflection of the moon in water, a dream, an echo, an apparition, an image in the mirror, a magical creation"; Conze, *The Large Sutra on Perfect Wisdom*, p. 38. A Tibetan list of twelve adds to these eight a castle in the air, lightning, rainbows, and bubbles; Sarat Chandra Das, *A Tibetan-English Dictionary* (Delhi: Motilal Banarsidass, 1976), s.v. *sgyu-ma'i dpe bcu gnyis*, p. 329. See also the list of twelve similes in Herbert V. Guenther, *The Life and Teachings of Nāropa* (New York: Oxford University Press, 1963), p. 63. Magical creations, or displays by realized beings, and apparitions of deities or other beings or objects appear frequently in Buddhist literature in order to impart a lesson on the nature of reality. Dreams serve this didactic purpose as well, but, unlike the other similes, they break out into additional meanings, in part perhaps because more people dream than experience apparitions or magical creations.

32 For an example of the Mahāyāna view see the *Aṣṭasāhasrikā Prajñāpāramitā*, one of the most ancient Mahāyāna sūtras, which contains a long passage equating magical illusion and dreams and then lists a variety of beings and ideas which are like both of these, e.g. all beings, all objective facts, the various classes of saints (including buddhas), buddhahood itself, and even nirvana. Quoted by MacQueen, "Inspired Speech," pt. 2, p. 57. At the same time, this text also affirms the revelatory importance of dreams, ibid., p. 52. Even Milarepa's songs contain a brief reference to the teaching that dreams are illusions in Prajñāpāramitā literature, Gtsaṅ smyon, *Mgur 'bum*, p. 645.

33 For a Tibetan example of the pervasiveness of this teaching see Deshung Rinpoche, *The Three Levels of Spiritual Perception*, trans. Jared Rhoton (Boston: Wisdom, 1995). This is a translation of the introduction to the "Path and Fruit" *(lam 'bras)* system of meditation, which frequently uses dreams to illustrate the illusory nature of all existence.

34 Conze, *The Large Sutra on Perfect Wisdom*, p. 247.

35 Ibid., p. 389.

36 Ibid., pp. 431–33.

37 Ibid., p. 433.

38 Ibid., p. 415.

39 Geshe Yeshe Thapkay of Deemed University in Sarnath explained that aspiring bodhisattvas meditate on emptiness in their dreams through the use of certain mantras, but they cease dreaming after the eighth stage. Conversation, Sarnath, April 8, 1995.

40 See Louis de La Vallée Poussin, "Studies in Buddhist Dogma: The Three Bodies of a Buddha *(Trikāya)*," *Journal of the Royal Asiatic Society* (1906): 943–77; Gadjin Nagao, "On the Theory of Buddha-Bodies," *Eastern Buddhist* 6, no. 1 (1973): 25–53; and Rockhill, *Life of the Buddha*, pp. 200–202. See also the Dalai Lama's uncontextualized comments on these three bodies in Varela, *Sleeping, Dreaming, and Dying*, p. 46, which are somewhat difficult to understand without having the Tibetan terms.

41 In the Tibetan tradition it also refers to incarnating deities and enlightened beings who choose to continually reincarnate, e.g., the Dalai Lama.

42 MacQueen, "Inspired Speech," pts. 1 and 2.

43 This point is echoed by Paul Williams, *Mahāyāna Buddhism*, pp. 30 and 33. See also Raoul Birnbaum, *The Healing Buddha* (Boulder: Shambhala, 1979), pp. 44, 130, and 214.

44 MacQueen, "Inspired Speech," pt. 2, pp. 54–55.

45 An important source of information on the mahāsiddhas is the biographical collection of the eighty-four siddhas by Abhayadatta, the *Caturaśīta-siddha-pravṛtti*, written between the end of the eleventh century and the beginning of the twelfth. Smon-grub Shes-rab made a Tibetan translation, from which both James Robinson and Keith Dowman have made translations into English. Reginald Ray, "Mahāsiddhas," in *EOR*, 9: 122–26, offers an excellent, brief overview of the siddhas. See also Tāranātha, *The Seven Instruction Lineages*, trans. David Templeman (Dharamsala: Library of Tibetan Works and Archives, 1983), for his account of fifty-nine siddhas and their lineages.

46 For more on Tantra see David White, ed., *The Religion of Tantra* (Princeton: Princeton University Press, in press).

47 See Samuel, "Early Buddhism in Tibet," pp. 390–94, for some of the shamanic characteristics of the mahāsiddhas.

48 Perhaps because the biographies in Abhayadatta's collection are short, dreams do not often appear in them, though they are prominent in Virūpa's short biography and in longer biographies. This is true for the jātakas in which dreams appear more frequently in the longer jātakas than in the shorter ones.

49 Janet Gyatso, "Genre, Authorship, and Transmission in Visionary Buddhism: The Literary Traditions of Thang-stong rGyal-po," in *Tibetan Buddhism: Reason and Revelation,* ed. Steven D. Goodman and Ronald M. Davidson (Albany: State University of New York Press, 1992), pp. 96–98.

50 There is a tradition that in the eighth century King Srongtsan Gampo held a medical conference in Tibet, which included physicians from Persia, India, China, and elsewhere. See Robert Sachs, *Health for Life: Secrets of Tibetan Ayurveda* (Santa Fe: Clear Light, 1995), p. 20; and Anthony Aris, ed., *Tibetan Medical Paintings* (New York: Harry N. Abrams, 1992), 1: 3. See also Winternitz, *History of Indian Literature*, 3: 665–68, for a discussion of some of the Buddhist medical texts found in Central Asia. For the very interesting and semi-legendary view of how medicine came into the world in general and Tibet in particular see Rechung Rinpoche, *Tibetan Medicine* (1973; Berkeley: University of California Press, 1976), pp. 8–28. This work also contains a biography of a famous Tibetan doctor that includes a semi-legendary record of the origins of medical knowledge and healing plants (pp. 147–327) and a lengthy bibliography on studies of Tibetan medicine in Western languages (pp. 98–102).

51 Healing has often been associated with spiritual power—for instance, in Jesus' miraculous healing powers and the widespread and enduring cult of Asklepios. For these and other examples see Lawrence E. Sullivan, "Healing," in *EOR*, 6: 226.

52 Birnbaum, *The Healing Buddha*, pp. 3–19. This study of the celestial Medicine Buddha Bhaiṣajyaguru is essential reading for the understanding of healing in Mahāyāna Buddhism. His cult was widespread in Tibet; see Anthony Aris, *Tibetan Medical Paintings*, 1: 17–18, 2: 173–74.

53 Kenneth Zysk, *Asceticism and Healing in Ancient India: Medicine in the Buddhist Monastery* (New York: Oxford University Press, 1991).

54 Discussed in Birnbaum, *The Healing Buddha*, esp. pp. 26–34.

55 The historical Buddha is believed to have manifested as the Medicine Buddha in order to teach healing practices; see Rechung, *Tibetan Medicine*, pp. 8–11.

56 For more information on these texts see A. L. Basham, "The Practice of Medicine in Ancient and Medieval India," in *Asian Medical Systems: A Comparative Study*, ed. Charles Leslie (Berkeley: University of California Press, 1976), pp. 20–21. For a useful overview of Indian medical literature see Winternitz, *History of Indian Literature*, 3: 664–79.

57 Kakar, *Shamans, Mystics, and Doctors*, pp. 227–29, 246.

58 For Galen see Miller, *Dreams in Late Antiquity*, p. 46; for the Mesopotamian doctors and Hippocrates see Kilborne, "Dreams," pp. 483, 485.

59 Kilborne, "Dreams," p. 486. A valuable record of this process is the dream journal of Aelius Aristedes (b. 117 C.E.), which contains two hundred of his dreams while he sought a cure for various illness at the temple of Asklepios over a twenty-seven-year period. For an English translation see Charles A. Behr, *Aelius Aristedes and the Sacred Tales* (Amsterdam: Adolf M. Hakkert, 1968); see also Miller's useful discussion of this work in *Dreams in Late Antiquity*, pp. 184–204.

60 For the temple of Isis see Manabu Waida, "Miracles: An Overview," in *EOR*, 9: 544–45; for the temple of Ptah see J. G. Davis, "Architecture," in *EOR*, 1: 388.

61 See Eliade, *Shamanism;* and Irwin, *The Dream Seekers.*

62 *Dṛṣṭaṃ śrutanubhūtaṃ ca prāthirtaṃ kaplitaṃ kathā / bhāvikaṃ doṣajaṃ caiva svapnaṃ saptavidhaṃ. CS,* v. 43, 2: 551. See also Jadunath Sinha, *Indian Psychology: Perception* (London: Kegan Paul, Trench, Trubner, 1934), pp. 314–15, for a brief discussion of this passage. O'Flaherty summarizes this system by saying that the "seven categories of the Caraka thus cover waking experience, somatic impulses, imagination, and the influence of the supernatural." *Dreams,* p. 24.

63 *CS*, 2: 552.

64 In the *Brāhmaṇas* the gods have the direction of north, while "the south becomes the horizontal equivalent to the underworld; so that by transference it

also becomes the region of death." Gombrich, "Ancient Indian Cosmology," p. 116. Beings or things that go toward or come from the south are almost always given a negative interpretation in Indian dream theory, both Hindu and Buddhist.

65 *CS*, v. 8–24, 2: 545–48. See Dange, ed., *Encyclopaedia of Puranic Beliefs and Practices*, 2: 448, for more dreams threatening death and illness.

66 *CS*, v. 27–39, 2: 549–50.

67 *Pūrvarūpāṇyatha svapnān ya imān venti dāruṇān / na sa mohādasādhyesu kamārṇyārabhate bhiṣak*; ibid., v. 47, 2: 552.

68 On this belief in India see *Bṛhadāraṇyaka Upaniṣad* 4.3.14 and also William Crooke, *The Popular Religion and Folklore of Northern India*, 2d. ed. (1896; Delhi: Munshiram Manoharlal, 1968), 1: 231.

69 Hesiod, *Theogony* 211–13, 756–66; cited by Jonathan Z. Smith, "Sleep," in *EOR*, 13: 362. This article contains many useful comments on the connections between dreams, sleep, and death.

70 This point is brought out in the *Bṛhadāraṇyaka Upaniṣad*, where the discussion on dreams and sleep inevitably leads to the discussion of death (4.3.13–38 and 4.4). See more on the connections between death and dreaming in chapter 10 below.

71 *CS*, vv. 44–45, 2: 551. As we shall see in chapter 9, not sleeping again after an auspicious dream is one way of ensuring its promised outcome.

72 See Somadeva, *The Ocean of Story*, trans. C. H. Tawney (London: Chas. J. Sawyer, 1924), 8: 99–100 n. 2, which lists examples of similar beliefs in other cultures, as well as the Indian belief that dreams occurring in the first watch of the night take a year to come true, while those occurring at dawn will be fulfilled immediately. The immediate fulfillment of dawn dreams occurs time and again in the literary dreams that follow.

73 *Suśrutasaṃhitā of Suśruta*, ed. and trans. Vidya Jādavji Trikamji Āchārya, 4th ed. (Varanasi: Chowkhamba Orientalia, 1980), chap. 23, p. 135, ll. 54–57, hereafter the *SS*; trans. as *The Sushruta Samhita* by Kaviraj Kunjalal Bhishagratna, 2d ed. (Varanasi: Chowkhamba Sanskrit Series, 1963), 1: 279–80. The text continues with additional examples of dreams, most of which follow those in the *CS*.

74 *SS*, chap. 29, pp. 135–36, ll. 71–74.

75 Zysk, *Asceticism and Healing*, pp. 21–24.

76 Ibid., pp. 43–48.

77 Ibid., p. 51. An explicit example of this can be found in the preamble to the

biography of the Tibetan doctor Yuthog Yontan Gonpo, trans. in Rechung, *Tibetan Medicine*, pp. 179–82.

78 Zysk, *Asceticism and Healing*, p. 3. Todd Fenner challenges this view; see "The Origin of the *rGyud bzhi:* A Tibetan Medical Tantra," in Cabezón and Jackson, *Tibetan Literature*, pp. 458–69, especially pp. 466–67.

79 Aris, *Tibetan Medical Paintings*, pp. 4, 14–16.

80 *Rgyud bzhi: A Reproduction of a Set of Prints from the Eighteenth Century Zuṅ-cu Ze Blocks from the Collections of Raghu Vira, by O-rgyan Namgyal* (Leh, India: S. W. Tashigangpa, 1975), p. 10, f. 3, ll. 3–6 to p. 9, f. 4, l. 1. Rechung, *Tibetan Medicine*, p. 48, has translated part of this text, though he drew on a slightly different manuscript. Compare these dreams and the auspicious ones that follow to the excerpt from another Tibetan medical text, *The Ambrosia Heart Tantra*, in Chophel, *The Folk Culture of Tibet*, pp. 92–94, and *The Quintessence Tantras of Tibetan Medicine*, trans. Barry Clark (Ithaca: Snow Lion, 1995), pp. 69–70.

81 *Rgyud bzhi*, p. 9, f. 4, l. 1.

82 Ibid., p. 9, f. 4, ll. 2–3.

83 Even though Monier-Williams glosses *vaiḍūrya* as "a cat's-eye gem," and the translators of Sangye Gyatso's commentary as "beryl," I am influenced in taking this as lapis lazuli by Raoul Birnbaum's discussion of lapis lazuli in *The Healing Buddha*, pp. 80–81, and his translations of this term from Chinese texts. I will, however, continue to use *The Blue Beryl*, since this is the title of the only English translation (in Aris, *Tibetan Medical Paintings*).

84 For more information on Sangye Gyatso, an extremely important and very enigmatic figure, see Snellgrove and Richardson, *Cultural History of Tibet*, pp. 204–8.

85 Aris, *Tibetan Medical Paintings*. Aris has translated much of what follows somewhat out of sequence with the Leh edition that I used, and he incorporated material from the *Rgyud bzhi*, 1: 49.

86 Saṅs rgyas rgya mtsho, *Vaiḍūrya sṅon po*, ed. T. Y. Tashigangpa (Leh: 1973), vol. 1, f. 222, l. 5.

87 Other interpretations of the three times for dreaming can be found in Chophel, *The Folk Culture of Tibet*, p. 95, who cites Longdol Lama's *Sung-bum* as saying that dusk dreams reflect previous experiences, midnight dreams are caused by ghosts and other spirits, while dawn dreams are prophetic. The *Milam Tagpa* says that "in the first part of the night habitual propensities *(bag chags)* are agitat-

ed; in the second part of the night ghosts are active; so examine the dream that comes in the third part of the night." Tanjur, vol. *tshi*, f. 130a.

88 *Vaiḍūrya sṅon po*, f. 224–25.

89 Ibid., f. 225.

90 Significantly, given the emphasis on seeing dreams, among its many bodily functions, the *srog rlung* maintains good eyesight; Rechung, *Tibetan Medicine*, pp. 103–21.

91 In addition to the foregoing citations, important discussions of South Asian perspectives of the body are Gerald James Larson, "Āyurveda and the Hindu Philosophical Systems," in *Self as Body in Asian Theory and Practice*, ed. Thomas P. Kasulis et al. (Albany: State University of New York Press, 1993), pp. 102–21; and Shasi Bhushan Dasgupta, *An Introduction to Tantric Buddhism* (1958; Berkeley: Shambhala, 1974), pp. 146–58.

92 Rechung, *Tibetan Medicine*, pp. 187–88 (dreams of Yuthog's mother); 210, 235, 256, 259 (Yuthog); 148–49, 223 (others).

93 See, for example, Tashi Tsering Josayma and K. Dhondup, *Dolma and Dolkar: Mother and Daughter of Tibetan Medicine* (New Delhi: Yarlung, 1990), which details the medical practices (such as pulse taking and urine analysis) of two well-known Tibetan doctors but never mentions dreams. Yet when I asked Dr. Lozang Tenzin, the staff physician at the Central Institute of Higher Tibetan Studies, if he used dreams in his practice, he said that he does not use them very much but that he does pay attention to his dreams for his own health, and sometimes he dreams about other people's health. Personal communication, Sarnath, India, March 10, 1997.

94 D. L. Snellgrove, *Four Lamas of Dolpo* (Cambridge: Harvard University Press, 1967), 1: 183–230. An example of a monk dreaming the *cause* of someone's illness can be found in Chophel, *The Folk Culture of Tibet*, pp. 94–95; here it is said, however, that monks cannot dream a cure to the illness.

95 This is not the place to attempt to sort out the ongoing practices and relationships of monks, lamas, and shamans. Sherry B. Ortner has succinctly summed up the similarities and differences in their roles in the Tibetan Buddhist Sherpa communities of present-day Nepal in *Sherpas through Their Rituals* (Cambridge: Cambridge University Press, 1978), p. 179 n. 2. See also the discussion in Kapstein, "The Illusion of Spiritual Progress," passim. For a brief discussion of dreaming among oracles, who are frequently consulted to find the cure for illness, see Hildegard Diemberger, "Lhakama *(lha-bka'-ma)* and Khandroma *(mkha'-'gro-ma)*: The Sacred Ladies of Beyul Khenbalung *(sbas-yul mKan-pa-lung)*," in *Tibetan History and Language: Studies Dedicated to Uray Géza on His Seventieth Birthday*, ed. Ernst

Steinkellner (Vienna: Arbeitskreis für Tibetische und Buddhistische Studien, Universität Wien, 1991), pp. 143, 146–47.

96 Snellgrove, *Four Lamas of Dolpo*, p. 220.

97 Ibid., p. 205.

Chapter 5

1 Charles F. Keyes, "Death of Two Buddhist Saints," p. 152. Tambiah takes a similar position in his discussion of three general features of Buddhist sacred biographies; *Buddhist Saints of the Forest*, p. 124.

2 Lincoln, *The Dream in Primitive Cultures*, pp. 6–7. Otto Rank's study of the hero also includes such dreams; "The Myth of the Birth of the Hero," in *In Quest of the Hero*, pp. 18–42; and Jones, *On the Nightmare*, has a short discussion of the belief in conception dreams.

3 See Bitel, *"In Visu Noctis,"* p. 52; and Bulkeley, *The Wilderness of Dreams*, p. 234 n. 9, for a bibliography from several traditions.

4 Other examples include Hagar (Gen. 16: 11–12), Abraham and Sarah (Gen. 17: 19–20, 18: 9–10), Samson's mother (Judg. 13: 3–5), and John the Baptist's father (Luke 1: 13–17). The main purpose of these annunciations is to predict the future of the child, usually male, and to describe the part he will play in God's divine plan.

5 This tradition continues today as can be seen in a recent Tibetan autobiography that describes the conception dream of the subject's mother: "The night of my conception my mother had a very significant dream that a being had entered her body with a flash of light." Chögyam Trungpa, *Born in Tibet* (Harmondsworth, U.K.: Penguin, 1971), p. 25, and by a story Namkhai Norbu tells of such a conception, *Dream Yoga*, pp. 106–7.

Conception dreams also figure in the biographies of Buddhists in other cultures as well. For instance, in his remarks at the Conference on Medieval Japanese Buddhist Women held at Columbia University in December of 1989, Prof. Kazuo Osumi said that the biographies of Chinese Buddhist monks often contain the dreams of their mothers, in which a deity tells them they will have a child that the mother promises to raise as a monk. An example of a Chinese nun's mother having such a dream and acting on it can be found in the biography of the fifth-century nun Seng-Ching, in Pao-ch'ang, *Lives of the Nuns: Biographies of Chinese Buddhist Nuns from the Fourth to Sixth Centuries, trans.* Kathryn Ann Tsai (Honolulu: University of Hawai'i Press, 1994), p. 69.

6 See David-Neel and Yongden, *The Superhuman Life of Gesar of Ling*, pp. 71–72, though it is a rather ambiguous passage.

7 *Tibetan Folk Opera: Drowa Sangmo,* trans. C. B. Josayma (Dharamsala: Library of Tibetan Works and Archives, 1983), p. 2.

8 Recall, though, Brahmā's guide to the symbols of conception dreams which includes predictions about future kings; *MV,* II.13. See also *AS,* pp. 38–39.

9 The Sanskrit word for this type of birth is *svayambhū,* meaning self-existent and indicating a divine birth. In Buddhist iconography the lotus is almost always the seat of buddhas and bodhisattvas, and it is ubiquitous in Buddhist art either as a seat or as held in the hand; it is representative of purity, beauty, and *bodhicitta* (mind of enlightenment). See Adrian Snodgrass, *The Symbolism of the Stupa* (1985; New Delhi: Motilal Banarsidass, 1992), p. 204. For examples of other births from lotuses and for lotus symbolism in general, see pp. 97–100 and 203–8. See also the excellent discussion in E. Dale Saunders, *Mudrā: A Study of Symbolic Gestures in Japanese Buddhist Sculpture* (New York: Pantheon Books, 1960), pp. 159–64; Alice Getty, *The Gods of Northern Buddhism: Their History and Iconography* (1914; New York: Dover, 1988), pp. 192–93; Coomaraswamy, *Elements of Buddhist Iconography,* pp. 17–19.

10 The importance of conception dreams in the biographies of Buddhist heroes can be seen in the biographical collection of the eighty-four siddhas in the story of Sakara, another name for Padmasambhava. In this story Padma does have a mother who has a conception dream *and* he is still born from a lotus. See Robinson's translation of Abhayadatta's *Caturaśīta-siddha-pravṛtti, Buddha's Lions,* pp. 227–28.

11 *Padma,* f. 45b.6 to 46a.1. W. Y. Evans-Wentz's translation of another edition of Padmasambhava's biography contains an additional dream. After Indrabhūti dreams, "the Buddhist priests, too, had an auspicious dream, which perturbed the non-Buddhist priests: they beheld a thousand suns illuminating the world"; Evans-Wentz, *The Tibetan Book of the Great Liberation,* p. 107.

12 For more on this ritual object and its meanings see Saunders, *Mudrā,* pp. 184–91; and Getty, *The Gods of Northern Buddhism,* p. 200. See also Agehananda Bharati, *The Tantric Tradition* (1965; New York: Samuel Weiser, 1975); and Snellgrove, *Indo-Tibetan Buddhism,* pp. 128–34. The bell is the complementary female ritual object.

13 *Mtsho skyes rdo rje, Padma,* f. 46a.6.

14 *Padma,* f. 127b.5–6. *Life and Liberation of Padmasambhava,* trans. Kenneth Douglas and Gwendolyn Bays (Berkeley: Dharma, 1978), p. 309, afterwards *Life and Liberation.*

15 *Padma,* f. 136a.4–6. *Life and Liberation,* p. 350.

16 *Padma,* f. 81a.6–81b.2. *Life and Liberation,* p. 183.

17 *Padma,* f. 125a.1–2. *Life and Liberation,* p. 303.

18 Eva M. Dargyay, *The Rise of Esoteric Buddhism in Tibet* (Delhi: Motilal Banarsidass, 1977), p. 19.

19 *Padma,* f. 94b.5–6. *Life and Liberation,* p. 236.

20 See Das, *Tibetan-English Dictionary,* s.v. *bdud-rtsi.*

21 For more on the symbolism of the vessel, sometimes also translated as vase or chalice, see Saunders, *Mudrā,* pp. 192–95; and "The Life of Tilopa," trans. Nālandā Translation Committee, in *Religions of Tibet in Practice,* ed. Donald S. Lopez (Princeton: Princeton University Press, 1997), pp. 138, 144–45.

22 Even though the sexual symbolism of nectar in a vessel should not be ignored, especially since these are fairly common elements in conception dreams (see, e.g., the dream of Gesar's mother in David-Neel and Yongden, *The Superhuman Life of Gesar of Ling,* pp. 71–72; and Marpa's dream in Gtsaṅ smyon, *Mi la,* 53.13.25, and Gtsaṅ smyon, *The Life of Milarepa,* trans. Lobsang P. Lhalungpa [Boulder: Shambhala, 1984], p. 43), symbols are rarely restricted in meaning. For instance, Snellgrove says that a vase containing consecrated water "symbolizes the whole of existence in its perfected state"; *Four Lamas of Dolpo,* p. 20. They are, though, most frequently used in initiation *(abhiṣeka)* ceremonies.

23 Keith Dowman, *Sky Dancer: The Secret Life of the Lady Yeshe Tsogyel* (London: Routledge and Kegan Paul, 1984), p. 11.

24 A similar conflation occurs in the *Four Treatises* when it recommends drinking milk as one of the ways to increase sperm. Rechung, *Tibetan Medicine,* pp. 44, 58, 60. This text also often conflates semen with menstrual blood (pp. 44–45).

25 Robert A.F. Thurman, *The Life and Teachings of Tsong Khapa* (Dharamsala: Library of Tibetan Works and Archives, 1982), p. 5. These dreams are also preserved in Blo bzaṅ 'phrin las rnam rgyal, *'Jam mgon chos kyi rgyal po tsoṅ ka pa chen po'i rnam thar thub bstan mdzes pa'i rgyan gcig ṅo mtshar nor bu'i 'phreṅ ba* (Sarnath, Varanasi: Mongolian Lama Guru Deva, 1967), hereafter Blo bzaṅ 'phrin las rnam rgyal, *'Jam mgon,* pp. 88–89.

26 Thurman, *Tsong Khapa,* p. 5 and Blo bzaṅ 'phrin las rnam rgyal, *'Jam mgon,* pp. 88–89.

27 Thurman, *Tsong Khapa,* p. 5 and Blo bzaṅ 'phrin las rnam rgyal, *'Jam mgon,* pp. 88–89.

28 Thurman, *Tsong Khapa,* p. 5 and Blo bzaṅ 'phrin las rnam rgyal, *'Jam mgon,* pp. 88–89.

29 Keith Dowman, *Sky Dancer,* p. 22. For more on these two see the discussion of polarity symbolism in Bharati, *Tantric Tradition,* pp. 199–227. See also more on the tantric meaning of blood in Diemberger, "Lhakama," p. 151 n. 39.

30 Thurman, *Tsong Khapa,* p. 6.

31 Vaidya, *LV,* 44.15.

32 For some early scriptural references to Mañjuśrī see Hirakawa, *History of Indian Buddhism,* pp. 291–93. His name in Tibetan is 'Jam dpal dbyangs, pronounced Jampalyang. See also Williams, *Mahāyāna Buddhism,* pp. 238–41; Getty, *The Gods of Northern Buddhism,* pp. 110–13.

33 For a discussion of celestial bodhisattvas, see Snellgrove, "Celestial Buddhas and Bodhisattvas," pp. 133–43. One of the best known scriptural descriptions of Avalokiteśvara is contained in chapter 27 of the *Lotus Sūtra.* See Hirakawa, *History of Indian Buddhism,* pp. 282–85, for a discussion of this important Mahāyāna text. Avalokiteśvara pervades Tibetan cultural and religious life, especially through his popular mantra, *oṃ maṇi padme hūṃ,* and he is believed to manifest repeatedly in human form in the person of the Dalai Lamas. His name in Tibetan is *sPyan ras gzigs,* pronounced Chenresig. For more information on him see Getty, *The Gods of Northern Buddhism,* pp. 57–70.

34 Vajrapāṇi is known as the great subduer of demons and is the guardian of the nectar of immortality. Getty, *The Gods of Northern Buddhism,* pp. 50–53.

35 Thurman, *Tsong Khapa,* p. 9.

36 The text does, however, remark on the astral signs. Gtsaṅ smyon, *Mi la,* p. 29; Gtsaṅ smyon, *The Life of Milarepa,* p. 15.

37 Gtsaṅ smyon, *Mi la,* 53.13–25; Gtsaṅ smyon, *The Life of Milarepa,* p. 43.

38 Gtsaṅ smyon, *Mi la,* 53.29–54.9; Gtsaṅ smyon, *The Life of Milarepa,* p. 44.

39 This is similar to the motif in earlier biographies of husbands who sidestep their wives' dreams, which later turn out to be true. For example, the Buddha and Padmasambhava both do this, as does Prince Vessantara.

40 Gtsaṅ smyon, *Mi la,* 54.10–11.

41 Gtsaṅ smyon, *Mi la,* 82.24–31; Gtsaṅ smyon, *The Life of Milarepa,* pp. 73–74.

42 See Snodgrass, *The Symbolism of the Stupa,* p. 189, for a brief discussion of womb symbolism in stūpas.

43 Gérard Fussman, "Symbolism of the Buddhist *Stūpa,*" *Journal of the International Association of Buddhist Studies* 9, no. 2 (1986): 44–45. This article also has

a helpful summary of recent studies of stūpas and a useful critique of Irwin's work on *stūpas*. See also Peter Harvey's critique of Irwin in "Symbolism of the Early Stūpa," *Journal of the International Association of Buddhist Studies* 7, no. 2 (1984): 67–93, and most recently Jonathan Walters's analysis of the relation of text and stūpa, "Stūpa, Story, and Empire: Constructions of the Buddha Biography in Early Post-Aśokan India," in *Sacred Biography*, ed. Schober, pp. 160–92.

44 See Yael Bentor, "Literature on Consecration *(Rab gnas)*," in Cabezón and Jackson, *Tibetan Literature*, p. 291, although on pp. 295–96 she cites texts that classify stūpas as emanation bodies *(nirmāṇakāya, sprul sku)* of the buddhas.

45 See Ray, *Buddhist Saints*, pp. 325–27, for a useful summary of the scholarly literature supporting this view and pp. 324–57 on stūpas in general and the particular practices of different schools. See also the important recent contribution of Gregory Schopen, "An Old Inscription from Amarāvatī and the Cult of the Local Monastic Dead in Indian Buddhist Monasteries," *Journal of the International Association of Buddhist Studies* 14, no. 2 (1991): 281–329, which broadens the discussion of stūpas to include those of other Buddhist saints. See also Snodgrass, *The Symbolism of the Stupa*, pp. 360–71 and passim, for a somewhat meandering discussion of the symbolic meanings of various parts of the stūpa.

46 This idea goes back to the early days of Buddhism, in fact to the first rule attributed to the Buddha when he has individual senior monks undertake teaching novices. The rule, in part, states: "The preceptor, monks, should arouse in the one who shares his cell the attitude of a son; the one who shares his cell should arouse in the preceptor the attitude of a father. Thus these, living with reverence, with deference, with courtesy towards one another, will come to growth, to increase, to maturity in this *dhamma* and discipline." *Vinaya Piṭaka,* trans. by Horner as *The Book of Discipline*, 4: 58–59; *Vinaya*, Oldenberg, I.45.

47 Gtsaṅ smyon, *Mi la,* 66.3–6.

48 This is not to deny the gendered structure of this biography, in which Milarepa's biological mother is an evil but dominant influence in the early parts of the text, while Marpa, the father figure, is the seemingly evil, but really beneficial, influence of the middle parts.

Robert Paul's discussion of this biography and, indeed, his understanding of hereditary and spiritual lineages is thought provoking in connection with Milarepa's filial relationship with Marpa and Dakmema. Paul sets out the dilemma in the following way: "the doctrines of karma versus descent in Sherpa culture express the contradictory view that fathers and sons both are and are not related to each other"; Paul, *Tibetan Symbolic World*, p. 29. His point is that one is physically connected to one's biological family (descent) but karmically driven to incarnate. However, one is also spiritually (karmically) connected to the biological family, a point Paul does not mention, and spiritually connected to others outside the biological family unit. Even though the relationship of guru and disciple parallels the relationship of father and son, my thinking differs from Paul's on this text when he emphasizes Marpa and Dakmema in terms of Milarepa's reconciliation of his Oedipal problems. This may or may not have been part of that very complex relationship, but more significantly Milarepa in all ways rejected a biological family by surviving the death of his biological parents (the earlier generation), rejecting his planned marriage (any later generations are proscribed), and by establishing himself as the guru of his remaining family: his aunt and sister. In other words, he transforms his biological family into part of his spiritual family.

49 *LV*, Vaidya, 44.15.

50 Blo bzaṅ 'phrin las rnam rgyal, *'Jam mgon*, p. 90.

51 In Tibetan, *Mi bskyod pa*, one of the five cosmic Buddhas, see Tucci, *Religions of Tibet*, p. 97; Getty, *The Gods of Northern Buddhism*, pp. 36–37. Akṣobhya is identified with the historical Buddha Śākyamuni, who showed himself to be imperturbable *(akṣobhya)* in the face of Māra's assault on the night of enlightenment; Snellgrove, "Celestial Buddhas and Bodhisattvas," p. 136. See also Williams, *Mahāyāna Buddhism*, pp. 243–47, for more on him and especially for a description of his Pure Land of Abhirati.

52 Gtsaṅ smyon, *Mi la*, 24.12–13.

53 Ibid., 24.17–19.

54 These five ḍākinīs refer to the goddess Tseringma, who was converted by Milarepa, and the four female companions who usually accompany her. She and her companions became protectors of the Buddhist religion, and they make frequent appearances in Milarepa's life.

55 A brief reference to these events in contained in song 38 of Gtsaṅ smyon, *Mgur 'bum*. The physician-saint Yuthog's biography begins in the same way, when his disciple dreams he is in the heaven of the Medicine Buddha; Rechung, *Tibetan Medicine*, pp. 148–52; but his mother also has a conception dream (pp. 187–88).

Chapter 6

1 For examples of shared dreams in other cultures see Bitel, *"In Visu Noctis,"* pp. 39–40, which discusses shared dreams in medieval Christian experience; an elaborate and amusing variant of a shared dream is contained in the Arabian story collection, *The Thousand and One Nights*, trans. Edward William Lane (London: Chatto and Windus, 1883), 2: 460–61; and Manabu Waida "Miracles," in *EOR*,

9: 544, cites an example from one of Asklepios's temples where a mother slept on behalf of her sick daughter who remained in another city: The mother had an elaborate dream in which Asklepios cured her daughter, and when she returned home, the daughter had recovered her health and had seen the same dream! The dreaming of Australian aborigines, however, appears to be closest to South Asian shared dream experiences; see Diane Bell, *Daughters of the Dreaming,* 2d ed. (1983; Minneapolis: University of Minnesota Press, 1993).

2 O'Flaherty, *Dreams,* chap. 2.

3 *MV,* Senart, II.133–36.

4 *LV,* Vaidya, chap. 14.

5 *AS,* pp. 111–12, 126–28.

6 *MSV,* I.92.

7 *LV,* Vaidya, 142.29–143.3.

8 *MV,* Senart, I.205.

9 Kanjur, vol. *ka,* text 48.

10 *Saddharmapuṇḍarīka,* trans. H. Kern, p. 278. This is at the end of chap. 13.

11 Ibid., p. 279.

12 A. L. Basham, *History and Doctrines of the Ājīvikas* (London: Luzac, 1951), p. 252.

13 Sikdar, *Studies in the Bhagawatīsūtra,* pp. 197–98.

14 Ibid., p. 198.

15 Ibid., pp. 198–99.

16 Ibid., p. 199.

17 Ibid., p. 197.

18 For further discussion of this story, see (Mrs.) Sinclair Stevenson, *The Heart of Jainism* (1915; Delhi: Munshiram Manoharlal, 1970), p. 22.

19 "Kalpa Sūtra," in *Jaina Sutras,* trans. Hermann Jacobi (1884; New York: Dover, 1968), 1: 219–20, 231–38.

20 Stevenson, *The Heart of Jainism,* p. 22 n. 2.

21 Colette Caillat, "Mahāvīra," in *EOR,* 9: 128–29.

22 Ibid., 9: 129.

23 The Digambaras say there were sixteen dreams. See Stevenson, *The Heart of Jainism*, p. 24.

24 Jacobi, "Kalpa Sūtra" in *Jaina Sutras*, 1: 231–38. J. P. Sharma discusses the symbolic meaning of these fourteen dreams in "Symbolism in the Jinist Dream-World," in Sharma and Siegel, *Dream-Symbolism in the Śrāmaṇic Tradition*, pp. 27 ff., while Stevenson, *Heart of Jainism*, pp. 22–25, provides various versions and interpretations of these dreams.

25 "Kalpa Sūtra," in *Jaina Sutras*, 1: 247. This is, of course, quite similar to the interpretation of the dream of the Buddha's mother.

26 Ibid., p. 246. See also Sharma, "Symbolism in the Jinist Dream-World," in Sharma and Siegel, *Dream-Symbolism in the Śrāmaṇic Tradition*, p. 3, for a discussion of these various categories of Jain heroes.

27 Quoted in Sharma and Siegel, *Dream-Symbolism in the Śrāmaṇic Tradition*, p. 13.

28 *Padma*, f. 56a.6. *Life and Liberation*, p. 131.

29 *Padma*, f. 57b.4–5. Robert Paul offers a psychoanalytic reading of this dream, which, unfortunately, misses the point in several important ways. First, he says the dream occurs on the wedding night of Padmasambhava and Bhāsadharā, which is a misreading of the text; according the *Padma* they had been married for at least five years when Bhāsadharā has her dream. Second, Paul interprets the dream as if it were Padmasambhava's. Paul, *Tibetan Symbolic World*, pp. 171–72. He is relying on Toussaint's French translation (*Le Dict de Padma=Padma thang yig*, trans. Gustave-Charles Toussaint [Paris: E. Leroux, 1933]), which, however, correctly translated the *Padma*.

30 *Padma*, at f. 57b.5–6. Bhāsadharā's dream and Padmasambhava's dismissal of it seem to be clearly based on the dream of the Buddha's wife preserved in the *MSV* and the *LV*, both of which were known in Tibet.

31 *Padma*, f. 142b.3–4. *Life and Liberation*, p. 366.

32 *Padma*, f. 168a.3. *Life and Liberation*, p. 452–53.

33 *Padma*, f. 168b.2.

34 Ibid., f. 168b.4–5.

35 Ibid., f. 182a.1–3. *Life and Liberation*, p. 483.

36 Mkhas grub Rje presents another dream of departure, which King Ajātaśatru has when Ānanda is preparing to enter nirvāṇa. He dreams that the handle of his parasol, one of his marks of state, is broken. F. D. Lessing and A. Wayman, *Introduction to the Buddhist Tantric Systems* (New York: Samuel Weiser, 1968), pp. 60, 61.

37 Gtsaṅ smyon, *Mi la'i mgur 'bum*, p. 625, hereafter *Mgur 'bum*. These dreams are translated in Gtsaṅ smyon, *The Hundred Thousand Songs of Milarepa*, trans. Garma Chen Chi Chang, 2 vols. (Boulder: Shambhala, 1977), pp. 467–68, hereafter Gtsaṅ smyon, *Hundred Thousand Songs*.

38 Gtsaṅ smyon, *Mgur 'bum*, pp. 623–24.

39 The exception occurs in Padmasambhava's biography where two of the shared dreams are about tantric masters other than Padmasambhava: Vairotsana and Vimalamitra.

Chapter 7

1 Lincoln, *The Dream in Primitive Cultures*, p. 68; Eliade, *Shamanism*, pp. 67, 102–4; La Barre, *Ghost Dance*, passim.

2 Alex Wayman comments on this text as follows: "This agrees with other Buddhist tantras, where auspicious dreams that come true indicate approach of the tutelary deity and success in the meditative process as contrasted with the bad dreams indicating that the deity stays far away as does the success *(siddhi)*." Wayman, "The Significance of Dreams in India and Tibet," in *Buddhist Insight*, ed. George Elder (New Delhi: Motilal Banarsidass, 1984), pp. 405–6. Mkhas grub Rje (1385–1438) also mentions this role of dreams in revealing the approach and withdrawal of the deity in his "Fundamentals of the Buddhist Tantras," translated by Lessing and Wayman as *Introduction to the Buddhist Tantric Systems*, pp. 202, 203. Tucci also lists dreams as one of the ways the tutelary deity *(yi dam)* is revealed; *Religions of Tibet*, p. 97.

3 *MV*, Senart, ii.133.15–136.12.

4 Guenther, *Life and Teachings of Nāropa*, p. 67.

5 Kelsang Gyatso, *Guide to the Dakini Land* (London: Tharpa, 1991), p. 26.

6 Deshung Rinpoche, *Three Levels*, p. 480. The introduction of this text also provides examples of dreams that lead to spiritual accomplishments, such as Dagpa Gyaltsen's learning of the *Hevajra Tantra* (p. xxix) and Sakya Pandita's dreams of Vasubandhu and Dignāga (p. xxix).

7 *LV*, Vaidya, 142–143.29–32.

8 *AN*, Hardy, iii.196.8–11.

9 Chapters 8 and 9 round out this study by exploring more formal practices preserved in other kinds of texts.

10 Gtsaṅ smyon, *Mi la*, 91.2–5.

11 Ibid., 91.7.

12 Detlef Ingo Lauf shows a detail of these pillars taken from another, though unfortunately unidentified, painting; *Tibetan Sacred Art: The Heritage of Tantra* (Berkeley: Shambhala, 1976), p. 210.

13 *Sñan rgyud kyi gdams ṅag thebs pa yin.* Gtsaṅ smyon, *Mi la,* 95.29. Marpa says the same thing about each dream.

14 *Thar pa'i gliṅ du gśegs pa yin.* Ibid., 96.4. Marpa again says the same thing about each dream.

15 Gtsaṅ smyon, *The Life of Milarepa,* p. 83. Gtsaṅ smyon, *Mi la,* 92.22–93.1.

16 Gtsaṅ smyon, *The Life of Milarepa,* p. 86. Gtsaṅ smyon, *Mi la,* 95.24–96.6.

17 Actually, this is a collection of only fifty-eight songs or stories, all of various lengths, having Milarepa as their subject, which were collected between the twelfth and thirteenth centuries by an unknown compiler (Gtsaṅ smyon, *Hundred Thousand Songs,* pp. 679 ff.). Chang's translation of Gtsaṅ smyon, *Mgur 'bum* has sixty-one songs because here the long story cycle of the goddess Tseringma is divided into four separate songs (nos. 28–31); therefore, from that point on, the numbers of Chang's translation (that is, Gtsaṅ smyon, *Hundred Thousand Songs*) vary from their sequence in Gtsaṅ smyon's *Mgur 'bum.* Consequently, the stories up to no. 28 will be referred to by Chang's numbers and after that by a slash between Chang's numbers and the story's position in the *Mgur 'bum.*

18 Gtsaṅ smyon, *Mgur 'bum,* p. 618. Song 41 in Gtsaṅ smyon, *Hundred Thousand Songs.*

19 Gtsaṅ smyon, *Mgur 'bum,* pp. 658–59.

20 For more on Gampopa and his disciples see Snellgrove, *Cultural History of Tibet,* pp. 135–36. One can make an interesting connection between dreams and Gampopa's earlier profession as a physician; dreams were a significant diagnostic tool in Tibetan medical theory and one with which Gampopa may have been familiar.

21 Gtsaṅ smyon, *The Life of Marpa the Translator,* trans. Nālandā Translation Committee (Boulder: Prajñā Press, 1982), pp. 181–88.

22 *Mnal lam du...sa bcu thob pa'i snga ltas rnams ji lta ba bzhin byung ngo.* Gtsaṅ smyon, *Mgur 'bum,* p. 623.

23 Gtsaṅ smyon, *Mgur 'bum,* pp. 623–24.

24 Ibid., pp. 642 ff.

25 I have followed Chang's translation, Gtsaṅ smyon, *Hundred Thousand Songs,*

p. 481, which relies on Milarepa's interpretation, for clarification of some particularly obscure phrases. Gtsaṅ smyon, *Mgur 'bum,* pp. 642–43.

26 See the discussion of Prajñāpāramitā literature above in chapter 4.

27 These are similes used to illustrate emptiness: an illusion, a mirage, a reflection of the moon in water, a dream, an echo, an apparition, an image in the mirror, a magical creation.

28 Gtsaṅ smyon, *Hundred Thousand Songs,* pp. 483–84; Gtsaṅ smyon, *Mgur 'bum,* pp. 645–46.

29 Gtsaṅ smyon, *Mgur 'bum,* p. 650.

30 Gtsaṅ smyon, *Mgur 'bum,* p. 784; Gtsaṅ smyon, *Hundred Thousand Songs,* pp. 641 ff.

31 Blame and fame, gain and loss, and so on.

32 Gtsaṅ smyon, *Mgur 'bum,* p. 784.

33 Ibid., p. 784.

34 Ibid., pp. 784–85.

35 Ibid., p. 785. The interpretations sometimes use a different vocabulary than the dreams, which often enhances the imagery.

36 Gtsaṅ smyon, *Mi la,* 121.23–28; Gtsaṅ smyon, *The Life of Milarepa,* pp. 112–13.

37 Gtsaṅ smyon, *Mi la,* 121.29–122.1.

38 Gtsaṅ smyon, *Mi la,* 122.1–2.

39 Gtsaṅ smyon, *The Life of Milarepa,* p. 113. Gtsaṅ smyon, *Mi la,* 122.4–20.

40 Collins, *Selfless Persons,* pp. 219–24, has an interesting discussion of agricultural imagery in Buddhist thought. It is particularly tempting to relate the imagery of this dream and Marpa's activity to the canonical passages in which the Buddha uses similar images—when, for example, he says: "My seed is faith, austerity the rain; insight is my yoke and plough, my pole modesty, mind the strap; mindfulness my plough-share and goad; ...energy is for me the ox which bears the yoke, drawing on towards rest from work." Quoted by Collins, p. 221, from the *Saṃyutta Nikāya* 1.172 ff. and the *Suttanipāta* 12 ff.

41 Gtsaṅ smyon, *Mgur 'bum,* p. 363.

42 Ibid., p. 363.

43 Ibid., p. 323.

44 Ibid., p. 323.

45 Thurman, "Tsoṅ-kha-pa," in *EOR,* 15: 73. The dream itself is in Mkhas grub Rje's "Rje rin po che'i gsaṅ ba'i rnam thar," in *The Collected Works (gsuṅ 'bum) of Rje Tsoṅ-kha-pa Blo-bzaṅ-grags-pa,* vol. 1 (New Delhi: 1979), f. 184.5.

46 Palden, "Song of the Mystic Experiences," in Thurman, *Tsong Khapa,* p. 52. The dream is in Mkhas grub Rje's "Rje rin po che'i gsaṅ ba'i rnam thar," f. 187.5 ff.

47 Thurman, *Tsong Khapa,* pp. 14–15.

48 Gtsaṅ smyon, *Mi la,* 53.13–54.11.

49 Gtsaṅ smyon, *Mgur 'bum,* p. 625. However, Gampopa, the disciple, also dreams of Milarepa, the guru, pp. 623–24.

50 Ibid., p. 363.

51 Ibid., p. 323.

52 Thurman, *Tsong Khapa,* pp. 14–15.

53 Ibid., p. 15.

54 Alaka Chattopadhyaya, *Atīśa and Tibet* (Calcutta: Indian Studies, 1967), p. 407.

55 Ibid., pp. 357, 388.

56 Tucci, *Religions of Tibet,* p. 45.

57 Namkhai Norbu, *Dream Yoga,* pp. 105–6 and passim.

58 Thinley, *The History of the Sixteen Karmapas,* pp. 42–44, 56, 62, 63, 66, 75, 80, 114.

59 Conversation, Kathmandu, April 2, 1997. When I asked him about the conception dreams of their mothers, he explained that they occur "through the power of the Bodhisattva," in other words, the incarnating Karmapa causes his future mother to dream.

60 Keith Dowman, *The Divine Madman* (Clearlake, CA: Dawn Horse, 1983), p. 119.

61 D. S. Ruegg, *The Life of Bu ston rin po che* (Roma: Istituto italiano per il medio ed estremo oriente, 1996), p. 158, ff. 36a and b.

62 See, for example, the textual and iconographic representations of this event in John C. Huntington, "Sowing the Seeds of the Lotus: A Journey to the Great Pilgrimage Sites of Buddhism," part 3, *Orientations* 17, no. 3 (March 1986): 32–46.

63 Ruegg, *Life of Bu ston,* p. 107, f. 18b.

64 La Barre, *Ghost Dance*, p. 199; Eliade, *Shamanism*, p. 109.

65 Discussed in chapter 2 above. A reading from the point of view of gender suggests some additional perspectives; see chapter 10.

66 *MV*, Senart, II.12.

67 *Kuṇāla Jātaka*, no. 536, V.239; *Mahāsupina Jātaka*, no. 77, I.192; *Vessantara Jātaka*, no. 547, IV.265.

68 *LV*, Vaidya, 156.17; *Vinaya* I.x.2.15.

69 Gtsaṅ smyon, *Mi la*, 88.32–89.7; Gtsaṅ smyon, *The Life of Milarepa*, p. 80.

70 Gtsaṅ smyon, *Mi la*, 98; Gtsaṅ smyon, *The Life of Milarepa*, p. 89.

71 Gtsaṅ smyon, *Mi la*, 119.26–27; Gtsaṅ smyon, *The Life of Milarepa*, p. 110.

72 Gtsaṅ smyon, *Mi la*, 121.29–122.1; Gtsaṅ smyon, *The Life of Milarepa*, p. 112–13.

73 See chapter 9 for a discussion of these dream lists and manuals.

74 Gtsaṅ smyon, *Mgur 'bum*, p. 625.

75 Ibid., p. 650.

76 Ibid., p. 651.

77 Ibid. This surprisingly positive interpretation of Gampopa's dream reminds one of Buddha's deceptively positive interpretation of his wife's harrowing dream, which correctly predicts his departure from home; *LV*, Vaidya, 140.16–142.28.

78 Gtsaṅ smyon, *Mgur 'bum*, pp. 650–51.

79 Ibid., p. 651.

80 *Padma*, ff. 94b.5–6, 45b.6–46a.1, and 68b.3.

81 There are certainly enough references to the auspicious meaning of seeing the sun *and* moon in dreams. For example, Rechungpa's dream that Milarepa interprets to mean he will abide in the state of realization (Gtsaṅ smyon, *Mgur 'bum*, p. 785, quoted above) and dreams described by Deshung Rinpoche (*Three Levels*, p. 480), not to mention several dreams in Padmasambhava's biography in which the sun and moon represent Padmsambhava (ff. 68b.34, 142b3–4) or a great teacher (f. 168b.2). See also Brahmā's list of dream symbols in *MV* II.13, those in the *AS*, pp. 38–39, and Nebesky-Wojkowitz's listing of a rising sun as foretelling happiness, wealth, and fame (*Oracles and Demons*, p. 465). On the other hand, there are frequent references to the inauspicious meaning of seeing the sun and moon set or fall from the sky or be eclipsed, as when the wife of the Buddha dreams of his departure in the *LV*, *MSV*, and *AS*.

82 Gtsaṅ smyon, *Mgur 'bum,* p. 651.

83 Ibid., p. 784.

84 Ibid., p. 651.

85 See, especially, song no. 38/35, "The Story of the Yak-Horn," but also the several songs that have Rechungpa's name in the title.

Chapter 8

1 Tylor, *Primitive Culture,* 2: 24, 49, 75 ff. See also the work of the early psychoanalyst Ernest Jones, *On the Nightmare,* esp. pp. 65, 73. The folklorist Alexander H. Krappe also found dreams and nightmares to be a source for fairy tales and local legends; *The Science of Folklore* (1929; New York: W. W. Norton, 1964), pp. 12 ff., 79.

More recently, anthropologist Weston La Barre argued that dreams are a source of religion itself, not just parts of a religion such as knowledge of the afterlife or the introduction of a new ritual; *Ghost Dance,* pp. 12–13. This is all actually a rather ancient idea. The *Epinomis,* a work attributed to Plato, says that "many cults of many gods have been founded, and will continue to be founded, because of dream-encounters with supernatural beings"; quoted in Kilborne, "Dreams," p. 483.

2 Lincoln, *The Dream in Primitive Cultures,* pp. 51–93. See also Dodds, *The Greeks and the Irrational,* p. 108, on a variety of religious items owing their origins to dreams among the Greeks.

3 Lincoln, *The Dream in Primitive Cultures,* p. 50.

4 In *The Interpretation of Dreams,* Freud says: "At bottom, dreams are nothing other than a particular *form* of thinking.... The fact that dreams concern themselves with attempts at solving the problems by which our mental life is faced is no more strange than that our conscious waking life should do so" (pp. 544–45 n. 2, emphasis in original; see also pp. 82–84, 97). C. G. Jung also supports the cognitive function of dreams, especially in his theory of their "prospective" function; see "General Aspects of Dream Psychology," in Jung, *Dreams,* pp. 41–42.

Our increasingly sophisticated understanding of cognition and cultural process substantiates these earlier views. In his study of modern South Asian ascetics, Gananath Obeyesekere brings together dreaming as a form of cognition and dreaming as a source of religious items. He argues, in part, that in their dreams people not only validate cultural symbols but reinterpret them and sometimes innovate. For instance, the ecstatic priestesses and priests in his study are continually incorporating *and* redefining the iconography of the gods through their subjective experiences of trance and dream; *Medusa's Hair,* pp. 113, 177–79.

5 Eliade, *Shamanism,* pp. 103–4. La Barre also brings out the problem-solving function of dreams among shamans who, "when asked about a problem will 'dream on it' themselves and supply the answer later." (*Ghost Dance,* p. 178.) See also Lincoln, *The Dream in Primitive Cultures,* pp. 68–98, for a survey of such problem-solving dreams, especially among Native American tribes where they are quite common.

6 Nebesky-Wojkowitz, *Oracles and Demons,* p. 549. See also Matthew Kapstein's excellent discussion of Tibetan shamanism and in particular the relationship between shamanic power and the Buddhist *bla-ma,* or guru, in which the *bla-ma* must demonstrate his mastery of these shamanistic techniques; "The Illusion of Spiritual Progress," in *Paths to Liberation,* pp. 197–98. Examples from other Asian cultures can be found in Laurel Kendall, *The Life and Hard Times of a Korean Shaman* (Honolulu: University of Hawai'i Press, 1988), e.g., pp. 56, 57, 69, 70, 73, 76. For Japan see Blacker, *Catalpa Bow,* pp. 168–77. For a Brazilian example, see Ellen B. Basso, "The Implications of a Progressive Theory of Dreaming," in Tedlock, *Dreaming,* pp. 89–90. Most of the South Asian participants in Obeyesekere's study had dreams in which they received instructions about their religious activities. See, for example, *Medusa's Hair,* pp. 25, 26, 57, 92–93, 94, 144, and 184–87.

7 See, for instance, Gilbert Herdt, "Selfhood and Discourse in Sambia Dream Sharing," in Tedlock, *Dreaming,* pp. 66–67; Stanley Krippner, "Dreams and Shamanism," in *Shamanism: An Expanded View of Reality,* comp. Shirley Nicholson (Wheaton, IL: The Theosophical Publishing House, 1987), pp. 129–31.

8 Lincoln, *The Dream in Primitive Cultures,* pp. 22 ff.

9 Dodds, *The Greeks and the Irrational,* pp. 103–4.

10 Both Tedlock, *Dreaming;* and von Grunebaum and Caillois, *The Dream and Human Societies,* offer a wealth of data on how various cultures in different time periods have incorporated dreams into reality.

11 Hans Peter Duerr, *Dreamtime: Concerning the Boundaries between Wilderness and Civilization,* trans. Felicitas Goodman (1978; New York: Basil Blackwell, 1987), p. 133, emphasis in original.

12 Peter Worsley, *The Trumpet Shall Sound: A Study of "Cargo" Cults in Melanesia,* 2d ed. (New York: Schocken, 1968); see especially pp. 56, 69, 72–73, 88, 109, 111, 115, 214, and 216, where cult leaders describe their dreams; Bryan R. Wilson, *Magic and the Millennium: A Sociological Study of Religious Movements of Protest among Tribal and Third-World Peoples* (New York: Harper and Row, 1973); and La Barre, *Ghost Dance,* esp. pp. 288–89.

13 Michael F. Brown, "Ropes of Sand: Order and Imagery in Aguaruna Dreams," in Tedlock, *Dreaming,* pp. 167–68.

14 The mastery or control of dreams has precedence in various parts of the world, for instance the incubation dreams of the ancient Greeks, the sought dreams of Native Americans, and others discussed above. See also Domhoff, *The Mystique of Dreams,* for his careful unravelling of the belief that the Senoi people of Malaysia have techniques for the control of dreams, pp. 13–34, and his analysis of why such a technique has great appeal to Americans, pp. 79–95.

15 Conversation, Losang Chogyen (a monk from Namgyal, the Dalai Lama's monastery), Columbia University, February 5, 1996. The Dalai Lama also mentions this practice in Varela, *Sleeping, Dreaming, and Dying,* pp. 103–29.

16 The history of this lineage is contained in book 9 of 'Gos Lo tsa ba, *Blue Annals,* pp. 728–52. Jamgon Kongtrul seems to suggest a third lineage through Sukāsiddhī when he refers to the Six Doctrines of Sukāsiddhī *(Su kha chos drug);* Koṅ sprul Blo gros mtha' yas, *Jamgon Kongtrul's Retreat Manual,* trans. Ngawang Zangpo (Ithaca: Snow Lion, 1994), pp. 93, 210, hereafter Koṅ sprul, *Retreat Manual. The Blue Annals* says she was a disciple of Virūpa and another one of Khyungpo Naljor's teachers, see pp. 729–31 for more on her.

See also Kapstein, "The Illusion of Spiritual Progress." Kapstein notes a difference in Tilopa's and Niguma's traditions of the Six Yogas, which "is the relative emphasis in the former on inner heat and luminosity, in the latter on apparition and dream"; ibid., p. 201. Kapstein's forthcoming study of Niguma along with his translation of the treatise attributed to her, *Māyādhvakrama,* should provide further valuable information. See also Miranda Shaw, *Passionate Enlightenment: Women in Tantric Buddhism* (Princeton: Princeton University Press, 1994), pp. 107–10; and Dge 'dun rgya mtsho, Dalai Lama II, *Selected Works of the Dalai Lama II,* ed. and trans. Glenn H. Mullin (Ithaca: Snow Lion, 1985), pp. 99–151, for more on Niguma.

17 A traditional explanation is that Nāropa received them directly from the primordial Buddha Vajradhara; Gtsaṅ smyon, *The Life of Marpa,* p. xxxii. Vajradhara is a form of Samantabhadra, who is also the traditional source for both Dzogchen and Mahāmudrā teachings. For a more pedestrian and complicated tradition, including his teacher Tilopa, see ibid., note on pp. xxxii–xxxiii. For a discussion of Tilopa's biography and translations of two of his short biographies, see "Life of Tilopa," in *Religions of Tibet in Practice,* ed. Donald S. Lopez, pp. 137–56. Another biography is *The Life of the Mahāsiddha Tilopa,* trans. Fabrizio Torricelli and Sangye T. Naga (Dharamsala: Library of Tibetan Works and Archives, 1995). Nāropa's biography provides some of the earliest oral teachings on the Six Yogas in the instructions given to him by Tilopa; Guenther, *The Life and Teachings of Nāropa,* pp. 67–69.

18 For some discussion by a contemporary Nyingma practitioner see Tarthung

Tulku, *Crystal Mirror* (Emeryville: Dharma, 1975), 4: 178–85. See also Longchenpa (Klong chen Rab 'byams pa, 1308–1364), *Kindly Bent to Ease Us*, trans. Herbert Guenther (Emeryville, CA: Dharma, 1975), pp. 42–48; and David Germano's exposition and translation of Longchenpa's teaching on dreams, "Food, Clothes, Dreams, and Karmic Propensities," in *Religions of Tibet in Practice*, pp. 293–312.

19 The order of this list follows Tucci, *Religions of Tibet*, pp. 98 ff., and Gtsaṅ smyon, *The Life of Milarepa*, pp. 214–15 n. 10. The order of the last two yogas is reversed in Garma Chen Chi Chang, *Teachings of Tibetan Yoga* (New Hyde Park: University Books, 1963), p. 54, and in Evans-Wentz, *Tibetan Yoga and Secret Doctrines* (New York: Oxford University Press, 1935), pp. 155–252. In his commentary on these yogas, Tsongkhapa never actually lists them, but he discusses them in the following sequence: Heat Yoga, Dream and Illusory Body, Bardo, Light, and Transference. His commentary is entitled the *Zab lam nā ro'i chos drug gi sgo nas 'khrid pa'i rim pa yid ches gsum ldan* and has been translated by Garma Chen Chi Chang in *Esoteric Teachings of the Tibetan Tantra*, ed. C. A. Musès (1961; York Beach, Maine: Samuel Weiser, 1982), discussed below, and Tsoṅ kha pa Blo bzaṅ grags pa, *Tsongkhapa's Six Yogas of Naropa*, trans. Glenn H. Mullin (Ithaca: Snow Lion, 1996). In his translation Mullin subsumes Dream Yoga under Illusory Body Yoga and adds projection of consciousness Yoga; see p. 97 for a brief discussion of this. Additional commentaries on the Six Yogas are listed in Evans-Wentz, *Tibetan Yoga*, pp. xxxii–xxxiii; and Tsoṅ kha pa Blo bzaṅ grags pa, *Tsongkhapa's Six Yogas*, pp. 36–44.

20 Gtsaṅ smyon, *The Life of Milarepa*, pp. 86–87.

21 Gtsaṅ smyon, *The Life of Marpa*, pp. 146–55. See also the Dalai Lama's discussion of this in Varela, *Sleeping, Dreaming, and Dying*, pp. 173–75.

22 See the discussion of these bodies from the perspective of Anuttarayoga in Daniel Cozort, *Highest Yoga Tantra: An Introduction to the Esoteric Buddhism of Tibet* (Ithaca: Snow Lion, 1986), esp. pp. 94–105.

23 Garma Chen Chi Chang, "Yogic Commentary," in Evans-Wentz, *Tibetan Yoga*, pp. xxxi–xxxii.

24 Chang, *Teachings of Tibetan Yoga*, p. 54. See also his translation of Tsonkgkhapa's commentary on these yogas in Chang and Musès, *Esoteric Teachings of the Tibetan Tantra*, pp. 123 ff.

25 Ibid., p. 122 n. 12.

26 Ibid., pp. 115–16.

27 Conversation, Sarnath, March 15, 1995. See also Koṅ sprul, *Retreat Manual*, for a detailed exposition of a three-year retreat. See also Tucci, *Religions of Tibet*,

p. 265 n. 137; and Chang and Musès, *Esoteric Teachings*, passim, which makes frequent reference to the various positions of different teachers and schools with regard to these yogas. Most recently, in answer to the question of a Western dream scholar, His Holiness the Dalai Lama said that Dream Yoga could be practiced "without a great deal of preparation"; Varela, *Sleeping, Dreaming, and Dying*, p. 45. However, his formal presentation of Dream Yoga was within the context of very advanced tantric practices. Clearly there are different traditions about Dream Yoga.

For a more detailed discussion of these yogas see Chang, *Teachings of Tibetan Yoga*, pp. 55–120; Evans-Wentz, *Tibetan Yoga*, pp. 155–276; and Glenn Mullin's translation of the Six Yogas of Sister Niguma in Dge 'dun rgya mtsho, Dalai Lama II, *Selected Works of the Dalai Lama II*, pp. 92–151; and Tsoṅ kha pa Blo bzaṅ grags pa's *Tsongkhapa's Six Yogas*.

28 Tucci, *Religions of Tibet*, p. 99. For more on the practices related to the divine body see Kelsang Gyatso, *Clear Light of Bliss: A Commentary to the Practice of Mahamudra in Vajrayana Buddhism* (1982; London: Tharpa, 1992).

29 Namkhai Norbu summarizes this from the point of view of the Dzogchen school, *Dzogchen: The Self-Perfected State*, ed. Adriano Clemente (Ithaca: Snow Lion, 1996), p. 74. See also Sogyal, *Tibetan Book of Living and Dying*, pp. 107–8.

30 Namkhai Norbu, *Dzogchen*, p. 63.

31 Chang, *Teachings of Tibetan Yoga*, pp. 88–94, 101–15. See also Gyatrul Rinpoche, *Ancient Wisdom: Nyingma Teachings on Dream Yoga, Meditation, and Transformation*, trans. B. Alan Wallace and Sangye Khandro (Ithaca: Snow Lion, 1993), pp. 104–19.

32 Kelsang Gyatso, *Clear Light of Bliss*, p. 129. See also his *Guide to the Dakini Land*, pp. 26–38, for the related practices of the yogas of sleeping and rising.

33 Gtsaṅ smyon, *The Life of Marpa*, p. 33, mentions this transmission.

34 His biography refers to her as "the Yoginī Adorned with Bone Ornaments"; ibid., pp. 32, 63, 80, 235, 202.

35 Gtsaṅ smyon, *The Life of Milarepa*, p. 80; Gtsaṅ smyon, *Mi la*, 88.32–89.7. This dream is also preserved in Gtsaṅ smyon, *The Life of Marpa*, p. 73; however, there it is preceded by Marpa's own dream of three ḍākinīs, who explain an obscure part of Nāropa's teachings.

Other examples of the transmission of the Six Yogas, especially Dream Yoga, through dreams can be found in the biography of Niguma's disciple Kyungpo Naljor in the Second Dalai Lama (Dge 'dun rgya mtsho), *Selected Works of the Dalai Lama II*, p. 98; Kapstein, "The Illusion of Spiritual Progress," pp. 195–96; and in the biographies of Sonam Lodo and Paldon Lodo in Snellgrove, *Four Lamas of Dolpo*, pp. 100, 205. The latter is a wonderful record of the consistent practice of Dream Yoga.

36 Gtsaṅ smyon, *Mi la*, 89.7–8; Gtsaṅ smyon, *The Life of Milarepa*, p. 80.

37 Gtsaṅ smyon, *The Life of Milarepa*, pp. 80–81; Gtsaṅ smyon, *Mi la*, 89.

38 Gtsaṅ smyon, *Mgur 'bum*, pp. 650 ff.; Gtsaṅ smyon, *Hundred Thousand Songs*, pp. 487ff.

39 Gtsaṅ smyon, *Mgur 'bum*, p. 198.

40 Ibid., p. 394. This is the only instance of the Six Yogas being referred to as *rnal 'byor drug* instead of *chos drug* that I have found in either the *Mgur 'bum* or the *Mi la*.

41 Ibid., p. 424.

42 For more on this practice see the 9th Karmapa (Dbaṅ phyug rdo rje), *The Mahāmudrā: Eliminating the Darkness of Ignorance*, trans. and ed. Alexander Berzin, commentary by Beru Kyentze Rinpoche (Dharamsala: Library of Tibetan Works and Archives, 1978).

43 Snellgrove and Richardson, *Cultural History of Tibet*, p. 247. This story has also been represented in the graphic arts. In Dharamsala in April 1995, for instance, I came across a greeting card with a lovely folk painting of this story.

44 Gtsaṅ smyon, *Mgur 'bum*, p. 432.

45 The *Mgur 'bum* continues the coupling of the Six Yogas and Mahāmudrā in two additonal songs, nos. 17 and 38/35, pp. 349, 580, 588.

46 Gtsaṅ smyon, *Mgur 'bum*, Chang, p. 352.

47 Thinley, *The History of the Sixteen Karmapas*, p. 42. There are many examples of the importance of dreams in this lineage, especially as a means of receiving esoteric teachings, e.g., pp. 51, 56, 61, 62, 63, 66, 75, 89, 90, 113–14.

48 See the references in Ruegg, *Life of Bu ston*, pp. 74, 80, 105–7, and 124.

49 Ibid., p. 107, f. 18b.

50 He was instructed by the Chennga Trakpa Jangchub; Alex Wayman, *Calming the Mind and Discerning the Real* (New York: Columbia University Press, 1978), pp. 19–20.

51 Thurman, *Tsong Khapa*, p. 23.

52 The *Zab lam nā ro'i chos drug gi sgo nas 'khrid pai rim pa yid ches gsum ldan*, which has been translated by Garma Chen Chi Chang in Chang and Musès, *Esoteric Teachings of the Tibetan Tantra*, and by Mullin (Tsoṅ kha pa Blo bzaṅ grags pa, *Tsongkhapa's Six Yogas*).

53 Chang and Musès, *Esoteric Teachings*, p. 213.

54 See, for example, the dream ritual texts from the Tanjur and Kanjur translated and discussed in chapter 9.

55 Chang and Musès, *Esoteric Teachings*, p. 213.

56 Ibid., p. 217.

57 Ibid., pp. 219–20.

CHAPTER 9

1 See the works of Lincoln, Irwin, Dodds, Miller, and Eliade discussed in chapter 1; for some early Jewish practices see Joshua Trachtenberg, *Jewish Magic and Superstition: A Study in Folk Religion* (1939; New York: Atheneum, n.d.), pp. 241–43.

2 A similar discussion and ritual occurs in the *Bṛhadāraṇyaka Upaniṣad* (6.1–6), where there is mention of going to sleep by the ritual fire but not of having a dream.

3 See Olivelle, *Upaniṣads*, pp. xlix–lvi.

4 Olivelle glosses this as suggesting "he should let himself fall asleep and not attempt to keep awake"; ibid., p. 344 n. 2.8.

5 *Chāndogya Upaniṣad*, 5.2.8–9.

6 *Svapna nidrā jñānālambanaṃ vā* I.34–38; quoted by Sarvepalli Radhakrishnan and Charles A. Moore, *A Sourcebook in Indian Philosophy* (Princeton: Princeton University Press, 1957), p. 460.

7 See the brief discussion of these states in chapter 3 above based on *Chāndogya Upaniṣad*, 8.7–12 and *Māṇḍūkya Upaniṣads*, 1–12.

8 Eliade, *Yoga*, pp. 55–57.

9 See ancient Indian medical texts, such as the *CS*, v. 43, 2: 551; the *SS*, chap. 23, ll. 54–57, p. 135; the Tibetan medical text *Rgyud bzhi*, f. 3, ll. 3–6 to f. 4, l. 1; and its commentary, the *Vaiḍūrya sṅon po*, vol. 1, f. 222, l. 5. These texts are discussed in chapter 4 above.

10 *Nāradaparivrājaka Upaniṣad* 181, in Olivelle, *Upaniṣads*, p. 203. Another example is found in the same text, 188–89, p. 207.

11 *Turīyātītāvadhūta Upaniṣad* 244, ibid., p. 240; *Paramahaṃsaparivrājaka Upaniṣad* 285, ibid., p. 262.

12 *Brahma Upaniṣad* 79, ibid., p. 148; *Nāradaparivrājaka Upaniṣad* 179, ibid., p. 202.

13 For more information on this text, especially the dating problems, see *Sāmavidhāṇa Brāhmana*, ed. A. C. Burnell (London: Trübner, 1873), pp. v–x.

14 Ibid., p. 82. I have had to rely on the commentary to elucidate some of the text; unfortunately it does not say anything more about this deity.

15 Ibid., iii.4.2.

16 This last phrase comes from the commentary; ibid., pp. 82–83.

17 Ibid., iii.4.3.

18 Ibid., p. 82.

19 *Kūrma Purāṇa*, ed. Sri Anand Swarup Gupta (Varanasi: All India Kashi Raj Trust, 1972), i.9.6–13. *Mahābhārata* III.194, 8–14, contains another version of this myth. See figure 5.

20 For additional variants of this myth and some examples of other sleeping gods see Jonathan Z. Smith, "Sleep," in *EOR*, 13: 362.

21 This is an important point made in the *Bṛhādaraṇyaka Upaniṣad*, 4.3.9–10, and discussed by O'Flaherty, *Dreams*, p. 14.

22 The *Bṛhat-kathā* of Guṇāḍhya. For more information about this text see Winternitz, *History of Indian Literature*, 3: 346 ff.

23 See the discussions in Charles Rockwell Lanman, *A Sanskrit Reader* (Cambridge, MA: Harvard University Press, 1884), pp. 332–33; and in Arthur A. Macdonell, *A History of Sanskrit Literature* (1899; Delhi: Motilal Banarsidass, 1971), who notes that *taraṅgas* (chapters) 60–64 are a recasting of the first three books of the *Pañcatantra*; and in Winternitz, *History of Indian Literature*, 3: 353–65.

24 Somadeva Bhaṭṭa, *Kathāsaritsāgara*, ed. Jagadīśa Lāl Śāstrī (Delhi: Motilal Banarsidass, 1960), bk. 12, chap. 5; Somadeva, *Ocean of Story*, 6: 76–77.

25 Somadeva, *Kathāsaritsāgara*, bk. 1, chap. 6.137; Somadeva, *Ocean of Story*, 1: 70–71.

26 Compare also the similar understandings of dreams in the Indian (Hindu) and Tibetan (Buddhist) medical texts quoted in chapter 4. This practice of dream ideologies crossing religious lines also occured in the Hellenistic world between Judaism, Christianity, and Paganism, see Miller, *Dreams in Late Antiquity*, passim.

27 I am very grateful to (Pema) Losang Chogyen for bringing this text to my attention and sharing his notes with me. Before his untimely death in 1996, he was preparing an English translation and a definitive edition of this text through a study of Sanskrit and Tibetan manuscripts.

28 Gtsaṅ smyon, *Mi la,* 91.2–5; Gtsaṅ smyon, *The Life of Milarepa,* p. 82.

29 Gtsaṅ smyon, *Mgur 'bum,* p. 625; Chang, p. 467.

30 Gtsaṅ smyon, *Mgur 'bum,* p. 650ff.

31 I have followed *Kālachakra Tantra: Rite of Initiation for the Stage of Generation,* ed. and trans. Jeffrey Hopkins (London: Wisdom, 1985), p. 192, which is in accord with my own cursory notes from this occasion.

32 Dodds refers to a similar use of a branch of laurel in the dreambooks of antiquity. See *The Greeks and the Irrational,* p. 110.

33 Namkhai Norbu distinguishes between women and men for this posture, recommending women sleep on their left side, *Dream Yoga,* pp. 52–53. The Dalai Lama, however, made no such distinction, even though there were many women present. When I questioned Geshe Lozang Jamspal about this position, he said one sleeps on the right side to avoid pressure on the heart, thereby assuring a sound sleep. Pressure, like other physical discomfort, presumably would influence dreams and thus not lead to a prophetic dream. Conversation, August 18, 1995, New York City. See also Kelsang Gyatso, *Guide to the Dakini Land,* p. 29, where he elaborates on the symbolic meaning of sleeping postures and attitudes.

34 Hopkins, *Kālachakra Tantra,* pp. 201–2.

35 Ibid., pp. 207–8.

36 See Tarthang Tulku's very clear exposition of this idea from the point of view of Yogācāra philosophy in *Crystal Mirror,* 4: 178–87.

37 See Bolling, "Dreams and Sleep"; and *Rig Veda,* 2.28.10, 10.37.4, 5.82.4–5, etc.

38 *SS,* chap. 19, vv. 26–27. These texts are discussed in chap. 4 above. See Barbara Tedlock, "Zuni and Quiché Dream Sharing and Interpreting" in Tedlock, *Dreaming,* for a discussion of some of the meanings involved in telling or not telling dreams, pp. 116–17 and 128. Tedlock found that in order not to disperse the good luck promised by a good dream the Zuni do not tell it until after it has been realized. However, they immediately tell their bad dreams in order to disperse and thereby weaken what they promise. Laurel Kendall's field work also reports this point of view in Korea, see "Dreaming of Solutions," p. 519. The only other recommendation not to tell a dream that I have come across in an Indian text occurs in the *Brahmavai Purāṇa,* which says "if a good dream is told to a person of the Kāśyapa *gotra* it becomes fruitless...also if told to a woman, there is a loss of wealth," quoted in Dange, ed., *Encyclopaedia of Puranic Beliefs and Practices,* vol. 2, p. 448. Interestingly enough, a Jewish text also advises against the telling of a dream to anyone, especially one's wife, Trachtenberg, *Jewish Magic,* p. 236. Irwin, *The Dream*

Seekers, has a thoughtful discussion of the meaning of silence in relation to the highly verbal dream experiences of various Native American people, pp. 163–84.

39 Dange, ed., *Encyclopaedia of Puranic Beliefs and Practices,* 2: 450.

40 Lamotte, *History of Indian Buddhism*, p. 92. A Tanjur text dealing with dreams (vol. *sha*, f. 88b) instructs that the "three sweets of sugar, honey, and molasses" among other things, should be offered to Tārā in order to have a good dream. This text is discussed below.

41 Strong, *The Legend of King Aśoka*, pp. 274–75, discussed above.

42 *The Jātaka*, Cowell, 1: 187.

43 This text is attributed to the historical Buddha, who manifested as the Medicine Buddha in order to teach it. It is said to have been written in Sanskrit about 400 C.E. and rediscovered in Tibet in the eleventh century.

44 The *Rgyud bzhi*, f. 3, ll. 3–6 to f. 4, l. 1. See also the lists in its commentary, the *Vaiḍūrya sṅon po*, vol. 1, f. 222, l. 5. Rechung Rinpoche has translated part of this text, though he drew on a slightly different manuscript; *Tibetan Medicine*, p. 48.

45 Koṅ sprul, *Retreat Manual*, p. 123 and n. 42. Additional remedies can be found in Chophel, *The Folk Culture of Tibet*, pp. 90–95.

46 Nebesky-Wojkowitz, *Oracles and Demons*, p. 503.

47 Quoted in Jacobi, *Jaina Sutras*, 1: 240. As has been shown in chapter 4, the medical texts state that not being able to sleep again after a dream indicates its promise will come to pass. Other Jain examples can be found in the *Triṣaṣṭiśalākāpuruṣacarita or the Lives of Sixty-Three Illustrious Persons*, vol. 2, trans. Helen M. Johnson (Baroda: Oriental Institute, 1937), pp. 29–35, 122–24, 233, 258.

48 *Payakkhitta* = *prakyaskitta*. The commentators explain it by "*padakhupta*, touching their feet in order to avoid the wicked eye." Jacobi, *Jaina Sutras*, 1: 245.

49 Ibid., 1: 245.

50 See Gonda, *The Ritual Functions and Significance of Grasses*, p. 6.

51 Tun-huang was an important junction on the Silk Route under the control of Tibet from about 786 to 848. See Crescenzi and Torricelli, "A Tun-huang Text on Dreams," pp. 31–37. I am grateful to the authors for allowing me to read an early draft of their paper, which contains the transliterated Tibetan text.

52 See, e.g., S. T. Kazi's introduction to Bo-doṅ Paṇ-chen Phyogs-las-rnam-rgyal, *Encyclopedia Tibetica;* and Paul Harrison, "A Brief History of the Tibetan bKa' 'gyur," in Cabezón and Jackson, *Tibetan Literature*, pp. 70–94.

53 This is the same term that was used in Abhayākaragupta's *Vajrāvalīnāmamaṇḍalapāyikā* on constructing mandalas.

54 This is probably the tantric Nāgārjuna, not the philosopher of the same name. For more information on both Nāgārjunas, see Reginald A. Ray, "Nāgārjuna's Longevity," in Schober, *Sacred Biography*, pp. 129–59.

55 The author does not say what these are; they would be given as part of the oral teachings.

56 Presumably a nursing mother.

57 Tanjur, vol. *tshi*, f. 130a. Stephan Beyer mentions magical eye ointment as one of the eight great magical attainments of Buddhism and explains that it is believed to enable one to "see the entire triple world." Beyer, *The Cult of Tārā: Magic and Ritual in Tibet* (Berkeley: University of California Press, 1973), pp. 247, 252. The *Sādhanamālā* lists "*añjana*, an eye salve that removes ignorance" as one of the eight great siddhis (powers), the attainment of which is one of the goals of tantric practitioners (*Sādhanamālā*, ed. Benyotosh Bhattacharyya, Gaekwad's Oriental Series, vol. 2, no. 41 [Barodo: Oriental Institute, 1928], cited by Elisabeth Anne Benard, *Chinnamastā: The Aweful Buddhist and Hindu Tantric Goddess* [Delhi: Motilal Banarsidass, 1994]), while the *Atharva Veda* 4.9 mentions using an eye ointment *(aṣana)* as *protection* from troubled dreams. The use of kohl around the eyes, especially in children, is ubiquitous in South Asia for protection against the evil eye.

58 Dodds, *The Greeks and the Irrational*, p. 105.

59 See also Milarepa's teachings to Gampopa on *bag chags* in relation to dreaming; Gtsaṅ smyon, *Mgur 'bum*, p. 649.

60 Tanjur, vol. *tshi*, f. 130a.

61 See the discussion of this in chapter 4 herein.

62 Ibid., vol. *tshi*, f. 130a.

63 Ibid., vol. *tshi*, f. 130b.

64 Ibid., vol. *tshi*, f. 130b.

65 See, for example, excerpts from various texts and from the oral tradition in Chophel, *The Folk Culture of Tibet*, pp. 89–102, and the excerpts from Nebesky-Wojkowitz, *Oracles and Demons*, quoted in chapter 4 above.

66 Kanjur, vol. 25, text 48, f. 410. Bracketed material refers to a translation of the Chinese edition given to me by Dr. Natalie Hauptman.

67 Tanjur, vol. *tshi*, f. 130b, ll. 5–6.

68 See, for example, Thurman, "Worship and Cultic Life," p. 472, whose discussion of Buddhist missionary activity highlights some of the ways the elite Buddhist tradition merged and blended with the indigenous folk traditions; and Ramesh Chandra Tewari, "Pre-Buddhist Elements in Himalayan Buddhism: The Institution of the Oracles," pp. 135–55, for his study of the incorporation of a popular and indigenous oracle into mainstream Buddhist practice. Geoffrey Samuel's work is also relevant in this context; see "Early Buddhism in Tibet" and *Civilized Shamans.*

69 Reginald Ray has argued persuasively for a distinction and a tension in ancient and medieval India between the charismatic Buddhism of the forest saints, or virtuoso meditators, and the scholastic Buddhism of an elite, settled monasticism, which pursues textual studies. He stresses the innovative nature of the former and the conservative tendencies of the latter. *Buddhist Saints*, e.g., pp. 379–80, though he softens this argument somewhat on pp. 413–14 and 438–47, which include relevant comments on Tibetan Buddhism. Geoffrey Samuel has a closely related discussion in the Tibetan context in "Early Buddhism in Tibet."

70 Paul Williams has characterized the growth of Mahāyāna as a "'doctrinal widening,' rendering doctrinally respectable certain activities and beliefs that some monks viewed with disdain, and associated primarily with the ultimately useless activities of lay people." Williams, *Mahāyāna Buddhism*, pp. 24–25. From its earliest days Buddhism adapted to the local conditions to which its missionary activities inevitably led, and Mahāyāna developed more as a highly diverse federation of cults based on different sūtras and their attendant practices than as a univocal movement; ibid., pp. 1–33. On this point see also Schopen, "The Phrase 'sa pṛthivipradeśaś caityabhūto bhavet.'"

71 Tanjur, vol. *nu*, ff. 176b–177b. A virtual duplicate of this text appears at ff. 152b–153a.

72 Ibid., f. 176b.

73 Ibid., f. 176b.

74 Ibid., f. 176b.

75 Compare the two *sādhanas* to Tārā translated and discussed by Luis O. Gomez, "Two Tantric Meditations: Visualizing the Deity," in Donald S. Lopez, ed., *Buddhism in Practice* (Princeton: Princeton University Press, 1995), pp. 266–70, 318–27.

76 See Janet Gyatso's thoughtful discussion of *sādhanas*: "An Avalokiteśvara Sādhana," in Lopez, *Religions of Tibet in Practice*, pp. 266–70.

77 Tanjur, vol. *sha*, ff. 88b–89a, pp. 175–77.

CHAPTER 10

1 This truism of gender studies is effectively argued by Rita Gross in "Methodological Remarks on the Study of Women in Religions: Review, Criticism and Redefinition," in J. Plaskow and J. N. Romero, eds., *Women and Religion* (Missoula: Scholars Press, 1974).

2 See the discussion above in chapter 4 and also the copious dream lists from Sangye Gyatso's commentary (the *Vaiḍūrya sṅon po*) on the Tibetan medical text, *Rgyud bzhi*, the *Four Treatises*, translated into English in Aris, *Tibetan Medical Paintings*, 2: 205–7

3 Liz Wilson discusses some female ghouls in early Buddhist literature in *Charming Cadavers*, pp. 58–60; and Ann Gold discusses wrathful yoginīs in the Gopi Chand story, in "Gender and Illusion in a Rajasthani Yogic Tradition" in Arjun Appadurai, et al., eds., *Gender, Genre and Power in South Asian Expressive Traditions* (Philadelphia: University of Pennsylvania Press, 1991), pp. 102–35; Tibetan literature is, of course, filled with wrathful ḍākinīs, demons, and ogresses; see, e.g., Janet Gyatso, "Down with the Demoness," in Janice Willis, ed., *Feminine Ground: Essays on Women and Tibet* (Ithaca: Snow Lion, 1989), pp. 35–51.

4 Hari Prasad Shastri, trans., *The Ramayana of Valmiki*, 3d. ed. (London: Shantisadan, 1962), V.27, p. 400. Trijaṭā's dream is for the most part also recorded in the *Mahābhārata* III.264.61–70.

5 Shastri, *Ramayana*, II.69, p. 331.

6 These were based on an earlier (circa first century C.E.) collection, now lost.

7 Somadeva, *Ocean of Story*, 1: 99–100. For further discussion of dreams in this text and in other South Asian folklore, see Serinity Young, "Dreams," in *South Asian Folklore* (forthcoming).

8 *Mahabhārata, Sauptika Parva* 8.65–68.

9 *Chāndogya Upaniṣad*, 5.2.8–9.

10 See the discussion of red as a dream symbol in chapter 5 herein.

11 See June Campbell's discussion of the secret role of women in Tantra in *Traveller in Space: In Search of Female Identity in Tibetan Buddhism* (New York: George Braziller, 1996).

12 For more information on ḍākinīs see Victoria Urubshurow, "Dakinis," in *The Encyclopedia of Women and World Religion*, ed. Serinity Young (New York: Macmillan, 1998), 1: 231–32; Diemberger, "Lhakama," pp. 137–53; and Nathan Katz,

"Anima and mKha'-'gro-ma: A Critical Comparative Study of Jung and Tibetan Buddhism," *Tibet Journal* 2, no. 3 (1977): 13–43.

13 Guenther, *Life and Teachings of Nāropa*, p. 67.

14 Kelsang Gyatso, *Guide to the Dakini Land*, p. 26.

15 See Nebesky-Wojkowitz, *Oracles and Demons;* Diemberger, "Lhakama," p. 141 and n. 19. See also *Padma*, f. 182a.1–3, where a possessed woman interprets omens for a community.

16 *Na chuṅ mdzes ma dkar sṅo ser dmar ljan ba lṅa*, Gtsaṅ smyon, *Mi la*, 25.21–22.

17 Ibid., 194.

18 See Gtsaṅ smyon, *Mgur 'bum*, no. 28, for their story.

19 Nebesky-Wojkowitz, *Oracles and Demons*, chap. 13, is devoted to the exposition of these and similar goddesses.

20 Gtsaṅ smyon, *Mi la*, 88.32–89.2. This dream is also preserved in Gtsaṅ smyon, *The Life of Marpa*, p. 73. Milarepa's other dreams of ḍākinīs are in Gtsaṅ smyon, *Mgur 'bum*, pp. 323, 363.

21 See references in n. 16 of chapter 8 herein.

22 Gtsaṅ smyon, *The Life of Marpa*, pp. 22–23.

23 Ibid., pp. 72–73.

24 Aris, *Hidden Treasures*, pp. 27–28, 37, 54–56, 79–80.

25 Ibid., p 40.

26 Thinley, *The History of the Sixteen Karmapas*, p. 45. Additional examples (from this lineage) of dreams about female deities are on pp. 45, 62, 66, 80, 90.

27 For instance, Jamgon Kongtrul refers to a third Dream Yoga lineage which he calls "The Six Doctrines of Sukāsiddhī" *(Su kha chos drug);* Koṅ sprul, *Retreat Manual*, pp. 93, 210. For more on Niguma, see 'Gos Lo tsā ba, *Blue Annals*, pp. 728–52. For Sukāsiddhī see ibid., pp. 729–31.

28 Jérôme Edou, *Machig Labdrön and the Foundations of Chöd* (Ithaca: Snow Lion, 1996), pp. 37, 136, 138.

29 Kelsang Gyatso, *Guide to the Dakini Land*, passim.

30 See the brief discussion of her in "Life of Tilopa," in *Religions of Tibet in Practice*, ed. Donald S. Lopez, pp. 138–41, and her appearances in Tilopa's biographies. See also the references to her in Shaw, *Passionate Enlightenment.*

31 Kelsang Gyatso, *Guide to the Dakini Land*, p. 2.

32 "Life of Tilopa," in *Religions of Tibet in Practice*, ed. Donald S. Lopez, p. 146.

33 Alaka Chattopadhyaya, *Atīśa and Tibet*, p. 135; and see p. 418 for two more of his dreams about Tārā. She also offers protection from frightening dreams; see Lopez, *Religions of Tibet in Practice*, p. 552.

34 Dowman, *The Divine Madman*, p. 119.

35 For a brief discussion and reference to some further examples, see "Wisdom as Feminine" in Serinity Young, *An Anthology of Sacred Texts by and about Women* (New York: Crossroad, 1993), pp. xxi–xxii, and various entries in the index under "Feminine." Katz, "Anima and mKha'-'gro-ma," pp. 13–43, has an interesting discussion of ḍākinīs as guides.

36 For more information on women's dreams see two articles by Carol Schreier Rupprecht, "Women's Dreams: Mind and Body," in *Feminist Archetypal Theory: Interdisciplinary Re-Visions of Jungian Thought*, ed. Estella Lauter and Carol Schreier Rupprecht (Knoxville: University of Tennessee Press, 1985), and "Sex, Gender and Dreams: From Polarity to Plurality," in *Among All These Dreamers: Essays on Dreaming and Modern Society*, ed. Kelly Bulkeley (Albany: State University Press of New York, 1996). See also Miller's discussion of Perpetua's dreams in *Dreams in Late Antiquity;* and Kagan, *Lucrecia's Dreams*, a well-documented study of a prophetic female dreamer. For more examples of conception dreams from around the world, see the bibliography on conception dreams in Bulkeley, *The Wilderness of Dreams*, p. 234 n. 9; and Otto Rank "Myth of the Birth of the Hero," pp. 18–42.

37 At least in the popular *LV* version.

38 Similarly, Bruce Lincoln, *Authority: Construction and Corrosion* (Chicago: University of Chicago Press, 1994), pp. 96–101, has presented some relevant and pervasive examples of dream discourse as one of the few authoritative voices available to women in the Roman world, albeit an easily challenged one.

39 Ilango Adigal, *Shilappadikaram*, trans. Alain Danielou (New York: New Directions, 1965), pp. 53–54.

40 Ibid., p. 55.

41 Ibid., p. 126.

42 Ibid., pp. 126, 129.

43 In addition to the examples discussed below, in the Jain tradition, after Mahāvīra's mother has her conception dream she tells it to her husband, who interprets it. This seems to be such a stock formula that it takes place even though the

king later sends for dream interpreters. Of course, the influence of the Queen Māyā's dream on this story (or vice versa) is apparent.

44 Other examples of gendered battles over the power to interpret dreams can be found in Young, "Dreams," in *Encyclopedia of Women and World Religion*, 1: 271–73.

45 See Lynn Bennett, *Dangerous Wives and Sacred Sisters: Social and Symbolic Roles of High-Caste Women in Nepal* (New York: Columbia University Press, 1983), pp. 261–308, for an intriguing discussion of Hindu men's control and pacifying worship of the fierce goddess Durgā as a way of confronting and overcoming their anxieties about real women.

46 This, despite the fact that the *Kāma Sūtra* lists dream interpretation as one of the sixty-four arts of a courtesan. However, courtesans are a significantly different category of women than wives. The privileging of male dream interpreters in South Asian texts contrasts with the prominence of female dream interpreters in many other cultures; see examples in Young, "Dreams," in *Encyclopedia of Women and World Religion*, 1: 271–73.

47 *LV*, Vaidya, 141.9–142.28. See the discussion of these two dreams in chapter 2 above.

48 *MSV*, 1: 83.

49 *Jātaka*, Fausbøll, 6: 540–41.

50 For further discussion of women's important and complicated relation to alternate states of consciousness see Lincoln, *Authority*, pp. 96–101; Lewis, *Ecstatic Religion: An Anthropological Study of Spirit Possession and Shamanism* (Middlesex, U.K.: Penguin 1971); Janice Boddy, *Wombs and Alien Spirits: Women, Men and the Zār Cult in Northern Sudan* (Madison: University of Wisconsin Press, 1989); and Laurel Kendall, *Shamans, Housewives, and Other Restless Spirits: Women in Korean Ritual Life* (Honolulu: University of Hawai'i Press, 1985), esp. pp. 23–25.

51 *Padma*, f.57b.6.

52 See, for instance, Kirin Narayan, *Mondays on the Dark Night of the Moon: Himalayan Foothill Folktales* (New York: Oxford University Press, 1997), p. 167; William Sax, *Mountain Goddess: Gender and Politics in a Himalayan Pilgrimage* (New York: Oxford University Press, 1991), esp. pp. 115–26; Bennett, *Dangerous Wives*.

Nancy Chodorow's work offers some meaningful psychological insights into women's greater connectedness to others; *The Reproduction of Mothering: Psychoanalysis and the Sociology of Gender* (Berkeley: University of California Press, 1978), esp. pp. 173–85.

53 Liz Wilson persuasively argues "that the objectification of women for the edification of men is truly a pan-Buddhist theme"; see *Charming Cadavers*, p. 4. A work that suggests some alternatives to this pattern in male biographies is *The Lives and Liberation of Princess Mandarava: The Indian Consort of Padmasambhava*, trans. Lama Chonam and Sangye Khandro (Boston: Wisdom Publications, 1998). This is a terma text discovered by Bsam gtan gliṅ pa in the early part of the twentieth century in eastern Tibet, a region that had been in the throes of religious change for several decades. This text contains chapters on Mandarava's past lives in which she and others dream, but the dreams are very woman-centered (see, for example, the complete reversal of gender imagery in a conception dream, p. 25). Whether this can be attributed to the religious climate of eastern Tibet will have to await further research. Along these lines, Donatella Rossi is researching female biographies discovered by a female terton in eastern Tibet.

54 Luce Irigaray is one of the most elegant articulators of the male co-optation of women's speech and subjectivity. See, for example, "The Three Genres," in *The Irigaray Reader*, ed. Margaret Whitford (Oxford: Blackwell, 1991), pp. 140–53, and *Sexes and Genealogies* (New York: Columbia University Press, 1993). In a Buddhist context, this point is made repeatedly by Wilson, *Charming Cadavers*, and Campbell, *Traveller in Space*, esp. pp. 189–91. See also Campbell's discussion of Irigaray in relation to female identity in Tibetan Buddhism.

55 On this belief in India see Crooke, *The Popular Religion and Folklore of Northern India*, 1: 231.

56 See, e.g., *LV*, Vaidya, 148.25–149.2. This imagery is duplicated in the story of Yasa, one of the earliest Buddhist monks. This and similar stories are recounted in Wilson, *Charming Cadavers*, pp. 77–82.

57 *Theogony* (211–13, 756–66), cited by Jonathan Z. Smith, in "Sleep," *EOR*, 13: 362. This article contains many useful comments on the connections between dreams, sleep, and death, pp. 361–64.

58 See Wilson, *Charming Cadavers*, which is devoted to this topic.

59 *Mahābhārata*, 12.248.13–21, etc., cited and translated by Wendy Doniger O'Flaherty, *The Origins of Evil in Hindu Mythology* (Berkeley: University of California Press, 1976), p. 228. For more Indian goddesses associated with death see Mary Storm, "Death," in *Encyclopedia of Women and World Religion*, 1: 243–44.

60 For example, Nebesky-Wojkowitz includes a black woman in his list of dreams foretelling death that he collected in Sikkim in the 1950s, *Oracles and Demons*, p. 466.

61 See Wilson, *Charming Cadavers*, for the negative configuring of this imagery in early Buddhism.

62 Bennett, *Dangerous Wives*, makes this point in relation to male worship and propitiation of fierce female deities in Nepal, pp. 261–308.

63 See, for example, Francoise Pommaret's discussion of the Tibetan *'das log* (mostly female mediums who travel to hell, talk to the deceased, and return with messages), in Lopez, *Religions of Tibet in Practice*, pp. 499–510. For more general comments on women and death in world religion see Storm, "Death," and Gail Holst-Warhoff, "Mourning and Death Rituals," both in *Encyclopedia of Women and World Religion*, 1: 243–44; 2: 682–85, respectively.

64 Cited by James H. Sanford, "The Abominable Tachikawa Skull Ritual," *Monumenta Nipponica* 46, no. 1 (spring 1991): 14. See Sanford's discussion of the conflation of women and death in this ritual.

65 For a brief discussion of these ideas within the context of world religions, see Young, *Anthology of Sacred Texts*, pp. xx–xxi.

66 See Wendy Doniger O'Flaherty, *Women, Androgynes and Other Mythical Beasts* (Chicago: University of Chicago Press, 1980), passim, for her discussion of the connections between women and death, and pp. 53–55 for the ambiguities of women's milk.

Appendix

1 Stephen LaBerge, *Lucid Dreaming: The Power of Being Awake and Aware in Your Dreams* (New York: Ballantine Books, 1986).

2 I am grateful to Antonella Crescenzi for helping me to clarify my thoughts on this topic.

3 LaBerge, *Lucid Dreaming*, has a chapter on the history of lucid dreaming; see pp. 21–41, 55–77. See also Hunt, *The Multiplicity of Dreams*, pp. 80–81.

4 This discussion of Kilton Stewart follows Domhoff, *The Mystique of Dreams*, pp. 35–64.

5 See the discussion of these later scholars, ibid., pp. 14–34.

6 An actual example of this comes from another culture, that of the Quichua people of Ecuador, who have an ongoing process of dream sharing, especially between husband and wife, that integrates the mythic and practical realms of their lives. Of particular interest, they required the anthropological team studying them to participate in this process. Norman E. Whitten, Jr., *Sacha Runa: Ethnicity and Adaptation of Ecuadorian Jungle Quichua* (Urbana: University of Illinois Press, 1976), esp. pp. 18, 51, 58–59, 67–68, 296–99. I am grateful to Lawrence Sullivan for bringing this research to my attention.

7 See Domhoff, *The Mystique of Dreams*, pp. 63–64, for his generous, and probably realistic, evaluation of Stewart's motives.

8 Stewart's influence continues today. At the annual conference of the Association for the Study of Dreams, held in New York City, June 20–24, 1995, literature on his publications and "Dream Education Workshops" was prominently displayed through an organization run by his widow and her new husband.

9 Domhoff, *The Mystique of Dreams*, pp. 65–78.

10 Ibid., p. 75. For a survey of experiments (which are rather inconclusive) on the control of dreams, see ibid., pp. 79–95.

11 Recently, in answer to the question of a western dream scholar, the Dalai Lama said that Dream Yoga could be practiced "without a great deal of preparation." Varela, *Sleeping, Dreaming, and Dying*, p. 45. However, in his formal presentation of Dream Yoga he presented it within the context of very advanced tantric practices. Clearly, there are different traditions about Dream Yoga, and it can be an extremely elastic term. Here I am presenting Dream Yoga as historically understood within the tradition of the Six Yogas of Nāropa.

12 LaBerge, *Lucid Dreaming*, p. 121. For more on the cognitive relation of lucid dreaming and the nightmare, as well as to meditational states, see Hunt, *The Multiplicity of Dreams*, pp. 118–27.

13 LaBerge, *Lucid Dreaming*, p. 127.

14 Dreams with a sexual content seem to be very well represented in lucid dream experience; LaBerge, *Lucid Dreaming*, pp. 89–95. Wendy Doniger O'Flaherty is particularly elegant and witty in her comparative discussion of South Asian and Western sexual dreams; "Western Dreams About Eastern Dreams" in *Among All These Dreamers*, pp. 169–76.

15 See Bulkeley, *Wilderness of Dreams*, pp. 59–63, for a discussion of LaBerge's impact on modern dream studies and an enthusiastic evaluation of his work. Bulkeley's enthusiasm for lucid dreaming is based, in part, on LaBerge's affirmation of the religious meaning of dreams.

16 LaBerge, *Lucid Dreaming*, pp. 23–24.

17 For a review of the cultural and linguistic issues, among others, of dream research across cultures, see Tedlock, *Dreaming*, pp. 1–30; and O'Flaherty, "Western Dreams about Eastern Dreams."

18 LaBerge, *Lucid Dreaming*, p. 193. In this regard, see also the brief discussion of Stewart and Carlos Castenada in Hunt, *The Multiplicity of Dreams*, pp. 430–31 n. 4.

19 LaBerge, *Lucid Dreaming*, pp. 145–46.

Texts and Translations

The bibliography has been divided into primary and secondary sources and arranged by the primary entry element as it appears in standard library catalogs. Because the Wylie romanization scheme for Tibetan differs slightly from the system adopted by the Library of Congress and the American Library Association, this standard LC-ALA romanization for main entries and uniform titles has been used in the bibliography when these are the forms used in catalogs. Further, original authors and titles have been given precedence over translators, editors, and translated titles. Thus the Pali edition of the *Anguttara Nikaya* made by E. Hardy and the E. H. Hare translation published under the title *The Book of Gradual Sayings* have been grouped together.

Abhayadatta. *Buddha's Lions = Caturaśīta-siddha-pravṛtti: The Lives of the Eighty-Four Siddhas.* Translated into Tibetan as *Grub thob brgyad cu rtsa bzhi'i lo rgyus.* Trans. James B. Robinson. Berkeley: Dharma, 1979.

———. *Masters of Mahāmudrā.* Trans. Keith Dowman. Albany: State University of New York Press, 1985.

Abhiniṣkramaṇasūtra. Trans. from the Chinese edition as *The Romantic Legend of Śākya Buddha* by Samuel Beal. 1875; Delhi: Motilal Banarsidass, 1985.

Adigal, Ilango. *Shilappadikaram.* Trans. Alain Danielou. New York: New Directions, 1965.

Aṅguttara Nikāya. Ed. E. Hardy. London: Pali Text Society, 1896.

Aṅguttara Nikāya. Trans. as *The Book of the Gradual Sayings* by E. H. Hare. Vol. 3. London: Pali Text Society, 1934.

Āryaśūra. *Jātakamālā.* Trans. J. S. Speyer. 1895; New Delhi: Motilal Banarsidass, 1971.

Aśvaghoṣa. *Buddhacarita.* Ed. and trans. E. H. Johnston. 1936; Delhi: Motilal Banarsidass, 1984.

Atharva-Veda Saṃhitā. Ed. Svami Satya Prakash Sarasvati. 3 vols. New Delhi: Veda Pratishthana, 1992. Trans. as *Hymns of the Atharva-Veda* by Maurice Bloomfield. 1897; Delhi: Motilal Banarsidass, 1979.

Blo bzaṅ 'phrin las las rnam rgyal. *'Jam mgon chos kyi rgyal po tsoṅ ka pa chen po'i rnam thar thub bstan mdzes pa'i rgyan gcig ṅo mtshar nor bu'i 'phreṅ ba.* Sarnath Varanasi: Mongolian Lama Guru Deva, 1967.

Bo-doṅ Paṇ-chen Phyogs-las-rnam-rgyal. *Encyclopedia Tibetica: The Collected Works of Bo-doṅ Paṇ-chen Phyogs-las-rnam-rgyal.* Vol. 2. New Delhi: Tibet House Library, 1969.

Bsam gtan gliṅ pa. *The Lives and Liberation of Princess Mandarava: The Indian Consort of Padmasambhava.* Trans. Lama Chonam and Sangye Khandro. Boston: Wisdom Publications, 1998.

Bsod nams rgyal mtshan, Sa skya pa Bla ma Dam-pa. *Rgyal rabs gsal ba'i me loṅ.* Trans. as *The Clear Mirror: A Traditional Account of Tibet's Golden Age* by McComas Taylor and Lama Choedak Yuthok. Ithaca: Snow Lion, 1996.

Bu ston Rin chen grub. *The History of Buddhism in India and Tibet.* Trans. E. Obermiller. 1932; Delhi: Sri Satguru, 1986.

Buddhaghosa. *Manorathapūraṇī.* Ed. Hermann Kopp. Vol. 3. London: Pali Text Society, 1936.

———. *Samantapāsādikā.* Ed. J. Takakusu and M. Nagai. London: Pali Text Society, 1930.

Caraka Saṃhitā. Ed. and trans. Ram Karan Sharma and Vaidya Bhagwan Das. Varanasi: Chowkhamba Sanskrit Series, 1977.

Chang, Garma Chen Chi, trans., and C. A. Musès, ed. *Esoteric Teachings of the Tibetan Tantra.* 1961; York Beach, ME: Samuel Weiser, 1982.

Chuang-tzu. *Chuang Tzu: Basic Writings.* Trans. Burton Watson. New York: Columbia University Press, 1964.

Conze, Edward, trans. *The Large Sutra on Perfect Wisdom, with the Divisions of the Abhisamayālaṅkāra.* Berkeley: University of California Press, 1975.

Dge 'dun rgya mtsho, Dalai Lama II. *Selected Works of the Dalai Lama II.* Ed. and trans. Glenn H. Mullin. Ithaca: Snow Lion, 1985.

Le Dict de Padma=Padma thang yig. Trans. Gustave-Charles Toussaint. Paris: E. Leroux, 1933.

Divyāvadāna. Ed. E. B. Cowell and R. A. Neil. Cambridge: Cambridge University Press, 1886.

Divyāvadāna. Ed. P. L. Vaidya. Darbhanga: Mithila Institute, 1959.

Dowman, Keith. *The Divine Madman.* Clearlake, CA: Dawn Horse, 1983.

———. *Sky Dancer: The Secret Life of the Lady Yeshe Tsogyel.* London: Routledge and Kegan Paul, 1984.

Evans-Wentz, W. Y., ed. *Tibet's Great Yogi Milarepa.* New York: Oxford University Press, 1928.

———. *The Tibetan Book of the Dead.* New York: Oxford University Press, 1927.

———. *The Tibetan Book of the Great Liberation.* New York: Oxford University Press, 1954.

———. *Tibetan Yoga and Secret Doctrines.* New York: Oxford University Press, 1935.

Freemantle, Francesca, and Chögyam Trungpa, trans. *The Tibetan Book of the Dead: The Great Liberation through Hearing in the Bardo.* Boston: Shambhala, 1975.

The Gilgit Manuscript of the Saṅghabhedavastu, Being the 17th and Last Section of the Vinaya of the Mūlasarvāstivādin. Ed. Raniero Gnoli. Rome: Istituto italiano per il medio ed estremo oriente, 1977.

'Gos Lo tsa ba Gźon nu dpal. *The Blue Annals.* Trans. George N. Roerich. 1949; Delhi: Motilal Banarsidass, 1976.

The Grihya-Sūtras. Trans. Hermann Oldenberg. 1886; Delhi: Motilal Banarsidass, 1981.

Gtsaṅ smyon He ru ka. *The Life of Marpa the Translator.* Trans. Nālandā Translation Committee. Boulder: Prajñā Press, 1982.

———. *The Life of Milarepa.* Trans. Lobsang P. Lhalungpa. Boulder: Shambhala, 1984.

———. *Mi la ras pa'i rnam thar.* Ed. J. W. de Jong. 's-Gravenhage: Mouton, 1959.

———, comp. *The Hundred Thousand Songs of Milarepa.* Trans. Garma Chen Chi Chang. 2 vols. Boulder: Shambhala, 1977.

———, comp. *Mi la'i mgur 'bum.* Delhi: Sherab Gyaltsen, 1983.

Guenther, Herbert V. *The Life and Teachings of Nāropa.* New York: Oxford University Press, 1963.

Gzi brjid. The Nine Ways of Bon: Excerpts from gZi brjid. Ed. and trans. David Snellgrove. London: Oxford University Press, 1967.

Ibn Hisham 'Abd al-Malik. *The Life of Muhammad.* Trans. A. Guillaume. Karachi: Oxford University Press, 1955.

Jacobi, Hermann. *Jaina Sutras.* 2 vols. 1884; New York: Dover, 1968.

The Jātaka. Ed. E. B. Cowell. 1895; London: Pali Text Society, 1973.

The Jātaka Together with Its Commentary. Ed. V. Fausbøll. London: Trübner, 1877.

Kālachakra Tantra: Rite of Initiation for the Stage of Generation. Ed. and trans. Jeffrey Hopkins. London: Wisdom, 1985.

Kanjur. Sde dge edition. Reprinted Oakland: Dharma, 1980. Vol. 25.

Kathāvatthu. Ed. Arnold C. Taylor. 1894; London: Pali Text Society, 1979.

———. Trans. as *Points of Controversy* by Shwe Zan Aung and C. A. F. Rhys Davids. 1915; London: Luzac, 1960.

Koṅ sprul Blo gros mtha' yas. *Jamgon Kongtrul's Retreat Manual.* Trans. Ngawang Zangpo. Ithaca: Snow Lion, 1994.

———. *Kongtrul's Encyclopaedia of Indo-Tibetan Culture.* Ed. Lokesh Chandra. New Delhi: International Academy of Indian Culture, 1970.

Kūrma Purāṇa. Ed. Sri Anand Swarup Gupta. Varanasi: All India Kashi Raj Trust, 1972.

Lalitavistara. Ed. P. L. Vaidya. Darbhanga: Mithila Institute, 1958.

———. Trans. as *The Voice of the Buddha: The Beauty of Compassion* by Gwendolyn Bays. Oakland: Dharma Press, 1983.

Life and Liberation of Padmasambhava. Trans. Kenneth Douglas and Gwendolyn Bays. Berkeley: Dharma, 1978.

The Life of the Mahāsiddha Tilopa. Trans. Fabrizio Torricelli and Sangye T. Naga. Dharamsala: Library of Tibetan Works and Archives, 1995.

"The Life of Tilopa." Trans. Nālandā Translation Committee. In *Religions of Tibet in Practice.* Ed. Donald Lopez. Princeton: Princeton University Press, 1997.

Longchenpa. *Kindly Bent to Ease Us.* Trans. Herbert Guenther. Emeryville: Dharma, 1975.

Mahābhārata. Ed. Vishnu S. Sukthankar et al. 19 vols. Poona: Bhandarkar Oriental Research Institute, 1933–66.

———. Trans. and ed. J. A. B. Van Buitenen. 3 vols. Chicago: University of Chicago Press, 1973–78.

Mahā-parinibbānasuttanta. Trans. T. W. Rhys Davids. *Buddhist Suttas.* 1881; Delhi: Motilal Banarsidass, 1965.

Mahāvastu. Trans. J. J. Jones. 3 vols. London: Pali Text Society, 1949–56.

Le Mahāvastu. Ed. É. Senart. Paris: L'Imprimerie nationale, 1890.

Majjhima Nikāya. Ed. V. Trenckner. 1888; London: Routledge and Kegan Paul, 1979.

———. Trans. as *Middle Length Sayings* by I. B. Horner. 3 vols. London: Pali Text Society, 1954–59.

Milindapañha. Ed. V. Trenckner. London: Williams and Norgate, 1880.

———. Trans. as *The Questions of King Milinda* by T. W. Rhys Davids. 1894; Delhi: Motilal Banarsidass, 1965.

Mkhas grub Rje. "Master of the Three Worlds." *Tibet Society Bulletin* 13 (June 1979): 11–17, 18–21. Tibetan text of his eulogy (Tib. *bstod pa*) to Tsoṅ ka pa with translation by Glenn H. Mullin and L. N. Tsonawa.

———. "Rje rin po che'i gsaṅ ba'i rnam thar." *The Collected Works (gsuṅ 'bum) of Rje Tsoṅ-kha-pa Blo-bzaṅ-grags-pa.* Vol. 1. New Delhi: 1979.

Mūlasarvāstivādavinayavastu. Ed. S. Bagchi. Darbhanga: Mithila Institute, 1967.

Nidānakathā. Trans. as *Buddhist Birth Stories* by T. W. Rhys Davids. 1880; New York: E. P. Dutton, 1925.

Padma bka' thang shel brag ma. Leh, India, 1968.

The Ramayana of Valmiki. Trans. Hari Prasad Shastri. London: Shantisadan, 1962.

Ṛgveda Saṃhitā. Ed. Svami Satya Prakash Sarasvati and Satyakam Vidyalankar. New Delhi: Veda Pratishthana, 1977.

———. Trans. as *The Rig Veda: An Anthology* by Wendy Doniger O'Flaherty. Middlesex, U.K.: Penguin, 1981.

Rgya cher rol pa. Tibetan translation of *Lalitavistara.* Tog Palace Manuscript of the Tibetan Kanjur. Vol. 53. Leh, India: C. Namgyal Tarnsergar, 1979.

Rgyud bzhi: A Reproduction of a Set of Prints from the Eighteenth Century Zuṅ-cu Ze Blocks from the Collections of Raghu Vira, by O-rgyan Namgyal. Leh, India: S. W. Tashigangpa, 1975.

———. *The Quintessence Tantras of Tibetan Medicine.* Trans. Barry Clark. Ithaca: Snow Lion, 1995.

Ruegg, D. S. *The Life of Bu ston rin po che.* Roma: Istituto italiano per il medio ed estremo oriente, 1996.

Saddharmapuṇḍarīka or the Lotus of the True Law. Trans. H. Kern. 1884; New York: Dover, 1963.

Sāmavidhāna Brāhmaṇa. Ed. A. C. Burnell. London: Trübner, 1873.

Saṃyutta Nikāya. Trans. as *The Book of the Kindred Sayings* by C. A. F. Rhys Davids and F. L. Woodward. 5 vols. London: Pali Text Society, 1917–30.

Saṅs rgyas rgya mtsho. *Vaiḍūrya sṅon po.* Ed. T. Y. Tashigangpa. Leh, India, 1973.

Shan-Chien-P'i-P'o-Sha: A Chinese Version by Sanghabhadra of Samantapāsādikā. Trans. F. V. Bapat and A. Hirakawa. Poona: Bhandarkar Oriental Research Institute, 1970.

Sikdar, Jogendra Chandra. *Studies in the Bhagawatisutra.* Muzaffarpur: Research Institute of Prakrit, Jainology and Ahimsa, 1964.

Somadeva Bhaṭṭa. *Kathāsaritsāgara.* Ed. Jagadīśa Lāl Śāstrī. Delhi: Motilal Banarsidass, 1960. Trans. as *The Ocean of Story* by C. H. Tawney. London: Chas. J. Sawyer, 1924.

Strong, John S. *The Legend and Cult of Upagupta: Sanskrit Buddhism in North India and Southeast Asia.* Princeton: Princeton University Press, 1992.

———. *The Legend of King Aśoka: A Study and Translation of the Aśokāvadāna.* Princeton: Princeton University Press, 1983.

Suśrutasaṃhitā of Suśruta. Ed. and trans. Vidya Jādavji Trikamji Āchārya. 4th ed. Varanasi: Chowkhamba Orientalia, 1980. Trans. as *The Sushruta Samhita* by Kaviraj Kunjalal Bhishagratna. 2d ed. Varanasi: Chowkhamba Sanskrit Series, 1963.

Tanjur. *Rgyud 'grel: The Corpus of Indian Commentaries on Vajrayana Buddhist Literature Translated into Tibetan.* Delhi: Delhi Karmapae Chodhey, Gyalwae Sungrab Partun Khang, 1982–1985.

Tāranātha. *The Seven Instruction Lineages.* Trans. David Templeman. Dharamsala: Library of Tibetan Works and Archives, 1983.

———. *The Origin of the Tārā Tantra.* Trans. David Templeman. Dharamsala: Library of Tibetan Works and Archives, 1981.

The Thousand and One Nights. Trans. Edward William Lane. London: Chatto and Windus, 1883.

Thurman, Robert A. F., ed. *The Life and Teachings of Tsong Khapa.* Dharamsala: Library of Tibetan Works and Archives, 1982.

Triṣaṣṭiśalākāpuruṣacarita or The Lives of Sixty-Three Illustrious Persons. Vol. 2. Trans. Helen M. Johnson. Baroda: Oriental Institute, 1937.

Tsai, Kathryn Ann. *Lives of the Nuns: Biographies of Chinese Buddhist Nuns from the Fourth to Sixth Centuries.* Honolulu: University of Hawai'i Press, 1994.

Tsoṅ kha pa Blo bzaṅ grags pa. *The Collected Works (gsuṅ 'bum) of Rje Tsoṅ-kha-pa Blo-bzaṅ-grags-pa.* Vol. 1. New Delhi, 1979.

———. *Tsongkhapa's Six Yogas of Naropa.* Trans. Glenn Mullin. Ithaca: Snow Lion, 1996.

Upaniṣads. Trans. Patrick Olivelle. Oxford: Oxford University Press, 1996.

———. Trans. as *One Hundred and Twelve Upaniṣads and Their Philosophy* by A. N. Bhattacharya. Parimal Sanskrit Series, no. 26. Delhi: Parimal Publications, 1987.

———. Trans. as *Saṃnyāsa Upaniṣads: Hindu Scriptures on Asceticism and Renunciation* by Patrick Olivelle. New York: Oxford University Press, 1992.

Vimalakīrtinirdeśa. Trans. as *The Holy Teaching of Vimalakīrti* by Robert A. F. Thurman. University Park, PA: Pennsylvania State University Press, 1976.

Vinaya Piṭaka. Ed. Hermann Oldenberg. Vol. 1. 1879; London: Pali Text Society, 1969.

———. Trans. as *The Book of the Discipline* by I. B. Horner. London: Oxford University Press, 1938.

Wayman, Alex, ed. and trans. *Yoga of the Guhyasamājatantra.* Delhi: Motilal Banarsidass, 1977.

Secondary Sources

Alphonso-Karkala, John B., ed. *An Anthology of Indian Literature.* Middlesex, U.K.: Penguin, 1971.

Amore, Roy C. "Comparative Study of Buddha's Pre-enlightenment Dreams: Implications for Religion." *The Notion of "Religion" in Comparative Research.* Ed. Ugo Bianchi, pp. 541–46. Selected Proceedings of the XVIth Congress of the International Association for the History of Religions, Rome, 1990.

Appadurai, Arjun, et al., eds. *Gender, Genre, and Power in South Asian Expressive Traditions.* Philadelphia: University of Pennsylvania Press, 1991.

Aris, Anthony, ed. *Tibetan Medical Paintings.* 2 vols. New York: Harry N. Abrams, 1992.

Aris, Michael. *Hidden Treasures and Secret Lives: A Study of Pemalingpa (1450–1521) and the Sixth Dalai Lama (1683–1706).* Shimla: Indian Institute of Advanced Study, 1988.

Aziz, Barbara. "Reincarnation Reconsidered: Or the Reincarnate Lama as Shaman." In *Spirit Possession in the Nepal Himalayas.* Ed. John T. Hitchock and Rex L. Jones, pp. 343–60. 1976; New Delhi: Vikas Publishing House, 1996.

Aziz, Barbara, and Matthew Kapstein, eds. *Soundings in Tibetan Civilization.* New Delhi: Manohar, 1985.

Babu, D. Sridhara. "Reflections on Andra Buddhist Sculptures and Buddha Biography." In *Buddhist Iconography,* pp. 97–101. Delhi: Tibet House, 1989.

Banerjee, P. "The Story of the Birth of Gautama Buddha and Its Vedic Parallel." In *Buddhist Iconography,* pp. 1–5. Delhi: Tibet House, 1989.

Bareau, André. "Buddhism, Schools of: Hīnayāna." In *EOR,* 2: 444–57.

———. *Recherches sur la biographie du Buddha dans les Sūtrapiṭaka et les Vinayapiṭaka anciens.* 2 vols. Paris: École française d'extrême-orient, 1970.

———. "Un personnage bien mysterieux: l'épouse du Buddha." In *Indological and Buddhist Studies, Volume in Honour of Professor J. W. de Jong on His Sixtieth Birthday.* Ed. L. A. Hercus et al., pp. 31–59. Canberra: Australian National University, 1982.

Basham, A. L. *History and Doctrines of the Ājīvikas.* London: Luzac, 1951.

———. "The Practice of Medicine in Ancient and Medieval India." In *Asian Medical Systems: A Comparative Study.* Ed. Charles Leslie, pp. 18–43. Berkeley: University of California Press, 1976.

———. *The Wonder That Was India: A Survey of the Culture of the Indian Subcontinent Before the Coming of the Muslims.* New York: Grove, 1959.

Basso, Ellen B. "The Implications of a Progressive Theory of Dreaming." In *Dreaming: Anthropological and Psychological Interpretations.* Ed. Barbara Tedlock, pp. 86–104. Cambridge: Cambridge University Press, 1987.

Bechert, Heinz, ed. *The Dating of the Historical Buddha.* 2 vols. Göttingen: Vandenhoeck and Ruprecht, 1991–92.

Behr, Charles A. *Aelius Aristedes and the Sacred Tales.* Amsterdam: Adolf M. Hakkert, 1968.

Bell, Diane. *Daughters of the Dreaming.* 2d ed. Minneapolis: University of Minnesota Press, 1993.

Benard, Elisabeth Anne. *Chinnamastā: The Aweful Buddhist and Hindu Tantric Goddess.* Delhi: Motilal Banarsidass, 1994.

Bennett, Lynn. *Dangerous Wives and Sacred Sisters: Social and Symbolic Roles of High-Caste Women in Nepal.* New York: Columbia University Press, 1983.

Bentor, Yael. "Literature on Consecration (*Rab gnas*)." In *Tibetan Literature: Studies in Genre.* Ed. José Ignacio Cabezón and Roger R. Jackson, pp. 290–311. Ithaca: Snow Lion, 1996.

Beyer, Stephan. *The Cult of Tārā: Magic and Ritual in Tibet.* Berkeley: University of California Press, 1973.

Bhagat, M. G. *Ancient Indian Asceticism.* New Delhi: Munshiram Manoharlal, 1976.

Bharati, Agehananda. *The Tantric Tradition.* New York: Samuel Weiser: 1975.

Bhattacharyya, D. C. "Metamorphosis of a Central Asian Symbolism." In *Buddhist Iconography,* pp. 149–53. Delhi: Tibet House, 1989.

Birnbaum, Raoul. *The Healing Buddha.* Boulder: Shambhala, 1979.

Bitel, Lisa M. "*In Visu Noctis:* Dreams in European Hagiography and Histories, 450–900." *History of Religion* 31, no. 1 (August 1991): 39–59.

Blacker, Carmen. *The Catalpa Bow: A Study of Shamanistic Practices in Japan.* London: Unwin Paperbacks, 1982.

Blondeau, A. M. "Analysis of the Biographies of Padmasambhava." In *Tibetan Studies in Honour of Hugh Richardson.* Ed. Michael Aris and Aung San Suu Kyi, pp. 45–52. Warminster, U.K.: Aris and Phillips, 1979.

Boddy, Janice. *Wombs and Alien Spirits: Women, Men, and the Zār Cult in Northern Sudan.* Madison: University of Wisconsin Press, 1989.

Bolling, G. M. "Dreams and Sleep (Vedic)." In *The Encyclopaedia of Religion and Ethics.* Ed. James Hastings, 5: 38–40. New York: Charles Scribner, 1913.

Brown, Michael F. "Ropes of Sand: Order and Imagery in Aguaruna Dreams." In *Dreaming: Anthropological and Psychological Interpretations.* Ed. Barbara Tedlock, pp. 154–70. Cambridge: Cambridge University Press, 1987.

Buddhist Iconography. New Delhi: Tibet House, 1989. Papers presented at an international seminar organized by Tibet House.

Bulkeley, Kelly. *The Wilderness of Dreams.* Albany: State University of New York Press, 1994.

Cabezón, José Ignacio, and Roger R. Jackson, eds. *Tibetan Literature: Studies in Genre.* Ithaca: Snow Lion, 1996.

Caillat, Colette. "Jainism." In *Encyclopaedia of Religion,* 7: 507–14.

———. "Mahāvirā." In *Encyclopaedia of Religion,* 9: 128–31.

Campbell, June. *Traveller in Space: In Search of Female Identity in Tibetan Buddhism.* New York: George Braziller, 1996.

Carrithers, Michael. "Hell-Fire and Urinal Stones: An Essay on Buddhist Purity and Authority." In *Contributions to South Asian Studies 2.* Ed. Gopal Krishna, pp. 25–52. Delhi: Oxford University Press, 1982.

Carter, John Ross. "Buddhaghosa." In *Encyclopedia of Religion* 2: 332–33. Ed. Mircea Eliade. 16 vols. New York: Macmillan, 1987.

Chakraborti, Haripada. *Asceticism in Ancient India in Brahmanical, Buddhist, Jaina, and Ajivika Societies, from the Early Times to the Period of Sankaracharya.* Calcutta: Punthi Pustak, 1973.

Chan, Victor. *Tibet Handbook: A Pilgrimage Guide.* Chico: Moon Publications, 1994.

Chang, Garma Chen Chi. *Teachings of Tibetan Yoga.* New Hyde Park: University Books, 1963.

———. "Yogic Commentary." In *Tibetan Yoga and Secret Doctrines.* Ed. Evans-Wentz. New York: Oxford University Press, 1935.

Chattopadhyaya, Alaka. *Atīśa and Tibet.* Calcutta: Indian Studies, 1967.

Chodorow, Nancy. *The Reproduction of Mothering: Psychoanalyis and the Sociology of Gender.* Berkeley: University of California Press, 1978.

Chophel, Norbu. *The Folk Culture of Tibet.* Dharamsala: Library of Tibetan Works and Archives, 1983.

Collins, Steven. *Selfless Persons: Imagery and Thought in Theravāda Buddhism.* Cambridge: Cambridge University Press, 1982.

Cone, Margaret, and Richard Gombrich. *The Perfect Generosity of Prince Vessantara: A Buddhist Epic.* Oxford: Oxford University Press, 1977.

Coomaraswamy, A. K. *Elements of Buddhist Iconography.* 1935; Delhi: Munshiram Manoharlal, 1972.

Courtright, Paul B. *Gaṇeśa: Lord of Obstacles, Lord of Reason.* New York: Oxford University Press, 1985.

Couture, André. "A Survey of French Literature on Ancient Indian Buddhist Hagiography." Trans. Robert Jollet. In *Monks and Magicians: Religious Biographies in Asia.* Ed. Phyllis Granoff and Koichi Shinohara, pp. 9–44. 1988; Delhi: Motilal Banarsidass, 1994.

Cozort, Daniel. *Highest Yoga Tantra: An Introduction to the Esoteric Buddhism of Tibet.* Ithaca: Snow Lion, 1986.

Crescenzi, Antonella, and Fabrizio Torricelli. "A Tun-huang Text on Dreams: Ms Pelliot tibétain 55 1 IX." *Tibet Journal* 20.2 (summer 1995): 3–17.

Crooke, William. *The Popular Religion and Folklore of Northern India.* 2 vols. 2d. ed. 1896; Delhi: Munshiram Manoharlal, 1968.

Dange, Sadashiv Ambadas, ed. *Encyclopaedia of Puranic Beliefs and Practices.* New Delhi: Navrang, 1987.

Dargyay, Eva M. *The Rise of Esoteric Buddhism in Tibet.* Delhi: Motilal Banarsidass, 1977.

———. "Srong-Btsan Sgam-Po of Tibet: Bodhisattva and King." In *Monks and Magicians: Religious Biographies in Asia.* Ed. Phyllis Granoff and Koichi Shinohara, pp. 99–117. Delhi: Motilal Banarsidass, 1994.

Das, Sarat Chandra. *A Tibetan-English Dictionary.* Delhi: Motilal Banarsidass, 1976.

Dasgupta, Shasi Bhushan. *An Introduction to Tantric Buddhism.* 1958; Berkeley: Shambhala, 1974.

David-Neel, Alexandra, and Lama Yongden, eds. and trans. *The Superhuman Life of Gesar of Ling.* Boston: Shambhala, 1981.

Davis, J. G. "Architecture." In *Encyclopedia of Religion* 1: 382–92. Ed. Mircea Eliade. 16 vols. New York: Macmillan, 1987.

Dayal, Har. *The Bodhisattva Doctrine in Buddhist Sanskrit Literature.* 1932; Delhi: Motilal Banarsidass, 1970.

Dbaṅ phyug rdo rje, Karma pa 9. *The Mahāmudrā: Eliminating the Darkness of Ignorance.* Trans. and ed. Alexander Berzin. Commentary by Beru Kyentze Rinpoche. Dharamsala: Library of Tibetan Works and Archives, 1978.

de Bary, William Theodore. *The Buddhist Tradition.* 1969; New York: Vintage, 1972.

Denny, Frederick M., and Rodney L. Taylor, eds. *The Holy Book in Comparative Perspective.* Columbia: University of South Carolina Press, 1985.

Deshung Rinpoche. *The Three Levels of Spiritual Perception.* Trans. Jared Rhoton. Boston: Wisdom, 1995.

Deussen, Paul. *The System of the Vedānta.* Trans. Charles Johnston. 1912; New York: Dover, 1973.

Diemberger, Hildegard. "Lhakama (*lha-bka'-ma*) and Khandroma (*mkha'-'gro-ma*): The Sacred Ladies of Beyul Khenbalung (*sbas-yul mKan-pa-lung*)." In *Tibetan History and Language: Studies Dedicated to Uray Géza on His Seventieth Birthday.* Ed. Ernst Steinkellner.Vienna: Arbeitskreis für Tibetische und Buddhistische Studien, Universität Wien, 1991.

Dobbins, James C. "The Biography of Shinran: Apotheosis of a Japanese Buddhist Visionary." *History of Religions* 30, no. 2 (November 1990): 179–96.

Dodds, E.R. *The Greeks and the Irrational.* 1951; Berkeley: University of California Press, 1973.

———. *Pagan and Christian in an Age of Anxiety.* New York: W. W. Norton, 1965.

Domhoff, G. William. *The Mystique of Dreams: A Search for Utopia through Senoi Dream Theory.* Berkeley: University of California Press, 1985.

Douglas, Nik, and Meryl White. *Karmapa: The Black Hat Lama of Tibet.* London: Luzac, 1976.

Dudjom Rinpoche. *The Nyingma School of Tibetan Buddhism: Its Fundamentals and History.* Trans. Gyurme Dorje and Matthew Kapstein. London: Wisdom, 1990.

Duerr, Hans Peter. *Dreamtime: Concerning the Boundary between Wilderness and Civilization.* Trans. Felicitas Goodman. New York: Basil Blackwell, 1987.

Eck, Diana L. *Darśan: Seeing the Divine Image in India.* Chambersburg: Anima, 1981.

———. "Mountains." In *Encyclopedia of Religion* 10: 130–34. Ed. Mircea Eliade. 16 vols. New York: Macmillan, 1987.

Edgerton, Franklin. *Buddhist Hybrid Sanskrit Grammar and Dictionary.* 1953; Delhi: Motilal Banarsidass, 1985.

Edou, Jérôme. *Machig Labdrön and the Foundations of Chöd.* Ithaca: Snow Lion, 1996.

Eichenbaum, Patricia D. "The Development of a Narrative Cycle Based on the Life of the Buddha in India, Central Asia, and the Far East: Literary and Pictorial Evidence." Ph.D. diss., New York University, 1979.

Eliade, Mircea. *Shamanism: Archaic Techniques of Ecstasy.* Trans. Willard R. Trask. Princeton: Princeton University Press, 1972.

———. *Yoga: Immortality and Freedom.* Trans. Willard R. Trask. Princeton: Princeton University Press, 1958.

Encyclopaedia of Puranic Beliefs and Practices. Ed. Sadashiv Ambadas Dange. New Delhi: Navrang, 1987.

Encyclopedia of Buddhism. Ed. G. P. Malalasekera. 4 vols. Ceylon: Government of Ceylon, 1961–1979.

Encyclopedia of Religion. Ed. Mircea Eliade. 16 vols. New York: Macmillan, 1987.

Encyclopedia of Women and World Religion. Ed. Serinity Young. New York: Macmillan, 1998.

Esnoul, Anne-Marie. "Les songes et leur interprétation dans l'Inde." In *Les songes et leur interprétation.* Ed. Esnoul et al. Paris: Éditions du Seuil, 1959.

Feldhaus, Anne. *Water and Womanhood: Religious Meanings of Rivers in Maharashtra.* New York: Oxford University Press, 1995.

Fenner, Todd. "The Origin of the *rGyud bzhi:* A Tibetan Medical Tantra." In *Tibetan Literature: Studies in Genre.* Ed. José Ignacio Cabezón and Roger R. Jackson, pp. 458–69. Ithaca: Snow Lion, 1996.

Fleet, J. F. "The Tradition about the Corporeal Relics of the Buddha." *Journal of the Royal Asiatic Society* (1906): 655–913.

Freud, Sigmund. *The Interpretation of Dreams.* Trans. and ed. James Strachey. New York: Avon, 1965.

Freud, Sigmund, and D. E. Oppenheim. *Dreams in Folklore.* Trans. Bernard L. Pacella. New York: International Universities Press, 1958.

Frye, Northrup. *Fearful Symmetry: A Study of William Blake.* 2d ed. Princeton: Princeton University Press, 1970.

Fussman, Gérard. "Symbolism of the Buddhist *Stūpa.*" *Journal of the International Association of Buddhist Studies* 9, no. 2 (1986): 37–53.

Gay, Peter. *Freud: A Life for Our Time.* New York: W. W. Norton, 1988.

Geertz, Clifford. *The Interpretation of Cultures.* New York: Basic, 1973.

Geiger, Wilhelm. *Pāli Literature and Language.* Trans. Batakrishna Ghosh. Delhi: Oriental Books Reprint, 1968.

Germano, David. "Food, Clothes, Dreams, and Karmic Propensities." In *Religions of Tibet in Practice.* Ed. Donald Lopez, pp. 293–312. Princeton: Princeton University Press, 1997.

Gerth, H. H. and C. Wright Mills, trans. and ed. *From Max Weber: Essays in Sociology.* New York: Oxford University Press, 1946.

Getty, Alice. *The Gods of Northern Buddhism: Their History and Iconography.* 1914; New York: Dover, 1988.

Ghurye, Govind Sadashiv. *Indian Sadhus.* 2d. ed. Bombay: Popular Prakashan, 1964.

Glassé, Cyril. "Night Journey." In *The Concise Encyclopedia of Islam.* Ed. Cyril Glassé, pp. 301–2. San Francisco: Harper and Row, 1989.

Gokhale, Balkrishna Govind. *Buddhism in Maharashtra: A History.* Bombay: Popular Prakashan, 1976.

Gold, Ann. "Gender and Illusion in a Rajasthani Yogic Tradition." In *Gender, Genre and Power in South Asian Expressive Traditions.* Ed. Arjun Appadurai, et al., pp. 102–35. Philadelphia: University of Pennsylvania Press, 1991.

Goldstein, Melvyn C., and Matthew T. Kapstein, eds. *Buddhism in Contemporary Tibet: Religious Revival and Cultural Identity.* Berkeley: University of California Press, 1998.

Gombrich, Richard F. "Ancient Indian Cosmology." In *Ancient Cosmologies.* Ed. Carmen Blacker and Michael Loewe, pp. 110–42. London: Allen and Unwin, 1975.

———. "The Significance of Former Buddhas in the Theravādin Tradition." In *Buddhist Studies in Honour of Walpola Rahula.* Ed. Somaratna Balasooriya et al., pp. 62–72. London: Gordon Fraser, 1980.

———. *Theravāda Buddhism: A Social History from Ancient Benares to Modern Colombo.* London: Routledge and Kegan Paul, 1988.

Gomez, Luis O. "Buddhism: Buddhism in India." In *Encyclopedia of Religion* 2: 351–85. Ed. Mircea Eliade. 16 vols. New York: Macmillan, 1987.

———. "Two Tantric Meditations: Visualizing the Deity." In *Buddhism in Practice.* Ed. Donald S. Lopez, Jr., pp. 318–27. Princeton: Princeton University Press, 1995.

Gonda, Jan. *Change and Continuity in Indian Religion.* The Hague: Mouton, 1965.

———. *The Ritual Functions and Significance of Grasses in the Religion of the Veda.* Amsterdam: North-Holland Publishing, 1985.

Goodman, Steven D., and Ronald M. Davidson, eds. *Tibetan Buddhism: Reason and Revelation.* Albany: State University of New York Press, 1992.

Goudriaan, Teun. *Māyā Divine and Human.* Delhi: Motilal Banarsidass, 1978.

Gross, Rita. "Methodological Remarks on the Study of Women in Religions: Review, Criticism and Redefinition." In *Women and Religion.* Ed. J. Plaskow and J. N. Romero. Missoula: Scholars Press, 1974.

Gupta, S. K. *The Elephant in Indian Art and Mythology.* New Delhi: Abhinav Publications, 1983.

Gyatrul Rinpoche. *Ancient Wisdom: Nyingma Teachings on Dream Yoga, Meditation, and Transformation.* Trans. B. Alan Wallace and Sangye Khandro. Ithaca: Snow Lion Publications, 1993.

Gyatso, Janet. "An Avalokiteśvara Sādhana." In *Religions of Tibet in Practice.* Ed. Donald Lopez, pp. 266–70. Princeton: Princeton University Press, 1997.

———. "Down with the Demoness." In *Feminine Ground: Essays on Women and Tibet.* Ed. Janice Willis, pp. 35–51. Ithaca: Snow Lion, 1989.

———. "Drawn from the Tibetan Treasury: The *gTer ma* Literature." In *Tibetan Literature: Studies in Genre.* Ed. José Ignacio Cabezón and Roger R. Jackson, pp. 147–69. Ithaca: Snow Lion, 1996.

———. "Genre, Authorship, and Transmission in Visionary Buddhism: The Literary Traditions of Thang-stong rGyal-po." In *Tibetan Buddhism: Reason and Revelation.* Ed. Steven D. Goodman and Ronald M. Davidson. Albany: State University of New York Press, 1992.

———. "A Literary Transmission of the Traditions of Thang-stong rGyal-po: A Study of Visionary Buddhism in Tibet." Ph.D. diss., University of California at Berkeley, 1981.

———. "Signs, Memory, and History: A Tantric Buddhist Theory of Scriptural Transmission." *Journal of the International Association of Buddhist Studies* 9, no. 2 (1986): 7–35.

Gyatso, Kelsang. *Clear Light of Bliss: A Commentary to the Practice of Mahamudra in Vajrayana Buddhism.* 1982. London: Tharpa, 1992.

———. *Guide to the Dakini Land.* London: Tharpa, 1991.

Harrison, Paul. "A Brief History of the Tibetan bKa' 'gyur." In *Tibetan Literature: Studies in Genre.* Ed. José Ignacio Cabezón and Roger R. Jackson, pp. 70–94. Ithaca: Snow Lion, 1996.

Harvey, Peter. "Symbolism of the Early Stūpa." *Journal of the International Association of Buddhist Studies* 7, no. 2 (1984): 67–93.

Hawley, John Stratton. *At Play with Krishna: Pilgrimage Dramas from Brindavan.* Princeton: Princeton University Press, 1981.

Herdt, Gilbert. "Selfhood and Discourse in Sambia Dream Sharing." In *Dreaming: Anthropological and Psychological Interpretations.* Ed. Barbara Tedlock, pp. 66–67. Cambridge: Cambridge University Press, 1987.

Hirakawa, Akira. *A History of Indian Buddhism: From Śākyamuni to Early Mahāyāna.* Trans. and ed. Paul Groner. 1990; Delhi: Motilal Banarsidass, 1993.

Hoffmann, Helmut. *The Religions of Tibet.* Trans. Edward Fitzgerald. New York: Macmillan, 1961.

Holland, Norman N. Foreword to *The Dream and the Text.* Ed. Carol Schreier Rupprecht. Albany: State University of New York Press, 1993.

Holst-Warhoff, Gail. "Mourning and Death Rituals." In *Encyclopedia of Women and World Religion* 2: 682–85. Ed. Serinity Young. New York: Macmillan, 1998.

Hopkins, P. Jeffrey. "Dge-lugs-pa." In *Encyclopedia of Religion* 4: 326–29. Ed. Mircea Eliade. 16 vols. New York: Macmillan, 1987.

———. *The Kālachakra Tantra: Rite of Initiation for the Stage of Generation.* London: Wisdom, 1985.

Hunt, Harry T. *The Multiplicity of Dreams: Memory, Imagination and Consciousness.* New Haven: Yale University Press, 1989.

Huntington, John C. "Pilgrimage as Image: The Cult of the Aṣṭamahāprātihārya." Part 1. *Orientations* 18, no. 4 (April 1987): 55–63.

———. "Sowing the Seeds of the Lotus: A Journey to the Great Pilgrimage Sites of Buddhism." Part 3. *Orientations* 17, no. 3 (March 1986): 32–46.

Irigaray, Luce. *Sexes and Geneaologies.* New York: Columbia University Press, 1993.

———. "The Three Genres." In *The Irigaray Reader.* Ed. Margaret Whitford, pp. 140–53. Oxford: Blackwell, 1991.

Irwin, Lee. *The Dream Seekers: Native American Visionary Traditions of the Great Plains.* Norman: University of Oklahoma Press, 1994.

Ivanhoe, Philip J. "Zhuangzi on Skepticism, Skill, and the Ineffable Dao." *Journal of the American Academy of Religion* 61, no. 4 (winter 1993): 640–43.

Jaini, Padmanabh S. "*Śramaṇas*: Their Conflict with Brāhmaṇical Society." In *Chapters in Indian Civilization.* Ed. Joseph W. Elder, 1: 39–82. Dubuque: Kendall/Hunt, 1970.

Jayatilleke, K. N. *Early Buddhist Theory of Knowledge.* London: George Allen and Unwin, 1963.

Jones, Ernest. *On the Nightmare.* New York: Liveright, 1951.

Josayma, C. B., trans. *Tibetan Folk Opera: Drowa Sangmo.* Dharamsala: Library of Tibetan Works and Archives, 1983.

Josayma, Tashi Tsering, and K. Dhondup. *Dolma and Dolkar: Mother and Daughter of Tibetan Medicine.* New Delhi: Yarlung, 1990.

Joshi, Lal Mani. *Studies in the Buddhistic Culture of India.* Delhi: Motilal Banarsidass, 1967.

Jung, C. G. *Dreams.* Trans. R. F. C. Hull. 1974; Princeton: Princeton University Press, 1990.

———. *Memories, Dreams, and Reflections.* Trans. Richard and Clara Winston. New York: Vintage, 1965.

———. *Psychology and Religion.* New Haven: Yale University Press, 1938.

Kagan, Richard L. *Lucrecia's Dreams: Politics and Prophecy in Sixteenth-Century Spain.* Berkeley: University of California Press, 1990.

Kakar, Sudhir. *Shamans, Mystics, and Doctors: A Psychological Inquiry into India and Its Healing Traditions.* Delhi: Oxford University Press, 1982.

Kalupahana, David J. "Consciousness." In *Encyclopedia of Buddhism,* 4: 230–42. Ed. G. P. Malalasekera. 4 vols. Ceylon: Government of Ceylon, 1961–1979.

Kane, P. V. *History of Dharmaśāstra.* Poona: Bhandarkar Oriental Research Institute, 1962.

Kapstein, Matthew. "The Illusion of Spiritual Progress: Remarks on Indo-Tibetan Buddhist Soteriology." In *Paths to Liberation: The Mārga and Its Transformations in Buddhist Thought.* Ed. Robert E. Buswell, Jr., and Robert M. Gimello, pp. 193–224. Honolulu: University of Hawai'i Press, 1992.

———. "The Purificatory Gem and its Cleansing: A Late Tibetan Polemical Discussion of Apocryphal Texts." In *History of Religions* 28, no. 3 (February 1989): 217–44.

Karetzky, Patricia Eichenbaum. *The Life of the Buddha: Ancient Scriptural and Pictorial Traditions.* Lanham: University Press of America, 1992.

———. "Māra, Buddhist Deity of Death and Desire." *East and West,* no. 32 (1982): 75–92.

Kariyawasam, A. G. S. "Buddha Nature." In *Encyclopedia of Buddhism* 1: 435–38. Ed. G. P. Malalasekera. 4 vols. Ceylon: Government of Ceylon, 1961–1979.

Katz, Nathan. "Anima and mKha'-'gro-ma: A Critical Comparative Study of Jung and Tibetan Buddhism." *Tibet Journal* 2, no. 3 (1977): 13–43.

———. *Buddhist Images of Human Perfection.* Delhi: Motilal Banarsidass, 1982.

Kawamura, Leslie. "Padmasambhava." In *Encyclopedia of Religion* 11: 148–49. Ed. Mircea Eliade. 16 vols. New York: Macmillan, 1987.

Kaysic, Mik. "Dream Interpretation in Tibetan Buddhism." *Dreloma,* no. 11 (1984): 21–34.

Keith, A. B. *The Religion and Philosophy of the Veda and Upanishads.* 2 vols. 1925; Delhi: Motilal Banarsidass, 1970.

Kendall, Laurel. "Dreaming up Solutions: The Interpretations of Dreams in Korean Shamanism." In *Yi Tu-Hyon Paksa Hwan 'Gap Kinyom Nonmunjip, Papers in Honor of Prof. Yi Tu-Hyon's Hwan 'Gap.* Seoul: Hakyonsa, 1984.

———. *The Life and Hard Times of a Korean Shaman.* Honolulu: University of Hawai'i Press, 1988.

———. *Shamans, Housewives, and Other Restless Spirits: Women in Korean Ritual Life.* Honolulu: University of Hawai'i Press, 1985.

Keyes, Charles F. "Death of Two Buddhist Saints in Thailand." In *Charisma and Sacred Biography.* Ed. Michael A. Williams. Chambersburg: American Academy of Religion, 1982.

Khandalavala, Karl. "Heralds in Stone: Early Buddhist Iconography in the Aśokan Pillars and Related Problems." In *Buddhist Iconography.* Delhi: Tibet House, 1989.

Kieckhefer, Richard. "Sainthood." In *Sainthood: Its Manifestation in World Religions.* Ed. Richard Kieckhefer and George D. Bond. Berkeley: University of California Press, 1988.

Kilborne, Benjamin. "Dreams." In *Encyclopedia of Religion* 4: 482–91. Ed. Mircea Eliade. 16 vols. New York: Macmillan, 1987.

Klein, Anne C. *Meeting the Great Bliss Queen: Buddhists, Feminists and the Art of the Self.* Boston: Beacon, 1995.

———. *Path to the Middle: Oral Mādhyamika Philosophy in Tibet.* Albany: State University of New York Press, 1994.

Kosambi, D. D. *Ancient India: A History of Its Culture and Civilization.* New York: Pantheon Books, 1965.

Krappe, Alexander H. *The Science of Folklore.* 1929; New York: W. W. Norton, 1964.

Krippner, Stanley. "Dreams and Shamanism." In *Shamanism: An Expanded View of Reality.* Comp. Shirley Nicholson, pp. 129–31. Wheaton, IL: The Theosophical Publishing House, 1987.

Kris, Ernst. *Psychoanalytic Explorations in Art.* New York: International Universities Press, 1952.

Kvaerne, Per. "Bon." In *Encyclopedia of Religion* 2: 277–81. Ed. Mircea Eliade. 16 vols. New York: Macmillan, 1987.

———. *The Bon Religion of Tibet.* Boston: Shambhala, 1996.

———. "The Literature of Bon." In *Tibetan Literature: Studies in Genre.* Ed. José Ignacio Cabezón and Roger R. Jackson, pp. 138–46. Ithaca: Snow Lion, 1996.

La Barre, Weston. *The Ghost Dance: Origins of Religion.* New York: Dell, 1972.

LaBerge, Stephen. *Lucid Dreaming: The Power of Being Awake and Aware in Your Dreams.* New York: Ballantine Books, 1986.

Lamotte, Étienne. *History of Indian Buddhism: From the Origins to the Śaka Era.* 1958; Louvain-La-Neuve: Institut orientaliste, 1988.

Lang, A., and A. E. Taylor. "Dreams and Sleep: Introductory." In *The Encyclopaedia of Religion and Ethics,* ed. James Hasting, 5: 28–33. New York: Charles Scribner's Sons, 1913.

Lanman, Charles Rockwell. *A Sanskrit Reader.* Cambridge: Harvard University Press, 1884.

Larson, Gerald James. "Āyurveda and the Hindu Philosophical Systems." In *Self as Body in Asian Theory and Practice.* Ed. Thomas P. Kasulis et al. Albany: State University of New York Press, 1993.

Lauf, Detlef Ingo. *Tibetan Sacred Art: The Heritage of Tantra.* Berkeley: Shambhala, 1976.

La Vallée Poussin, L. de. "Cosmogony and Cosmology (Buddhist)." In *Encyclopaedia of Religion and Ethics.* Ed. James Hastings, 4: 129–38. New York: Charles Scribner's Sons, 1914.

———. "Studies in Buddhist Dogma: The Three Bodies of a Buddha *(Trikāya).*" *Journal of the Royal Asiatic Society* (1906): 943–77.

Lessing, F. D., and A. Wayman, *Introduction to the Buddhist Tantric Systems.* New York: Samuel Weiser, 1968.

Levering, Miriam. "Scripture and Its Reception: A Buddhist Case." In *Rethinking Scripture: Essays from a Comparative Perspective.* Ed. Miriam Levering, pp. 58–101. Albany: State University of New York Press, 1989.

Lewis, I. M. *Ecstatic Religion: An Anthropological Study of Spirit Possession and Shamanism.* Middlesex, U.K.: Penguin, 1971.

Lincoln, Bruce. *Authority: Construction and Corrosion.* Chicago: University of Chicago Press, 1994.

Lincoln, Jackson Steward. *The Dream in Primitive Cultures.* 1935; New York: Johnson Reprint, 1970.

Ling Rinpoche. "The History of Ganden, Drepung, and Sera." *Tibet Society Bulletin* 13 (June 1979): pp. 1–6.

Lopez, Donald S., Jr. Introduction to *Buddhist Hermeneutics.* Ed. Donald S. Lopez, Jr., pp. 1–10. 1988; Delhi: Motilal Banarsidass: 1993.

———. "Sanctification on the Bodhisattva Path." In *Sainthood: Its Manifestation in World Religions.* Ed. Richard Kieckhefer and George D. Bond, pp. 172–217. Berkeley: University of California Press, 1988.

———, ed. *Buddhism in Practice.* Princeton: Princeton University Press, 1995.

———, ed. *Religions of Tibet in Practice.* Princeton: Princeton University Press, 1997.

Lorenzen, David N. *The Kāpālikas and Kālāmukhas: Two Lost Śaivite Sects.* 2d ed. Delhi: Motilal Banarsidass, 1991.

Lüders, H., ed. *Bhārhut Inscriptions.* Rev. ed. Ootacamund: Government Epigraphist for India, 1963.

Luhrman, T. M. *Persuasions of the Witch's Craft: Ritual Magic in Contemporary England.* Cambridge: Harvard University Press, 1989.

Luther, Martin. *Luther's Works,* vol. 54, *Table Talk.* Ed. and trans. Theodore G. Tappert. Philadelphia: Fortress, 1967.

Macdonell, Arthur A. *A History of Sanskrit Literature.* 1899; Delhi: Motilal Banarsidass, 1971.

MacQueen, Graeme. "Inspired Speech in Early Mahāyāna Buddhism." Parts 1 and 2. *Religion* 11, no. 4 (1981): 303–19; 12, no. 2 (1982): 49–65.

Manser, A. R. "Dreams." In *Encyclopedia of Philosophy.* Ed. Paul Edwards, 1: 414–17. New York: Macmillan, 1967.

McGill, Forrest. "Painting the 'Great Life.'" In *Sacred Biography in the Buddhist Traditions of South and Southeast Asia.* Ed. Juliane Schober, pp. 195–217. Honolulu: University of Hawai'i Press, 1997.

Miller, Patricia Cox. *Dreams in Late Antiquity: Studies in the Imagination of a Culture.* Princeton: Princeton University Press, 1994.

Mitra, Jyotir. *A Critical Appraisal of Ayurvedic Material in Buddhist Literature.* Varanasi: Jyotiralok Prakashan, 1985.

Monier-Williams, Monier. *Sanskrit-English Dictionary.* 1899; Oxford: Oxford University Press, 1976.

Nagao, Gadjin. "On the Theory of Buddha-Bodies." *Eastern Buddhist* 6, no. 1 (1973): 25–53.

Nakamura, Hajime. "Buddhism, Schools of: Mahāyāna Buddhism." In *Encyclopedia of Religion* 2: 457–72. Ed. Mircea Eliade. 16 vols. New York: Macmillan, 1987.

———. *Indian Buddhism: A Survey with Bibliographic Notes.* 1980; New Delhi: Motilal Banarsidass, 1987.

———. *Ways of Thinking of Eastern Peoples: India, China, Tibet, Japan.* 1948–49; Honolulu: University of Hawai'i Press, 1964.

Namkhai Norbu. *Dream Yoga and the Practice of Natural Light.* Ithaca: Snow Lion, 1992.

———. *Drung, Deu, and Bon: Narrations, Symbolical Languages, and the Bon Tradition in Ancient Tibet.* 1982; Dharamsala: Library of Tibetan Works and Archives, 1995.

———. *Dzogchen: The Self-Perfected State.* Ithaca: Snow Lion, 1996

Narayan, Kirin. *Mondays on the Dark Night of the Moon: Himalayan Foothill Folktales.* New York: Oxford University Press, 1997.

Nebesky-Wojkowitz, René de. *Oracles and Demons of Tibet: The Cult and Iconography of the Tibetan Protective Deities.* 1956; Graz, Austria: Akademische Drück- u.Verlagsanstalt, 1975.

Neihardt, John G. *Black Elk Speaks: Being the Life Story of a Holy Man of the Oglala Sioux.* 1932; New York: Pocket Books, 1972.

Nietzsche, Friedrich. *Human, All-too-Human.* Trans. Walter Kaufman. In *The Portable Nietzsche.* New York: Viking, 1954.

Nock, A. D. *Conversion: The Old and the New in Religion from Alexander the Great to Augustine of Hippo.* 1933; Oxford: Oxford University Press, 1961.

Norbo, Samten. "A Short History of Tibetan Translated Literature." *Tibet Journal* 1, nos. 3 and 4 (autumn 1976): 81–84.

Norman, K. R. *Pali Literature.* Wiesbaden: O. Harrassowitz, 1983.

Obeyesekere, Gananath. *Medusa's Hair: An Essay on Personal Symbols and Religious Experience.* Chicago: University of Chicago Press, 1981.

O'Flaherty, Wendy Doniger. *Dreams, Illusion, and Other Realities.* Chicago: University of Chicago Press, 1984.

———. *The Origins of Evil in Hindu Mythology.* Berkeley: University of California Press, 1976.

———. "Western Dreams About Eastern Dreams." In *Among All These Dreamers: Essays on Dreaming and Modern Society.* Ed. Kelly Bulkeley, pp. 169–76. Albany: State University Press of New York, 1996.

———. *Women, Androgynes and Other Mythical Beasts.* Chicago: University of Chicago Press, 1980.

Oldenberg, Hermann. *Buddha, sein Leben, seine Lehre, seine Gemeinde.* Stuttgart: Cotta Verlag, 1959.

———. *The Religion of the Veda.* Trans. Shridhar B. Shrotri. 1894; Delhi: Motilal Banarsidass, 1998.

Ong, Walter. *Orality and Literacy: The Technologizing of the Word.* London: Methuen, 1982.

Oppenheim, A. Leo. "Mantic Dreams in the Ancient Near East." In *The Dream and Human Societies.* Ed. G. E. von Grunebaum and Robert Caillois, pp. 341–50. Berkeley: University of California Press, 1966.

Ortner, Sherry B. *Sherpas through Their Rituals.* Cambridge: Cambridge University Press, 1978.

Parsifal-Charles, Nancy. *The Dream: 4,000 Years of Theory and Practice: A Critical, Descriptive and Encyclopaedic Bibliography.* West Cornwall, CT: Locust Hill, 1986.

Paul, Robert A. F. "Some Observations on Sherpa Shamanism." In *Spirit Possession in the Nepal Himalayas.* Ed. John T. Hitchock and Rex L. Jones, pp. 141–51. 1976; New Delhi: Vikas Publishing House, 1996.

———. *The Tibetan Symbolic World: Psychoanalytic Exploration.* Chicago: University of Chicago Press, 1982.

Plato. *The Dialogues of Plato.* Trans. B. Jowett. 2 vols. 1892; New York: Random House, 1937.

Pobozniak, T. "Genesis of the Milindapañha." In *Sanskrit and World Culture.* Schriften zur Geschichte und Kultur des Alten Orients, no. 18. Berlin: Akademie Verlag, 1986.

Prats, Ramon. "Some Preliminary Considerations Arising from a Biographical Study of the Early *Gter-ston.*" In *Tibetan Studies in Honour of Hugh Richardson.* Ed. Michael Aris and Aung San Suu Kyi, pp. 256–60. Warminster, U.K.: Aris and Phillips, 1979.

Radhakrishnan, Sarvepalli, and Charles A. Moore. *A Sourcebook in Indian Philosophy.* Princeton: Princeton University Press, 1957.

Raglan, FitzRoy Richard Somerset. "The Hero: A Study in Tradition, Myth, Myth and Drama." Part 2. In *In Quest of the Hero.* Ed. Robert A. Segal, pp. 89–175. Princeton: Princeton University Press, 1990.

Rahula, Telwatte. *A Critical Study of the Mahāvastu.* Delhi: Motilal Banarsidass, 1978.

Ramanujan, A. K., ed. *Folktales from India: A Selection of Oral Tales from Twenty-two Languages.* New York: Pantheon, 1991.

———. *Speaking of Śiva.* Baltimore: Penguin, 1973.

Rank, Otto. "The Myth of the Birth of the Hero." In *In Quest of the Hero.* Ed. Robert A. Segal, pp. 3–86. Princeton: Princeton University Press, 1990.

Ray, Reginald. "Buddhism: Sacred Text Written and Realized." In *The Holy Book in Comparative Perspective.* Ed. Frederick M. Denny and Rodney L. Taylor, pp. 148–80. Columbia: University of South Carolina Press, 1985.

———. *Buddhist Saints in India: A Study in Buddhist Values and Orientations.* New York: Oxford University Press, 1994.

———. "Mahāsiddhas." In *Encyclopedia of Religion* 9: 122–26. Ed. Mircea Eliade. 16 vols. New York: Macmillan, 1987.

———. "Mi-la-ras-pa." In *Encyclopedia of Religion* 9: 519–21. Ed. Mircea Eliade. 16 vols. New York: Macmillan, 1987.

———. "Nāgārjuna's Longevity." In *Sacred Biography in the Buddhist Traditions of South and Southeast Asia.* Ed. Juliane Schober, pp. 129–59. Honolulu: University of Hawai'i Press, 1997.

Rechung Rinpoche. *Tibetan Medicine.* 1973; Berkeley: University of California Press, 1976.

Reynolds, Frank. "The Many Lives of Buddha: A Study of Sacred Biography and Theravāda Tradition." In *The Biographical Process: Studies in the History and Psychology of Religion,* ed. Frank E. Reynolds and Donald Capps, pp. 37–61. The Hague: Mouton, 1976.

———. "Rebirth Traditions and the Lineages of Gotama: A Study in Theravāda Buddhology." In *Sacred Biography in the Buddhist Traditions of South and Southeast Asia.* Ed. Juliane Schober, pp. 19–39. Honolulu: University of Hawai'i Press, 1997.

Reynolds, Frank, and Donald Capps, ed. *The Biographical Process: Studies in the History and Psychology of Religion.* The Hague: Mouton, 1976.

Reynolds, Frank, and Charles Hallisey. "Buddha." In *Encyclopedia of Religion* 2: 319–32. Ed. Mircea Eliade. 16 vols. New York: Macmillan, 1987.

Reynolds, Frank, and Charles Hallisey. "Buddhism: An Overview." In *Encyclopedia of Religion* 2: 334–51. Ed. Mircea Eliade. 16 vols. New York: Macmillan, 1987.

Rhys Davids, T. W. *Buddhism: Its History and Literature.* New York: G. P. Putnam's Sons, 1896.

———. *Buddhist India.* 1903; Delhi: Motilal Banarsidass, 1971.

Rhys Davids, T. W., and William Stede. *Pali-English Dictionary.* 1921–1925; Delhi: Motilal Banarsidass, 1993.

Richard, Naomi Noble, ed. *Masters of Japanese Calligraphy.* New York: Asia Society, 1984.

Robinson, Richard H., and Willard L. Johnson. 3d ed. *The Buddhist Religion: A Historical Introduction.* Belmont, CA: Wadsworth, 1982.

Rockhill, W. W. *The Life of the Buddha.* Varanasi: Orientalia Indica, 1972.

Roland, Alan. *In Search of Self in India and Japan: Toward a Cross-Cultural Psychology.* Princeton: Princeton University Press, 1988.

Rupprecht, Carol Schreier, ed. *The Dream and the Text: Essays on Literature and Language.* Albany: State University of New York Press, 1993.

———. "Sex, Gender and Dreams: From Polarity to Plurality." In *Among All These Dreamers: Essays on Dreaming and Modern Society.* Ed. Kelly Bulkeley. Albany: State University Press of New York, 1996.

———. "Women's Dreams: Mind and Body." In *Feminist Archetypal Theory: Interdisciplinary Re-Visions of Jungian Thought.* Ed. Estella Lauter and Carol Schreier Rupprecht. Knoxville: University of Tennessee Press, 1985.

Russell, James R. "The Dream Vision of Anania Sirakac'i." *Revue des études armeniennes, nouvelle serie* 22 (1988): 159–70.

Sachs, Robert. *Health for Life: Secrets of Tibetan Ayurveda.* Santa Fe: Clear Light, 1995.

Samuel, Geoffrey. *Civilized Shamans: Buddhism in Tibetan Societies.* Washington, DC: Smithsonian Institution Press, 1993.

———. "Early Buddhism in Tibet: Some Anthropological Perspectives." In *Soundings in Tibetan Civilization.* Ed. Barbara Aziz and Matthew Kapstein, pp. 383–97. New Delhi: Manohar, 1985.

———. "The Gesar Epic of East Tibet." In *Tibetan Literature: Studies in Genre.* Ed. José Ignacio Cabezón and Roger R. Jackson, pp. 358–67. Ithaca: Snow Lion, 1996.

Sandars, N. K., trans. *The Epic of Gilgamesh.* Baltimore: Penguin Books, 1960.

Sanford, James H. "The Abominable Tachikawa Skull Ritual." *Monumenta Nipponica* 46, no. 1 (Spring 1991): 1–20.

Saunders, E. Dale. *Mudrā: A Study of Symbolic Gestures in Japanese Buddhist Sculpture.* New York: Pantheon Books, 1960.

Sax, William. *Mountain Goddess: Gender and Politics in a Himalayan Pilgrimage.* New York: Oxford University Press, 1991.

Schiefner, F. Anton, trans. *Tibetan Tales Derived from Indian Sources.* London: George Routledge, n.d.

Schlingloff, Dieter. *Studies in the Ajanta Paintings: Identifications and Interpretations.* Delhi: Ajanta, 1987.

Schmid, Toni. *The Cotton-Clad Mila: The Tibetan Poet-Saint's Life in Pictures.* Stockholm: Statens Etnografiska Museum, 1952.

Schober, Juliane, ed. *Sacred Biography in the Buddhist Traditions of South and Southeast Asia.* Honolulu: University of Hawai'i Press, 1997.

Schopen, Gregory. "Archaeology and Protestant Presuppositions in the Study of Indian Buddhism." *History of Religions* 31 (August 1991–May 1992): 1–23.

———. "Burial *Ad Sanctos* and the Physical Presence of the Buddha in Early Indian Buddhism: A Study in the Archaeology of Religion." *Religion,* no. 17 (1987): 193–225.

———. "An Old Inscription from Amarāvatī and the Cult of the Local Monastic Dead in Indian Buddhist Monasteries." *Journal of the International Association of Buddhist Studies* 14, no. 2 (1991): 281–329.

———. "The Phrase 'sa pṛthivipradeśaś caityabhūto bhavet' in the Vajracchedikā: Notes on the Cult of the Book in Mahāyāna." *Indo-Iranian Journal* 17, nos. 3/4 (November/December 1975): 147–81.

Schuhmacher, Stephen, and Gert Woerner, eds. *The Encyclopaedia of Eastern Philosophy and Religion.* Boston: Shambhala, 1989.

Schumann, H. W. *The Historical Buddha.* Trans. M. O'C. Walshe. London: Penguin, 1989.

Segal, Robert A. *In Quest of the Hero.* Princeton: Princeton University Press, 1990.

Shakabpa, W. D. *Tibet: A Political History.* New Haven: Yale University Press, 1967.

Sharma, Chandradhar. *A Critical Survey of Indian Philosophy.* Delhi: Motilal Banarsidass, 1960.

Sharma, Jagdish, and Lee Siegel. *Dream-Symbolism in The Śrāmaṇic Tradition: Two Psychoanalytical Studies in Jinist and Buddhist Dream Legends.* Calcutta: Firma KLM, 1980.

Sharma, Sharmistha. *Astrological Lore in the Buddhist Śārdūlakarṇāvadāna.* Delhi: Eastern Book Linkers, 1992.

Shastri, Biswanarayan. "The Philosophical Concepts and the Buddhist Pantheon." In *Buddhist Iconography*, pp. 52–59. Delhi: Tibet House, 1989.

Shaw, Miranda. *Passionate Enlightenment: Women in Tantric Buddhism.* Princeton: Princeton University Press, 1994.

Sikdar, Jogendra Chandra. *Studies in the Bhagawatīsūtra.* Muzaffarpur, Bihar: Research Institute of Prakrit, Jainology, and Ahimsa, 1964.

Sinha, Jadunath. *Indian Psychology: Perception.* London: Kegan Paul, Trench, Trubner, 1934.

Smart, Ninian, and Richard D. Hecht. *Sacred Texts of the World.* New York: Crossroad, 1982.

Smith, Jonathan Z. "Sleep." In *Encyclopedia of Religion* 13: 361–64. Ed. Mircea Eliade. 16 vols. New York: Macmillan, 1987.

Snellgrove, D. L. "Buddhism, Schools of: Tibetan Buddhism." In *Encyclopedia of Religion* 2: 493–98. Ed. Mircea Eliade. 16 vols. New York: Macmillan, 1987.

———. "Celestial Buddhas and Bodhisattvas." In *Encyclopedia of Religion* 3: 133–43. Ed. Mircea Eliade. 16 vols. New York: Macmillan, 1987.

———. *Four Lamas of Dolpo.* 2 vols. Cambridge: Harvard University Press, 1967.

———. *Indo-Tibetan Buddhism: Indian Buddhists and Their Tibetan Successors.* London: Serindia, 1987.

———. *The Nine Ways of Bon: Excerpts from gZi brjid.* London: Oxford University Press, 1967.

———. "Śākyamuni's Final Nirvāṇa." *Bulletin of the School of Oriental and African Studies* 36 (1973): 399–411.

Snellgrove, D. L., and Hugh E. Richardson. *A Cultural History of Tibet.* Boston: Shambhala, 1986.

Snodgrass, Adrian. *The Symbolism of the Stupa.* 1985; New Delhi: Motilal Banarsidass, 1992.

Sogyal Rinpoche. *The Tibetan Book of Living and Dying*. San Francisco: Harper-SanFrancisco, 1993.

Spiro, Melford E. *Buddhism and Society: A Great Tradition and Its Burmese Vicissitudes*. 2d. ed. Berkeley: University of California Press, 1982.

Stablein, William. "Mahākāla the Neo-shaman Master of the Ritual." In *Spirit Possession in the Nepal Himalayas*. Ed. John T. Hitchock and Rex L. Jones, pp. 361–75. 1976; New Delhi: Vikas Publishing House, 1996.

Stevenson, (Mrs.) Sinclair. *The Heart of Jainism*. 1915; Delhi: Munshiram Manoharlal, 1970.

Storm, Mary. "Death." In *Encyclopedia of Women and World Religion* 1: 243–44. Ed. Serinity Young. New York: Macmillan, 1998.

Streng, Frederick J. *Emptiness: A Study in Religious Meaning*. Nashville: Abingdon Press, 1967.

Strong, John S. *The Experience of Buddhism*. Belmont, CA: Wadsworth, 1995.

———. "A Family Quest: The Buddha, Yaśodharā, and Rāhula in the *Mūlasarvāstivāda Vinaya*." In *Sacred Biography in the Buddhist Traditions of South and Southeast Asia*. Ed. Juliane Schober, pp. 113–28. Honolulu: University of Hawai'i Press, 1997.

Stutley, Margaret and James, eds. *Harper's Dictionary of Hinduism: Its Mythology, Folklore, Philosophy, Literature, and History*. San Francisco: Harper and Row, 1984.

Sullivan, Lawrence E. "Healing." In *Encyclopedia of Religion* 6: 226–34. Ed. Mircea Eliade. 16 vols. New York: Macmillan, 1987.

Swearer, Donald K. "Folk Religion: Folk Buddhism." In *Encyclopedia of Religion* 5: 372–78. Ed. Mircea Eliade. 16 vols. New York: Macmillan, 1987.

Sweet, Michael J. "Mental Purification *(Blo sbyong)*: A Native Tibetan Genre of Religious Literature." In *Tibetan Literature: Studies in Genre*. Ed. José Ignacio Cabezón and Roger R. Jackson, pp. 244–60. Ithaca: Snow Lion, 1996.

Takeuchi, Yoshinori, and John P. Keenan. "Buddhist Philosophy." In *Encyclopedia of Religion* 2: 540–47. Ed. Mircea Eliade. 16 vols. New York: Macmillan, 1987.

Tambiah, Stanley Jeyaraja. *The Buddhist Saints of the Forest and the Cult of Amulets*. Cambridge: Cambridge University Press, 1984.

Tanaka, Kenneth K., and Raymond E. Robertson. "A Ch'an Text from Tun-huang: Implications for Ch'an Influence on Tibetan Buddhism." In *Tibetan Buddhism: Reason and Revelation.* Ed. Steven D. Goodman, and Ronald M. Davidson, pp. 57–78. Albany: State University of New York Press, 1992.

Tarthang Tulku. *Crystal Mirror.* Vol. 4. Emeryville: Dharma, 1975.

Tedlock, Barbara. "Zuni and Quiché Dream Sharing and Interpreting." In *Dreaming: Anthropological and Psychological Interpretations.* Ed. Barbara Tedlock, pp. 105–31. Cambridge: Cambridge University Press, 1987.

———, ed. *Dreaming: Anthropological and Psychological Interpretations.* Cambridge: Cambridge University Press, 1987.

Tewari, Ramesh Chandra. "Pre-Buddhist Elements in Himalayan Buddhism: The Institution of the Oracles." *Journal of the International Association of Buddhist Studies* 10, no. 1 (1987): 135–55.

Thinley, Karma. *The History of the Sixteen Karmapas of Tibet.* Boulder: Prajñā, 1980.

Thomas, Edward J. *The Life of Buddha as Legend and History.* London: Routledge and Kegan Paul, 1969.

Thupten Ngodup, the Nechung Kuten. Interview by Lotsawa Tsepak Rinzin and Tashi Tsering. *Tibetan Bulletin* (Dharamsala), July–August 1992, 26–28.

Thurman, Robert A. F. "Buddhist Hermeneutics." *Journal of the American Academy of Religion* 46, no. 1 (1978): 19–39.

———. "Magico-Religious Powers." In *Encyclopedia of Religion* 9: 115–18. Ed. Mircea Eliade. 16 vols. New York: Macmillan, 1987.

———. "Tsoṅ-kha-pa." In *Encyclopedia of Religion* 15: 72–74. Ed. Mircea Eliade. 16 vols. New York: Macmillan, 1987.

———. "Worship and Cultic Life: Buddhist Cultic Life in Tibet." In *Encyclopedia of Religion* 15: 472–75. Ed. Mircea Eliade. 16 vols. New York: Macmillan, 1987.

Trachtenberg, Joshua. *Jewish Magic and Superstition: A Study in Folk Religion.* 1939; New York: Atheneum, n.d.

Trungpa, Chögyam. *Born in Tibet.* Harmondsworth, U.K.: Penguin, 1971.

Tsonawa, Losang Norbu. *Indian Buddhist Pandits from "The Jewel Garland of Buddhist History."* Dharamsala: Library of Tibetan Works and Archives, 1985.

Tsultrim Gyamtso, Khenpo. *Comparison of View and Four Songs of Milarepa.* Trans. and ed. Shenpen Hookham. N.p.: Marpa Institute, n.d.

Tucci, Giuseppe. *The Religions of Tibet.* Trans. Geoffrey Samuel. Berkeley: University of California Press, 1980.

———. *The Theory and Practice of the Mandala.* Trans. Alan Houghton Brodrick. New York: Samuel Weiser, 1973.

Tylor, Edward B. *Primitive Culture: Researches into the Development of Mythology, Philosophy, Religion, Language, Art and Custom.* New York: Henry Holt and Company, 1865.

Urubshurow, Victoria Kennick. "Dakinis." In *Encyclopedia of Women and World Religion* 1: 231–32. Ed. Serinity Young. New York: Macmillan, 1998.

———. "Symbolic Process on the Buddhist Path: Spiritual Development in the Biographical Tradition of Milarepa." Ph.D. diss., University of Chicago, 1984.

Van Tyl, Charles D. "An Analysis of Chapter Twenty-Eight of the Hundred Thousand Songs of Mila-Raspa, a Buddhist Poet and Saint of Tibet." Ph.D. diss., Indiana University, 1971.

Varela, Francisco J., ed. *Sleeping, Dreaming, and Dying: An Exploration of Consciousness with the Dalai Lama.* Boston: Wisdom, 1997.

von Grunebaum, G. E., and Robert Caillois, eds. *The Dream and Human Societies.* Berkeley: University of California Press, 1966.

Wach, Joachim. *Sociology of Religion.* Chicago: University of Chicago Press, 1962.

Wadley, Susan S. "No Longer a Wife: Widows in Rural North India." In *From the Margins of Hindu Marriage: Essays on Gender, Religion, and Culture.* Ed. Lindsey Harlan and Paul B. Courtright. New York: Oxford University Press, 1995.

Waida, Manabu. "Miracles: An Overview." In *Encyclopedia of Religion* 9: 541–48. Ed. Mircea Eliade. 16 vols. New York: Macmillan, 1987.

Walters, Jonathan S. "Stūpa, Story, and Empire: Contructions of the Buddha Biography in Early Post-Aśokan India." In *Sacred Biography in the Buddhist Traditions of South and Southeast Asia.* Ed. Juliane Schober, pp. 160–92. Honolulu: University of Hawai'i Press, 1997.

Wangyal, Geshe. *The Door of Liberation: Essential Teachings of the Tibetan Buddhist Tradition.* New York: Maurice Girodias, 1972.

Wayman, Alex. *Calming the Mind and Discerning the Real.* New York: Columbia University Press, 1978.

———. "The Parents of Buddhist Monks." *Bharati,* 1966–1968, pp. 25–36.

———. "The Significance of Dreams in India and Tibet." In *Buddhist Insight.* Ed. George Elder, pp. 399–412. New Delhi: Motilal Banarsidass, 1984.

Weber, Max. *The Religion of India: The Sociology of Hinduism and Buddhism.* Trans. and ed. Hans H. Gerth and Don Martindale. New York: Free Press, 1958.

———. *The Sociology of Religion.* Trans. Ephraim Fischoff. Boston: Beacon, 1964.

Weinstein, Donald, and Rudolph M. Bell. *Saints and Society: The Two Worlds of Western Christendom, 1000–1700.* Chicago: University of Chicago Press, 1982.

White, David, ed. *The Religion of Tantra.* Princeton: Princeton University Press. In press.

Whitten, Norman E., Jr. *Sacha Runa: Ethnicity and Adaptation of Ecuadorian Jungle Quichua.* Urbana: University of Illinois Press, 1976.

Williams, Michael A., ed. *Charisma and Sacred Biography.* Special issue of *Journal of the American Academy of Religion Thematic Studies* 48, nos. 3 and 4 (1982).

Williams, Paul. *Mahāyāna Buddhism: The Doctrinal Foundations.* London: Routledge, 1989.

Willis, Janice D. *Enlightened Beings: Life Stories from the Ganden Oral Tradition.* Boston: Wisdom, 1995.

———, ed. *Feminine Ground: Essays on Women and Tibet.* Ithaca: Snow Lion, 1989.

———. "On the Nature of Rnam-Thar: Early Dge-Lugs-Pa *Siddha* Biographies." In *Soundings in Tibetan Civilization.* Ed. Barbara Aziz and Matthew Kapstein, pp. 304–19. New Delhi: Manohar, 1985.

Wilson, Bryan R. *Magic and the Millennium: A Sociological Study of Religious Movements of Protest Among Tribal and Third-World Peoples.* New York: Harper and Row, 1973.

Wilson, Liz. *Charming Cadavers: Horrific Figurations of the Feminine in Indian Buddhist Hagiographic Literature.* Chicago: University of Chicago Press, 1996.

Windisch, Ernst. *Māra und Buddha.* Leipzig: S. Hirzel, 1895.

Winkler, John J. *The Constraints of Desire: The Anthropology of Sex and Gender in Ancient Greece.* New York: Routledge, 1990.

Winson, Jonathan. "The Meaning of Dreams." *Scientific American* (November 1990): 86–96.

Winternitz, Maurice. *A History of Indian Literature.* 3 vols. 1927; Delhi: Oriental Books Reprint, 1977.

Worsley, Peter. *The Trumpet Shall Sound: A Study of "Cargo" Cults in Melanesia.* 2d. ed. New York: Schocken, 1968.

Young, Serinity, ed. *An Anthology of Sacred Texts by and about Women.* New York: Crossroad, 1993.

———. "Dreams." In *Encyclopedia of Women and World Religion,* 1: 271–73. Ed. Serinity Young. New York: Macmillan, 1998.

———. "Dreams." In *South Asian Folklore: An Encyclopedia.* Ed. Peter J. Claus and Margaret A. Mills. New York: Garland, forthcoming.

———. "Gendered Politics in Ancient Indian Asceticism." *Union Seminary Quarterly Review* 48, nos. 3–4 (1994): 73–92.

———. "Rejection and Reconciliation: Human and Divine Females in the Biographical Literature of the Buddha." Paper presented at the Seventeenth Annual Conference on South Asia, Madison, WI, November 1988.

Zimmer, Heinrich. *Myths and Symbols in Indian Art and Civilization.* Ed. Joseph Campbell. 1946; New York: Harper, 1962.

Zopa Rinpoche, Thubten, and Brian Beresford. "The Course of Study at Sera-Je." *Tibet Society Bulletin* 13 (June 1979): 7–10.

Zysk, Kenneth. *Asceticism and Healing in Ancient India: Medicine in the Buddhist Monastery.* New York: Oxford University Press, 1991.

Index

collecting, 168
conception, 3, 21, 75–85, 173, 214, 224
counteracting bad, 59, 133–37, 139
of Dakmema, 81–84, 93, 151, 156–57, 162
death-related, 124–25, 160–62, 210
emptiness of, 17
of Gampopa, 93, 99–102, 106, 112
gods as cause of, 34, 45, 200, 226
of Gopā, 24, 35–37, 40, 155
and illness, 67–68
instructions for obtaining, 137–38, 162
instruction to observe, 110
in the *jātakas,* 3, 37–39
of King Indrabhūti, 77
of King Kosala, 2, 45–46, 109
of kings, 8
of Māra, 39–41
mastering, 27, 120
meaning in, 2, 9, 45, 67, 101, 183
in medical textx, 3, 65–72, 130, 135, 208–9
men's, 148–52
of Milarepa, 3, 97–100, 109–11, 133, 162
moral responsibility for, 43–44
pollution from, 44, 135
psychoanalytic study of, 11, 18–19, 185–86, 220
of Queen Māyā, 3, 6, 10, 16, 21–24, 28, 33, 74, 88
of Rechungpa, 83–85, 102–4, 112, 150
and religious innovation, 117–20
seeking during initiation process, 55
shared, 3–4, 87–94, 156–57, 168, 243
as signs of spiritual accomplishment, 4, 95–113
sought, 110, 129–35, 165–66
as source of divine communication, 8
stages in, 48
studies of, 173–74
textual survival of, 9
that indicate liberation, 89
of Tsongkhapa, 106–7
typology of, 11, 66–67
validity of, 16
valuing, 56, 157
of Viṣṇu, 2

ABOUT WISDOM

WISDOM PUBLICATIONS, a not-for-profit publisher, is dedicated to making available authentic Buddhist works for the benefit of all. We publish translations of the sutras and tantras, commentaries and teachings of past and contemporary Buddhist masters, and original works by the world's leading Buddhist scholars. We publish our titles with the appreciation of Buddhism as a living philosophy and with the special commitment to preserve and transmit important works from all the major Buddhist traditions.

If you would like more information or a copy of our mail-order catalog, please contact us at:

Wisdom Publications
199 Elm Street
Somerville, Massachusetts 02144 USA
Telephone: (617) 776-7416 • Fax: (617) 776-7841
Email: info@wisdompubs.org • www.wisdompubs.org

THE WISDOM TRUST

As a not-for-profit publisher, Wisdom Publications is dedicated to the publication of fine Dharma books for the benefit of all sentient beings and dependent upon the kindness and generosity of sponsors in order to do so. If you would like to make a donation to Wisdom, please do so through our Somerville office. If you would like to sponsor the publication of a book, please write or e-mail us for more information.

Thank you.

Wisdom Publications is a non-profit, charitable 501(c)(3) organization and a part of the Foundation for the Preservation of the Mahayana Tradition (FPMT).